THE BED AND
BATH BOOK

THE BED AND BATH BOOK

Terence Conran

Crown Publishers Inc., New York

Contributors
Barbara Chandler
Andrew Duff
Lawrence Wright, MA B Arch

Charlotte Baden-Powell, AA Dip RIBA
Angela Coles
Andrew Duncan
Janet Fitch
Maria Kroll
Bettina McNulty
Suzanne Slesin
Alexandra Towle
Cynthia Wickham

Roger Baresel
Bonnie Molnar
Ian Oswald, MD, DSc

Consultants
Prof. Alexander Kira
Peter Martin
David Salter, Dip Arch RIBA, FSIAD

The Bed and Bath Book was edited and designed by
Mitchell Beazley Publishers Limited, Mill House,
87-89 Shaftesbury Avenue, London W1V 7AD

Editor	Alexandra Towle
Assistant editor	Dian Taylor
Editorial assistants	Gillian Abrahams
	Fiona Grafton
	Rosamond Massie
Art editor	Val Hobson
Associate art editor	Mike Rose
Designers	Rozelle Bentheim
	Pete Saag
Design/editorial assistant	Tony Spalding
Picture research	Marilynn Zipes
Production	Julian Deeming
Executive editor	Iain Parsons

Library of Congress Cataloging in Publication Data
Conran, Terence.
   The bed and bath book.   Includes index.
1. Bedrooms. 2. Bathrooms. 3. Interior decoration. I. Title.
NK2117.B4C66 1978   747'.77   77-28086
ISBN 0 517 53399 5

Typeset by Tradespools Ltd, Frome, Somerset, England
Reproduced by Gilchrist Brothers, Leeds, England
Printed by Smeets BV, Weert, Netherlands

Contents

Introduction

The bedroom and the bathroom are the most private rooms in the house
– and it seems appropriate to consider them together. They are rooms in
which we spend a great deal of time, rooms in which we should be able to
relax and feel totally at ease with ourselves and the surroundings. Yet,
perhaps because they are seldom on public show, the bedroom and the
bathroom are often the most neglected areas of the house – traditionally
designed purely for function, all too rarely for self-indulgence. The
purpose of this book is to help you make the most of your bedroom and
bathroom and to bring your personal style and invention to your most
intimate rooms.

Terence Conran

Bedding & bathing—a modest history

I make no excuse for including a substantial section on the development of bedding and bathing habits in a practical book about the design of bedrooms and bathrooms. I believe a thorough understanding of the way our social behaviour has evolved is necessary before one can tackle a contemporary problem. It is surprising how often the simple solutions arrived at in the past through necessity throw a whole new light on the complexities of modern life. We all too easily assume that our bathing habits are "civilized" because cleanliness has become an obsession in the Western World. Large industries have been built on the dictum that "cleanliness is next to Godliness", but rising pollution levels caused by "cleansing" chemicals may lead to a major reassessment of this attitude. This brief history takes a look, too, at the effective use artists have always made of the bed and the bath in their work and the influence on modern thinking of that great dream machine—Hollywood.

The ancients

Sleeping is unavoidable. Washing is not. History has many examples of unwashed human communities, usually—but not always—primitive ones. The resistance of many modern children to the routine of personal hygiene is quite similar to the behaviour of ancient peoples. There is no clear mention of a bath-tub, for instance, in the Old Testament. Even when the Hebrews had ample fresh water they seem to have had little inclination to use it. Leviticus' "He shall bathe his flesh in running water, and shall be clean" was not about having a good wash but, rather, a euphemism for the careful purification of various parts of the body by water sprinkled from a pitcher. Washing was ritual, not routine—to ablute was to wash away sins rather than dirt.

For ancient nomadic tribes, water was so scarce that the defence of a clean watering place was something of a sacred duty, and in warfare a favourite tactic was to sully the enemy's water supply. These people beautified their bodies not with water but with asses' milk and alkaline mixtures like soda-ash.

The Egyptians, who had the Nile, were luckier. They did bathe in the river, although their knowledge of hydraulics—the conveyance of water through channels—was largely confined to irrigation. The carriage of water was arduous and, even with slaves, improbable over a long distance. The Egyptians, therefore, relied on a lot of perfume to make their bodies as attractive as their homes and palaces. Egyptian beds, too, were quite sophisticated, and royalty might even have been protected by mosquito netting. Ordinary people, however, had to be content with sleeping as high up a building as possible, where the bugs would hopefully be blown away.

According to Herodotus, there was a bedroom at the top of the Tower of Babel where God could commune with a fair (earthly) maiden. In general, however, the poorer classes had to share their own company and make do with less elaborate bedsteads and rush matting. Most of the beds, and all the bedding, were light enough to be moved easily. Saul orders David's bed to be carried up (with David in it) that he may slay him.

Royal beds were, as always, unique. We are told that King Og of Bashan had an "iron bedstead"—although this was probably made of basalt. Solomon had a bed carved from Cedar of Lebanon. Homer's Odysseus slept in a bed decorously carved out of the trunk of an olive tree. As befits a hero, it was lined with ox-hide and covered with linen sheets.

Later, and quite separately, a remarkable civilization flourished in the Indus Valley. In the ruins at Mohenjo-Daro, in what is now Pakistan, great brick-built, dome-shaped buildings proclaim the memory of a wealthy, disciplined and domesticated society. There is evidence of public bathing in heated water, almost certainly as part of a religious ceremony rather than a desire to be clean.

But it was in the Mediterranean, on Crete, that we know of man's earliest achievements in advanced hydraulic and sanitary engineering. When King Minos built his palace at Knossos in about 2000 BC he installed an ingenious system of baths, sinks, water-closets and cisterns linked with pipes made of terracotta. Minoan plumbing was not rivalled for many hundreds of years; nor was the beauty of the royal beds and baths.

The abundance of evidence in Crete and in the Indus Valley suggests a regularity of bathing which was certainly not emulated by the Greeks of Athens. The Athenians scorned private domestic luxury: baths were taken after competitive athletics and were invariably cold. The very idea of a household was strange to the Greeks, a militaristic race, who were noted neither for their marital fidelity nor for the personal collection of material possessions.

It was several hundred years before the Romans shed the simplicity they had inherited from Greece. Rome was a mercantile and military power, not an industrial one, and increasing prosperity and peace encouraged her citizens to develop an agreeable way of life. Domestic comforts were as much enjoyed as aesthetic pleasures. Most Roman homes had attractive daytime couches for conversation, eating and drinking. Beds for sleeping were usually more plain, and set apart in cubicles. Ceremonial marriage beds, however, were vehicles for the display of the household silk. Romans slept in their underwear, and on rising would quickly wind their togas about them—bathing was an afternoon activity and, of course, Rome was famous for her baths: here the social attitude of the citizens was happily combined with their impressive technological ingenuity.

Lavishly draped day bed in the Grecian style, depicted on a Corinthian vase.

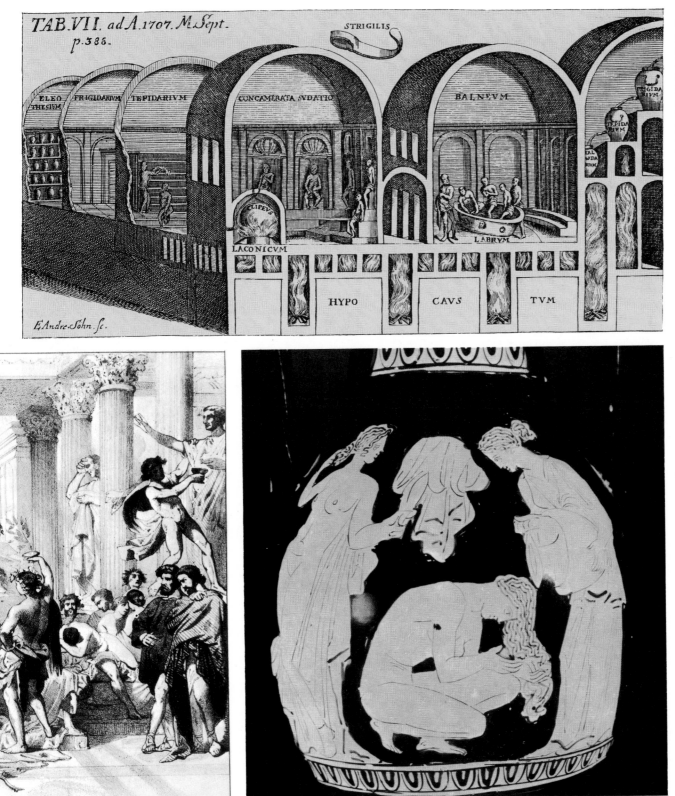

The Romans mastered the passage of water over long distances and over difficult terrain with the use of aqueducts, most of which were built underground. Roman piping—usually of lead—has in many instances survived in working order until the 20th century. Although several rich Roman villas had private baths (and some private bedrooms even had their own wash-basin) most citizens would go each afternoon to the public baths. Some of the biggest, such as the ones built during the rules of the Emperors Caracalla and Diocletian, could take thousands of bathers. Some were heated by hot springs, such as those at Bath in England; others, like the Baths of Hadrian in Rome, had fierce fires beneath the terracotta floors of the pools.

There was room for ball games and plenty of opportunity for relaxation and social intercourse: the baths also housed shops, and even libraries and museums. The experience, therefore, corresponded to one of the highest ideals of Roman life, *mens sana in corpore sano* ("a healthy mind in a healthy body"). Roman society was bisexual, in many ways immodest, and above all supremely self-confident. This very self-assurance was the basis for the formidable quality of domestic life. The evangelical Early Christians posed a threat to the stability of the Empire by railing constantly against the wastefulness of the city, epitomized by the extravagance of its public bathing places. And the thanks they got for their criticism was a barbarous death in the arena.

Left: *5th-century* BC *vase showing a Grecian at her toilet. Washing was a primitive and irregular affair for the Greeks, who considered it an indulgence.*

Far left: *a Roman orgy painted by the French artist Thomas Couture, in 1847.*

Top left: *reconstruction of the baths of Titus, Rome. Bathing was a highly sociable event and the Romans enjoyed uniquely sophisticated bathing practices: here, the bather would rub himself with oil from the* eleothesium, *move into the warm* tepidarium *and through to the steamy* laconicum, *where he sat and sweated until ready to enter the hot balneum. After scraping dirt from his body with the* strigilis, *he rinsed in the bath-tub before plunging into the chill waters of the* frigidarium.

The Dark Ages

It is quite a respectable generalization to say that when Rome was sacked by the barbarians in AD 476 there followed a thousand years in which Europe went unwashed—but only as far as Western Europe is concerned. For while the Empire's aqueducts and public baths were crumbling in what are known today as Britain, France and Germany, Roman civilization's hallmark of clean (in the physical, not moral sense) and luxurious living had reached its zenith in the Eastern Roman Empire at Constantinople. This magnificent city, known today as Istanbul, was not blessed with indigenous supplies of water, but relied on an ambitious system of conduits, fountains and cisterns completed during the rule of the Emperor Justinian around AD 550, when the "Dark Ages" were already well established in the West. When, in the 11th century, the Eastern Roman Empire in turn faced destruction, its invaders, the Turks, were far more civilized than the Germanic hordes who had overrun the West.

The Seljuk Turks already had a reputation as builders of the *caravanserai* on the inhospitable Anatolian Plain of central Turkey, oases of comfort designed for the bathing, resting and feeding of travellers. Turkish baths, like Roman baths, had warm-rooms, hotrooms and steam-rooms. If anything, they had more in common with the modern "gourmet" bather's ideal, because they were designed more for luxurious, recreational bathing than those of their Roman predecessors, where the emphasis shifted towards physical fitness.

Meanwhile, Christendom endured the Dark Ages. No significant advances were made on the Roman way of life, especially in terms of plumbing and sanitation, and in many areas, notably Britain, there were significant retreats. Life for man, as Thomas Hobbes, a 17th-century historian, said, was solitary, poor, nasty, brutish and short. On saints' days, eating and drinking took precedence over cleansing.

Feudal society was a subsistence society in which the provision of food and drink was the preoccupation of the bulk of the people. Separate rooms for bathing and sleeping were non-existent in both merchants' houses and serfs' hovels. In the great halls of castles and manors, retainers and servants slept communally around the fire. Only the master and his lady, and perhaps their immediate family, had private apartments. The two cornerstones of decent living in modern times—one's own, clean bed and regular supplies of hot water for bathing—were in this period exclusive prerogatives of rank rather than common necessities.

A bed was a badge of wealth for the feudal baron to take with him on his travels. A bedroom, or privy-chamber—because it was one of the most secure rooms in a castle—became a hallowed sanctuary, somewhere to keep the treasure strongbox or conduct secret business. Thus the lord or lady's chamber became a place loaded with significance, and right of entry was a special mark of favour, requiring a code of conduct.

Sewage disposal was elementary—usually by chute into the castle moat—and plumbed water all but nonexistent; food was taken by hand (forks were not introduced to England until the 17th century) so that cleanliness at table was of some importance. As in earliest times, people of quality, who had servants to carry water, were in the best position to cultivate the necessary washing of face, hands and teeth at meals. Predictably enough, this carried a significance beyond mere cleansing: it was one of the outward indications of *courtaisie* (a specialized medieval word meaning something like good breeding) and involved a considerable ritual with all the paraphernalia of rose water, napkins and large, ornamental ewers.

As for bathing the entire body, much labour was required for heating water to fill a tub, and consequently it did not

Left: *medieval woodcut of soldiers relaxing on a remarkably sophisticated air bed during a siege. The bellows at one corner were used to inflate the bed.*

Above: *approximately once every three weeks, medieval families congregated for a communal bath. Small, bucket-shaped "balers" were used to carry hot water to and from the wooden tub.*

Right: *in the 14th-century home, bathing was an event to be savoured: eating and drinking from a plank placed across the tub was quite common.*

happen very often. A 13th-century monarch, such as England's King John, bathed once every three weeks. When the tub was filled with hot water in a modest household, the entire family would forgather to make maximum use of the water. Once again, a basic human activity, by the scarcity of its occurrence, achieved the importance of a great occasion, worthy of celebration. So, naturally enough, in houses where there were ample means, bath-time was accompanied by music, food and, afterwards, in all likelihood, sex.

The general squalor of the Dark Ages was not quite unrelieved. In the monasteries, the standard of welcome for a traveller was almost certainly better than at the local inn. Monks, unlike their lay contemporaries, slept in separate beds in rooms designed for that purpose—dormitories. Baths were taken in the warm-water *calefactory*, usually in wooden tubs padded with linen, and routine washing before meals took place in a wash-basin or *laver*.

Of course, it is necessary to look at the Dark Ages as a whole and realize that, among the nobility, standards did gradually improve, and especially after the Crusaders had reported at home the Turkish habits they had witnessed in the East. By the end of the 14th century, Turkish baths were quite common in London and Paris, the first opportunity for the populaces of those cities to bathe in fulsome supplies of hot water since

Roman times. Known as "stews" or "bordellos", these baths rapidly became haunts of prostitution and all kinds of vice. The Church campaigned against them vigorously, eventually achieving their closure in France and England during the early 16th century. Although the Church's action was justified on purely practical grounds—stews were spreading grounds of plague and venereal disease—it does characterize a fascinating attitude to washing prevalent in the Dark Ages, for which the Church, with its enormous influence, was responsible. In Ancient Rome, maintaining a clean, beautiful body was a mark of that society's self-confidence: a tribute to the earthly carcass, which had achieved such wonders of culture. To the churchmen of the Dark Ages that followed Rome's fall, this hedonism signified, ironically enough, the heathen's fatal pride. Christianity, as interpreted by the medieval Church, understood no true purity except that of the redeemed soul in the life hereafter. In this it was largely influenced by the early Christian ascetics, among them the Stylites like St Simeon of Syria, who lived on his pillar rejoicing in the rejection of things temporal as he witnessed the worms drop from his decaying hulk. Extolling this example, the medieval Church taught its flock to have no faith in the earthly condition of man. These were times in which to wash, and to enjoy it, were signs of heresy.

Above: *illustration from a book written c. 1470. At this time, ordinary people had only one warm room where they both slept and ate. A wooden bench for use during the day often doubled as a bed when spread with a straw mattress.*

Right: *a possession as handsome as this kingly balustrade bed was highly prized in medieval times. Those fortunate enough to have their own bed—a great status symbol—would often take it with them on their travels, and they would certainly take their bedding.*

Far right: *a public bath, or "stew", portrayed by the medieval artist H. S. Beham. A Turk's head street sign was used to indicate a public bath because it was the Crusaders returning to England from Turkey who introduced the idea.*

A modest history
Enlightenment

"*Il fait caca dans sa chambre,*" and, moreover, used the curtains for wiping, wrote Ernst August, Elector of Hanover, of the Tsarevitch in a letter to his wife in 1712. The Tsarevitch, son of Peter the Great of Russia, was in Dresden for his marriage to a German princess—causing wonder and amusement among the assembled potentates of the "civilized" world by his unkempt appearance and dirty personal habits, another example of which was his unfamiliarity with handkerchiefs.

The Elector's wife, at pains to defend the Tsarevitch, replied to her husband with characteristic wit that if the King of France took to blowing his nose on his fingers, it would at once be considered the height of fashion by all Europe.

In doing so, she unknowingly summed up a period whose attitudes to cleanliness and personal appearance were amazingly contradictory. For this, at the Court of Louis XIV, France's magnificent Sun King, was a time of enlightenment. Louis' court considered itself to have initiated a revolution in manners by which it led the known world in cultivated living. When speaking of outsiders, Louis' courtiers would use the same words again and again: "They do not know how to live."

Since 1682, this *savoir-vivre* had been practised in a custom-built setting of fantastic splendour—Versailles. Not only was its furniture and plate the envy of Europe, but money and craftsmanship were lavished on giving ornamental beauty to the less glamorous effects of living: the close stool, the shaving table, the bidet and chamber-pot.

Strict rules governed dress and personal appearance. At various times, dressing the hair high by means of ridiculously uncomfortable metal frames, or painting the face a deathly white, were obligatory for the ladies of the court. Different styles of dress were as numerous as the ceremonial occasions for which they were required. The men would sprinkle themselves with diamonds as liberally as the women.

The King's basic domestic activities, such as rising and going to bed, were imbued with sanctity and converted into ceremony. The day began with the *grand lever* and ended with the *coucher*, at which the greatest privileges, such as the handing of the royal shirt or gloves, were reserved for the monarch's closest family. Lesser favours, such as holding the royal candle, or chamber-pot, were distributed among lucky courtiers. To accommodate the onlookers on these occasions there was a special outsize bedroom (a room for sleeping in led off the back) with, as its centre-piece, the enormous *lit de parade*, from which certain categories of state business might also be conducted.

Such ceremony, however, had nothing to do with honouring the restorative value of a good night's sleep, or even with going to bed in style. It was practical politics. There was fierce competition for the leading roles in these little court

Above: *the popular hot baths at Leuk, in 18th-century Valais, bore a close resemblance to a cultured, if somewhat submerged, drawing-room.*

Left: *the practice of receiving friends in the bed-chamber, popularized by the Royal courts of England and France, allowed a lady confined by pregnancy to socialize in comfort.*

Right: *Gardez l'eau! In the 18th century, it was considered only good manners to precede the daily discharge of excrement and dirty water from one's window with the well-known cry of "Gardy-loo!" This London street at night with all its insalubrious detail was recorded by Hogarth.*

dramas, and the King deliberately encouraged it. For when the nobles spent their days competing for such small honours, there remained less time for serious intrigue.

There was an equally human reality behind the fine clothing. Standards of cleanliness and knowledge of how to care for the body were still all but medieval, even among the few who practised this high etiquette. Most doctors were quacks and medicine was crude. In a letter, written at the time, the Duchess of Orleans commented: "My doctor gave me a purge which was so effective that I had to retire to my close stool no less than 30 times."

Among the lower classes, the human propensity for fouling the nest was as consistently displayed as in the Middle Ages. Once again, the Duchess put it succinctly: "There is one dirty thing at Court I shall never get used to: the people stationed in the galleries in front of our rooms piss into all the corners. It is impossible to leave one's apartment without seeing someone pissing."

The supposed high point of cleanliness reached at Louis XIV's court occurred, of course, two centuries after the close of the Middle Ages, and the years which had intervened were not particularly significant in terms of the story of human cleanliness. Peasants continued, as ever, unwashed. Among well-born Europeans, one might surmise, there was a broadening of attitudes coincidental with the Renaissance of the second half of the 15th century. News brought back by explorers from other continents might, for example, have shown that one hot bath every three weeks—the norm in the Middle Ages—did not amount to a great deal of washing.

In the following century, during the reign of Elizabeth I in England, a gentleman named Sir John Harington drew plans for a flushing water closet, generally regarded as the first of its kind, and certainly the most sophisticated Europe had known since the Minoan era on Crete. In Elizabethan and Jacobean England there was a surge of country-house building: these structures were cleaner, lighter and warmer than their medieval counterparts, but in many fine houses too much attention was paid to the construction of costly follies in the grounds and not enough on domestic and sanitary essentials.

If the ancient world's standards of cleanliness and care for the body were the result of self-confidence, and medieval squalor the reverse, it might seem correct to think of this period as one of gradually restored self-confidence. The truth, however, is perhaps best personified by the Elizabethan dandy, whose passion for heavy clothes, wigs and powder all too often concealed a stinking body, pock-marked skin and hair absent through the ravages of syphilis.

Above: *18th-century baths for the rich were designed like the finest pieces of furniture, complete with draperies and submerged cushions.*

Below: *newly-weds, understandably reluctant to rise from the warm pleasures of the honeymoon bed.*

Right: *mixed bathing in the hot springs at Bath could be something less than decorous, accompanied by food, music and the obvious enjoyment of the onlookers.*

Among the Victorians who succeeded in the 19th century to the wealth of the industrial revolution, many were appalled by the conditions it had brought to the labouring masses. The invention of machines for the cheap mass-production of goods had created the vast blots of filth known as manufacturing towns, and a rapidly growing birth rate added to the congested misery caused by the drift of country folk to industrial centres.

Wages were minimal, poverty intense. In dark, overcrowded tenements, beds were shared once again by whole families rather than, as previously, just by the children. Bath-tubs were almost unknown. Disease and pests bred by dirt spread at great speed and cholera epidemics were common, carried by the giant rats that thrived in the decaying sewers. Gin was still generally cheaper and safer to drink than water. In London, water was rationed until the 1850s.

In the wealthy middle-class houses, life was altogether different. Hot baths with liberal use of soap gradually replaced freezing douches, and bathrooms were serviced by armies of servants. The stylish Victorian bedroom was cluttered with screens, mirrors and potted plants, and chamber pots and tiled wash-stands proliferated. The coil-spring mattress was invented in the 1860s, and iron and brass bedsteads replaced wooden frames. This, and the widespread manufacture of cheap cotton sheets, more or less purged the civilized bed of the pestilential bug. The rooms of children and servants were more simple, even Spartan, but the same code of prudery that segregated books on their shelves by the sex of the author and covered unchaste piano legs with crinoline skirts ostensibly applied to all classes and all ages.

While moral virtue was the great leveller of Victorian society, philanthropy and social reform became major preoccupations. Together with education, enfranchisement and the abolition of child labour, public hygiene became, if belatedly, a crusading matter. Parliament seriously turned its attention to public hygiene in the 1840s, when the build-up of sewage in the River Thames made the atmosphere at Westminster unbearably fetid. George Jennings, the

Left: *bedecked in shower caps like witches' hats, the children are forced, in the true Victorian manner, to wash.*

designer of sanitary appliances, ran a campaign for the installation of public conveniences in London which finally succeeded just over a century after Joseph Bramah had patented his hydraulic water closet in 1778.

This was also the era when the building of public wash-houses began in earnest. Admission was at a modest price and regular attendance was regarded as part of the working man's civic duty. The baths were, in fact, temples in brick, brass and marble to the birth of a new attitude to keeping clean—one which is familiar today. To the zealous Victorian social worker, washing was the baptism through which common man had to pass before he could improve his social condition, his mind and, ultimately, save his soul.

Northumberland and Durham miner, scrubbing up after his toils, 1871.

"Dirty Father Thames" ploughing his way through the filthy river, taken from an 1848 Victorian periodical.

London nightmen, 1861, whose twilight task it was to empty private cesspits.

In 19th-century literature, especially the novels of Dickens and Zola, there are many examples of this attitude in operation, but the clearest of all is found, fittingly enough, in *The Water Babies*, the children's classic by Charles Kingsley. Tom, the child chimney-sweep—not just dirty, but black with soot from head to toe—goes down the wrong chimney in a big country house and enters a girl's bedroom.

"The next thing he saw was a washstand, with ewers and basons [Kingsley's spelling], and soap and brushes and towels; and a large bath, full of clean water—what a heap of things all for washing!" Then he notices the girl asleep in bed, marvels at the vision of cleanliness and asks himself, "'Are all people like that when they are washed?' And looking round, he suddenly saw, standing close to him, a little, ugly, black, ragged figure, with bleared eyes and gaping white teeth. . . . And behold, it was himself, reflected in a great mirror . . . and Tom, for the first time in his life, found out that he was dirty; and burst into tears with shame and anger."

Kingsley's emphasis on the fact that dirtiness was a product of ignorance, from which chimney-sweeps, like heathens, needed saving, was entirely typical of the morally concerned Victorian's attitude to hygiene. Attitudes had come full circle: cleanliness, rather than squalor, was prerequisite to Godliness.

A modest history
How clean is decent?

Early in the 1900s, a popular ballad ran:

"One day I met a dirty tramp, the
dirtiest that could be.
"I said, why don't you ever wash and
he ups and says to me,
"Never have a bath till you need one,
you know what I mean.
"Never have a bath till you need one,
if it only makes you clean."

By contrast, 20th-century man today
believes himself to be about the fresh-
est, most ideally clean of creatures. More
or less everyone in the Western demo-
cracies has access to that most desirable
of domestic facilities, private indoor
plumbing. In the USA, 94.6 per cent of
houses have bathrooms. In the UK, the
figure is 95.3 per cent. House design has
become so functional that almost every
new home or apartment, regardless of
aesthetic considerations, is built around
the all-important "plumbed core" that
carries the sanitary essentials. Equally,
the thought of whole families sharing
beds or even bedrooms today causes
horror and raised eyebrows.

In all this, the 20th century owes much
to the Victorians, whose practical skills
in the pursuit of comfort *en famille* were
continued in the work of such architects
as Sir Edwin Lutyens—and, usually,
with a memorable sense of style (although Lutyens's own enthusiasm for
giving each bedroom its adjoining bathroom was still considered eccentric). The
Victorian spirit of bold experimentation
was also sustained by architects like
Aalto, Le Corbusier and their followers,
who made imaginative use of the new
synthetic building materials that were
fast becoming available.

But perhaps our greatest debt is to the
Victorians' eye for commerce. As a result of the work of such men as William
Morris and the Heals, who were both
craftsmen and tradesmen, the pleasures
of interior decoration and domestic comfort were made readily available to the
new, 20th-century middle classes.
Fashion ceased to be a luxury and became a business. For the first time, there
was more money in the popular market
than in the exclusive world of high
society, and it was no coincidence that
the wave of *art nouveau* was decadent,
passionate—and brief: styles with a more
universal appeal quickly took its place.

Improved technology and techniques
of mass production played an increasingly important role in domestic life. The
year 1910 saw the first cheap manufacture of cast-iron enamelled bath-tubs.
Mass-produced nightwear was immediately popular and, being more comely
and liberating than the equivalent Victorian garments, it was fortunate that the
new trend coincided with the first
cautious steps towards contraception.
Modern interest in sexual behaviour began immediately after the First World
War with Marie Stopes's well-publicized
work on the medical, social and psychological aspects of sex. It coincided with
the publication of the work of Freud and
Jung on dreams, and the growing fascination with the psychiatry of sleep and
sex received a frank expression in art and
literature.

The catalysts for drastic adaptations
of domestic life were two world wars.
Domestic servants hung up their aprons
and flocked to the factories, and the im-
practicability of maintaining large homes
and the acute housing shortages meant
that tall city houses were broken up into
flats or single, all-purpose rooms. But
the boost that war gave to technological
development was impressive, and had its
results for the householder in terms of
electrical gadgets, aerosol deodorants
and other aids to personal hygiene.

Left: *hot running water made life easier
for both the wealthy and their servants.*

Above: *an early example of endorsement
advertising from a soap manufacturer.*

Indeed, deodorization became a 20th-century cleansing phenomenon. Besides the under-arm roll-on, spray-on or pat-on, there are deodorants for the feet, the mouth, the vagina, the house. Deodorant has been added to diesel fuel in an attempt to make exhaust fumes smell sweeter, ashtrays have been impregnated with a chemical to deodorize the ash, and a deodorant company has offered to spray the lockers in Grand Central Station, New York, with a chemical that would allegedly give them a pleasant "outdoorsy odour".

The deodorant story began in the 1920s with an antiseptic introduced by the English surgeon Lord Lister. An American, Gerard Lambert, realized its potential as a mouth wash, but despaired of marketing it because he knew of no acceptable description for the unmentionable complaint it was meant to cure —until he heard the word *halitosis* and discovered it was simply Latin for bad breath. To Lambert, it had the sweet smell of success. Shrewd advertising, based on human insecurity, did the rest: the pictures showed despondent girls wondering why men were avoiding them. With minor refinements, this was to be the pattern for all future deodorant advertising, and quite possibly a root cause of the 20th century's often muddled, even perverse attitude towards personal cleanliness.

Employment of the mass media to dispense persuasive pictures of how the other—the successful—half lived led to other 20th-century phenomena. Conformity became the ideal, gently satirized in the early 1960s in the song about little boxes made of ticky tacky, and rejected by the hippy movement, which deliberately discarded so-called conventional cleanliness.

But while general standards of health and comfort have unquestionably improved, there is still enormous scope for further progress. A very large gap has developed between the standards of living of the richer and poorer communities of the world. Even in the industrialized West, the provision of civilized amenities is by no means universal. The need to husband energy resources has led to rapid advances in the techniques of heating, lighting and insulating houses, but the overcrowding of towns and the toxic effluence of heavy industry have caused problems of environmental pollution on an unprecedented scale.

And what of the future? Will there be still greater conformity to fashionable trends, until we are all sleeping on water beds, surrounded by the paraphernalia of hi-fi sets, televisions, cocktail cabinets and sexual aids? Or will there, by the close of the 20th century, be a reversion to simpler habits?

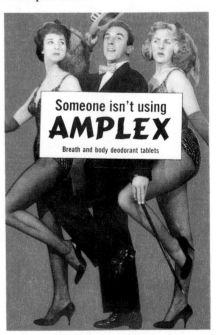

Above: *ever since the 1920s we have been led to believe that our popularity depends upon the deodorant we use.*

Left: *modern painting of the San Francisco baths in the early 1900s, when prudery still forbade mixed bathing.*

19

A modest history
Other cultures

Standards of domestic comfort in Europe have been generally higher than elsewhere since the European Renaissance. However, in cleanliness and decency, many civilizations have nothing to learn from the West, particularly in countries where religion plays a major role.

As a matter of strict religious observance, Hindus wash three or more times a day. There are even elaborate rules regarding the length of a man's toothbrush, which in rural areas consists of a freshly cut twig. The correct length twig for the average Hindu is ten inches; it is shorter for the lower castes and longer for a Brahmin. The Muslim practice of ritual washing of the hands, mouth and nose before prayer has continued unceasing through the centuries. Even in the poor villages of Bangladesh or Morocco the mosque is equipped with a pool in its outer courtyard.

In those Islamic countries once subjected to Iranian or Turkish rule, great importance is attached to personal hygiene; the communal Hamman is still popular as a place for regular bathing and recreation, and it is even used for marriages and churchings (the thanksgiving service given for women after childbirth). Also, in rural areas of Turkey there is a tradition, which still persists, where a boy's mother will examine her future daughter-in-law minutely from top to toe in the public baths before allowing the girl to marry her son.

Farther afield, in South-East Asia, water is credited with spiritual qualities and is thought to endow purity, wealth and fertility.

The Japanese have always been scrupulously clean. Traditionally, baths are square and deep and big enough to hold several people at once, but the communal bath is only for soaking, every bather washes scrupulously before getting in. The hot water is perfumed and medicated with flowers and seaweed, sulphur and soda. Fresh iris leaves floating in the bathwater are thought to bring health and happiness. Sand baths are popular in Kyushu, where bathers relax on the beach, buried to the neck in the sub-sands, which are heated by thermal activity to 35°C (90°F).

It is an unhappy feature of the modern world that improved communications and increasing prosperity break down the customs of traditionalist communities. Even Japan, with all its age-old traditions, has been affected by rapid "Americanization". Unfortunately, statistics have shown that a greater conformity to Western ways does not necessarily lead to a consequent rise in the quality of living standards.

In the Soviet Union, for example, many modern apartments look well but work badly. Guests to Russian hotels are well advised to take their own bath plugs with them, although the Russians excuse themselves by maintaining that, to be hygienic, one should wash only in clear, running water.

The holy River Ganges is not the only bathing place resembling nothing so

much as an open sewer: modern industry has polluted the bathing grounds of many primitive, river-based communities. All over the world, the authorities are trying to persuade primitive peoples to abandon tradition and use newly built washrooms. Even hardened United Nations' officials have been known to baulk at the Ethiopian habit of washing beneath the warm stream of a urinating cow. The Australians have had a measure of success in stopping the Aborigines from daubing their bodies with rancid snake fat.

The "hard sell" of a Western scrubbed, deodorized and shiny clean ideal poses a threat to the infinite variety of human vanity throughout the world. Woe the day when Moroccan nomads feel they can no longer paint their women blue.

The effect of all social change on sleeping habits is clear enough. Husbands and wives the world over seek the privacy and modesty which are the hallmarks of the modern Western bedroom. Today, only a few primitive communities, mostly jungle and nomadic tribes, adhere to their traditional customs of communal sleeping. In the forests of New Guinea the sexes are still strictly segregated, with the men and the boys sleeping in large round huts and the women, girls and babies in large rectangular huts. Lovemaking takes place privately in secluded spots on the edge of the forest. How long such practices continue depends very much on the availability of practical alternatives, as all primitive social customs are utilitarian in origin.

Perhaps the day will yet dawn when even the most rigidly traditional Japanese peasant will come to prefer feathers and down, rather than rice husks, in his pillows. In Pakistan bottled hair conditioners and bath oils may replace yogurt and mustard oil. The Burmese may discover the delights of coil-sprung mattresses and forsake bare wooden planks. The civilized security of the modern jungle may entice the natives of the Philippines to come down from their tree-houses. In the Arctic, certainly, purpose-built centrally heated houses are proving more attractive than igloos. The Eskimos have at last discovered the cure for their chronic bronchitis, a disease that was endemic to their previous way of life.

A Kamaiura Indian from Haut Xindu in the state of Mato Grosso, Brazil, takes to his hammock for a midday rest.

Above: *for this West African tribe, a bank of earth built against the hut wall serves as a bed for all the family.*

Left: *a Mongolian herdsman's Gher. The portable beds are curtained off around the edge of the hut.*

Centre right: *Kang bed in a commune high in the cold hills of North China. The family sleep on the brick plinth, which is warmed by a fire beneath.*

Right: *Hindu pilgrims bathe in the Ganges at the holy city of Benares, India.*

The artist's view

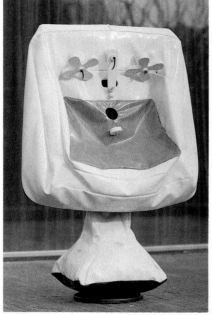

Oldenburg, "Soft Wash Basin", 1966

The step from any painted or sculpted classical Venus rising from the foam to Hockney's young men under the shower is shorter than might be immediately obvious. Painters have always been inspired by nudes, just as they have liked to paint people in their less public moments—showing them unselfconsciously absorbed in their private affairs, emotions and situations. The Old Masters, of course, imbued even their off-duty nudes with heroic attributes borrowed from mythology and the Bible —hence luscious Ledas with attendant swans, and naked Susannahs surrounded by Elders. But by the time everyday subjects became fit meat for art, sleepers and bathers were shown simply and unadorned. More recently still, the very objects of daily life have entered the repertoire of serious art—from Marcel Duchamp's urinal (via Warhol's soup can) to Oldenburg's PVC wash-basin.

David Hockney, detail from "Domestic Scene Los Angeles", 1963

Henri de Toulouse-Lautrec, "Le lit", 1893

Jean Huber, "Le lever de Voltaire", 1770

Ingres, "La petite baigneuse", 1826

Berthe Morisot, "Le berceau", 1872

A modest history
The camera's eye

Movie-makers have done a great deal for manufacturers of bedroom furniture and even more for those of bathroom hardware. In the early days of the cinema, producers and directors soon discovered that sexploitation accompanied by lush settings brought in box-office money—and where the movie-makers trod, the manufacturers were quick to follow.

Cecil B. De Mille was the true discoverer of the screen bathroom, where a woman undressed not for wicked sex but for that best of motives, hygiene. In *Male and Female* (1919), De Mille needed a way to reveal the delights of Gloria Swanson without risking the wrath of the censor. He achieved it by lingering lovingly over a scene of Swanson disrobing—and in the process brought bathing out into the open and turned it into an art.

The sexy bath—and, later, the shower—became a routine cinema device, and for many years De Mille remained the supreme interpreter of his own idea. It is possible that he actually nudged manufacturers of bathroom hardware into "discovering" the bathroom. Until the 1920s, bathrooms had not been linked—at least publicly—with glamour and sex appeal. Now, display windows became filled with fittings curiously similar to those which De Mille created for the exotic bathrooms in which he set his famous disrobing scenes. Towards the end of the 1920s, glossy magazines were carrying advertisements for bathrooms modelled on De Mille's cinema temples to soap and water.

While the cinema bathroom was reserved for disrobing, the screen bedroom provided a natural setting for seduction. Producers and directors competed to create extravagant sets against which to display their stars in glamorous states of *déshabillé*. A quite wicked line in styles to vamp by was pioneered by Theda Bara, and when Mae West simmered seductively on the screen beds of the 1930s the sales potential of satin sheets soared.

As time, and the golden days of Hollywood, passed by, so did a great many of the extravagant props. Reality was the new theme, screen settings became more utilitarian and the kitchen-sink drama was "in"—until James Bond appeared on the scene and led to the happy rediscovery that the attractions of high style are—like diamonds—forever.

Left and bottom left: *since the early days of cinema history, interior designers have been heavily influenced by screen bedrooms. In the twenties they borrowed ideas from the exotic furnishings of "The Golden Bed" (1925). More recently, films like "Diamonds are Forever", starring Sean Connery (1971), introduced the glossy, space-age look.*

Right: *Carroll Baker as thirties star Jean Harlow, who exuded eroticism without actually revealing much—even in the bedroom. Screen bedrooms were still large and lavish in the thirties, but were moving increasingly within the bounds of reality and the settings against which cinema stars played out their roles were becoming easier for the cinemagoer to adapt at home.*

Bottom right: *when Marilyn Monroe made "The Seven Year Itch" in 1955, screen bathers still had to immerse themselves to the chin in chaste suds to please the censor. In the privacy of their own bathrooms, cinemagoers were able to emulate the stars in their bubble baths.*

Below: *Burt Lancaster in "The Hallelujah Trail" (1965) does not look entirely comfortable in his enclosed tub, but it provides a useful surface for whisky glasses and other bath-time luxuries. Movies that tread the nostalgia trail have contributed to a revival of interest in such antique trappings as tin tubs and brass bedsteads.*

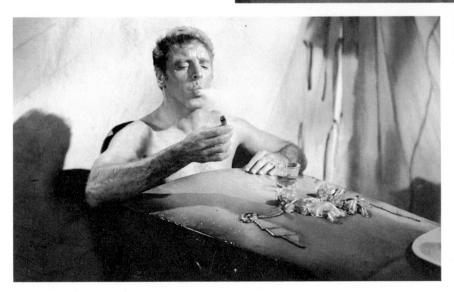

Find your style

When you come to plan your bedroom or bathroom, one of the first things you ask yourself is, "What will it look like in the end?" There are a host of factors, financial, spatial and social, that will influence the final appearance of your rooms, and unless you have a clear picture of what you want to achieve before you start, you could end up with a hodge-podge of compromises. The rooms pictured here are not intended as blueprints to be slavishly followed, detail for detail—the vital touch that makes a room special is the contribution of your own personality and ideas. The purpose of this chapter is to help you to analyse the various ingredients that make up a particular style. Once you have understood just what it is that distinguishes, for instance, the "country house" look from the "cottage", or the "town house" from the "seduction den", you will be able to marry up the various elements that together create a successful scheme.

Find your style
Country cottage

The scale of a cottage is one of the most important ingredients of its charm. Because a cottage is so compact, the most quirky spaces and detailing occur in an innocent effort to cram a quart into a pint pot. This quirkiness should never be lightly obliterated in a misguided attempt to make things more convenient, because there is usually little to gain. For instance, cottage windows are small and may not admit much air during the summer—but their size also helps to prevent heat loss in winter.

The furnishing of cottages and their bedrooms will, of course, be simple and unpretentious and inexpensive, but it must also be charming and reasonably comfortable. Walls look good if white, coloured or prettily papered; doors, windows and woodwork glossy white or stripped pine; pine-boarded, polished floors with simple patterned or striped rugs; beds in enamelled iron or pine; crisp white sheets and stripped pine or bentwood chairs and tables.

Lighting is important since there tend to be few outlets unless the place has been rewired. Small lights with brass bases and glass shades look right by the bedside, as will glass or enamelled shades for the ceiling light. In the bathroom, tungsten strip lights behind a pine fascia work well.

If installing a bathroom, be sensitive to the character of the cottage. Old baths and basins can sometimes be saved, or if you use new ones, choose the simplest designs with the simplest fittings. Jugs of wild flowers add their own charm and reinforce the countrified feel.

Left: *in a tiny cottage room, it is essential to keep everything to scale. Prints and furniture should be small; miniature patchwork may be used to visually reduce the size of a big bed, the only large piece of furniture.*

Far left: *natural pine slats and planks give this unelaborate washroom continuity and depth. Splashes of colour set off the room's neutral tones and useful baskets soften the modern style.*

Above: *illustrating that the cottage style does not have to be pretty-pretty: exciting, checkerboard tiles are used here to brighten a confined area. Taps are installed on the wall in order to leave the curved lines of the tub unbroken.*

Top left: *large windows admit plentiful fresh air and sunshine. A curvilinear bedframe, cane chair and floral bedspread blend well with the peaceful country setting.*

An airier and grander version of the cottage style, where furniture tends to be large and comfortable, especially the beds. Natural wood, usually pine, is used for the cabinet work, floors, ceilings and even as tongued-and-grooved boarding for walls. Alternatively, walls might be rough-plastered or whitewashed, or washed in faded colours. Wallpapers would be sprigged and flowered.

Windows should be easy to fling open, allowing curtains of sprigged muslin to flutter about in the breeze.

Lighting is indirect, with pools of light and dark. Bedside lights made from old stoneware jars with drum shades would be appropriate and a Japanese paper globe with flex looped across the ceiling rafters will work well.

The floor would have its old pine boards sealed and polished or perhaps painted in a pale colour.

Above: *essentially bare furnishings would leave this a sombre room if it were not for the strong repeat print, enhanced by generous light. Dried herbs, although predictably symbolic of the style, add a charm of their own.*

The bathroom is large, with an old-fashioned, comfortable bath and basin. These are often an interesting shape, but with simple tiles around them, or maybe pine boarding, either left natural, painted glossy white, or stained dark brown and varnished. The floor might be cork or quarry tiles and the taps and towel rails polished brass. Rather than smart, patterned or coloured towels, large white ones, probably the worse for wear, hang around, or are stuffed in willow laundry baskets.

One thing always found in the farmhouse bedroom is a jug of daffodils.

Above: *an ingenious transformation of what might have been an obtrusively bulky piece of furniture. Left in their natural state, these wooden bunk beds would surely have swamped the small room with their sombre colour.*

Above left: *an ingenious space-saving idea, though perhaps for agile members of the family only. The modernity and sophistication of the bath and shower fittings blend perfectly with the plain beauty of the steps and surrounds, which are a sympathetic mixture of varnished and stained wood.*

Left: *there are no concessions to slick modernity in this oddly situated bathroom—a splendid old tub is the focal point. A potentially rather characterless and uncomfortable room is given a feeling of warmth by the dusky pink colourings, soft lighting and yellowish glow of the semi-circular window.*

Far left: *surely made for a countryman, the sturdy bed is effectively contrasted against a background of creamy walls and curtains; a contrast strikingly emphasized by the white bedspread, which helps to give the room its delightfully prim and old-fashioned character.*

31

Country house

This style may well depend on fabrics with an air of faded grandeur and on furniture that has a certain patina. All has been lovingly assembled over generations and is the antithesis of *nouveau riche*. Although more elegant than cottage or farmhouse, it is a development of the latter with recognizable overtones of the town-house style.

The floors might still have the austerity of painted or polished old boarding, or, equally, be close-carpeted in one colour. Walls might be painted with pastel colours or papered in pale stripes or a gentle, hardly distinguishable pattern. The fabrics would be chintzy, with sheets, blankets and bedcovers all matching or co-ordinated in a scheme that is soothing and comfortable.

Soft lighting with lampshades covered in pleated fabric; lots of large mirrors and cushions; the dressing table covered with silver-backed hair brushes and large bottles of toilet water (not perfume); framed prints of birds and wild flowers; piles of magazines and books on the bedside tables; rattan chairs and stools and large vases of roses or peonies all add up to make life comfortable for the unostentatiously well-heeled incumbents.

Gentle colours and a feeling of space are the essential elements.

The bathroom is similar, with bath, basin and bidet in the same matching pastel shade, certainly a fitted carpet and again plenty of mirrors. A decorative laundry bin, free-standing mirrors and an interesting cabinet, with jars and bottles, will add charm. The towels would be large and in plain colours.

Right: *the open spaces of the country house successfully translated into a modern idiom: here nothing diverts the eye from the magnificent vaulted ceiling.*

Below: *spaciousness is an important element of this style and should be exploited. In this case, a pretty iron bedstead makes a strong focal point in an uncluttered expanse of floor.*

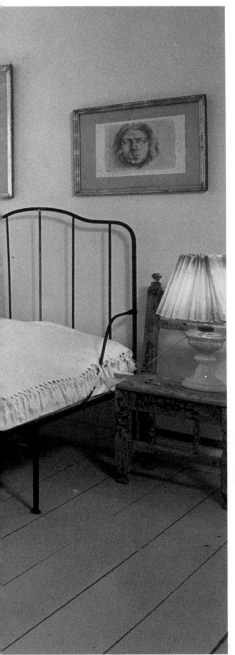

Above: *inlaid boxes, Persian rugs, watercolours and candlesticks abound in large houses, and here these trappings of country life spill over into the bathroom.*

Below left: *with plenty of space at one's disposal, it is possible to position the bath where one pleases. Here the bather enjoys a vista of rolling acres.*

Below: *the country way—softness and prettiness are achieved by means of plump cushions and natural materials.*

Find your style
Town house

A town house ought to be as restful and comfortable as possible—an escape from the rat-race outside.

It has an affluent air, helped along with dark, rich colours in paint and wallpaper; subtle textures of hessian and grasspaper; wall-to-wall carpeting in tiny, neat patterns; gleams of chrome and brass and shafts of brilliant light from concealed spotlights or downlighters illuminating precious objects such as stone carvings or shells.

Beds will be divans with braid-edged, tailored covers and bedheads to match. Bedclothes might be marked with a neat YSL significant only to the eye of the informed beholder. The bedside table will undoubtedly have controls for the lights, perhaps for the television too.

Clothes, in quantity, will be neatly stored in fitted, wall-to-wall closets with hidden doors on touch latches. One of these doors is more than likely a large, full-length mirror in smoked glass. The dressing table is also built into this fitted wall, with concealed striplighting over the make-up mirror.

The bathroom will be very compact and well planned with neat, built-in cabinets. Its walls are almost certainly lined in dark, shiny tiles or maybe dark cork and the ceiling is white to reflect the maximum amount of light if the window is small. Complex bathroom fittings, if they are of shining chrome, add sparkle and eye-catching detail. The floor is probably carpeted to match or to reflect that of the bedroom.

Left: *making the most of the narrow proportions typical of some town houses: "railway tracks" down the ceiling unify the room's extremities. The tiled stove is reminiscent of a wardrobe. Designed by Eliel Saarinen, the Finnish architect.*

Above: *custom-fitted bath and bordered door panels, the essence of this style.*

Top: *a potentially gloomy bathroom compensates for its deficiency of natural light with cheerfully picked out details.*

Left: *a sophisticated, urban blend of colour is achieved by the pinkish-beige of the carpet echoed in the Persian rug. Furniture and objects are kept to a dramatic minimum and arranged well.*

Below: *smart compactness achieved by a partition and checkered border in cork.*

Above: *capitalizing on sparse, urban light: the extendable magnifying mirror permits making-up or shaving with the face well lit by natural light. Additional light is reflected by the wall mirror.*

35

This is the abode of the jet-set entrepreneur, who lays his head down in Olympic Towers, Manhattan, one night and Chester Square, London, the next. Usually it is a total environment dreamt up by a decorator or designer after a quick brief, so that it tends to be his interpretation of jet-set life, an opportunity for him to use his skills in some extravagant and imaginative detailing.

Multilevels are often built into the apartment to increase the feeling of space and luxury: the bed will be on a dais, the bath two steps down and sunken. Deep carpet creeps up walls and the bed itself is ocean going in its self-sufficiency, with every conceivable remote-control gadget within easy reach.

The mood of an international bedroom is dark, rich, silent and mysterious. Woodwork will be rosewood or perhaps ebonized. Walls might be covered in leather, suede or silk. The furniture might well include Bauhaus originals supplemented with Eames and Knoll and modern Italian pieces. The source of lighting will usually be invisible.

Walls, or sometimes a smoked-glass screen, divide bedroom from bathroom, which is lined with terrazzo, marble and expanses of mirror. Every individual detail, including the inset basins and baths, is an integral part of the architecture. Creamy-white blinds diffuse the light, enhancing the feeling of assured and controlled ostentation.

Above: *room to move—a bathroom entirely free from strictures of space. The generous bath is merely a shapely detail in the extensive floor area.*

Left: *simple but dramatic use of colour, reflected in a ceiling of mirror tiles.*

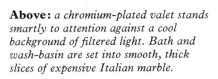

Above: *a chromium-plated valet stands smartly to attention against a cool background of filtered light. Bath and wash-basin are set into smooth, thick slices of expensive Italian marble.*

Right: *expanses of marble and mirror are the hallmarks of the ultra-sophisticated bathroom. Comfortable levels of heat and humidity are essential to obviate the inherent chill of marble and to keep the mirrors free of mist.*

Left: *a rich, sophisticated glow, pierced by a recessed downlighter and reflected in panels of tinted mirror. The sculptural shelving unit, forming a dual-purpose bedhead and room divider, displays a collection of "executive" objects, rather than piles of paperbacks and magazines.*

Above: *a little wash-bowl of smart stainless steel adds its own hard shininess to that of the tiles and mirror. Quality, precision materials are more important than colour in creating this style.*

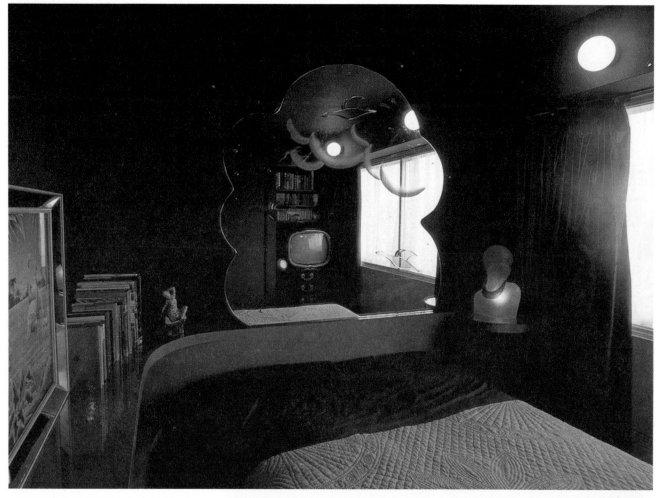

Eclectics were the class of philosophers who selected such doctrines as pleased them in every school. Today, designers of this persuasion widen our visual horizons by examining, then recycling, the artefacts of other ages and cultures, ordering them so that sometimes they become relevant to contemporary life. In this way they translate fads, such as art deco, into lasting styles, but only if they are truly talented people. Unfortunately, eclecticism is often a smokescreen for insincerity and bad taste.

The renaissance of, for example, *art nouveau* and Jugendstyle (known in Italy as Stile Liberty) started about ten years ago when a few designers and artists rediscovered the abundant creativity that occurred at the beginning of this century. They combined the original artefacts with new products that they designed in the same style. But because of the time lapse since the inception of the original ideas, these developed and changed subtly, and themselves became the prototypes of new styles.

This style is a highly personal one; the mark of people who are supremely confident of their own taste. They may be, and usually are, associated in some way with the arts, and it is they who are the creative innovators. Eclectics do not aim to keep up with the Joneses. And indeed, the Joneses have no wish to keep up with them—until an eclectic style has been given the official seal of approval by the glossy magazines.

Above: *the conventional treatment of a small, poky room is to create the illusion of space by making it light and airy. Here, a successful deviation from the rule has produced a womb-like retreat, bejewelled with curiously etched mirrors and dimly lit by an opalescent glass bust.*

Right: *a celebration of the 1950s, featuring the artist's palette, a motif reminiscent of bohemian coffee bars. The room hovers on the verge of being a museum of kitsch, but, perversely enough, is rescued by the riveting pop paintings from another decade.*

Far right: *a cavernous bathroom in the grand manner, generously over-furnished with swagged curtains, chandeliers and silver rocking chairs. Further oddities include an occult motif on the floor and a modernistic nude high on the wall.*

Above: *a curious corner, overrun with plastic hooks, which bring a touch of amusement to a potentially boring wall and are functional as well.*

Top left: *"Home is the sailor, home from sea, and the hunter home from the hill"; dramatic trophies and native artefacts are heaped about the place—flywhisks, swordfish, Indonesian batiks and Navajo rugs all help to transform this compact urban bedroom.*

Left: *beds like giant bonbons with candy-striped bows are the dominant feature in this personal decorative extravaganza. Despite the incongruous touches of pine, leather, chrome and cowhide, the effect has been to create an unforgettable, cohesive whole.*

Eastern bizarre

This look has recently emerged from the eclectic stable and gained glossy magazine recognition. At its best it can be an exciting *mélange* of pattern and colour, and, at its worst, a tatty hotchpotch of garish, oriental imports.

The knack of creating this look is knowing when to stop. Take as your standard the controlled elegance of Indian miniatures. Piles of highly patterned, colourful cushions will look that much better if they have a plain background. Remember that Sultans themselves usually wear a plain white, loose djellaba with a coloured sash. Pick up the look of their tents and drape fabrics to make a canopy for the bed.

When you select mirrors, or screens for the windows, remember the gracefully curved domes of mosques. Do not take short cuts with shutters made from fretcut hardboard, but construct them from slats of wood cross-hatched in a geometric lattice.

Big brass trays can look perfectly fine as bedside tables if they rest on a simple base and are not kitsched up with heaps of ethnic clutter.

In the bathroom, wall tiles in blue and white, Moorish patterns or mirror mosaic with a floor of buff quarry tiles, patterned, ceramic mosaic or pale cork would look just right. Bathrobes are a must, and towels should be in a mixture of neat, geometric patterns.

One advantage of this look is that it can quickly and economically endow rented rooms with a comfortable, casual and satisfying style, creating something of a home-made harem.

Left: *a many-faceted bejewelled extravaganza—an ordinary bathroom becomes a setting fit for the "Desert Song"—and all thanks to panels of tiny mirror tiles, a profusion of steam-loving plants and a magnificent, ostrich-egg chandelier.*

Right: *the bedroom of Zandra Rhodes, one of Britain's most innovatory dress designers. The walls and bed canopy are artfully draped with inexpensive Indian bedspreads hanging from a regal canopy supported by chains from the ceiling.*

Far right: *guest bedroom in the palace of the Maharajah of Udaipur, an Indian state famous for the beauty of its palaces. This serene room is a far cry from the overdecorated East of our imaginings.*

Left: *a ruby-red tent full of rich Eastern promise. A long, narrow room has been transformed with silk, ebony, gold and fur into a dream image of a maharajah's palace.*

Below: *the real thing. In a courtyard of the Alhambra, the fortified palace of the ancient Moorish kings of Granada, the royal bathtub is built-in behind pillars. The Alhambra is rich in the typical features of Moorish architecture— courtyards and gardens ornamented with marble, mosaic and fountains.*

Hollywood glamour

The shrines of the sex goddesses of Hollywood's silver screens in the 1920s and 1930s have much influenced the look of bedrooms. Unfortunately, this influence has mainly been bad, epitomized as it is in the tasteless frills around kidney-shaped dressing-tables and the hideous, barbola-work on mirror frames.

Possibly the style has its roots in the bedchambers of medieval kings and queens, when rough stone walls were covered with rich hangings, and a simple wood frame was converted by the art of the upholder (forefather of the upholsterer) into a splendid four-posted nuptial arena. The sex goddess, just like the queen, has to have an altar, but in her case it is reincarnated as a dressing-table covered in an embroidered cloth and set about with the artefacts of her religion.

When this style has been properly interpreted in a contemporary idiom, bedrooms and bathrooms of glamour and sensuousness have materialized.

The bedroom relies on space, with the bed dominating the room. The bed itself might well be sculptured into a shape reminiscent of love—but I have often wondered how one buys sheets to fit a heart-shaped bed. The floor would have voluptuously deep, close-carpeting, and the windows would be heavily curtained in a satin-finish fabric. There is very little pattern, only soft, subtle, plain colours. Padding is important, certainly on bed-heads and bed covers, but perhaps even as quilting on the walls, because sound, like light, has to be soft.

Furniture, lacquered cream or covered in a mosaic of bevelled-edge mirror, floats around like expensive yachts in Cannes harbour.

The light sources would be indirect, from strip-lights in the pelmet washing down the curtains, and from behind the headboard, or from the sides of the dressing-table mirror. Several table lamps with large, pleated fabric shades provide scattered pools of light. Lovingly signed photos in silver frames cover table tops and Marie Laurencin paintings decorate the walls. A large vase of red roses or spiky, pink gladioli from an admirer complete the luscious picture.

The bath, like the bed, is likely to be large, circular or heart shaped and it may in addition be sunken. Water might pour from gilded dolphins' heads and the walls be entirely of mirror or, even more sensuously, black glass. The floor and the bath-surround are of marble and the towels unbelievably large, in plain colours, monogrammed.

The basin can be part of another dressing-table, this time the serious work-centre where the war paint, that keeps the goddess on her throne, is applied. No frills this time: direct lighting around the sides of the mirror ensures maximum visibility, and neat cupboards and drawers stock the tools of her trade.

Above: *vanity satiated—a mirrored bed reflected in a mirrored wall. Pale pink and white have always been colours favoured by complexion-conscious stars—here the scheme is given oomph with lipstick-red scatter cushions.*

Right: *worthy of a Studio Charm School starlet, this is a dressing-table for serious grooming sessions.*

Top right: *flattering, low-level lights are reflected in mirrored table-tops and alcoves. Thick, padded silk covers are for those who drink champagne, not black coffee, for breakfast.*

Centre right: *pinkish-white marble bath facing a mirror so that Venus can admire herself arising from the waves.*

Far right: *the generously rounded curves of this magnificent dressing-table are a reminder of Hollywood's great and glorious past.*

Find your style
A period piece

Quality, solidity and pattern epitomized the Victorian attitude to the design of homes. It stemmed from a superb confidence that all was right with their world. Their homes were their castles.

Today, in a less stable world, that confidence seems rather attractive and this is one reason why this style of decoration is successfully reproduced, especially in bedrooms. Also, just because of its quality and solidity, much Victoriana remains intact.

The grand, ornate brass bedstead had pride of place. Walls were covered with a rich, coloured and patterned paper. Ornate plaster-work moulding framed the ceiling. Doors were heavy and closed with a clunk. The solid furniture was made of mahogany. Curtains were lined and interlined, obscuring light and deadening sound.

This cloying heaviness often seems excessive for contemporary life, and the remedy is to lighten the room by painting the walls or papering them with a paler, more charming pattern and close-carpeting the floor in a plain colour. The cumbersome furniture can be reduced in quantity, but the comfortable brass bedstead must remain, even if some of its ornate excesses are removed in the name of simplicity.

A Victorian bathroom really was a celebration of the plumber's art. Pipework and fittings were solid; large, comfortable, enamelled baths filled quickly with very hot water and their sides were panelled. Tiled walls in neat, geometric patterns; mosaic floors; solid brass towel rails; marble shelves; bevelled edges to mirrors and mahogany toilet seats added up to a comfortable, practical bathroom that works as well today as it ever did.

Above right: *the best of the Edwardian age—rich mahogany panelling and beautiful, etched mirrors—make an interesting setting for efficient modern equipment. There is no need to suffer cracked cisterns and leaky taps in the cause of authenticity—good modern design should blend into any setting.*

Right: *a pretty little Victorian washstand surrounded by knick-knacks in a specialist antique shop. Lamps with opalescent shades—emulating gaslight—sparkle in the mirrors, recreating the atmosphere of the period.*

Right: *charming brass and enamel four-poster, hung about with bits of antique lace and topped with a snow-white crochet cover. Because all the surrounding objects are so perfectly in period, it does not matter that there is a modern telephone. Victorian interiors were often somewhat gloomy and fusty. But in this modern translation, the white ceiling counters any feelings of oppression.*

45

Oriental simplicity

Different ages have borrowed different looks from the Orient: Chippendale his chinoiserie and bamboo chairs, Whistler the blue and white china. We have extracted the geometric, stark, low-level look of a traditional Japanese house. This involves a low, simple bed built on a platform, with a mattress rather like a karate pad. Light-diffusing screens cover the windows. It is a style only for the very tidy: clutter destroys the serenity.

Lighting may come from the modern Italian fittings that have an oriental flavour, especially those of the sculptor Noguchi and the fine, lacquered fan lights of Ingo Maurer. One large papyrus plant carefully placed in a corner, or a ceramic vase with a sprig of cherry blossom, completes the decoration.

Bathrooms in the oriental style differ, depending on whether they are in the town or country. If the former, then a continuation of austere geometry with exquisitely detailed closets and fittings is required. Baths and basins should be built into the whole rectilinear plan of things, with every knob and rail as unobtrusive as possible and the surfaces plain and unpatterned.

Above: *bathtime at a Japanese students' hostel. Having washed outside the bath, the students enjoy a communal soak in a modern version of the traditionally deep, rectangular Japanese tub.*

Above right: *the slatted platform is both a bench and bed-base, epitomizing the simple, linear style of the Orient.*

Right: *bedrooms in the oriental style require a subtle storage system to minimize the Western clutter of clocks, books and clothing. Here they are hidden in the bedside trunk and behind the painted screen.*

Left: *this French country bathroom is full of natural materials that evoke the native artefacts of steamy, Far-Eastern jungles. The primitive basin is gouged from a slab of Provençal stone. Copper piping and tap valves are encased in hollow bamboo sealed with polyurethane to prevent steamy rot. The room is bathed in a beautiful, diffused light filtering through a sheet of jute sacking material stretched taut across the ceiling skylight.*

Above: *held together with string—the efficient shower makes no concessions to modern plumbing components.*

47

Find your style
Mediterranean

As a style, Mediterranean can mean many things to many people, so it is important that I should clearly describe my interpretation.

It is associated with the simple, sunny life led by those lucky people who live around the Mediterranean. Lightness, airiness, clean, clear colours and subtle, natural shades make me think of the Mediterranean, as does a simple, uncluttered way of life.

It is perfectly possible to interpret the style in a modern or traditional way and indeed the traditional is often so timeless that both work well together.

A Mediterranean bedroom might have walls and arched door openings that are roughly plastered, or left with that sandy texture produced by strokes of the mason's trowel. The floor might be cool,

Left: *in a sticky, Mediterranean climate a ceramic- and terracotta-lined bathroom is cool and refreshing. The formal lines of the floor tiles and regal elevation of the bathtub strike a pleasing balance with the rounded curves of the simple French chair, wash-stand and bidet.*

Provençal terracotta tiles with a plain, lightly textured wool or cotton rug. A splash of vibrant colour in a painting or bedcover stimulates the senses.

The control of sunlight is important, so that curtains or blinds are likely to be plain white. At night time, shutters close out the insects and in the early morning, unwanted light. Furniture is extremely simple and sparse, made from olivewood or pine bleached silver or painted dull, subtle shades of dark green or blue.

In the bathroom, tiles are again the dominant decorative motif: they might be terracotta hexagons, rhomboids or just plain squares for the floor. Perhaps the same blue and white design may be used on both floor and walls. Towel rails, cabinets and shelves look good in both olivewood or pine.

Left: *tiles, mosaic and whitewashed stone are all characteristically Mediterranean. Here, however, the style has been adapted and modernized. The simple, attractive shapes and designs remain, but have been imaginatively reorganized to make a practical wash-basin unit, with adequate space for storage.*

Below left: *the rough texture of the chunky bedspread wittily matches the uneven wall and adds character to a spartan, Mediterranean holiday cottage bedroom. A potted fig tree breaks the white-on-white colour scheme and its glossy green leaves make the room feel more furnished and lived in.*

Below: *even the lampshade appears to be taking off in this jet-set, riviera bedroom. An abstract painting and the plain modernity of the bed and floor cushions constitute an up-to-the-minute version of the Mediterranean style. Some skill is required in avoiding total failure while juxtaposing such seemingly unconnected elements for maximum effect.*

Above: *located in a Grecian villa, this simple bedroom sets the scene for the daily siesta. Splashes of colour, provided by the indigenous woven rugs, jugged flowers and potted plants, off-set the typically stark stone cupboard surround and tiled floor.*

Find your style
Seduction den

Some Sybarites prefer to emphasize the secondary use of the bedroom—making love—to that of sleeping, but there is no reason why an overtly sexy bedroom should not be restful.

The primeval instinct to climb into a small, secure cave is one which bedrooms of this style often try to satisfy. This may be done by siting the bedroom in confined spaces like the loft, beneath the stairs, or even by building the bed on a dais. If space is at a premium the bed could be on a platform. In this case it is vital to make the ladder up to the bed really secure, and to create a sense of security on the platform itself: it is surprising how easily the seductive mood is destroyed when one is distracted by minor anxieties.

Mirrors, lighting and warmth are important components. Mirrors behind, above, alongside and at the end of the bed have always been used by those who like to add extra dimensions to the sex act. A soft, warm light that responds to the touch of a bedside dimmer switch can be delightful. Venetian blinds that control the moonlight or afternoon sun; thick curtains that obliterate them; warm air supplemented by an open fire in winter, and in the summer a cool breeze all help to stimulate the senses and serve the cause of eroticism.

The seductive bathroom must rely on a bath comfortably large enough for two, or alternatively a large shower. Fur on the floor is not practical, but a thick, absorbent carpet is an adequate substitute. Colours and lighting should be soft and peachy. A large mirror is in keeping, as are big bottles of scent, aftershave or talc and, of course, a bidet.

Above: *since Elinor Glyn, mistress of Lord Curzon, announced her predilection for making love on tiger skins, fur everywhere has become the popular idea of a sexy bedroom. Now that it is anti-social to use the real thing, fake fur is perfectly acceptable.*

Top: *the dedicated playboy or girl may decide to invest in audio-visual equipment. In this highly erotic room, its bed surrounded by a velvet-cushioned lip, sexy music and blue movies help to create a den for unbridled lust.*

Right: *an expanse of buff carpet that laps over the furniture creates a warm, seductive background for the centrepiece, an enormous bed dramatically lit by the skylight above.*

Above: *an adult's adventure playground in which the furniture is shaped and recessed, the textures soft and the colours muted.*

Far left: *embedded in a sea of shocking pink, the sunken bed is designed to be rolled on to from the floor in comfortable abandon. When one sits in the cockpit, the floor becomes a table for lamp and mirror.*

Left: *all roads lead to a double bed given the importance almost of a shrine. Emphatic, striped carpeting leads the eye unerringly towards a bed raised on two steps, with suitably discreet lighting.*

Find your style
Essentially masculine

Most men would like their rooms to be very neat and tidy with everything in apple-pie order, but they rarely are unless there is a woman or a Jeeves around. However, the essential of this style is neatness, straight lines and angles: curves and flounces are obviously feminine.

Everything in the truly masculine bedroom would be sober and architectural. Walls are probably covered with a dark paint or sombre paper, the bed with a tailored spread, maybe in corduroy, the close-fitted carpet either in one dark colour of Wilton or in a very neat pattern *à la* Hicks. The only contrast to this severity might be an old and comfortable leather club chair.

Clothes would be kept in good order, with shoes and ties in racks and shirts in shallow trays: a well-designed and efficient built-in closet of mahogany or teak, with interior lights, houses them all.

Lighting, in these circumstances, is for practical purposes, such as reading, dressing and shaving—not for flattery. A reasonable number of electronic gadgets, not gimmicks, are included to make life more comfortable.

Sporting prints and photos of football teams, speed-boats and skiing adorn the walls in neat black or aluminium frames, and on the bedside table are photos of the better-looking girlfriends and even mother. Silver trophies might, with luck, fill a bookcase or two in the room of a sportsman enjoying a winning streak.

The bathroom is again a model of neatness and architectural planning—everything is built-in and well made, framed in chrome, covered in glass, panelled in formica. The floor might be cork or the same geometric patterned carpet used in the bedroom, and the towels either plain or with a neat pattern.

If you were to open the mirror-faced bathroom cupboard, you might be surprised at the large number of different bottles of after-shave, toilet water, deodorant and hair-care potions that are apparently indispensable to the essentially masculine male.

This room exemplifies the male's well-known formal neatness. The bed is placed centrally like a sacrificial altar and there are no loose objects, save storage boxes and pouches, on any surface. The adjustable lamps, with their capacity for precise lighting, are super-masculine.

Above: *the most predictable way of achieving this style is to rig out a room with exclusively male objects.*

Left: *a masculine bathroom is here created by the presence of such male paraphernalia as the tape deck and Cologne bottle set and also by a particularly functional use of texture. The carpeted back rest behind the WC bowl and bidet really is comfortable and the clear circle in the smoked-glass mirror allows for a good view while shaving.*

Below left: *it is possible to create the masculine look solely with strong colours.*

Below: *the masculine way of treating space is to emphatically define the territory of each piece of hardware with solid partitions.*

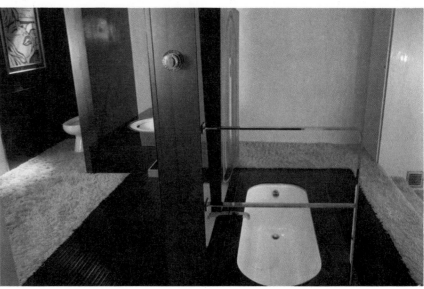

Find your style
Essentially feminine

I suppose women think of the bedroom more as "my room" than "our room", which is why there are so many essentially feminine bedrooms. Maybe men encourage women to make the rooms feminine because they find it sexy. I personally feel that the style would pall with married life, but might be quite charming in the first flowering of love.

Flowers, frills and softness are essential to the style, as are soft lights and soft beds. Pretty, sweetpea colours and pale, stripped pine furniture contribute to the air of guileless sweetness.

Floors might be of pine boards painted a pale colour and stencilled or covered here and there with a fluffy rug. Windows might have a lacy curtain or a pretty, flowered print. Table lamps with drum or pleated shades or even draped with scarves provide the soft, peachy background light.

If there is a fitted closet, its doors are likely to be louvred and painted white. Loose furniture might be of cane or rattan, well padded with loose cushions. Collections of small pictures, photographs and mementos decorate the walls and tops of chests of drawers and dressing-tables. Mirrors, usually in ornate frames, are placed so that they flatter. Romantic novelettes are always to be found on the bedside table.

Above: *girlie clutter : everything is well within reach while adding cheerful and interesting decoration to both table-top and mirror.*

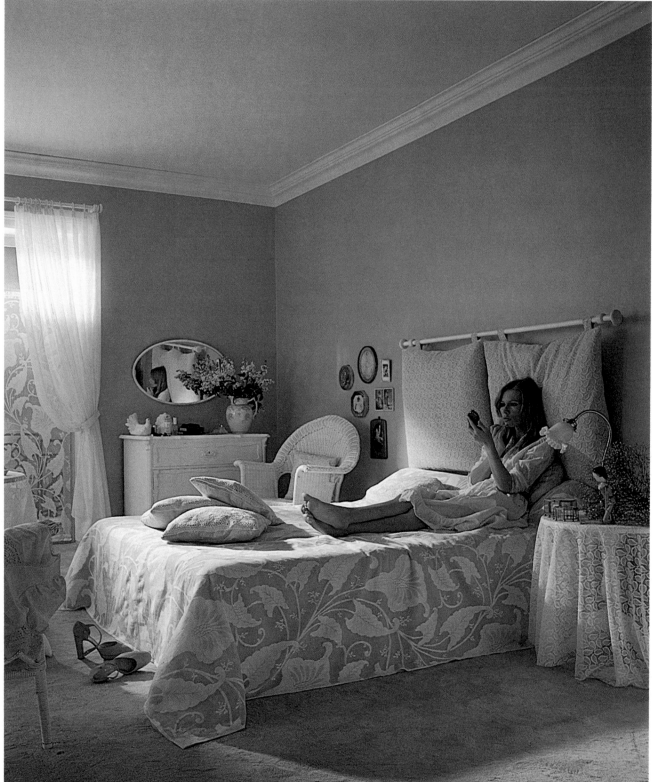

Left: *generously draped peach-coloured fabrics and embroidered lace create a particularly feminine form of luxury. Nothing disturbs the feeling of tranquillity and simplicity.*

Right: *fit for a starlet, plush rolls of padding head the bed. The combination of frills, flowers and a fancy print makes this room uncompromisingly feminine.*

Far right: *a woman's touch—it takes very little trouble to transform a shelf with flowers and an interesting selection of suitable objects.*

Below: *deliberately positioned plants create neat points of colour in sympathy with the design of the fabric. This bedroom is fresh and cool by day, but snug and intimate at night, with its cosy duvet and pendant lamp simply shaded with cotton lawn.*

The styling link

If your bedroom and bathroom are *en suite*, then I think it preferable to avoid a cultural shock as you move between the two areas. The difficulty is to achieve a sense of continuity between two very different places with distinct functions.

The open-plan bed/bathroom will undoubtedly be improved with some form of division, such as a built-in dressing-table back-to-back with a wash-basin unit, or a wardrobe facing into the bedroom that is backed by an airing cupboard on the bathroom side. But there is no need for the division to be a functional one. It could be purely decorative—a model ship in a glass case, a piece of interesting sculpture or a free-standing double-sided mirror. You might consider providing a private place for the wc unit and the bidet, screened off by a sliding panel or a curtain.

Colours, materials, finishes and lighting should flow, as far as possible, from one area to the other. Carpet, if used in the bedroom, should continue into the bathroom, as should wallpapers and fabrics. For instance, you may use a draped material for the bedroom curtains and a blind in the same fabric for the bathroom, and link the basic colours of the sheets and duvet covers to the bathroom towels. This co-ordination will have the synergistic effect of increasing the sensation of space, as the two rooms become welded into one.

If, on the other hand, you have to travel down a long corridor to reach your bathroom, then a real cultural shock is probably exactly what you need.

Right: *looking as compact as a lunar module, this circular bathroom, set in the middle of the bedroom, would appear quite incongruous without the scarlet bath mat and towels, which repeat the line and colour of the bedroom curtains.*

Below: *in this open-plan room, wood and brass are evident in both bed and bath areas. Sleeping and washing places are defined by a showcase for a much-valued possession.*

Above: *Victoriana, epitomized in the brass bedstead, is reiterated in the adjoining bathroom by the period pieces and heavy, mahogany fittings.*

Left: *a central, carpeted track links the sleeping area to the washing area; the glass turret, housing a screen of plants, acts as a decorative token divider between the two territories.*

Bedroom planning

It seems sadly incongruous that the bedroom, which is by far the most personal room in the house, is also the most neglected. The reason, I suspect, is that it is not usually on public view, and this becomes an excuse for taking shortcuts in design and planning. But this is a false economy. A good night's sleep in a comfortable bed, a leisurely selection of your clothes from a well-ordered wardrobe, a warm, well-lit room with a floor that is pleasant to touch and a bed that is easy to make and, above all, a room that looks good to your eyes, will help you to face the world in a relaxed frame of mind. This chapter deals with all those considerations that go into the planning of a comfortable and stimulating bedroom: where it should be located, where the bed should be, the calculation of storage requirements, and the practical elements such as heating, plumbing and lighting, and the choice of treatment for windows, walls and floors—in short, how to plan your bedroom so that you look forward to sleeping, waking and living in it.

Bedroom planning
Location

In the average urban home, the main bedroom is usually located directly above the living-room and facing the street. The reasons for this are primarily structural: the greatest floor area is to be found above the living-room, usually the largest room in the house, and both rooms can have common structural walls. Family behaviour has also influenced home design. Parents tend automatically to occupy the main bedroom because, being themselves the principal users of the living-room, they can then be sure that noise made in the bedroom will not disturb anyone downstairs. Conversely, they can relax in the living-room with their friends, unrestricted by the presence of sleeping children in the room above.

In reality, few households run on such ordered lines. One man's private haven might be an isolation cell to another. So consider what you want from your bedroom before you decide where to lay down your bed.

If the bedroom is to be used only for sleeping, then one of the largest areas of space in the house will be woefully under-used for the greater part of the day. If you are a light sleeper or a late riser, you will sleep better in a back bedroom, overlooking a quiet garden instead of a noisy street. And if you yearn for the sun on your face in the morning, you will have to move the bedroom accordingly.

Size: If you spend plenty of time in your bedroom—reading, dressing, watching television or just escaping from the general hubbub—you will need a room large enough to contain these activities, otherwise you will get little pleasure from them. If, on the other hand, you crash into bed after midnight and set off at dawn, then all you need is the smallest convenient space into which you can compress a bed and perhaps a clothes storage system. If you decide to keep your clothes in a separate dressing-room, this again will affect the size of the room you need.

Orientation: Morning sun lovers in the northern hemisphere should choose rooms facing the south-east, sunset worshippers the south-west, and those who dislike sunlight in their sleeping quarters should pick the northern side of the house.

Children: Parents and children do not have to sleep in adjacent rooms. In fact,

as adults and children keep such different hours, the farther they are from one another the more chance there will be of uninterrupted sleep all round. In this case, nervous parents can listen in to the baby's breathing on an intercom link, and on a two-way intercom they can mutter reassuring sounds to fretful children without leaving the warm comfort of their beds.

The bathroom: A bathroom near the bedroom is essential for a comfortable life, and the position of the bedroom is thus to some extent determined by the location of the plumbing: the bathroom and its pipework is expensive to move around. For economy and efficiency, kitchens, bathrooms and WCs are usually stacked neatly above one another on each floor or, in the case of apartments and one-storey houses, backed on to the same service wall, and share the same drains.

A typical two-child family in a three-bedroom house will have the parents in the large front bedroom and the children in a room each at the back. If the parents want to invite the occasional guest without disrupting the household, and they feel they would rather have a view of the patio than of the street, then the easiest solution is to turn the front bedroom into a dormitory for the children (possibly splitting it into two rooms), thus freeing the third bedroom to become a dressing-room-cum-guest-room, a study or even a second bathroom.

In many houses, the first-floor front room is the largest in the house because, unlike the front room on the ground floor, it does not have a hall or passageway from the front door, and it makes a better living-room than bedroom. So, unless your bedroom is the most important room in your life, consider sleeping downstairs and enjoying the views from a first-floor living-room.

Convention accepts that two adult people will share a bedroom, and indeed a bed, for most of their lives. But if the two people concerned have widely different life-styles, it is asking much of one room to accommodate them both.

One, perhaps, may like to sleep from 10.30 pm to 7.00 am, then leap out of bed to perform Canadian Air Force exercises. The other may be addicted to late-night horror films on the television over a couple of cognacs, then reading until 2.30 am. In which case, separate rooms may be well worth considering.

Many older houses have an enormous attic which will convert into an excellent main bedroom, a bathroom or both, liberating space below. Before attempting such a project, have a survey made of the roof space. Beds, and more particularly baths full of water, are very heavy. Attic floor joists are not as substantial as those in the rest of the house.

Basement bedrooms are potentially cosy, although they tend to be airless. Bathrooms may present a further problem. If the basement has never been connected to mains drainage before, have a plumber check the house drains: if they are placed above the basement floor level, you will have to install a sewage pump to clear the waste pipes from the new bathroom. Sewage pumps should be installed by a qualified plumber and, for your peace of mind, regularly serviced.

Above: *a platform overlooking the sitting area—an interesting location for the bedroom, provided the people who sleep there are the last to bed.*

Top: *on the ground floor, the hall wall has been removed and what was once the dining-room has become the main bedroom-cum-TV-room—more formal seating arrangements are upstairs. Roll-up pinoleum blinds give the sleepers a degree of privacy, protection from draughts and a sense of security.*

Right: *an architectural solution to the conflicting needs for space and privacy. On the galleried upper floor, walls are merely parapets—when required, panels of stiffened fabric slide across the ceiling track, affording privacy to the occupants of the main bedroom.*

Bedroom planning
Allocating space

A large bedroom, suitably furnished and heated, is delightful. But should a bedroom fail to measure up to the ideal of spacious living, you can, with careful planning, create for it at least an illusion of space.

Most floor space in most bedrooms is, quite rightly, taken up with the bed or beds. The narrow strip of extra floor space gained by cramming yourself and your mate into a bed a size smaller than is comfortable rarely compensates for the resulting sleeplessness.

Nevertheless, if a bed threatens to engulf the entire room, consider a tip-up variety which disappears into a closet during the day, or a bed on a platform, high enough to clear a useful area of floor for clothes storage or dressing-table space. If cantilevered beds and carpentry are out of the question, an easy way to diminish the size of the bed visually is to reduce its height by fitting very short legs or just castors to the bed frame. Head boards, four-posters and canopied drapes are only for rooms of generous proportions.

If the bedroom is of a size and shape to permit you to choose where the bed is placed, do not position the head of the bed under a window (unless the window shuts firmly and has been professionally double glazed): you will be exposing yourself to a neck-cricking draught. Equally, you will sleep in a draught if the bed is placed between the window and the door. If you like to sleep by a window in hot weather, choose a bed on skids or castors that can be moved around easily.

Clothing
After beds, clothing and shoes are the greediest consumers of space. Unless you provide adequate wardrobe or closet space, you will eventually drown in a sea of suits and dresses that belong nowhere. Hanging and drawer space are universally necessary, but clothes storage must always be planned for the individual: a cool dude with two pairs of jeans to his name will have a completely different set of priorities to the competition dancer who owns 20 pretty ball gowns stiffened with countless layers of tulle.

The sacrifice of one wall to fitted storage means you can forget about chests of drawers and wardrobes, which waste floor area by creating pockets of unusable space around and above them.

Wall-fixed storage at the head of the

Above and right: *an ingenious use of space with a strong linear effect. The position of the bed may be varied within* the open partition between the study and bedroom areas. The sliding screen neatly divides the two rooms.

bed with shelves for a radio, alarm clock, glass of water, books and a bedside light will prove less space-consuming than separate tables. It will also free the floor area for other activities such as bedmaking and early-morning press-ups.

Make room for a chair if you can—a bed makes an inadequate sitting place, and it is pleasant to sit in comfort to chatter or read. A chair also provides a good alternative to the floor as an overnight resting place for hastily discarded clothing.

Space-saving solutions
Planning a bedroom in an existing space, rather than designing one to your own requirements, is always difficult, but there are a few modest alterations you can make to any room that can make all the difference between a comfortable, workable bedroom and a nightmarish forest of clashing doors and drawers.

Doors, for example, can be re-hung to swing in the opposite direction, exchanged for sliding doors or even removed completely. Radiators can be repositioned without too much upheaval—the best place for them is under the window to heat the cold air as it sinks and push warmed air around the room. Fireplaces, unless in use or possessed of particular charm, should be removed and the space filled in to make a free wall

available for shelving or clothes storage.

The well-planned bedroom will also have contingency space for out-of-favour garments—shelves or closets, for instance fixed above windows or above the bed. It is a sad fact that all possessions expand to overflow the available space, and that human nature, on the whole, takes unkindly to any suggestion of discarding them.

Above: *bold use of available space. The well-lit room is given over almost entirely to the large bed. The frame helps to suggest a ceiling to the bedroom area.*

Right: *smart and compact, the bedroom becomes a casual study area with the duvet and pillows hidden neatly away during the day. The multi-purpose cabinets may be for clothes or office use.*

Layout

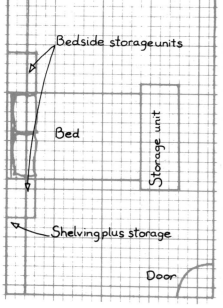

Bedside storage units

Bed

Storage unit

Shelving plus storage

Door

Above and right: *when designing a room, organize your master-plan first. To keep a large area of floor space clear, position the bed and storage units together and build in high-level shelves.*

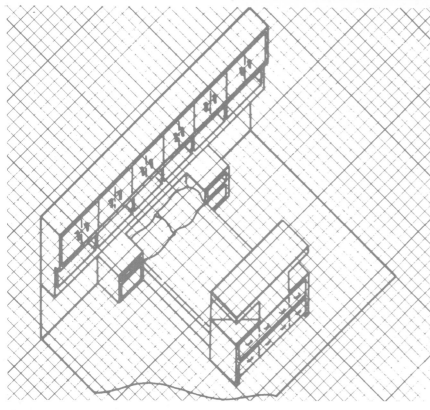

Much detailed research has been carried out to establish minimum space requirements for the use of individual pieces of furniture and equipment. This has been done to create a set of standards to help architects to design workable living spaces for people.

Drawing a plan

An accurate floor plan is immensely useful. It clears the mind and encourages imaginative solutions that the single-handed planner faced with a roomful of heavy furniture may never attempt. A good plan is also a great help to builders, carpenters and plumbers, who need all the help they can get if they are taking their brief from an amateur.

To make a plan, draw a rough, free-hand sketch of the floor area, then measure the room carefully, using a steel rule for accuracy. Transfer the plan on to grid paper, using the scale of 1:20—1 cm on paper equal to 20 cm of wall if you are working in metric; $\frac{1}{2}$ in to 10 in if you work in Imperial.

Measure up all the furniture and equipment and draw out each piece on thin card to the same scale as your room plan, then draw around each item the required circulation space as shown in our diagrams. Cut out the furniture pieces and shuffle them around on your plan. It will be difficult to produce a plan on which none of the circulation areas overlap, but what looks congested on paper can often work well in practice, especially if the furniture is low, as feet and ankles need less space than thighs.

Arranging furniture

Give some thought to your particular way of life, your activities, hobbies and habits, and aim to produce logical furniture groupings that relate to them.

If, for instance, you rise at leisure and spend an hour in front of the mirror preparing to face the day, you will need a large dressing-table with a comfortable seat that is well out of the main circulation route. The stay-in-bed, on the other hand, who dresses in seconds flat and performs essential grooming on the run, hardly needs to clutter up the bedroom with dressing-tables and stools as they will seldom justify their presence.

Wash-basins and showers, of course, have to be plumbed in where there is

Above: *compact, low-level bedroom planning : shelves surrounding the bed on all sides allow one to keep all manner of bedtime necessities close to hand.*

Top right: *displaying a simplicity associated with the Orient, this cuboid storage unit serves as bedroom shelves, drawers, wardrobe and bedhead.*

water, and their position will be more or less dictated by the existing pipework. Modern professional plumbing has put an end to pipes that gurgle in the night, so sleeping *en suite* with the bathroom is no longer a noisy affair.

Power points should be installed on either side of the bed for bedside lights, and if you intend to do the ironing, watch television, use a hair-dryer or vacuum the carpet, install a power point in the wall farthest from the bed. Make sure you can switch off the lights from a recumbent position, as there is little point in getting nicely soporific over your bedtime book if you have to wake yourself up to trip over to the light switch. Try to leave a clear route to the door : if you have to get out of bed blinded with sleep to get a glass of water or calm a crying child, you do not want to risk crashing into the sharp corner of a dressing-table.

Right: *a cool, low-level room, rightly revolving around the centrally placed bed. As the bed has a very low base, the surrounding shelves are correspondingly low and therefore within easy reach.*

Awkwardly shaped rooms

Spare a thought for the light-house keeper in his dizzying tower; for the sea-dog cramped into the sharp end of his ship; the artist in his cramped and low-ceilinged garret—and your own awkwardly shaped room will appear almost normal. There is a hidden bonus to a room of odd dimensions: it exercises the imagination to search for and find interesting solutions that could turn a Cinderella of a room into the most interesting in the house.

Too small

In a bedroom with a ceiling height of about 4.3 m/14 ft, a simple platform bed with space beneath for storage, dressing-table and so on could virtually double the room's capacity. Platforms can be constructed by a do-it-yourself enthusiast of moderate skill from either timber or a type of clamp-together layman's scaffolding. If you intend standing on the platform, allow headroom of 2 m/6 ft 6 in. If you are content to crawl into bed, leave a good 1.5 m/4 ft between your pillow and the ceiling, so you can sit up comfortably and read without feelings of oppression.

If you lack the headroom for a platform, a bed with storage facilities in the base is a good compromise. Several manufacturers make beds with drawers underneath, or you could get one made by a carpenter to your own specifications or build up a bed base yourself using a proprietary storage cube system. Reaching under the bed is not an easy action, so do not store daily essentials, such as underwear, in floor-level drawers. Reserve below-the-bed space for bulky sweaters and extra blankets, and all the space-consuming sports gear that normally congests the small closet.

In a small bedroom that doubles as space for daytime activities, it may be necessary to get rid of the bed altogether during daylight hours. A convertible sofa-bed is not a permanent solution: convertibles, being hybrids, rarely make good, supportive beds or comfortable sofas. In addition, the morning and evening rituals of folding and unfolding, unmaking and making, soon turn into a chore. Convertibles are best left for overnight guests and transitory one-room flats.

Tip-up beds have an institutional clang about their image, due to their popularity in youth hostels and colleges. Today's cantilevered beds, however, are both stylish and comfortable, and their great advantage is that they disappear into a wall-closet fully made up.

At the opposite end of the scale from the bedroom with a hidden bed is the room that is nothing but a bed, with clothes storage and dressing space banished to the landing or the bathroom. To turn a room into a bed, place a mattress or low bed in the centre of the room, and fill the gaps between bed and wall with upholstered blocks of foam of the same height as the bed so the whole floor area becomes a soft, bouncy surface. Use a duvet or quilt to eliminate bed-making, and if the bedroom door opens inwards, either re-hang it or cut out an arc from the foam so the door can swing unimpeded. If you have Sybaritic tastes, there's no limit to the size of room you can fill up with bed.

Long and thin/short and fat

A wall of fitted storage is a great righter of wrong proportions. Both manufactured unit furniture and purpose-built storage fitments can be made to accommodate doors, windows, built-in washbasins and even beds.

Platforms, screens and large plants will serve to break a long, thin space into a series of cosy, well-defined areas, and

much cosmetic surgery can be brought about by illusion. A wall of mirror glass, for example, will visually improve the proportions, as will the judicious use of colour. Dark walls and ceilings will appear to come closer, pale walls will seem to recede.

Too huge

The only "problem" with too much space is to ensure that none of it is frittered away. You have the opportunity in a large room to arrange furniture in a really interesting way. Do not fall into the traditional trap of distributing furniture all around the room—it makes even the largest space look cluttered. Use chests of drawers, blanket boxes or free-standing shelving units as bedheads, foot boards or room dividers. Set the bed in the middle of the room like an island, or across a corner and fill the angle with shelving. A low platform, like a dais, will define and contain the sleeping area, adding visual interest to a large room that lacks a focal point. Exploit the spaciousness and use the bedroom as a secondary living-room, a TV or hobbies room—it would be a great shame to leave a large chunk of space unoccupied for two-thirds of the day.

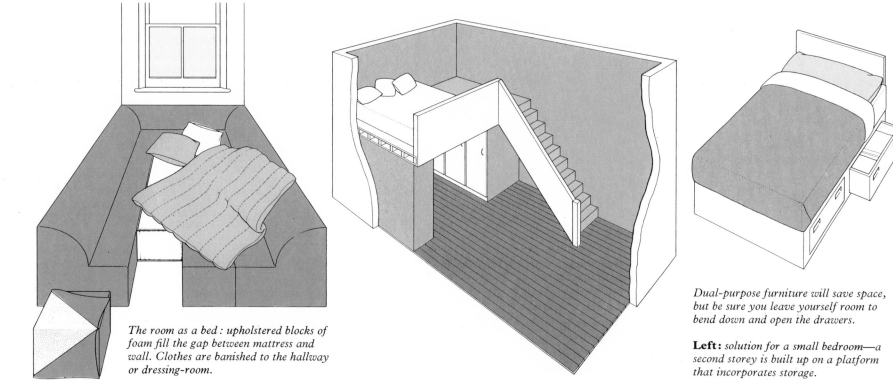

The room as a bed: upholstered blocks of foam fill the gap between mattress and wall. Clothes are banished to the hallway or dressing-room.

Dual-purpose furniture will save space, but be sure you leave yourself room to bend down and open the drawers.

Left: *solution for a small bedroom—a second storey is built up on a platform that incorporates storage.*

Above: *storage units can be made to slot into any awkward spot. Here, daylight falls on to the fitting from both sides, making the top an attractive focal point. The unit also cleverly hides the main bulk of an air-conditioning unit.*

Far left: *an interesting bedroom under the eaves, where the lower part of the ceiling has been used to house a sleeping recess. The beds have to be placed on very low bases, or directly on the floor, otherwise a hasty arousal in the morning may result in a sorely bruised head.*

Left: *problems arise with a narrow room —it can easily look like a corridor unless the furniture is placed crossways as well as lengthways. This bed is judiciously placed across the room.*

Calculating storage needs

A well-planned clothes storage system could transform your life. Even the untidiest of people could reform in the face of a tailor-made system where every garment has its allotted space. Clothes will benefit, too—they look smarter and last longer if air can circulate freely around them.

Whatever form of storage you choose, whether factory-made units or closets of your own design, do not skimp on the dimensions. The money you invest in good storage can only add to the value of your house.

In order to design the right kind of storage for your way of life, you must know what needs to be stored, how it should be stored, and the amount of

space your possessions will require.

You will need somewhere in the bedroom to keep dirty linen—a bag hanging in the closet or on the back of a door, a wicker basket or even a shelf or drawer—but not too discreetly hidden or you may forget about the contents altogether.

How much space

There is little sense in constructing a wardrobe that is out of scale with your own dimensions. Inevitably, there will be limitations based on human ability to stretch and bend. The dimensions given here are based on a person 1.6 m/ 5 ft 4 in tall.

To calculate how much hanging space, shelf and drawer space you need, count up your clothes, allow each article its relevant width and depth, then add ten per cent to the total for breathing space and new acquisitions.

Below: *the sizes of your clothes will dictate the size of your wardrobe. Each square represents 5 cm/2 in.*

Clothes to store

Men	Women
overcoats **H**	overcoats **H**
raincoats **H**	raincoats **H**
jackets **H**	jackets **H**
trousers **H**	trousers **H**
suits **H**	skirts **H**
shirts **H.S/D**	dresses **H**
knitwear **S/D**	long dresses **H**
underwear **S/D**	blouses **H.S/D**
nightwear **S/D**	knitwear **S/D**
sports clothes	underwear **S/D**
H.S/D	nightwear **S/D**
ties **H**	sports clothes
scarves **S/D**	**H.S/D**
belts **H.S/D**	scarves **S/D**
shoes **S/R**	belts **H.S/D**
boots **S/R**	shoes **S/R**
hats **S/R**	boots **S/R**
	hats **S/R**

H = hanging rail
S/D = shelves or drawers
S/R = shelves or racks

Right: *a sensible and well-planned storage arrangement that makes maximum use of available space.*

	1550
	1220
	920
	600
	300

Above: *take into consideration how far you can reach and how low you can bend before building a storage system.*

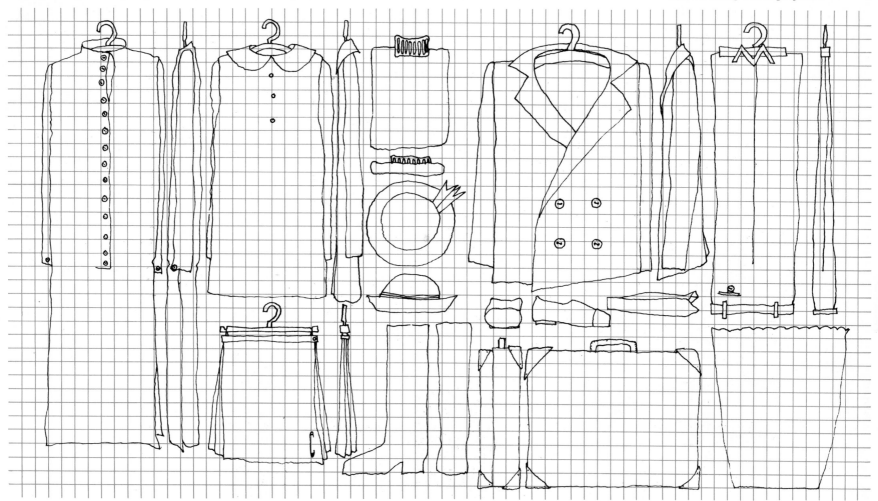

Bedroom planning
The inside story

How you organize the space inside your storage system makes a world of difference to the efficiency of your bedroom planning. If you are buying fitted storage units, study the manufacturers' choice of interior fitments: many offer a comprehensive and well-planned range of storage accessories. Sometimes, for example, better use is made of space by providing two tiers of hanging rods for clothes—one of them to take shorter items like jackets and skirts—than by keeping to the older idea of a single hanging rail.

Some systems have wire baskets or clear plastic trays or shelves to store folded clothes like sweaters and shirts or blouses; available in different depths, they slide along runners fixed to the sides of the wardrobe or are top-fixed to runners underneath shelves. For a touch of luxury, there are dovetailed sliding trays in solid mahogany.

The easiest systems, in fact, require no fixing to wardrobe or closet sides—they are supported by their own free-standing frame, slotted at regular intervals so that you can fit drawer runners or shelf clips wherever you decide you want them. An added advantage of these free-standing arrangements is that you can take them with you when you move, even though the storage units may be built in.

If you are designing your own storage system, whether building it yourself or employing a carpenter, browse through the catalogues of fitted furniture for ideas for organizing your space. Look through a good catalogue of cabinet fittings, too, and spend some time in a hardware store looking for ingenious fittings that will spark off a good idea you can incorporate in your own planning.

You can buy—or make yourself—all kinds of aids to wardrobe organization that you can incorporate in a new system or employ to make better use of existing storage. Simple ideas include providing a couple of hooks inside your wardrobe door to take skirt loops, or lining your wardrobe and closet doors with storage pockets—narrow, three-sided shelves to take jars, bottles and small items like gloves and hankies. Elastic stretched between two small hooks, or a length of narrow rod, will cope with belts, ties and cravats. You can buy special hangers that will give you storage for five skirts or five pairs of trousers for the space of one hanger, and "shoe caddies" that provide handy pockets for your shoes. Shoe racks can be fitted to the wardrobe floor.

Getting the most out of your storage requires careful thought and planning—but the result is well worth the effort.

Above: *each shirt is given its own clear plastic pull-out tray in this neatly laid out, well-lit closet.*

Right: *an odd corner is utilized as a storage area, with spacious shelving and a rail and hooks for hangers.*

Above: *a compact storage system includes pull-out wire racks and smaller plastic trays to provide room for everything from socks to jackets.*

Top left: *a double bed tilts upwards to reveal plenty of storage space underneath for bulky items such as duvets, blankets and pillows.*

Left: *Clothes rails, like the ones you find in dress shops, revolve so that your wardrobe circulates for you to see what you've got.*

Right: *most shoes end up higgledy-piggledy at the bottom of a closet. These have a happier fate in a special inset rack with shoe polish and stool.*

Designing a storage system

Above: *purpose-built storage units are expensive to install, but if, like these, they are carefully planned from the start, they are well worth the cost and effort.*

Below: *separate units, useful for ever-changing storage needs, are arranged across the length of the wall to resemble fitted closets and drawers.*

The choice of bedroom storage units is large, and time invested at the outset in weighing the pros and cons of the various systems available will result in well-organized storage that suits your particular needs.

Built-in storage

With built-in storage you can achieve a system that perfectly suits your life-style and possessions. You can fit the storage exactly to the room, making use of odd corners and concealing uneven or out-of-true walls, floors and ceilings. The room will undoubtedly appear better planned, and the feeling of space and organization will be increased. The choice of styles and decorative finishes is virtually unlimited, and you can supervise the work personally to achieve a high standard of finish. Built-in furniture will frequently (but not always) add to the value of your home: a "plus" to be featured in an estate agent's description of your property when you come to sell.

The disadvantages are that built-in furniture is expensive (with the exception of do-it-yourself projects) and, once installed, the units cannot be moved around. Finding a skilled carpenter can take time and trouble and, having found one, you may not be able to assess his skill until the job is done. You also need the ability to work out an effective storage system for yourself—and to explain it to the carpenter. If you are inexperienced, you can make disastrous mistakes. Building in furniture may take longer than you think and can be very disruptive to the household routine.

Free-standing storage

Paradoxically, it can be easier to choose an efficient storage system from a limited range of professionally designed units than it is to turn designer yourself, with unlimited choice but little experience. Furniture viewed in a showroom can be chosen relatively quickly, although delivery may be subject to delays, and the cost will be less than for professionally built-in furniture. Free-standing furniture can be used to change the layout of the room and can be moved from one room to another, and you can take it with you when you move.

The disadvantages are that your choice is limited to standard ranges, with little scope for indulging personal whims, and the furniture will not fit your room exactly or take account of uneven floors and walls that are out of true. With older styles or reproduction designs, extra cleaning under closets and on top of wardrobes may be involved.

Fitted storage

A compromise between built-in and free-standing furniture, fitted storage is undoubtedly growing in popularity. It consists of standard, mass-produced units, carefully designed so that once the system is installed the effect is virtually indistinguishable from that of built-in furniture. Some ranges offer a choice of as many as five door-panel widths so that any given space can be fitted to within about 75 mm/3 in. Single doors usually extend to a height of about 228 cm/7 ft 6 in, and there are two-door systems that consist of a lower wardrobe plus top closets so that storage can be provided from floor to ceiling. Provision is usually made for "fillet" or infill pieces that cover any small gaps left at the top or sides—these are usually simple to cut to size on site.

Decorative finishes include white, various wood veneers, mirrors and fabrics, and styles can be "Louis", "contemporary", "Spanish", "colonial" and "country"—although the originators of

these styles certainly didn't have fitted furniture. Manufacturers and stores specializing in fitted furniture often offer a design service to help you to make the best use of your space. Many shops also offer a fitting service, saving you the trouble of finding a carpenter, and also providing a guarantee of good workmanship. Installation can frequently be completed in a day.

Choosing built-in furniture: Look through as many books, magazines, brochures and catalogues as you can for ideas. Measure your room carefully, and draw your plans to scale: you can at least aim to eliminate expensive mistakes at the planning stage. Engage a carpenter who has been recommended or whose work you have seen—a good carpenter will also make helpful suggestions.

Choosing free-standing or fitted storage: Measure your available space carefully and collect as many brochures as possible —systems vary widely in flexibility and

some offer door panels or closet units in only one or two widths, which means that you may be left with large gaps. Others may offer as many as five widths so that virtually any space can be filled almost exactly.

Some systems come in only one depth; others can be ordered in up to four depths, making it possible, for example, to span a chimney breast with a flush-fronted run of doors while varying the depth of the storage. Wherever possible, go to a shop or showroom to see the system that attracts you: mail-order offers can deceive, not necessarily intentionally. Check measurements in catalogues very carefully—some manufacturers obviously believe they are selling to a nation of dwarfs, and the interiors of their wardrobes would only suit mini-clothes. Check on delivery dates and, if the store or manufacturer offers a fitting service, ask for a reference on a recent job so that you can check the quality.

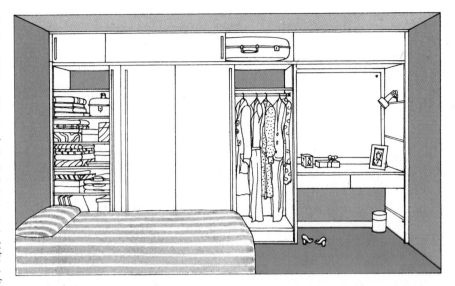

Above and below: *this built-in storage system has been specially designed by Terence Conran so that any semi-skilled enthusiast can build it at home. Conran's shops will be selling the component parts in a pre-finished state.*

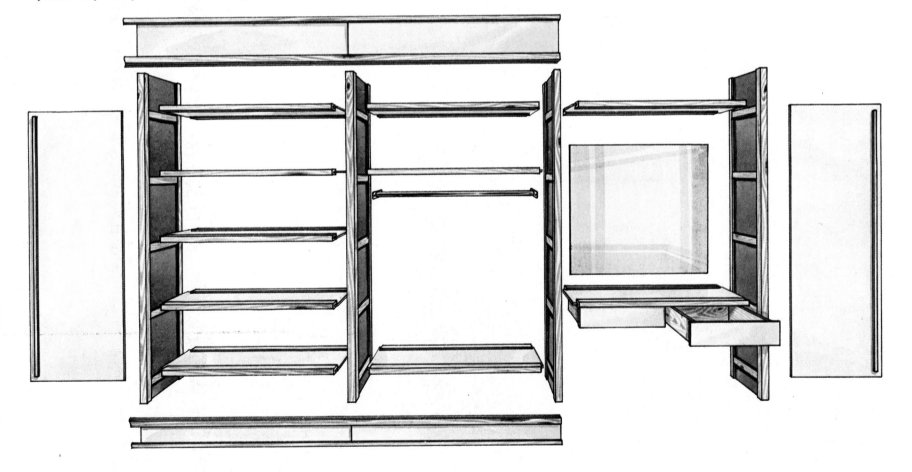

Bedroom planning
The door story

Although the manufacturers of fitted furniture offer a good selection of door styles and a reasonable choice of widths, you will obviously have far greater freedom of choice if you are designing your own storage. Here are some ideas.

Louvred doors are not expensive and always look attractive, with the natural wood simply sealed or painted. However, unless you buy the backed variety, dust will come through the slats.

Plain flush doors, made quite cheaply with hardboard over a framework of battening, can be made more decorative with panels created from strips of moulding pinned and glued into place, or there are ready-made panels that you simply glue on. An alternative is to wallpaper your doors to match the rest of the bedroom—to avoid joins, plan door sizes to tie in with the width of the wallpaper. For a more permanent finish you can varnish the paper or cover it with a sheet of clear plastic. Add moulding to protect the edges and fit handles that stand well clear of the door.

Fabric-covered doors look soft and pretty. Staple the fabric into place, then hide the staples with braid or moulding. Hessian and felt are available con-

Left: *brightly painted storage-unit doors flush with the wall make an exciting and colourful background feature.*

veniently paper-backed for easy application, but they should be protected with an edging strip.

Mirrors, in sheet or tile form, will give a feeling of space to the room and are useful for giving a full-length view of yourself. Make sure your doors are strong enough and have heavy-duty hinges to take the considerable additional weight.

Doors obviously need enough space in front of them so that they can be opened without knocking against the bed or other furniture. Pairs of narrow double doors take up less space than broad single doors, but may be more expensive to make and fit.

Sliding doors are the best choice in a tight squeeze, but they can be the cause of some annoyance: part of the wardrobe will always be concealed by one of the doors when open, and tracks can become jammed and clogged with dirt. A new and inexpensive idea is the "sliding wall" type of wardrobe—you use your own wall as the wardrobe back and fit large sliding doors between floor and ceiling tracks. The wardrobe can be any depth you like and can be kitted out with your own choice of interior storage fitments.

Doors that fold back concertina-fashion can be useful for a long run of closets. However, they take up a space half their depth inside the closet as well as out, so closets need to be deep.

Above: *louvred doors on fitted units add texture to one side of the room. One mirrored panel breaks the solid line.*

Right: *these doors have been papered to match the wall and are neatly outlined with wooden moulding strips.*

Above: *mirrored doors make a room feel more spacious—but remember that mirror glass is heavy and should only be hung on the most robust doors.*

Top right: *mirror panels extend a room visually and, when interspersed with glossy surrounds, give a wall of fitted storage units a very elegant and stylish frontage.*

Right: *the natural look of the doors on the built-in, floor-to-ceiling storage in this high, gabled bedroom is in harmony with the room's rugged rafters and exposed brick wall.*

Far right: *long, lacy curtains hung from a decorative pole across one corner of a room look very attractive and are a simple and economical way to conceal clothes and any bulky bedroom clutter.*

Drawers and bedside tables

Undoubtedly, the more storage you can fit behind a run of continuous closet fronts the more streamlined and neat your room will look, but you may well want extra drawers or small closet units.

Most fitted bedroom ranges have matching drawer units, which can be either butted together or supplied with continuous tops to form a low counter around the room. Special units are available that fit into corners. Mirror units will turn a chest of drawers into a dressing-table, or you can bridge the gap between two chests to make a dressing-table with a knee-hole.

Although the prevailing fashion has been for fully fitted, streamlined bedrooms, free-standing furniture with attractive shapes and detailing can add a great deal of charm to a room. They may not make the most efficient use of space, however, and may be more difficult to clean around than fitted units.

Some of the most attractive—and least expensive—chests are still to be found in junk shops, waiting to be restored to their original charm. You can also buy a good range of reproduction chests and dressing-tables in a wide range of styles, but the cost of labour today makes these very expensive. Simple whitewood chests remain relatively in-

expensive and, given a careful finish with stain, sealer or paint, look most attractive. You can add your own handles.

A clutter of bottles and jars on top of a chest or dressing-table can be awkward to clean and may look unsightly. They can often be stored in a deep drawer, sub-divided with thin strips of wood to keep the bottles upright.

Remember to provide storage close to the bed for a reading lamp, books, drinks, a clock and a radio. You can buy a variety of small cabinets, both modern and reproduction. The bedhead wall can often be called into service, too, to give extra storage space. Many head-board designs allow a certain amount of storage for small items, and a number of fitted furniture ranges provide matching head boards. If the bed stands between two tall closets, it is often possible to add an extra row of closets above the bed so that the bed has a recessed effect. Take care, though: any furniture placed above a bed, even the simplest set of shelving, must be very firmly fixed—heavy objects falling on sleeping people would obviously be unpleasant and even the thought of it could provoke a nightmare.

A very effective and inexpensive way of providing extra bedroom storage is simply to build open boxes, or pigeon

Above: *this stippled writing table tidily displays precious mementoes and knick-knacks that are too space-consuming for table tops.*

Right: *storage baskets, suitable for such things as large chunky sweaters and sports clothes, soften a room full of smart, fitted furniture.*

holes, or build up an open-box arrangement from one of the cube systems available. This can provide space for folded towels, linen, boots, sweaters, shirts and blouses, socks, or piles of newspapers.

Storage of awkward bulky items such as extra blankets or out-of-season clothing needs special thought. Blanket chests with lift-up lids are an old-fashioned but still sensible idea; whitewood versions are available quite cheaply, or you could convert an old trunk. If you add a foam cushion covered in a pretty fabric, you can use the chest for seating as well as for storage.

You can also use the top parts of wardrobes for storing bulky items; many fitted systems provide top closets for this purpose. In rooms with high ceilings, it is often possible to install top closets big enough to store suitcases, and sometimes a run of top closets can be continued above the door of the room. This kind of storage entails standing on steps or a sturdy chair to reach it, but it can be invaluable for objects that are not in constant use. Many beds are also designed to provide extra storage space. Some have generous drawers in the base; others are made so that the top of the base lifts up to reveal ample storage underneath.

Top right: *even a shallow alcove can be used to house a storage unit. This built-in wooden bunk doubles as a bedhead.*

This knobby chest of drawers has been designed to accommodate many items of different shapes and sizes.

Books and magazines are neatly stashed away in a pull-out bedside box—a space-saving idea for the small bedroom.

Wicker furniture—a folding chair, a hamper and a light table—are economical alternatives to streamlined units.

Heirlooms and hand-me-downs

Of course, it is lovely to start off with a clean slate, perfect taste and plenty of money, but life is not usually like that. Most of us, from the outset, own a number of things that do not at first glance fit into the decorative scheme we have in mind.

One man's heirloom, of course, is another man's white elephant: that is the trouble with the generosity of kind relations who come to the aid of those trying to set up house. The recipient must learn to make the best of pieces that turn up on the doorstep unbidden; luckily, there is no single piece that cannot be cut down, repainted or re-cycled in some useful way. Pleasant old pieces, small or medium, will cause no pain. An old chest, a painted *caisson*, a well-proportioned *armoire*, a roll-top desk—such things that are pretty in themselves are a joy to possess, especially if their interiors are rearranged to pro-vide a bit of modern convenience. Let the good pieces stand on their own, not squashed into a line-up of ill-matched furniture. There is no need to alter the style of the whole bedroom to match one exquisite find: a more stunning effect is achieved by showing off a lovely antique in a modern setting.

Do not worry overmuch if good hand-me-downs were not originally intended to do duty in the bedroom. A tallboy, the sort that used to be found in drawing-rooms, can be useful as a man's ward-robe: take out the shelves of the top part, fix a hanging rail for suits and one for ties against the inside of one of the doors, use the little twin top drawers for socks and handkerchiefs and the two large drawers for shirts and underwear. A Davenport desk can make a useful make-up table: fix your looking-glass to the inside of the put-up lid, and keep your jars and bottles inside. The little drawers marching down its flank can come in useful for tights and accessories.

Left: *the pleasant, simple exterior of an early refrigerator has been retained, but the inside has been converted into shelves for clothes and bed linen.*

Far left: *a marble-topped table and tall plant stands accentuate the nostalgic atmosphere of this bathroom.*

Opposite: *an heirloom may be full of potential, even if at first sight it seems to be a huge white elephant. Here, exquisitely grained, old wooden wardrobe doors have been removed and built into practical, modern cupboards.*

Below left: *in this bedroom, stripped wooden wall panelling sets off the richly coloured furniture and artefacts.*

Below: *deservedly given pride of place, this 19th-century painted armoire is surrounded by furniture in natural, unobtrusive colours.*

Bentwood furniture, whether it is kitchen chairs or a curvaceous coat-hanger stand, looks well in any room, and there is no reason why it should not lead a useful life in the bedroom. Garden chairs of the cane armchair variety, painted white, are delightful in a summery room, especially if equipped with a seat-cushion to match the rest of the room in colour. Even an old iron pot stand, the sort that used to make an obelisk of pots and pans in the kitchen, looks good in a bedroom if instead of saucepans it holds pots of fern or ivy. One of its real advantages is that you need only water the topmost pot: seepage through the hole in its bottom' will obligingly irrigate the rest.

Should you find yourself the reluctant heir to a bed with an impossible head-board, saw it off and replace it with your own wall-fixed bedhead made from a wide set of shelves, or possibly a screen or a wall-hanging. If your loot includes non-matching chairs, upholstered or otherwise, reduce their disparities by covering or painting them in the same colour. If you become heir to pictures you do not care for, consider whether the frames have some appeal in their own right. Simply replace the artwork with mirror-glass and hang them singly or in attractive groups.

Theoretically, heavy old master ward-robes can be gutted, sawn up and trans-formed into room dividers, benches, chests and all sorts of interesting rein-carnations that require real skill in carpentry. The simplest transformation is to remove the doors; if they are beautiful, preserve them and throw away the carcass; if not, replace the doors with a curtain and make use of the well-fitted and roomy interior.

And remember that, with the present popularity of pine, walnut and mahogany furniture is becoming increasingly rare and should never be thrown away.

Heating and ventilating

A book of household tips published in 1934 urges its gentle readers thus: "Night air is just as wholesome as day air, and bedroom windows should *always* be kept wide open." It is now generally accepted that this very British habit of sleeping in a cold draught, even in mid-winter, is a contributory cause of bronchitis and other chesty ills. The fact remains that the British do have an in-built mistrust of central heating and air conditioning, especially where the bedroom is concerned. Notwithstanding the climatic and cultural differences that prevail on either side of the Atlantic, most bedrooms need to be supplied with a source of heat (and, in some cases, a source of cooling).

Open fires
Most houses built before the Second World War have fireplaces in the bedrooms, but in the course of modernization and alteration the fireplace—which in itself provided a form of ventilation—is all too often regarded as an anachronism and bricked up. Open fires are welcoming and attractive, but only practical in large bedrooms, where they can be seen and appreciated to the full. They are not a very efficient form of heating, as a high percentage of heat disappears up the flue, unless a throat restrictor is fitted into the chimney. Escaping heat can be usefully harnessed if you install a back boiler to boost your hot-water supply.

Coal fires will, in time, deposit fine smuts of soot all over the room, and wood fires will emit a cloud of fine ash. Obviously a smoky fire in the bedroom would be intolerable, so keep the chimney regularly swept and invest in a grate that draws well.

Instant heat
Electric fires, convector heaters and gas fires will provide an effective amount of background heat to take the chill from the air. Combined with an electric time-switch, fires can be pre-set to turn on and give of their all when most needed. The quickest and hottest instant fire is the electric fan-heater, which can be either free-standing or wall-mounted.

Electric and gas heaters should not be left on through the night because they are a fire risk and they remove essential humidity. If fires are to be left on for considerable periods, some form of humidification will be welcomed, even if it is simply a dish of water placed near the source of heat.

Night-storage heaters, available only in the UK, are not suitable for bedrooms as their heat output during the night cannot be controlled. Thus if, anticipating a cold night, the heaters were turned on to receive and store heat, and the weather perversely changed for the better, you would be condemned to swelter through the night as the heater discharged its stored energy. Under-floor heating poses the same problems.

Central heating
Radiators normally run off a central boiler with a central temperature control, but thermostatic valves can be fitted to individual radiators if you wish to vary the degree of heat between living areas and bedrooms, and a time-clock will economically switch the whole system on and off according to your daily routine. The British, notoriously loath to sleep in a heated room, tend to set time-clocks to switch off late and cut in early to provide for a cosy bedtime and a warm awakening with plenty of hot water for the bath.

The positioning of the radiators will affect the planning possibilities of the room, as ideally furniture should not be placed directly next to a source of heat. The best place for a radiator is under a window; in this position it acts as a convector, heating the cold air that sinks on to it and pushing heated air outwards and upwards, keeping the whole room at a constant temperature rather than heating one little corner.

Central heating based on a duct that circulates warm air around the house through warm-air grilles is less popular than it was a few years ago because it is uneconomical, dusty and very drying. However, like a fan heater, it warms a cold room very quickly and thoroughly, but it should not be left on to blow you dry all night.

Air conditioning
If your air is to be conditioned, your windows must be double glazed and hermetically sealed or outside elements will interfere with your internal climate.

The simplest type of air conditioning is a "through-the-wall" unit, which deals with just one room. The self-contained unit is fixed to the wall with a duct through to the outside. It has its own heating coil and chiller and will keep the room at whatever temperature is selected on the built-in thermostat.

At its most sophisticated and expensive level, an air-conditioning system will service the whole house from a central plant room, with an outside cooling tower and a system of ducts, diffusers and air grilles to circulate filtered, humidified air at the required temperature. A simple computer controls the system and ensures that each room is maintained at the preselected degree of humidity and temperature.

Humidification
Most forms of heating are ultimately drying—both to the skin and to the mucous membranes of the nose and throat. Sleeping in an overheated, under-humidified room will make your skin dry and flaky and your head ache. The crudest humidifier is a saucer of water placed on a sill above the source of heat. The next best is a purpose-built reservoir that clips to the radiator and allows water to evaporate at a controlled rate. A clip-on reservoir is perfectly efficient and satisfactory. If you want a discreet, sophisticated piece of equipment, there are machines that squirt a fine, measured spray of water into the room at regular intervals. But perhaps the best way to keep the warmed night air in the bedroom breathable is simply to leave the window open—just a little.

Right: *boxed-in radiator makes a warm head board—but it could give you a headache unless turned off during sleeping hours. A bowl of flowers in water on the window-sill restores lost humidity to the air.*

Far right: *located under the windows, slender panel radiators with individual time-switches and thermostats provide a gentle background heat. The massive wood-burning stove adds plenty of character and winter warmth.*

Left: *a fire crackling in the bedroom hearth would tempt the most dedicated night bird to enjoy an early bedtime. Obviously, sensible precautions must be taken—chimneys must be swept regularly, and fire-guards moved into position before the lights go out.*

Below and below left: *outlet grilles from an air-conditioning system are best placed under windows to counteract the inevitable heat loss from a large area of glass (even if it is double-glazed). Curtains and blinds should be kept well clear of heat sources.*

Bedroom planning
Basins and showers

A bedroom with a private bathroom attached is indeed a luxury. One can emerge from one's night-time quarters prepared for a new day without exposing an unwashed, unshaven vulnerability to other members of the household. Unfortunately, there are houses and apartments where such an arrangement is simply not feasible, but a wash-basin or shower squeezed into an odd corner of the bedroom makes a very welcome compromise.

Position

The whereabouts of plumbed-in appliances depend on the existing pipework, and if a wash-basin or shower is located close to both water supply and drainage outlet then expenses can be kept to a minimum. In most houses, particularly modern ones, the plumbing is designed as economically as possible, so the upstairs bathroom and WC are positioned directly above the kitchen to ensure that pipes are kept as short as possible. Any new wash-basin or shower for the bedroom should be on the wall nearest the bathroom, or close by, to minimize the length of expensive drainage pipes. A corner location is usually the neatest.

Below: *if you do not want to dig into the floor to install the waste trap, it can be set at floor level and the shower base raised accordingly on a platform.*

Wash-basins

Factory-made vanity units abound, but unless you can find one that blends perfectly with your chosen style it is cheaper and more pleasing to build in your own. The pipework attached to wash-basins is seldom pretty to look at, however well plumbed. If possible, conceal your basin within a wall of built-in storage, or build out a false wall, leaving a 15 cm/ 6 in duct for the pipes—the top will form a useful ledge behind the basin.

Showers

Showers splash and wet people drip, so you will certainly need a waterproof area round the shower tray, and a well-designed door or shower curtains long enough to tuck into the tray. The drainage trap of the shower tray is a bulky item and should be built into a raised platform or recessed into the floor —but do ensure that the floor is not weakened by any modifications necessary to accommodate the plumbing. The weight of a shower tray, plus a person, plus a quantity of water could prove the floor's undoing if you happen to have sawn through vital timbers. Shower units are heavier than they appear to be.

Below right: *a low bedroom ceiling may preclude a raised shower unit, in which case it will be necessary to sink the waste trap into the floor.*

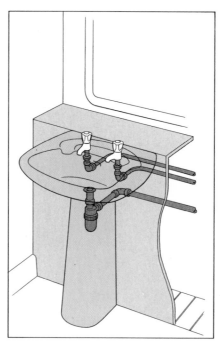

Above: *a duct behind the wash-basin neatly conceals the plumbing, eliminating the need for a cavity in the wall to accommodate the pipes. Not only does this avoid drastic structural alterations, it also gives the wash-basin a sturdy and compact appearance. As an added bonus, the top of the duct makes a useful shelf for storage.*

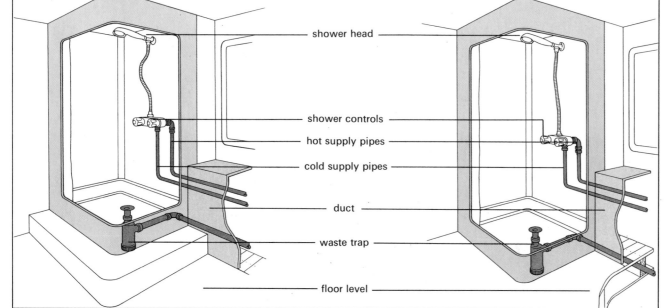

- shower head
- shower controls
- hot supply pipes
- cold supply pipes
- duct
- waste trap
- floor level

Above: *a bathroom en suite behind a sliding screen door makes a very private haven for the pampered users, with its generous mirror and well-planned lighting.*

Top left: *small children tend to take rather a long time—and make a mess—in the family bathroom, driving adults to a frenzy in the morning. A wash-basin in the children's room is the answer, fixed at the correct height for a child.*

Far left: *even the possessor of a one-room flat need not be denied the luxury of a private bath. The doors that conceal this carefully planned mini-bathroom when it is not in use open wide to help disperse the steam that accompanies a blissful soak.*

Left: *the guest-room is an obvious candidate for a wash-basin, especially if your house has only one bathroom.*

83

Bedroom planning
Lighting

In the days of fulsome draperies and candle-light, illumination of the bed-chamber was the cause of countless domestic fires. Now that our light source is both safe and infinitely flexible, it is sad that so many bedrooms, albeit safe from flare-ups, are as inadequately lit and shadowy as in our great-grand-parents' day.

Lighting requirements in the bedroom are as varied and complex as for any other room. Consider, for instance, all the activities that take place there, from reading to rummaging in the depths of the wardrobe. Almost every activity requires a source of light, or a power point to activate electrical equipment such as curling tongs, hair dryers, shavers, radio and TV.

A bedroom needs both general and specific lighting: not a uniformly bright glare, but several light sources controlled by dimmer switches, ranging in intensity from a strong overall light for dressing (so that you can check your clothes for stains, holes and crumples) to a subdued pool of illumination to read by while your partner sleeps. The traditional, single centre-hung pendant is as inappropriate in the bedroom as it is in any other well-planned room—more so, in fact: when you stand between a light source and a drawn blind, you unconsciously stage a shadow-play for the neighbours.

Power points

Count how many pieces of electrical equipment you use in the bedroom—including bedside lamps, radio, hair dryer, curling tongs, shaver, TV set, stereo—then work out where you will be using them and install power points accordingly. Sockets for heavy equipment such as the TV set, that is going to sit pretty well permanently at table height, should be positioned 45 cm/18 in from the floor. For shavers, hair dryers and other lightweights that will be waved about in the air, position sockets a good 10 cm/4 in above work-top height. (Shavers are normally fitted with 2-pin plugs that require special sockets or an adaptor.)

Double socket outlets are only marginally more expensive to install than single ones, so, if you are rewiring, it is worth doubling your outlets in case you acquire more equipment or feel moved to switch everything on at once.

General light

Ceiling pendants give an adequate but harsh and shadowy general light. They should be positioned close to the window to avoid the hazard of silhouetting your more intimate moments.

Tungsten strips, fitted around the perimeter of the room and concealed by baffle boarding, will give a pleasant, indirect light washing down the walls. Adjustable wall spotlights are a useful dual-purpose solution. Swivelled upwards, they bounce general light off the ceiling; turned down, they beam on to your bedtime book.

A bank of spotlights mounted on a ceiling track are a flexible and dramatic light source. Individual spots can be focused on areas that need attention, such as the dressing area, a favourite picture or a mirror. Obviously, spotlights you can reach are infinitely more adjustable than spotlights you can't, so position the ceiling track within arm's length of someone standing on the bed or a chair.

Whatever the source of general light, position an on-off switch by the door and another by the bed. There is nothing more aggravating than having to force yourself out of bed to turn lights off when you are warm and drowsy.

Specific light

Closets or wardrobes: A light within the closet or wardrobe, operated by a pressure switch, will probably reintroduce you to a lot of clothes you had forgotten you owned. A light above the hanging rail, protected by a baffle board from accidental knocks, is easy to install and very effective. If the closet is too tightly packed to take a light bulb, an external spotlight, angled to shine inside, is a good alternative. Recessed downlighters will shed attractive pools of light upon your clothing. Build them into a false top of the closet—they need about 20 cm/8 in clearance.

The full-length mirror: If you really want to see what you look like, if you want to know if there are threads hanging from your hemline or if you are interested in the creases in your trousers, then angle the light to shine on you—not on the mirror.

Shaving and making up: For a clear and shadowless view of your face, light should shine at you from a source close to the mirror. There are several ways of

achieving this without dazzle. The simplest mirror light is a purpose-made fitment with a plastic diffusing shade, and often a built-in power point for an electric shaver. It is designed to sit directly above the mirror. A more elegant solution is a fluorescent or tungsten tube fixed across the top of the mirror, or on three sides, and concealed by a baffle that blends with the decorative theme of the rest of the furniture.

Spotlights work well as mirror lights. They should be wall-mounted on either side of the mirror, facing downwards so the mirror gazer is not bedazzled. As every Thespian knows, naked tungsten bulbs set into a mirror surround cast an ideal light for making up. Bright, yellow light will make you squint, so choose small, white-light bulbs no brighter than 15–20 watts.

Reading and writing: There is no need to illuminate the whole room for these solitary pursuits. If sitting at a desk, an angled table or standard lamp is the most suitable lighting. In fact, a pool of

Sockets, switches, telephone and overhead strip lighting are all craftily positioned for bedtime convenience.

light gives a pleasant sense of intimacy and encourages concentration. If lying in bed, it becomes even more important to keep your light source localized—especially if your partner is less than keen on being kept awake until your last page is turned. Individual table lamps are the most common solution, but choose ones with heavy bases and sturdy stems, as free-standing bedside lights are vulnerable to knocks from groping hands seeking switches in the dark.

Wall-mounted lights leave bedside tables free for books, magazines and glasses of water. Choose adjustable spotlights (angled on to the page of the book, not on to the reader's face). For a wider field of light, fit a tungsten strip along the top of the bedhead, concealed by a continuous baffle—but fit two, so that one can be switched off by a partner who wants to sleep.

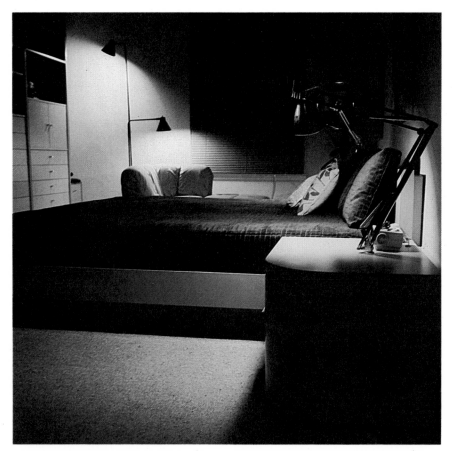

Above: *a combination of lighting from dimmers to track-mounted spotlights to wall lamps guarantees versatile results.*

Right: *a pretty flighty alternative to the conventional bedroom lamp gives a diffused light through its gauzy wings.*

Above: *adjustable lamps are ideal for bedtime reading and split up the room into pleasing pools of light.*

Below: *a low-hung pendant lamp can be used very successfully to spotlight an area, as long as it is placed to one side.*

A well-lit bedroom with a light for every purpose: a strip light or spotlights for the make-up mirror, angled lamps for reading, and recessed downlighters for the wardrobe.

Windows and shutters

Close-set windows are balanced by a centrally positioned bed. Painted shutters, hung inside, take the place of curtains which would mar both the *luxuriant view and the windows' elegant château arches. On warm, sultry nights, shutters are particularly advantageous, excluding light while letting in air.*

Top: *sophisticated louvres shade this picture window—they can be flipped down for complete blackout. A halo of extra light comes from an unusual skylight.*

Above: *a square, hinged pane has been inserted into a round attic window to create an interesting geometric pattern.*

Above: *slender vertical windows, fitted with adjustable glass louvres, which cleverly mimic the planking of the walls and floor. The light admitted is limited, making a cool and relaxing bedroom.*

Right: *diagonal louvres in sliding screens are pleasing to the eye and obliterate a dreary, city view. Painted a cheerful shade of yellow, these add an unusually exciting decorative touch to the room.*

Below: *window screens can easily be made in a wide variety of designs. From left to right: louvred timber panel, square timber trellis, diagonal timber trellis and narrow dowelling trellis.*

It is not generally advisable to alter the size or type of your windows, unless the house was badly designed in the first place. A house originally built to gaze out at the world from behind elegant Georgian sashes looks totally wrong if forced to adopt the unblinking stare of a picture window. Equally, a modern façade would be ill-at-ease if fitted with bow windows and random panes of bottle glass.

The best advice is to leave well alone, simply repairing and replacing damaged frames. If a change does prove necessary, remember that there are regulations governing the size of windows in relation to other ventilation arrangements and the floor area of the room, so check with your local building authority and planning department before you embark on any major structural changes.

Windows have several functions to perform—to let in fresh air and light, and to provide access to an interesting view. It must also be possible to black them out efficiently and to seal them against burglars, draughts, heat loss and noise. Proprietary window locks will discourage thieves, and efficient double glazing will certainly minimize heat loss—although double glazing will also cut off supplies of fresh air, so it will be necessary to combine it with an air-conditioning or forced-air ventilation system.

The sunnier European countries make great use of outside shutters, which block out light yet admit air, and do not obstruct the window at all when folded back. Efficient and lovely as they are in their home settings, however, outside shutters look absurd grafted on to inappropriate architectural styles. Period English houses sometimes have internal shutters that fold back into the reveal, leaving the daytime aspect uncluttered by bunched-up curtains or the hard line of blinds with dangling pull-cords.

The modern equivalent of shutters is the louvre panel, available in a variety of shapes, sizes and timbers from pine to mahogany. Louvre panels give a room a cohesive quality if teamed with louvred wardrobe doors, making them particularly useful in a room that has an awkward shape or in which there are a number of oddly shaped windows. Panels can be hinged to swing outwards like shutters, or they can be mounted on sliding tracks, provided there is enough wall space for them to retreat to.

A fixed screen will attractively obscure a dreary view, and is certainly a better solution than frosted or patterned glass, which always looks dismal. If your problem is lack of privacy, consider mirrored glass or a sheet of solar reflective film, so that you can see out but passers-by see only the reflection of their own inquisitive faces.

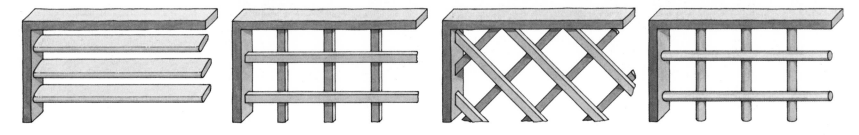

Bedroom planning
Curtains and blinds

In most rooms, curtains and blinds have several roles to fulfil, but nowhere more so than in the bedroom. A sheer blind, for example, that may serve its purpose admirably in the bedroom by day will be less popular with the rudely awakened occupants when the first light of dawn streams into the room.

The versatility of window treatments is such that they can be used to frame a pleasant outlook or to camouflage a bad one. A beautiful view can be emphasized by the window frame itself, with the role of the curtains played down or even no curtains at all if the window is a particularly handsome one, while an ugly view can be softened by pretty lace curtains. A dull interior can be enlivened by brightly patterned curtains or a painted blind, either toning with the wallpaper or standing out like a picture against a plain background.

There are only two lengths to which curtains should go: the sill or the floor. The length of the rail, however, is flexible, as is its position. Two small windows can be treated as one by using one pair of curtains (or a single large blind) for both. Curtains can also extend the whole length of the wall. A single window can be made to look larger by keeping the curtains well away from the frame at the sides, and by using a deep valance or pelmet that just meets the frame at the top. An awkwardly large window should have closely fitted curtains to bring it into proportion with the rest of the room.

When hanging curtains, pencil pleats will look tailored and modern; pinch pleats are more traditional, and gathered and looped headings are more informal. Curtains can be hung from a decorative pole or invisible tracks—these range from double tracks which allow two sets of curtains to be hung on the same fixture (and are excellent for blocking out light, as the edges are curved) to hinged tracks which swing outwards to allow awkward windows to be opened.

Blinds are versatile and give bedrooms a clean-cut look. Roller blinds are the easiest to assemble yourself; other types include roman, which give a valance effect when pulled up; pinoleum, made of fine strips of wood or cotton; pleatex, venetian, vertical louvred or wooden. Blinds can be sheer or opaque, but unless you're an early riser opaque will be the choice for a bedroom and, properly fitted, can make curtains unnecessary.

Left: *make a good impression from the outside where curtain linings are on show. For total darkness inside, line curtains with a light-obscuring and insulating fabric like Millium.*

Opposite: *stargazer's window, angled for a good view of the planets. Roller blinds, fixed into sliding tracks, are pulled down when the time comes to black out the heavens.*

Bottom left: *picture window with views of Manhattan obscured for sleep by curtains of gossamer-fine spun wool.*

Above: *effective night sky silk-screened on a plain roller blind.*

89

Walls – paper and paint

Of all wall coverings, the papers and paints are simplest to handle, making the transformation of a room a relatively cheap and painless exercise.

Papers can be self-adhesive, saving mess. If they have body to them—like the anaglyptas or the embossed papers—they can hide bumps and unevennesses in the wall itself, thus saving the expense of a plasterer. Paints are easier to apply than ever they were, and dry faster and more smoothly. Any number of papers and paints are wipable or washable, which extends their lifespan in reasonably pristine condition.

However, it is this very longevity of paper and paint which is a disadvantage if you have chosen unwisely and happen to hate the fruit of your labours. So be sure to do your homework before investing money and effort. Study your chosen shades and patterns by daylight and by the sort of artificial light that you are going to use *in situ*. Unless you are doing the room up altogether, with new curtains, new carpet, new furniture and new counterpane, your new walls must work in with your existing colour scheme; they are more likely to do so if they echo or pick up one of the existing colours. If you are starting from scratch, you will of course want to visualize the entire scheme; ensure that all is harmonious by pinning scraps of your proposed carpet, counterpane and curtaining on to a board.

Colour schemes

Before the great colour revolution swept through our homes, the choice of bedroom colour schemes could not have been simpler. Favourite colours were oyster pink, powder blue or eau de Nil: all colours that set off to perfection the cream-and-gilt dream-bedroom suites with a sprinkling of curlicues and swarms of cherubs perching in likely and unlikely places, the idea being to make every woman feel like Mme de Pompadour, and every man an amorous king.

Apart from the predictable oatmeal, browns and beiges, there are no longer any typical bedroom colour schemes. Indeed, there are hardly any typical bedrooms—just rooms in which we sleep, more private and personal than the other rooms in the house, rooms in which we should be able to feel especially safe, relaxed and happy. Therefore, any decorations that make the room look good and help you to feel good in it will

work for you, even if they break all the rules in the book.

Even the theory that bedrooms must look restful has been exploded in a firework burst of scintillating colour. And if you have a hankering for colour upon colour, but would not be happy to awake each morning in the interior of a kaleidoscope, remember that your bedhead and the wall against which it is placed are behind you. Your gaze will therefore not fall upon it first thing in the morning, so this is somewhere you can place a concentration of multicolour.

It is the neutrals, light or medium, that are considered to be restful colours. Really dark, deep tones cause the walls to embrace you.

The effects of colour

Colour psychologists—the people who help industrial concerns to create environments in which work is most efficiently done—tell us that the very dark browns, greens, blues and purples are soporific; that the cold colours, those which have no red in their make-up, make us feel physically cold and uneasy; that reds and oranges have an exciting effect on the human psyche and that the yellows, because of their association with sunlight, are pleasantly encouraging.

However, yellowish reflections on the average pink and white skin can have a less than cosmetic effect. One suspects that the well-used pastels, which, of course, started life as clear, sharp shades and only became tired and washed out with succeeding generations of decorators, clung to walls for so long because they were enormously flattering.

Optical illusions

So much for the effect of colour on people. What does it do for the space? Wall treatments can optically alter and improve the proportions of a room, and this is useful to know since few rooms are perfectly proportioned.

Bright and strong colours tend to look as if they are advancing towards the observer, while the cool neutrals recede, so that you can create the illusion of airiness or greater enclosure by a judicious choice of colour. You can visually lower the ceiling by painting it a darker tone than the walls and by introducing bands of the same colour below the cornice. Conversely, you can optically raise the floor by making your walls darker

than the floor-covering. Dissecting walls by means of colour, embellishing them with murals, introducing false perspective by means of colour, all *trompe l'oeil*, and patterns are, of course, a law unto themselves.

A tiny pattern on a large expanse of wall will fail to register even if it looked contrasty and strong in the wallpaper book: it is the huge number of repeats that cause the blur. On the other hand, a very large pattern on the walls of a smallish room can be claustrophobic. It will make the space look smaller by virtue of the small number of repeats—and this is a particularly glum outlook for insomniacs, who need plenty of repeats to count as they try fitfully to doze off in the cold light of dawn.

Right: *this room, which strongly reflects the turn of the century era, seems almost to stand still in time. The high wall is covered with a varnished collage, and panels of richly polished mahogany.*

Bottom right: *the wall is painted plain white to create a simple background, which clearly emphasizes the two enormous and colourful patchwork quilts on the wall, and the third on the bed.*

Below: *this pyramid shape looks rather as if it has been cut out of the brick wall with pinking shears. In fact, a disused chimney has been capitalized on to make an interesting effect.*

Above and left: *this pretty wallpaper, with its simple green sprig, tones in perfectly with the brighter green of the mantlepiece and the marbled effect of the fireplace surround. This effect is achieved by a method of applying paint known as stippling* **(left).** *For this you need emulsion paint and a sponge. The sponge should be quite dry, not wringing with paint. Dab the sponge lightly over the surface to be treated.*

Bedroom planning
Walls – fabrics, cork and wood

The theory is that because a bedroom suffers less wear and tear than other rooms, its decorations may be more delicate, more exquisite and more expensive. After all, if you can't indulge yourself in your most private room, where can you? Grass cloths or silks might well find a home there, except if there are very young children in the house who like to gravitate towards the parental bed for Sunday breakfast: tiny, eggy fingers and pale, watered silk do not mix.

Such hazards apart, the choice of fabrics for the wall has never been greater than now, quite apart from the co-ordinated fabrics and papers that combine to give a unity of design.

It is not only the furnishing counters, but also the dress fabric counters which provide a happy hunting ground for decorators and designers.

Fabrics have a softer, deeper texture than any other wall covering, making a room look immensely cared for. This is true whether the fabric is neat and tailored like hessian (which comes, self-adhesive, from furnishing stores) or something jolly from the local draper, like gingham. Anything with a checkerboard pattern is, of course, hell to fix since the crisp effect of the pattern will be spoilt if the weave is stretched out of its natural lie. So instead of trying to cover a whole wall, fix fabric on to frames. These can be laid flat for easier working. Then, when all is ramrod straight, fix the frames to the wall.

All fabrics for walls should be treated with a dirt-repelling silicone spray. Many wall-fabrics can be vacuum cleaned and lightly shampooed, but for something like felt, which comes in such excellent colours, or pile fabrics, such as velvet, a spraying is essential. Velvet and felt should, of course, be used flat, but many other, lighter weaves can be draped—ideal for catering to fantasies.

For those wishing to be wafted to dreamland on billowing diaphanous clouds, plain snow-white cambric or a white lacy fabric fixed not to the wall but gathered against the ceiling and surrounding the bed will do the trick. Or, instead of creating a total shroud, arrange the material only above the bed-head, like a tester: the long stoles either side of the bed can be caught up and a short frontal flounce suspended from the ceiling. Used in this way, fabric works best against plain white walls, or at most against a sharp little pattern on a white background.

Fabric, too, is an essential ingredient in creating the stark far eastern look. If the room contains little more than four walls and a low-level bed, or sleeping platform, it stands to reason that the more exquisite the material, the more dramatic the effect. It is here, too, that the straw papers come into their own.

Latter-day Elinor Glyns, loving to sin on tigerskins, but preservationists at heart, will go on safari to the fur-fabric counter. Bedspreads come printed like spotted cats—the other side of kitsch, indeed, but amazing when allied to other fake-furs or fur-printed fabrics.

On the subject of plushness: nothing is grander than carpeting taken right up the wall behind the bed—or even all around the room. This is a splendid insulating medium; your heating bills will plummet.

Cork and wood panelling

Cork has the same characteristics. Being a semi-soft material, it causes sound-waves to bounce from wall to wall, diffusing during their criss-cross travels. Poor Marcel Proust remained a martyr to noise in spite of having taken the precaution of spending the latter part of his life in a cork-clad bedroom. Since, in his day, it was not generally known that cork needs sealing if it is not to emanate fine dust, his asthma did not improve either. Nowadays, however, cork is a fine proposition for the walls of a bedroom: it comes in blonde and brown, and is simply glued to walls.

If you like the look of wood—and it can give a beautiful, warm glow to a room—take advantage of tongued-and-grooved boarding. It may be laid in a straight, horizontal or vertical pattern, or herringboned.

Few people will want to tamper with original panelling, but if it is for some reason unattractive, there is the possibility of making it look quite different by painting it and picking out the moulding in splendid colours.

And if your bedroom has a beamed ceiling, you are not obliged to have it the traditional mock-Tudor black and white. Pick out the beams in any colour you like, or even paint them white like the rest of the ceiling; the play of light and shade will delight you as you gaze contemplatively upwards.

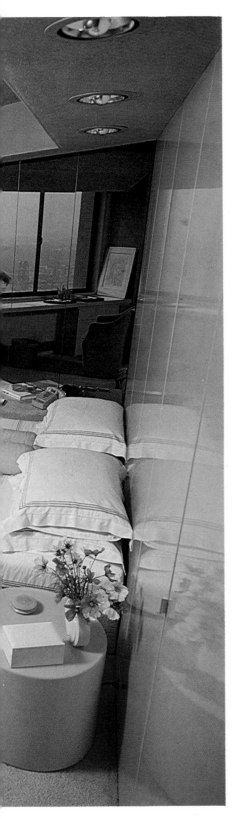

Left: *chequered print, enveloping the walls as well as the bed, gives the whole room a neat, tailored appearance. One panel of fabric is joined to the next with a smart, camouflaging border.*

Far left: *all-over suede bathes a room in luxury; this look could pall without the relief given by the contrasting, hard gloss over one wall. Felt can be used instead of suede to give the same soft covering at a fraction of the cost.*

Below left: *panels of wooden slats give walls texture and are ideal for picture hanging. Painted garden trellis can be used for this type of wall covering.*

Bottom: *stark, wooden boards, varnished on one wall and white-painted on the next, accentuate the interesting nooks and crannies of this rustic bedroom.*

Below: *gingham, when successfully hung—stretched on to frames before securing to the wall—is visually exciting in the bedroom.*

Floors – wood, vinyl and tiles

Traditionally, less hard-wearing floors are recommended for bedrooms than for living-rooms, on the assumption that bedrooms are used only in the morning and at night. Today's shrinking living space, however, may well mean that bedrooms are being pressed into service as double-duty rooms—bedroom-living-rooms, bedroom-studios, bedroom-hobby rooms—so choose a quality of flooring that will cope with the amount of wear you expect your bedroom to get.

Flooring in the bedroom must feel pleasant to the skin. Unless you have a passion for padding around the house in bare feet, the bedroom is one of the few places in your home where you actually touch the floor with bare skin. Touch and stroke samples with this in mind. In colder climates you may also want your bedroom flooring to add warmth to the room in the form of extra insulation and draught-proofing. And in a shared bedroom it is important that the flooring deadens as much noise as possible to minimize disturbance when one person has to get up in the middle of the night, or is an up-with-the-dawn lark or a last-to-bed owl. Deal with all squeaky floorboards before laying any kind of flooring on top of them. Screw boards through to the joists in two places, but make sure that you miss any underfloor cables or pipes—these are usually laid in the middle of the board.

Many types of smooth flooring are suitable for bedrooms. All of them can be teamed with rugs for softness at strategic points.

Original floorboards
These can be sanded, then sealed, stained or painted. Thorough sanding is essential to avoid splinters, especially in children's rooms, where the floor is likely to be an arena for games. Gaps between the boards can be filled with papier mâché stained to match the boards, or with wooden fillets glued into place. Gaps in skirtings can be stopped with quadrant moulding pinned into place. Filling of any kind, however, is time-consuming and to some extent spoils the appearance of the floor.
Wear, feel and appearance: Reasonably hard-wearing, but the surface finish (varnish) may need renewing fairly frequently. Feels hard but not too cold. Well-sanded floorboards assume a honey colour; sealed with clear varnish, they

blend with natural country styles of furnishing. You can stain boards a darker shade for a more formal look, which goes well with white furniture, and for a brighter look you can stain with colours and then varnish, or paint with polyurethane paint. Geometric designs are easy to do if you base them on the lines of the floorboards. You can use stencils to make patterns.
Warmth and noise: Give no extra insulation. With nothing to deaden footsteps, can be noisy.
Cost and maintenance: Relatively low-cost flooring finish—you can hire a sanding machine and do the job yourself. Boards show dust clearly, so frequent sweeping or vacuuming is essential. The surface finish may need renewing from time to time if the room gets hard wear.

Wood overlays
This is a long-lasting form of flooring finish which most people would reserve for their living-room floors. Unlike most carpeting, wood floors can add to the value of your home. Types of wood overlays include strips in widths varying from about 45 to 70 mm/2 to 3 in according to the wood. These fit together with tongues and grooves or with interlocking "ears" and are nailed or glued to the existing floorboards. Alternatively, there are parquet panels, usually about 8 mm/$\frac{1}{3}$ in thick. Some are felt-backed and can be stuck directly to the floor; others are tongued and grooved.
Wear, feel and appearance: Hard-wearing and long lasting. Feels hard but not too cold. Parquet panels are rather formal; wood strips blend in well with most styles of furnishing. A wide variety of wood colours is available from palest yellow shades to rich, reddish browns. All forms of wood floor look very good with rugs.
Warmth and noise: Seals over gaps between floorboards and adds a small amount of insulation. Relatively noisy.
Cost and maintenance: Medium to expensive—do-it-yourself versions of wood overlay flooring have helped to bring down costs. Sweep regularly.

Hardboard overlay
Available in a wide range of standard sizes, hardboard sheets laid smooth side up can make attractive, inexpensive floors. Alternatively, hardboard provides a useful sub-floor for other types of flooring such as vinyl and cork tiles, vinyl

sheeting and tiles of carpet or ceramics.
Wear, feel and appearance: Reasonably hard-wearing but the surface finish may need renewing from time to time. Feels hard but not too cold. Brown surface of board can simply be varnished for a natural effect, but this can look a little drab. Alternatively, use polyurethane floor paint to create areas of plain colour or even patterns. You can use smaller sizes of board for a tiled effect, or paint roads or fields or airports to add play potential to a child's room.
Warmth and noise: Seals over gaps between boards; gaps around skirtings can be blocked with quadrant moulding. Not as noisy as bare boards but not as quiet as carpet.
Cost and maintenance: Relatively inexpensive. Boards show dust clearly so frequent sweeping or vacuuming is essential.

Chipboard overlay
Make sure that you select a flooring grade of chipboard. This is a sturdier, more expensive and longer-lasting form of overlay than hardboard.
Wear, feel and appearance: Hard-wearing if well sealed or painted. Feels hard but not too cold. Varnished with clear polyurethane seal, the board has an attractive, honey-flecked appearance, which will blend with any pale wood, such as pine. Chipboard also takes coloured stains well and can then be given clear coats of varnish for extra wearability, or it can be painted with polyurethane paint for a glossy, colourful finish.
Warmth and noise: Seals over gaps between boards and adds small measure of insulation. Not as noisy as bare boards but not as quiet as carpet.
Cost and maintenance: Less cheap but more hard-wearing than hardboard, but still relatively inexpensive compared with quality carpet. Will show dust, in common with other forms of smooth flooring. Therefore needs frequent sweeping or vacuuming.

Vinyl tiles
The cheapest vinyl tiles are made with asbestos fillers in plain colours with a marbled effect. Although hard-wearing, these tiles are brittle and care must be taken in laying. Better quality tiles do not contain fillers and come in a wide range of colours, some with an adhesive backing, some with printed designs.

Wear, feel and appearance: Hard-wearing if correctly laid and maintained—always follow the makers' instructions carefully. A smooth, dry, clean and level sub-floor is essential—a hardboard underlay is usually necessary over old boards. Can feel rather cold and unwelcoming to bare feet, though the effect could be softened with rugs. Can look rather institutional in bedrooms. However, using two or more colours, it is possible to create interesting designs—borders around the bed, for example. Some printed versions imitate Italian and Spanish ceramic patterns, so you could achieve an exotic Mediterranean effect without the weight or excessive chilliness of ceramic tiles.
Warmth and noise: Will seal over gaps but add little extra insulation. Better than bare boards, but not as quiet as cushion vinyls or carpet.
Cost and maintenance: Better-quality tiles will cost as much as carpet. Remember to take into account the cost of hardboard underlay when estimating costs. As with all smooth floorings, vinyl tiles will show dust. They are easy to sweep and mop clean, but most types require regular polishing. Always follow the manufacturers' recommendations for the type of cleaning agents and polishes to use—some cleaners and polishes can cause irreversible yellowing. On the whole, avoid use of abrasive powders and liquids which contain ammonia.

Vinyl sheet
This is available in smooth, hard, printed forms in a wide variety of designs. Most of the points made for vinyl tiles apply, except that the range of designs is wider, although there is not the same opportunity to make your own patterns.

Cushioned vinyl sheet is far more resilient underfoot than other forms of sheet and vinyl tile: a foam interlayer is formed during the manufacturing process, and this type of flooring is often embossed or textured. Available in widths of 1,830 mm/6 ft and 3,660 mm/12 ft or in a new metric width of 2 metres.
Wear, feel and appearance: Hard-wearing if correctly laid and maintained—see points made for vinyl tiles. Feels warmer to the touch than other types of vinyl—can make a suitable flooring for children's bedrooms, where you expect frequent spills of paint water, etc. Attractive range of designs, but avoid those that

Left: in a hot climate, white ceramic tiles on the floor and the walls provide a crisp, cool background.

—reserve for rooms with little or short-term wear. Feels cold and unpleasant. On the whole only available in bright, garish designs.

Warmth and noise: Covers gaps. Slightly deadens noise.

Cost and maintenance: Inexpensive—its chief and virtually only virtue. Sweep or vacuum frequently.

Cork tiles

Warm and resilient, with a pleasant brown colour, cork blends well with many styles of furnishing. Cork tiling lends itself well to rugs. Shades range from pale and flecked effects to a rich, dark brown. Common tile size is 300 mm/76 in or 305 mm/77 in square.

Wear, feel and appearance: Properly sealed and properly laid on smooth, dry, level sub-floor, cork tiles are hard-wearing. Tile thickness is usually around 3 mm/$\frac{1}{8}$ in—thicker tiles are available but are not necessarily more hard-wearing, although they are more resilient and give a greater degree of insulation. Cork tiles are available finished with a wax polish, which may need renewing from time to time. For very heavy duty, you can buy tiles factory-finished with a layer of clear PVC. Unsealed tiles from cheaper ranges should be sealed with several coats of clear varnish before you walk on them. Warm, resilient, pleasant to the touch. Pleasant, natural appearance.

Warmth and noise: Adds good extra insulation and covers gaps. Deadens noise to some extent.

Cost and maintenance: Medium to expensive, but considered worth it by most people. Will show dust but easy to sweep or vacuum. Wax-finished variety may need repolishing from time to time. If you have applied your own sealer, this may need renewing after a while.

Ceramic tiles

On the whole, ceramic tiles are not suitable for bedroom floors unless you live in a very hot climate, for they are cold to the touch. There is also the problem of weight: many bedroom floors, being situated above ground level, would need strengthening to take the additional weight of ceramic tiles and the concrete bed in which they sit.

Sanded and sealed with clear varnish, rough, dark-stained floorboards become smooth and honey coloured.

Too beautiful to be covered, this old stone floor can be scattered with rugs to keep bare feet warm in cold weather.

imitate other materials, such as ceramic tiles, slate, wood and rush.

Warmth and noise: Cushion layer plus hardboard underlay create a certain degree of extra insulation. Seals out draughts. Cushion effect deadens noise appreciably, but not to the same extent as carpet plus underlay.

Cost and maintenance: More expensive than printed hard vinyls and will work out more expensive than cheaper forms of carpeting, but will last longer. Easy to maintain. Textured types disguise dust to some extent, and patterns conceal staining. As with all vinyls, follow carefully the makers' recommendations for cleaning. Polishing is not usually necessary—simply mop over with a damp cloth or squeezed-out mop.

Printed felt

This is the very cheapest kind of floor covering, not to be confused with vinyls, for it simply has a plastic coating over a printed felt base.

Wear, feel and appearance: Poor wearing

Bedroom planning
Carpets

Understandably, carpets are by far the most popular floor covering for bedrooms. Carpets feel good under bare feet, add warmth to the room, eliminate draughts and look inviting. Simple vacuuming once or twice a week is usually all that is required to keep bedroom carpets clean. The word "carpets", however, embraces a multitude of types, so here are some guidelines to steer you through what can seem to be a jungle of carpet terminology.

It is generally assumed that bedrooms can be satisfactorily furnished with carpets that are less hard-wearing and therefore cheaper than those needed for living-rooms. The more fibres packed into each square centimetre or inch of carpet pile the better, so if you do want a hard-wearing carpet look for a dense, tightly packed pile that does not "grin", i.e. show a lot of backing when the sample is bent back on itself.

A reputable store will guide you to the most suitable carpet for a particular location. In the UK, many carpets carry the British Carpet Mark as a guide to consumers: for example, Category I is considered suitable for "bedrooms and secondary rooms with light traffic". However, in a smaller home you may well want to use your bedroom during the day. In this case, look for a carpet in Category 2, "medium domestic/light contract". One-room flats, where the wear is heavily concentrated, benefit from Category 3, "general domestic/ medium contract, domestic situations with heavy traffic". And if the sky is the limit, you might go for Category L. This stands for luxury: L carpets "are superior to Category 3, created for comfort and aesthetic appeal, but not necessarily for areas of high durability".

Carpet descriptions in the shops are divided between descriptions of how the carpet is made and what it is made from. Keep the two definitions clear. On the whole, the latter is more important than the former.

How carpets are made

Woven carpets are what the description implies and take their names from the English towns where the traditional weaving processes originated, Axminster and Wilton. Axminster carpets are unique in the number of colours that can be incorporated in any one design. Wilton carpets are usually but not necessarily

plain. The important point to remember is that the words Axminster and Wilton are no guarantee of quality in themselves; you must also assess pile-fibre quality and content.

Tufteds are manufactured by a modern process in which needles working at high speeds punch the carpet pile into the ready-woven backing, which is then given a coating of latex to hold the tufts in place. The pile can then be left looped or can be shorn to create a cut pile. Sometimes only the higher loops are shorn, which creates a textured effect. Many tufteds have a foam backing, which cuts out the need for an underlay. Tufteds can be plain, mottled, in shaded colour effects and even patterned by overprinting.

Fibre-bonded (sometimes called needle-loom or needle-punch) carpet has dense layers of fibres punched into a backing; the layers are then impregnated with a bonding agent to hold them together. Depending on the fibres used, this provides a soft, hard-wearing surface. It is popular for carpet tiles.

Above: *unmistakable velvety pile of a Wilton carpet—honey-coloured luxury.*

Left: *the Conrans' bedroom is carpeted with a Berber-weave broadloom.*

Bottom left: *Flokati—shaggy white woollen room-size rugs from Greece.*

Below: *hard-wearing and practical cord carpeting made with looped animal hair.*

Cord carpets have an even, ridged surface which resists flattening. They can be made by weaving, tufting or by fibre-bonding with a ridged surface. Providing the fibre used is good and is used in sufficient quantity, any of these methods can produce a good cord.

What carpets are made from

Wool is the traditional but an expensive carpet fibre. Hard-wearing, it stands up well to flattening, shows good resistance to soiling and will not easily burn. It can be used in blends with other fibres.

Acrylics (e.g. Acrilan, Orlon, Dralon, Dolan) are also expensive and often resemble wool both to handle and to look at. They can be used on their own or in blends with other materials.

Modacrylics (e.g. Teklan) are a new fibre development with inherent flame-resisting properties.

Viscose, sometimes known as rayon (e.g. Evlan, Evlan M, Danuflor), when used on its own makes cheap carpeting which tends to soil and flatten, although it is reasonably hard-wearing. Used in blends it makes budget-priced, good-value, low-pile carpets.

Nylons (e.g. Bri-Nylon, Enkalon, Du Pont, Antron), being tough fibres, are often used in blends to add durability.

Developments in recent years have produced silky, lustrous nylons with "soil-hiding properties"—the nylons are constructed in such a way that light reflection from the fibres disguises dirt. (Older types of nylon tended to look dirty quickly, although they were easy to clean.) These new nylons are used for fine-denier effects in fabulous colours, but are expensive: ideally suited for really ritzy bedrooms. Printed loop piles, plain and printed cut-piles and newer velvety plush piles are all available now, so nylon is no longer necessarily nasty.

Polyesters (e.g. Terylene, Dacron) are only moderately hard-wearing, but have a pleasant feel and take colours well. They are used for good-value, shaggy-looking bedroom carpets.

Polypropylenes (e.g. Propathen, Ulstron) are a newer arrival on the carpet scene. Hard-wearing and usually budget priced, they show good resistance to staining. Some people complain that they feel a little harsh, and they can have an unpleasant glitter (like cheaper nylons); and they can cause a build-up of static electricity. A good-value plain carpeting for bedrooms.

Cotton, coir and sisal are natural fibres used for carpeting and matting. Cotton is used mainly for cheaper carpeting, which is not very hard-wearing and has poor resistance to soiling. Washable, long-pile cotton rugs, however, can be attractive and useful in bedrooms and bathrooms. Coir, from coconut shells, is woven into matting which, although very hard-wearing, is harsh to the touch and could feel unpleasant under bare feet. Sisal, too, would feel a bit harsh for bedrooms: it is usually used for hard-wearing cords and mattings.

Many of these fibres are used in complicated blends. Carpet technologists aim to incorporate the good qualities of each particular fibre into their blends, but it is difficult for an amateur to assess their success; you must put your trust in the name of a good maker or a good shop—preferably both.

Choosing colours and patterns

Try not to get carried away by colours and patterns when buying any kind of flooring; if a floor covering is poor-wearing, it is doomed speedily to dismal looks. Remember, too, that the colours and patterns you choose may have to last through changes of paper and paint.

Bedroom areas are broken up by the beds, storage, chairs and other furnishings, and large, jazzy patterns on the floor can be distressingly unsuccessful. With so many pretty patterns for papers, curtains and bed linen, all of which are seen to best advantage against a plain floor, it can be wiser to choose a plain or textured carpet for the bedroom. Pale colours, of course, show marks and stains, and dark colours show up "white dirt" made up of crumbs from bedtime biscuits and morning toast, bits of thread and fluff. Safest, if not necessarily the most stunning, is a medium shade.

Textured or flecked carpets can be a good compromise between the dirt-hiding properties of patterned carpets and the chic style of the plains. Deservedly popular are the Berber styles, woven or tufted from natural undyed wools in shades of cream and brown.

Finding a fit

Fitted carpets are the most practical proposition in a bedroom; they will make your room seem larger and more streamlined and will be easy to clean. You can use a low-cost cord and add extra interest with rugs. You can also fit carpets yourself if they are tufted with a foam back, in which case they will be virtually non-fraying. However, it is advisable to have woven, unbacked carpets fitted by a professional because they require stretching. Many types of cord also benefit from professional fitting.

It is essential that all carpets without a foam backing have an underlay. This should be dense and springy—ask to see a sample at your carpet store. Underlay cushions wear and prevents dirt penetrating from the back of the carpet. Traditional jute/hair mixtures are fine; more expensive are bonded felts impregnated with rubber; springiest of all are foam-rubber underlays, which are also the most expensive.

Carpet tiles are a relatively new development and well suited to bedrooms, where wear tends to get concentrated in narrow passage areas in front of wardrobes, around the bed and so on. Loose-lay carpet tiles can be moved around to even out the wear. They are simple for one person to lay, can be cut with scissors, and two colours can be used to make interesting border designs to outline a particular shape or area. You can even rinse them under the tap.

Rugs

Old or antique oriental rugs and their modern descendants are beautiful and hard-wearing floor coverings. For hundreds of years, rugs and carpets have been hand-knotted by nomad tribes and in town and village workshops over a huge area stretching from the Balkans in south-eastern Europe across the Middle East and Asia to China.

Designs were passed between tribes and communities through intermarriage, migration and by the traders of the Silk Route and they are known by the names of their place or tribe of origin. During this century, the craft of rug-making has been subject to more government supervision and control, ensuring high standards of workmanship, sometimes at the expense of individuality of design.

Bokara rug from Pakistan—a finely knotted rug of wool and goats' hair.

Antique rugs have a higher investment value than most modern rugs because of their natural vegetable dyes, scarcity and the unique beauty of each piece. However, they may be less hard-wearing and will almost certainly be more expensive than modern rugs.

Where to buy
Department stores usually employ approachable, fairly knowledgeable staff and are convenient for checking prices

Russian Seichor—a modern rug.

Turkish rug of artificial silk.

because of their range of stock, particularly moderns.

Antique shops and specialist carpet dealers are often very expert. Some deal in rugs of particular areas and will help in developing a collection. They will do valuations and repairs. Ask around for personal recommendations.

At auctions, catalogue descriptions can be informative. Don't expect to find bargains, but you may buy at reasonable prices if you learn the market by visiting local shops. Take great care in inspecting rugs—there are many pitfalls.

Persian rugs of good pedigree are as safe an investment as fine paintings.

How to buy
Examine rugs carefully in a good light, particularly the back. Lay the rug flat on the floor, not on a pile of rugs. Look for:

Mends or reweaving, not necessarily a bad thing if expertly done.

Tears, holes or "low" areas This is where the pile, often of a particular colour—frequently black—has worn, giving a relief effect.

Fineness of knotting This is not so important in tribal and old Caucasian rugs. Knots should be firm and even. In town rugs, like Isfahans, Kashans and modern Pakistani Bokharas, the finer the knotting the better. This can vary between

250 knots per square inch to 800 knots per square inch in a really good silk rug.

Silk or artificial silk (mercerized cotton) A simple test is to carefully remove a single strand and burn it with a match. Artificial silk will make a grey powdery ash and smell like paper burning, silk will burn and smell like human hair.

Softness and gloss on wool Chemical washing is occasionally used to mellow colours and make new rugs shine.

Abraschs This is a streak or patch of wool lighter or darker than its surrounding area. Skeins of yarn would have been taken from different dye lots and faded at varying speeds. Often charming and idiosyncratic in old rugs, this may be artificially imitated in new ones.

If your finances will not run to antique oriental rugs, consider buying a hand-woven Indian durry; they are stylish and within reach of any budget.

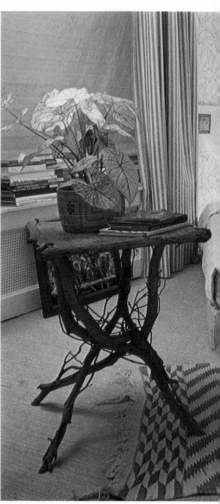

Left: *Indian durry, cheap and cheerful woven cotton rug available in an amazing variety of colourways.*

Top left: *coarsely woven wool rug from Ethiopia, which could have been made to order for this simple modern room.*

Above: *a pretty hand-made crocheted rug looks wonderful with stripped pine and white china. Obviously not intended to withstand hob-nail boots, but perfect for bare feet and bedroom slippers.*

Bedroom planning
Changes of level

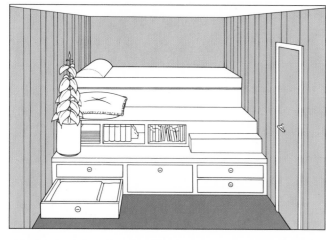

A bedroom without free-standing furniture : a cascade of varying levels provides sleeping and sitting platforms as well as plenty of useful shelf and drawer space.

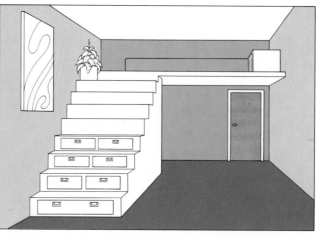

An architectural solution : the access steps to the sleeping platform double as drawers at the lower levels. Hanging space is accessible from the back of the stair unit.

The sculptural look : surrounding a neat, tailored bed base, dual-purpose seating and storage units hide away untidy bedside clutter, duvets and pillows.

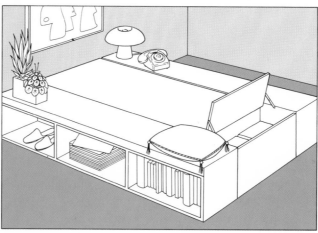

A continuous ledge around the bed provides seating and storage space and clears the bedroom of space-consuming furniture such as dressing-tables and bedside chairs.

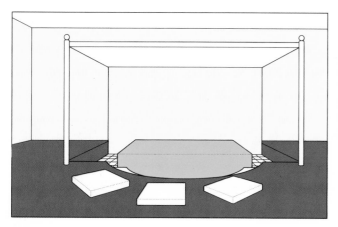

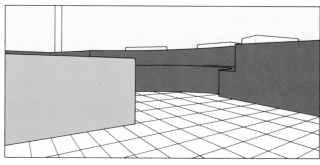

Above and left: *a platform, built above an existing floor, dips down to the original level to form a dramatic seating circle surrounding a sleeping well.*

Many modern architects do not like the idea of furniture: too many legs, too much cluttering of the space. Making an exception for one or two beautifully designed pieces, they prefer to provide pits and platforms at different levels which allow any number of people to relax in beds and seating areas that have no obvious furniture connotations.

Modulations of the floor plane can be simple or complex, occasional or progressive, subtle or striking. All can contribute qualities of landscaping that cannot be achieved by other means, allowing the eye to travel without hindrance, especially if the same floor covering is used up hill and down dale. Changing levels in the bedroom can create special places within the one room, without vertical division.

The easiest change of level is a simple platform dais for the bed. It can provide useful seating, can contain some useful storage and, more important, provide a focus within a dull space. Additions of this sort are generally feasible in terms of weight: the overall load of a timber-jointed platform on the floor structure should not exceed 25–30 kg per square metre/5–6 lb per square foot. The platform would have to be very elaborate and solid to exceed this limit, as weights are distributed, not concentrated.

A limiting factor in a floor-raising project is more likely to be height. In a room not more than 2.5 m/8 ft high—a common height in modern buildings—local building regulations may limit the floor area over which you can reduce that height. You will also have to consider if you will be happy nearer the ceiling—what is cosy to some is unbearable to others, but ceiling treatments can help to counteract such oppressiveness: shiny reflective paint adds visual height, and so does a mirror.

Right: *a low-level bed base raised on a carpeted dais makes an interesting focal point. Simple structures like this platform are easy to build, especially if you plan to cover them with carpet, which will conveniently conceal any unsightly flaws in the finish.*

All about beds

A bed hides all the mysteries of its construction within a sandwich of padding and a ticking cover. As we are denied a view of what is going on inside, it is difficult to judge when a bed has reached the end of its useful life, and even more difficult to compute the merits of different types of springing when investing in a new one. The facts we give you here will help you to ensure that all your family get a comfortable night's sleep on beds that take good care of their backs. Until quite recently, the choice of bed coverings was limited to plain pastel colours and the natural fibres of cotton, linen, silk or wool. With the advent of synthetic fibres and the intense competition between manufacturers to produce something new and different, bed coverings have become a focus for the fashion designers' attention. This chapter guides you through the panorama of possibilities to help you make the right decision on how your bed should be clothed, from the decorative and practical points of view.

All about beds
History of the bed

Making a bed originally meant just that. If you had belonged to an Anglo-Saxon household, soon after supper you would have stuffed your sack with straw and laid it on the floor or at best on a hard bench in the great hall, where family, servants and livestock lived, ate and slept. At curfew (*couvre-feu*) the central fire was covered and everybody literally "hit the hay". There was little opportunity or concern for privacy, except that the thane and his lady enjoyed the privilege of *bolstar*, *pyle*, *scyte* and *bedreaf* (bolster, pillow, sheet and coverlet) in a curtained-off apartment.

By the mid-11th century, there was a little more comfort. The invention of the chimney allowed the fireplace to be moved to the wall, and thus a bower or bedroom on an upper floor would be heated by a fireplace set into the main chimney. These upper rooms, however, were not very private places, as the field labourers would report there daily for their orders. The beds were grand and massive affairs; an important one would have a tester, or canopy, hung from the ceiling on chains to keep out the inevitable draughts. A full tester would protect the whole bed, a half tester only the head.

"Queen Elizabeth slept here", one is often informed when visiting English stately homes, and she quite likely did.

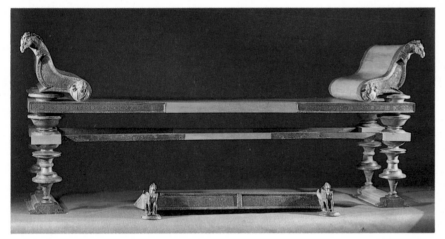

A Roman bed may look uncomfortable, but in use was amply piled with quilts, mattresses and, for extra warmth, a toga.

Medieval bed with a half-tester canopy. The bed was often the most valued possession in a medieval house and the bedchamber a place to receive guests.

Monarchs and great landowners travelled almost continually because their revenues were paid in kind, and the most reliable way to collect was to visit the source of income and collect the proffered goods before moving on to the next. On such progresses they took their own beds—not the heavy carved wooden bedsteads, but the feather mattresses, pillows, linen and curtains to bedeck the guest beds of their hosts.

It was in the 16th century—not before—that the four-poster appeared. At this time, Dutch craftsmen were making many of northwestern Europe's most notable beds, massive affairs in elaborately carved oak, coarse by Italian standards. The famous Great Bed of Ware, now in the Victoria and Albert Museum, bearing the date 1460 but actually made between 1575 and 1600, is about 11 feet/3.25 metres square, not unusually large by the standards of the time. For kings and nobles the bed had become a reception room, almost a throne, especially in France, where the *lit de parade* was the setting for the ceremonies of birth, marriage and death. An inventory of Louis XIV's possessions lists 25 different kinds of state bed.

In the 17th century, beds became lighter and more elegant in design. Increasingly commonplace were beds that could be corded—that is to say, the cords of the mattress were stretched with a tool called a bed twitch. The base might still

Artist's impression of American pioneer bed, or "jack bed", supported on one leg.

Hefty oaken four-poster, carved by Tudor craftsmen in emulation of the more delicate Italian Renaissance work.

be of straw, under a feather mattress, which had to be opened, aired and re-stuffed at intervals. When made, the bed was finally smoothed with a long wooden bed staff resembling a stout broomstick.

Early colonial beds in North America showed a strong Dutch influence. The *betste* was a press-bed set in a recess with doors, closed during the day. The *sloepbanck* was a folding bed hinged to disappear behind its tester curtains. Pioneers out West were content with the jack bed, which had only one leg, the other corners being supported by the log cabin walls. Its springing was flexible wooden poles and the mattress the familiar sack of straw. By contrast, a mayor of New York who died in 1690 left bed-linen valued at $500, including 61 pillowcases. By then the better-off had four-

Ludwig II (1845–86), the eccentric and insomniac King of Bavaria, commissioned this Gothic tomb of a bed in carved walnut, topped with a forest of tiny spires. The panelled bedroom, which occupied 17 woodcarvers for four and a half years, is in the fairy-tale Neuschwanstein castle.

Elegant American colonial bedroom for the whole family at the Shirley Plantation, Virginia—about 1770.

posters; in 18th-century America these were light, graceful and charming tent beds, often with an ogee canopy. Such colonial bedrooms often had a pleasing, puritan simplicity.

In 18th-century Europe, beds were often designed like classical temples. Mahogany replaced the rather intractable oak and the upholsterer began to contribute more than the joiner. Chippendale and the Adam brothers produced some superb examples, always as an integral feature of the bedroom's overall design.

The introduction of the metal bed—or rather its revival from Roman and Byzantine days—may be attributed mainly to the bed bug. This tenacious creature, and the flea also, was further deterred by the advent of cheap cotton

for sheets, which could be boiled without being spoiled. Used at first only in hospitals, prisons or servants' rooms, the iron bed appeared in the best bedrooms from about 1860, decorated with brass rods, knobs and medallions.

Under-mattresses improved steadily. In 1781, a box-shaped hair mattress appeared; in 1785, one of woven cane; in 1826, metal laths were replaced by coil springs. Woven wire was found to be very soft and comfortable, but sagged too quickly. This was overcome by mounting the mattress frame on two screw rods, so that by turning the screws with a bed key the wire was stretched tight again. A notable improvement to the vertical coil spring came with the packing of each spring into a separate fabric cylinder.

Some so-called recent bedding developments are not as new as they seem: the water-bed was a 19th-century invention, used in hospitals for the benefit

The spectacular state bed at Osterley Park, Middlesex, by Robert Adam.

of bed sore, bone fracture and paralysis cases. Louis XI adopted an air-bed, or *lit de vent*, in 1478, and in his turn was imitating Heliogabalus, the Roman emperor of the 2nd century AD. The *lit de parade* has reappeared, as a throne for sexy film stars. The advertiser of a divan bed with a built-in heater gives no credit to Sheraton for having invented it. Doctor Graham's Celestial Bed of 1778, fitted with electrical, mechanical and musical devices, antedates the stunt beds that are regularly featured at furniture exhibitions—which do not vibrate, as his did.

But apart from trendy freaks, what is the bed of today but a rectangular, fabric-covered shape, supplemented by no more than a headboard? Certainly it is comfortable as never before: as we know from the advertisements, it was perfected some years ago, and again last year and this; next year we shall no doubt be offered the really perfect bed.

Buying a bed

Just as a good night's sleep is essential for good health, good looks and an even temper, so a good bed is essential for a good night's sleep. A bed that is too hard or too soft can cause any one of a number of evils from restless nights to muscle strain, so it is worth taking time and trouble to ensure that you sleep on a bed that is not only comfortable but also supports every part of your body.

Children, in particular, need a good night's sleep for sound growth, concentrated study and active play. Their spines must be supported correctly at night, so make sure that outgrown, outworn beds and bunks are replaced as your child grows and develops.

The average bed does not last much longer than ten years, so if yours is creeping into double figures it is time to think of buying a new one. Spend as much money as you can afford on this basic element of the bedroom—frequently listed by experts as the number one home furnishing priority—and keep these general guidelines in mind. Ignore the fancy frills displayed in furniture windows and concentrate, instead, on the basic structure of the beds being offered.

Put your trust in a good name: You cannot see the working innards of a bed; these are concealed by dainty damask or bold stripes. Our explanation on pages 108 and 109 of how beds are constructed will help you to follow the manufacturers' brochures, but it is still important to buy from a reliable manufacturer, through a reputable retailer. You will benefit from the manufacturer's experience and research facilities and the retailer's expertise. If anything goes wrong, you can be sure of redress.

Lie before you buy: Comfort is an intensely subjective and personal matter. Do not go buying a bed when you are in a rush: it is essential to take your time when choosing a bed. There is no point in trying to make do with a timid prod, or by sitting on the edge. All you have to do is take off your shoes and lie full out on any bed that you are considering. After you have tried a few beds, you will start to build up your own ideas of what is and what is not comfortable.

Research shows that women in particular feel too inhibited to stretch out on a bed in a store, but this is an important enough matter for you to overcome your inhibitions. You will find that a store seriously dedicated to selling quality

beds will welcome your feet on their show pieces; they may even provide plastic mattress protectors for the purpose. If the bed is to be shared, you should take your partner along as well and both of you should try each bed together. If you are a full-blooded Wagnerian opera singer and your partner a fly-weight jockey, remember that double beds to suit different weights and comfort requirements can be made by combining two singles.

When buying beds for children, take them to the store with you. Let them try out the beds and take their comments into careful consideration—what you think of as comfortably firm may seem rock-hard to a small, skinny child.

Size: Make sure the bed you buy is big enough. Lie flat on the bed with your hands behind your head—your elbows should be contained within the width of the bed. Do not skimp on a double bed—regard a width of 1.5 m/5 ft as minimum, if space permits. The length of the bed depends on your height. There should be at least 15 cm/6 in to spare between your feet and the end of the bed.

Support: While you should not sleep on a bed that is too soft, it is possible that some people, influenced by publicity about the benefits of "firmness", are choosing beds that are too hard. Follow this simple procedure for assessing hardness or softness: lie down, and slide the flat of your hand into the small of your back. If there is a space between you and the mattress, the bed is probably too hard for you. If it is difficult to slide your hand into the small-of-the-back area, then the mattress has too readily filled the hollow and is probably too soft. The mattress that is right for you will give a little at the pressure points (shoulders and hips, for example), and will push upwards a little to fill the hollows, thus providing total body support. Since there is no one sleeping position, it is important to try a mattress by lying on it on your side and front as well as on your back in order to ensure complete comfort.

Remember, too, that the heavier you are the firmer a mattress needs to be. The bedding industry calculates that the average double bed can withstand 159 kg/350 lb; a single bed will take 82 kg/182 lb. If in doubt when choosing a bed, remember that mattresses will soften with use and err on the firm side.

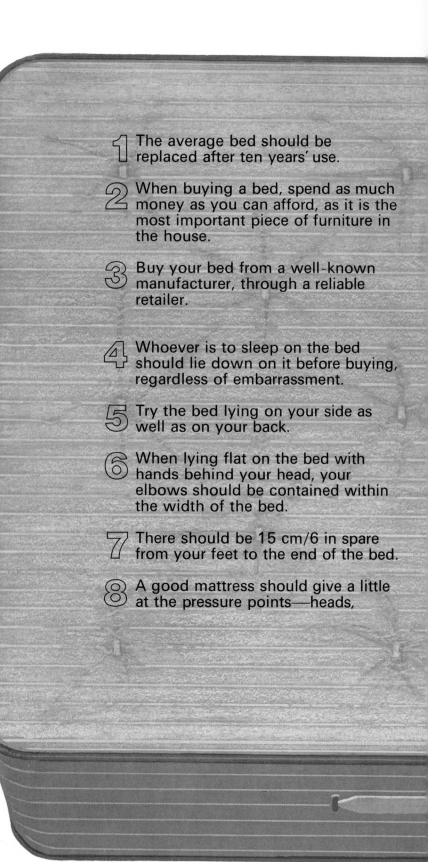

1 The average bed should be replaced after ten years' use.

2 When buying a bed, spend as much money as you can afford, as it is the most important piece of furniture in the house.

3 Buy your bed from a well-known manufacturer, through a reliable retailer.

4 Whoever is to sleep on the bed should lie down on it before buying, regardless of embarrassment.

5 Try the bed lying on your side as well as on your back.

6 When lying flat on the bed with hands behind your head, your elbows should be contained within the width of the bed.

7 There should be 15 cm/6 in spare from your feet to the end of the bed.

8 A good mattress should give a little at the pressure points—heads,

shoulders, hips and feet—and should push upwards a little to fill out the hollows of your body.

9 If the mattress fills out the hollows of your body completely, then it is too soft.

10 If the mattress does not fill out the hollows of your body at all, then it is too hard.

11 Heavier people need a bed firmer than average.

12 Children need a good night's sleep, so make sure that outgrown, outworn beds are replaced.

13 When buying a double bed, both partners should test it together.

14 Double beds to suit different weights and comfort requirements can be made by zipping together two singles.

15 Do not skimp on a double bed— regard 1.5 m/5 ft as the minimum width.

Do air your bed every day. Your body gives off moisture, so throw back the bed clothes for at least 20 minutes to allow your bed to dry out.

Do turn a spring mattress every week for the first month, and at three-monthly intervals thereafter. This helps the filling to settle evenly.

Do protect your mattress from stains.

Do check screw-in leg fittings; they may work loose with time.

Do use a soft brush to remove dust and fluff from your mattress, but do not pull at tufts and buttons.

Do clean under the bed; dust and fluff accumulate swiftly.

Do not leave the polythene wrapper on your new mattress or divan base. The bag will trap damp, causing mildew and eventual rotting.

Do not leave the wrapper within reach of young children.

Do not sit in the same place on the edge of the bed every day.

Do not bend or fold a mattress for any reason; the filling will be damaged.

Do not bounce on the bed.

Do not smoke in bed; this is one of the commonest causes of fires in the home.

All about beds
Mattresses

A bed is made up of a mattress and a base (a divan in the UK and sometimes called a sleep set in the USA) and it makes sense to buy the two together, since this is how they are designed to be used. You cannot hope to achieve the twin goals of comfort and support by placing a new mattress on an old base.

Types of mattress

Open springs are most commonly used for sprung mattresses. In a typical open-sprung mattress, rows of wire springs are held together at top and bottom by strong helical wires—very narrow-diameter continuous springs. This helps to spread the load more evenly across the mattress. The mattress unit is then reinforced around its edge for greater strength and support. There are about 288 springs in a 137 cm/4 ft 6 in wide mattress. The more expensive the mattress, the better the quality of the springs.

Posture springing is a special type of open springing manufactured under licence. It consists of a woven web of continuous wire, held in place by a wire framework top and bottom. The makers claim that the stress imposed by the body is more evenly distributed.

Pocket springing is a more expensive process. Each spring is sewn under tension into its own individual pocket made of a woven material such as heavy cotton. The pockets keep the springs under tension at all times, and stop the springs from spreading as they are compressed. Different manufacturers make different versions of pocketed springs, but the general principle is the same: that each spring can act independently of its neighbour to support the body as needed. This is claimed to be particularly beneficial in double beds, because movement made by one person is less likely to be passed on to the other.

A mattress with pocketed springs will contain far more springs than a mattress with open springs—there will be about 600 pocketed springs in a 137 cm/4 ft 6 in wide mattress, but more expensive mattresses will have as many as three times the number of springs as there are in an open-spring construction.

Upholstery. All types of sprung mattresses are enclosed in layers of upholstery that prevent you from feeling the springs and add insulation to the bed (it is important for the retention of body warmth that you should be insulated by your mattress as well as by your bedding). The upholstery is made of an initial layer of material such as coir (coconut fibre), sisal, curled hair or rubberized curled hair, polypropylene or a similar synthetic material. A secondary surface layer may be made of combinations of woollen-mixture felt, cotton felt, curled hair, white wool or polyether foam. Manufacturers who use the more expensive materials claim that they provide better insulation, better resilience and better absorption of the moisture given off by the body during sleep. Some mattresses have a "winter" and a "summer" side, with "warm" and "cool" upholstery.

Ticking, which can be made of natural fibres such as cotton or synthetics such as rayon, is put on top of the upholstery layers. Ticking can be traditionally tufted or buttoned to hold the upholstery in place, or the top of the mattress may be quilted in various patterns.

Hair mattresses (sprung or unsprung) are still available although they are considered to be rather old-fashioned, and are becoming expensive due to the cost of natural materials and labour. Hair for mattresses comes from the manes of horses, the tails of cattle and the backs of hogs. It is sterilized and given a crimp: spun first into a rope, it is given a steam treatment and finally dried in hot air. The result is an almost permanent wave.

Foam mattresses are available in latex, polyether foam or a mixture of both. Latex foam is the more expensive material and in general has a softer, bouncier feel. Many people, however, prefer polyether foam. Once again it is a question of trying out the different mattresses in the store until you find what you like. Foam mattresses are light to transport and are ideal for people who are allergic to the padding materials used in sprung mattresses.

Types of bed base

The base is usually a wooden structure filled in with springing to support the mattress above.

In a firm-edged base, the springing is contained within the wooden frame. The bed is usually set on screw-in wooden legs with castors, to give an overall height of about 50 cm/20 in. As an alternative, some bases are fitted with skids instead of legs; these give the bed a neater, lower look.

In a sprung-edged base, the springing is set on top of the wooden frame to make a base which is claimed to take the comfort of the bed right to its edges and therefore provides a greater sleeping area. Although sitting on a bed with either type of base is not recommended, a sprung-edged base is better for dual-purpose rooms such as one-room flats, where the bed is likely to double as a settee, but try to vary the point at which you sit on the bed.

For those who like a very firm bed, different types of unsprung bases are becoming increasingly popular. When these beds are called "orthopaedic" models, it is because the manufacturers wish to imply that these extra-firm beds will prevent or even cure back troubles, but always discuss the merits of this type of bed with your doctor if you have any kind of back disorder. Unsprung bases vary from wooden slats to simple wooden bases upholstered with foam or fibre. Alternatively, a double sheet of polypropylene may be stretched over a solid timber frame or perforated hardboard. Never put a mattress directly on the floor because condensation will cause it to rot.

Do-it-yourself beds

Many of the more advanced ideas for bedroom design depend on constructing your own bed. A wide range of ready-made foam mattresses can be bought for use with home-made bases. If, however, you want to make your own mattress, the type of foam you use will depend partly on personal preference and partly on the type of base with which it is to be used. With a sprung base, a minimum thickness of 10 cm/4 in is recommended. With a rigid base, you need a thicker mattress, minimum depth 13 cm/5 in.

Covering a mattress is not easy because such a large piece of foam is awkward to handle. The foam should be cut slightly larger than the required finished size of the mattress—allow an extra 19 mm/$\frac{3}{4}$ in on the length, and 12 mm/$\frac{1}{2}$ in on the width. When covered, the foam will be slightly compressed, ensuring clean lines and minimizing wrinkles. Because foam will not slide easily, leave a long seam open on the underside of the cover. Put the mattress inside and hand sew the seam.

If you are making the base for a foam mattress, it is most important to provide proper ventilation so that the mattress can "breathe". This is why foam mattresses should never be used directly on the floor for more than the occasional

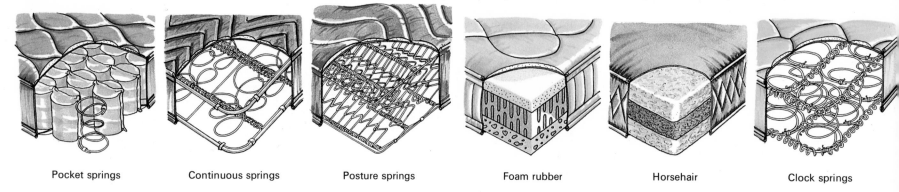

Pocket springs   Continuous springs   Posture springs   Foam rubber   Horsehair   Clock springs

night. A slatted base should have a minimum of 19 mm/¾ in between the slats, and a solid base should have 19 mm/¾ in diameter holes at 18 cm/7 in intervals across the width and 25 cm/10 in intervals down the length. All wood used should be untreated: preservatives, varnish or paint could stain the mattress cover and even cause deterioration of the foam.

Any type of rigid base should ideally have a 5 cm/2 in layer of polyether foam (the type used for camping mattresses which has indentations on the underside, giving an "egg-box" effect; you may have to order it specially). This should be upholstered on to the base, "egg-box" side down, to enable air to circulate properly under the mattress and eliminate all possibility of condensation forming on the underside: simply cover the foam with a stout, air-permeable fabric, turn under the edges and tack it or staple it with a heavy-duty stapler to the sides of the base. Any type of fabric can be used to cover the base, as long as it is air-permeable.

Dealing with stains

If an accident occurs, act quickly to stop water or other liquids from seeping into the mattress upholstery, where it could cause real problems. Strip off the bedclothes and stand the mattress on its side (seepage is slower on an upright surface). Blot off as much liquid as possible with an absorbent cloth, an old towel or plain paper towels.

Treat all stains quickly. The longer they are left, the more difficult they will be to remove.

Immediate sponging with cold water clears many liquid stains. Do not worry about leaving a small water mark; it will not show when the bed is made. A stain that has been allowed to dry is much

more difficult to remove than a fresh one.

If necessary, treat further as recommended here.

Leaking hot-water bottle or flood damage: To dry out the mattress, use a hair drier. If a large area has to be dried, put a protective covering on the floor and stand the mattress on its side, lengthways, in front of a carefully positioned fan-heater. Inspect frequently.

Tea, coffee and other milk-based drinks: Sponge the mattress first with warm borax solution (1 dsp. laundry borax to 0.3 litre/½ pint water) then with clear water. When dry, an aerosol grease solvent should remove any trace of grease, but use it sparingly on a foam mattress. Brush the cover lightly but thoroughly to clear the deposit.

Fruit juices and fruit-based drinks: Use a borax solution (see above) to remove the stickiness and the smell. It may be impossible to remove the colour left by blackcurrant and orange drinks.

Urine: Sponge the mattress with a warm solution of mild detergent (suitable for use on synthetic materials) or upholstery shampoo. Wipe with cold water to which a few drops of disinfectant have been added.

Oily marks (e.g. night creams, embrocations): Use an aerosol grease solvent to draw out and absorb the stain (see tea stains, above). Avoid using liquid grease solvents.

Vomit and excrement: Scrape and wipe up solid matter, trying not to spread the stain. Using a sponge or soft nail brush, treat as for urine, above.

Blood: Sponge first with cold salt water, then with clear cold water. Any upholstery cleaner that claims to remove blood stains is usually effective on fresh marks and may remove dried stains.

Never use hot water when treating a blood stain, as it will set the stain.

An illustration by Edmund Dulac from the classic fairy tale by Hans Andersen, "The Princess and the Pea". The young princess, visiting a prospective husband in another kingdom, meets with scepticism about her royal upbringing from her future mother-in-law, who devises the ultimate test: she places a dried pea under a huge pile of feather mattresses on which the princess is to sleep. In the morning the princess's backside is suitably covered in bruises, proving beyond doubt her truly royal sensitivity.

Wire lattice

Wooden slats

Sprung edge

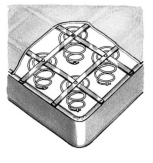

Firm edge

Standard shapes and sizes

When you consider the diversity of the human frame, it will come as no surprise to learn that the manufacturers of beds are in a turmoil over so-called standard sizes. Luckily for the consumer, there is plenty of choice without resorting to expensive custom-built beds and the resultant expensive bedding.

In the days of Imperial measurements, single beds ranged in width from 2 ft 6 in to 3 ft 6 in and doubles ranged from 4 ft to 6 ft 6 in; and then came metrication. In the UK, bedding manufacturers added the slightly larger metric sizes to their existing ranges when the industry went metric in 1971.

"King" size and "queen" size in the UK are arbitrarily applied to sizes bigger than 5 ft; there is no official measurement for these descriptions. When people say "king" size they simply mean big. When they say "queen" size they mean big, but not as big as "king" size.

The old 4 ft bed (sometimes called the three-quarter bed) is very rare, and is known in the trade as a "Landlady's double" because landladies were reputed to cram two people into a space fit only for one.

The old 2 ft 6 in bed is still made, often marketed under euphemistic labels such as "compact single" or "youth bed". The larger "standard" metric single bed, 100 cm/3 ft 3 in, has not proved popular; indeed, some manufacturers do not include it in their range at all. The 150 cm/5 ft standard metric double, however, is increasing its sales every year.

In the US, Imperial measurements are still used for standard bed sizes, but not all manufacturers make all models in all sizes, although special sizes can normally be ordered at extra cost.

If you are sleeping double, it is worth knowing that extremely comfortable double beds can be created from single beds designed for the purpose. The bases clip together with a bar, and the mattresses usually zip together. The undoubted advantage is that each person has a choice of firmness and can move about without disturbing the sleeping partner. This is particularly useful when one person is heavier than the other or suffers from back trouble. Better-quality zip-up beds have zips along both sides, so that mattresses, as recommended, can be turned in all directions—from side to side and from top to bottom.

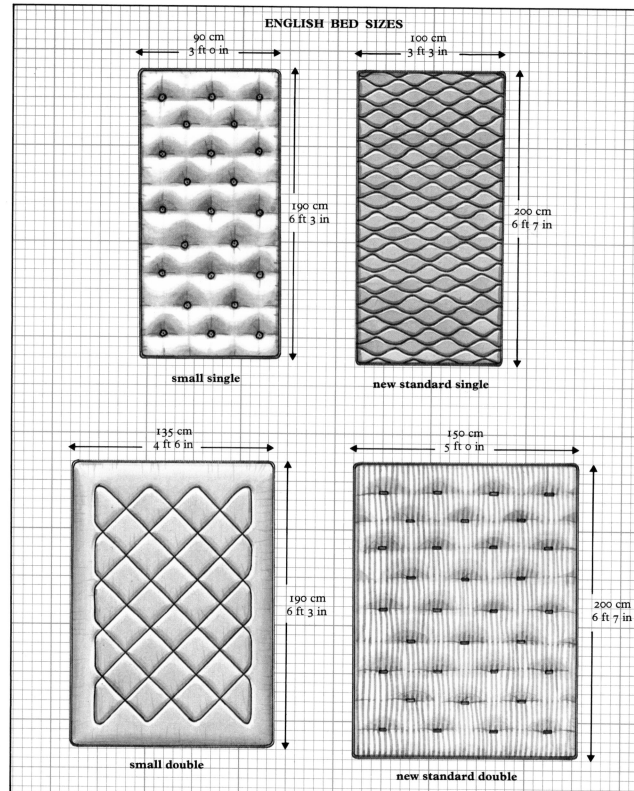

ENGLISH BED SIZES

90 cm / 3 ft 0 in — 190 cm / 6 ft 3 in
small single

100 cm / 3 ft 3 in — 200 cm / 6 ft 7 in
new standard single

135 cm / 4 ft 6 in — 190 cm / 6 ft 3 in
small double

150 cm / 5 ft 0 in — 200 cm / 6 ft 7 in
new standard double

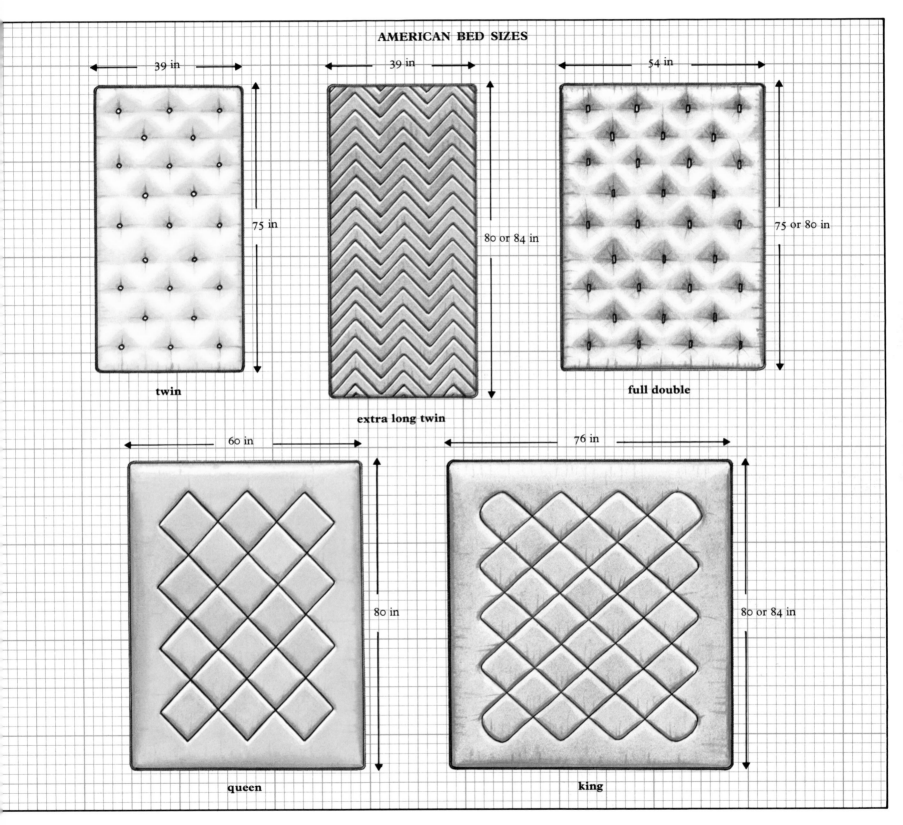

AMERICAN BED SIZES

twin — 39 in × 75 in

extra long twin — 39 in × 80 or 84 in

full double — 54 in × 75 or 80 in

queen — 60 in × 80 in

king — 76 in × 80 or 84 in

Distinctive beds

In days gone by, the bed itself was a status symbol, and inevitably the dominant feature in the bedchamber. Thanks to modern materials and methods of construction, however, furniture has become less bulky and far sleeker—fully fitted and less obtrusive. But many people are looking back to the bed to provide the focal point in the bedroom. Consequently, the market for hefty four-posters, modern-day *lits de parade* and exotic custom-built beds grows daily.

The bedstead

The old-fashioned bedstead has foot and head boards of metal or wood, joined by a framework and supported on legs. Nostalgia extends to the bedroom as to everywhere else, and although it is unlikely that original springing will still be suitable for use, you may be able to fit an old bedstead around a modern bed base, together with a new mattress. If this proves difficult, you could simply utilize the original head and foot boards. Some firms are still making bed bases that fit within an old-fashioned bedstead.

Wooden bedsteads made earlier this century can still be bought in junk shops; you can paint them in bright colours, cover the head boards with foam and fabric, or give them a new lease of life with paint stripper and varnish. Furniture manufacturers who specialize in reproductions make wooden bedsteads in traditional styles with cabriole legs in oak, curl mahogany or walnut veneers.

Ornate Victorian-style bedsteads in iron or brass have been enjoying such a vogue that the days are long past when you could pick them up for a song at an auction, but you may be lucky and have one in the family. Non-matching head boards and foot boards are easier to find. There are plenty of reproductions about, of course, but their proportions are less generous and the overall effect has less style than the real thing.

Top: *an attractive enamelled brass bedstead adds a positively old-fashioned charm to any bedroom.*

Left: *a canopied effect can be achieved by stretching fabric over the uprights at all four corners of the bed, or over the uprights of two single beds. The canopy is suspended at its centre from a hook firmly attached to the ceiling.*

The four-poster

Four-posters are available in both traditional and modern styles in metal, in white or black enamelled steel—often with brass trim—or complete in gleaming brass. Brasswork these days leaves the factory lacquered to cut out polishing, and these beds come complete with modern bed bases and mattresses in widths up to 183 cm/6 ft and lengths up to 213 cm/7 ft.

A four-poster bed may be called a "tester", which strictly speaking refers to the canopy over the bed, while a bed with two posts at the head supporting a small canopy may be referred to as a half-tester. When bedrooms were unheated and draughty to boot, it made good sense to have thick curtains suspended from your canopy top, to pull around the bed. Today, these curtains are either nonexistent or shortened to become simply a valance or frill around the top of the bed; some models have full-length drapes, but usually only for show. Modern reproductions often have drapes and valance in detachable Nottingham cotton lace, which can be hand-washed.

Most four-posters are less than 213 cm/7 ft high and will fit well into most rooms, although they look better if you have a high ceiling.

Reproduction four-posters are available to suit most tastes, from American Colonial to ornately carved Tudor styles, including scaled-down reproductions of the Great Bed of Ware, the original of which was the prized possession of a 17th-century inn-keeper and is alleged to have accommodated 26 butchers and their wives who were celebrating on the eve of William III's coronation.

Canopied beds

You can make your own canopied bed at considerably less expense than buying a four-poster, old or new. The simplest version has four wooden uprights with cross beams to contain any standard-sized bed. Line the top and ends with fabric of your choice, which could match your bed covers. For a more elaborate version, use carved wooden spindles for the uprights, available from stock from many timber merchants. If your ceiling is fairly low, you can dispense with the posts or uprights completely and simply suspend a wooden framework from the ceiling on chains, with canopy top and frilled valance. Make sure you make firm fixings through into ceiling joists—a poorly fixed structure could be very dangerous.

A less elaborate version of the canopied four-poster is made by using the bedhead wall to support a canopy just at the top of the bed. There are two basic ways to achieve this. You can buy from hardware or drapery stores a fitment called a coronet, which is a semi-circular curtain rail that can be fixed above the bed at its top to take a curtain. The curtain is then looped back over short lengths of protruding rods, fixed at right angles to the wall on either side. Alternatively, you can hang your draperies from a short length of curtain pole, which can be fixed with a bracket at right angles to the wall.

Exotic shapes

Evoking dreams of film-star glamour, beds in strange shapes can be made to order by some specialist firms. The truly round bed will need specially shaped pillows and sheets. Included in some manufacturers' "standard" ranges, however, are oval or D-shaped beds which offer a lot of the glamour with little of the inconvenience. Their flat end will sit neatly up against a wall, and they can even be fitted with head boards and kitted out with ordinary sheets and blankets in large sizes. A heart-shaped bed has been made for the incurably romantic, but unless the heart is of truly expansive proportions it does not offer as much scope for togetherness as a regular rectangle.

Padded beds

There is a growing trend towards padded bed bases, which contain the mattress in a well. These have been described as "fashion" beds or "the bed within a bed." Some padded beds feature elaborate buttoned or rolled head and foot boards, which may incorporate storage. Others have adjustable sections at both ends so that you can raise either your feet or your head. When the mattress is covered in smart fabric to match the base, the makers intend you to stow away all the bedding during the day and use the bed for lounging.

Right: *camels, date palms and sand dunes provide the sun-scorched theme for this desert bed, ideal for nomadic types.*

Above: *an unusual, modern four-poster bed made of cane and woven rattan with a firm, upholstered base.*

Right: *all laced up for the night—a bed with a difference for those who fancy a touch of the absurd.*

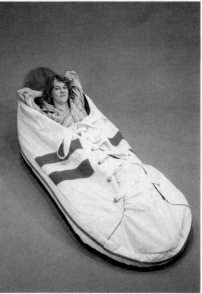

Water beds and hanging beds

It is not a great step from making the bed the focal point of the bedroom to its becoming the focal point of the household. Water beds and hanging beds are the latest conversation pieces, although water beds are not new—a gentleman called Mr Hooper was advertising his water-filled mattresses for the relief of bed sores as long ago as 1854. Nineteenth-century water beds must have been rather nerve-racking, but today, with improved technology, tough modern vinyls give the water-bed sleeper a deeper sense of security.

Water beds

A water bed consists of a vinyl water-filled mattress that rests in a safety liner contained within a stout frame. Frames vary in design from low-line modern to positively period. Happiness, gushes one manufacturer, is a warm water bed; the warmth emanates from a special electric pad fitted between the safety liner and the frame.

It is important to buy from a reputable manufacturer to ensure that your mattress is made from heavy-duty vinyl with properly sealed seams, and that the heater conforms to relevant safety standards. It is essential to contain the bed within a frame, to take the pressure off the seams. Water-bed converts claim that a water bed supports your entire body in a way impossible with conventional beds. Pressure points are eliminated; if you prefer a firmer bed, you just add more water. Bed-making is simple, as water beds usually take sheets in standard sizes. Once the mattress is filled, the water never needs changing—you simply add a bottle of chlorine or bleach every four to five months. Seasickness should not be a problem, as the water stops moving within minutes of boarding. Two people on a water bed are supposed to stabilize the bed, which then moulds itself to their bodies. Love-making on a water bed is allegedly a sensational experience.

The manufacturers dismiss as myths stories of floors collapsing under the weight of water beds. The average double water bed is supposed to be within the load-bearing requirements of most buildings, but if you live in an old property or have any misgivings, seek the advice of a reputable surveyor.

Manufacturers recommend water beds particularly for the overweight, the pregnant, both the old and the young, back sufferers, long-term sufferers, long-term convalescents, cardiac and stroke patients, and, not least, sufferers from bed sores.

Hanging beds

People who have slept in beds suspended from the ceiling say that it is very pleasant, and that you soon get used to the swinging sensation. It is essential to ensure that the bed is properly secured in the ceiling, and that the ceiling joists will take the weight of you and your bed. The position of the bed will be more or less determined by the position of these joists. If you are in any doubt about the stresses and strains and the weight loadings, do check with a surveyor and get the bed properly installed by a good carpenter or builder with some experience in this field.

Hanging beds offer undoubted novelty value and design cachet. They leave the floor clear for cleaning and, if a suitably designed pulley system is installed, the bed can be hauled right up to the ceiling, leaving the whole floor space beneath clear for other activities pursued during the day.

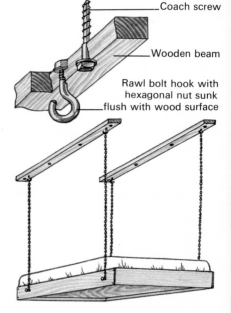

Coach screw

Wooden beam

Rawl bolt hook with hexagonal nut sunk flush with wood surface

Above and left: *to make sure your hanging bed is safe to sleep on, you must do some preliminary research on the state of your ceiling. The bed must be hung from joists that are strong enough to take the combined weight of you and your bed. Remember, too, that unlike an ordinary bed you cannot choose exactly where the bed will go, as its siting is determined by the positioning of the joists.*

Right and below: *as long as your floor is strong enough, a water bed is perfectly safe. The tough vinyl mattress, safety liner and stout frame are designed to ward off disasters.*

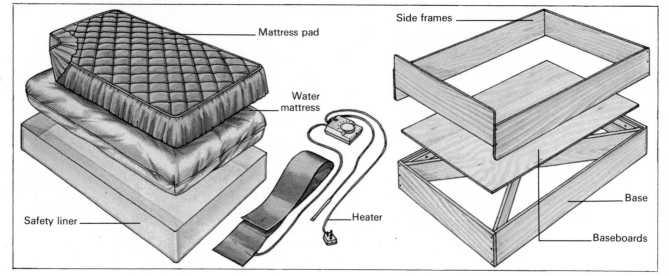

Mattress pad

Water mattress

Side frames

Safety liner

Heater

Base

Baseboards

Orthopaedic beds

Back problems unfortunately afflict many of us, and some sufferers mistakenly try to cure the trouble themselves by resorting to the old trick of putting a board under the mattress. Undoubtedly, beds that sag or are too soft will aggravate back trouble, but you should never try the trick with the board without first consulting your doctor. Then, if you do use a board, it must be the width of the bed and at least as long as the distance from your head to your buttocks, and it should be regarded only as a temporary measure.

If you are troubled with persistent back pain, you should—in consultation with your doctor—invest in a firmer bed. Most manufacturers offer at least one "orthopaedic" model in their standard range, but it is probably wisest to buy from a manufacturer who specializes in providing beds for this problem.

Beds designed specifically to combat back trouble have firm but resilient bases (a board, of course, lacks any degree of resilience). The resilience is achieved in various ways. There is, for example, a base sprung with "torsion bars", an alternative to coil springing, which the manufacturer claims is firmer and longer lasting. Extra heavy springs reinforce the edge of the base, and a special metal-strip underframe is available to prevent any distortion caused by uneven floors. Other manufacturers offer solid bases given resilience with layers of foam. There are also beds in which the mattress is supported by beechwood slats that rest between slits in the rubber suspension strips.

For those who must spend long periods in bed because of ill health, there are beds with adjustable sections for raising and lowering the head and the feet. These can be electrically operated by the occupant of the bed; the mechanisms are not particularly bulky, so the appearance of the bed (and the bedroom) need not suffer. One model can even be adjusted to form a wheelchair. For people who find getting in and out of bed impossible, there is a "stand-up" bed that can be tilted into an upright position by operating a hand lever. The occupant then stands on a foot board. The bed and the occupant can be lowered back in the same way.

When people who find it difficult to move are confined to bed for long periods, there is a danger that they will

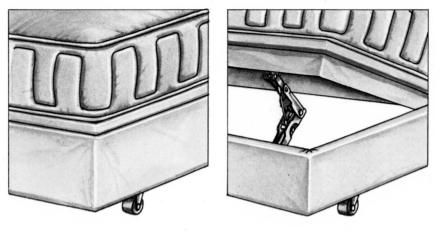

Electrically operated bed has a base divided into three sections so that backache sufferers can comfortably adjust their position. Electrically powered mechanisms, operated by a push-button control, slowly raise and lower the head or foot sections of the base, so that reading in bed or watching television is no longer a question of fighting a losing battle with piles of pillows and suffering the inevitable muscle tensions in the neck and back. The sectioned base of the bed is firm and flat, and the firmly sprung mattress is specially designed to withstand years of gentle bending.

develop "pressure sores". These occur at the areas that have to support most of the body weight when a person is lying down: the shoulder blades, the hips and the backs of the heels. Pressure sores can be avoided by changing a person's position every two hours, but even with the most dedicated home nursing this is not always possible. To prevent formation of pressure sores, body pads moulded from polyurethane foam have been specially developed. There are also "ripple mattresses" that have long channels filled with air to take the pressure of the body. The air pressure in the channels can be regulated to ensure that a heavy patient will not sink and that a light patient will not roll off.

A relatively new development for the treatment and prevention of pressure sores is the specially designed water bed for "fluid flotation therapy". These beds are rather similar in design and appearance to normal hospital beds. Slim-line, water-filled PVC mattresses fit into a fibre-glass frame, and the water temperature is thermostatically controlled. There are some models on the market equipped with adjustable head rests and safety sides, and with various devices for lifting the patient.

Making a bed can trigger off pain for back sufferers. Any bending should be done at the hips and the knees, keeping the back upright. It is better to kneel down when tucking in bed clothes; if you use a duvet and fitted sheets, tucking in is not necessary. High beds are easier to make than low ones, so you should consider raising your bed on blocks.

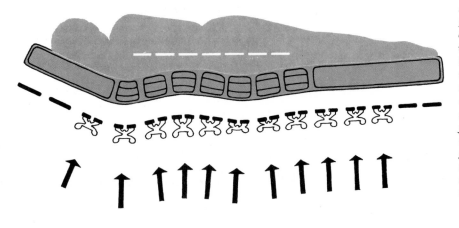

A bed base of flexible wooden slats *provides a resilient surface, leaving the choice of a hard or soft mattress up to whoever has to sleep on the bed. The beechwood slats, which are joined together with webbing, are not fixed to the frame, so they can easily adjust to the weight of a child or of a portly grandparent. The slats support the spine comfortably but firmly, thus avoiding strain to ligaments and muscles. Back-ache sufferers generally sleep better if their spines are straight. In order to achieve this, one needs a bed base that will accommodate the natural protrusions of the body.*

Coping with back trouble

The first thing to organize is a comfortable position in bed. It is important to try to rest horizontally, thereby taking the body's weight and a lot of stress off the back. Being propped up is probably a bad thing, so be prepared to lie on your back or side with one or, at the most, two pillows. It is not essential to lie flat on your back and, with severe back pain, you may not be able to do so. Try to get as comfortable as possible in a position that relieves the pain, making use of pillows or cushions to give support. For example, if you want to keep your spine supported, try putting a pillow in the small of your back. With a sagging mattress, it may be helpful to put a pillow or cushion under it to give it support. Some people, when they have sciatic pains, find lying on their side with the affected leg uppermost on a pillow a comfortable position. Others prefer to lie on their back, either flat or with a pillow under one or both knees. Some people find lying face down to be a relief.

If you want to read, lie on your front with your head over the end of the bed and the book on a chair or on the floor; if you lie on your back, hold the book above your face.

Although it may be possible to find a comfortable lying position, moving about from one position to another can put quite a stress on the spine unless you use your arms, so it helps to have something firm to hold on to. If you want to turn over in bed, you will need room to roll, so start by wriggling over to one side of the bed. Then bend your knees, bringing your heels up to your buttocks, fold the arm of the opposite side to which you intend to turn across your chest and, using the weight of your knees, roll, keeping your shoulders in line with your hips. For getting out of bed, come to the edge lying on your side, bend your knees up, then let your legs hang out to act as a counterweight as you push yourself upright. Have a chair at hand to lean on when you get to your feet.

Extract from *Avoiding Back Trouble* reproduced by courtesy of the Consumers' Association, publishers in the UK of *Which?* magazine.

Foldaway beds

In the distant days of silent films, Charlie Chaplin raised a big laugh when he folded himself up into the wall along with the bed he was sleeping on. More recently, in glorious technicolor, James Bond and friend used the same folding-bed trick to escape a hail of bullets. Amusing gimmicks though these beds may have been, there lies behind them a very sensible idea for those with acute problems of space.

Folding beds today range from beds that fold away under their twins to a bed that miraculously appears from the back of a drinks cabinet. Before you decide on the type you prefer, consider how often the bed will be needed and who is likely to be sleeping in it. If you want a bed for regular night-time use, you should have a model that folds away complete with made-up bedding. If you only want an extra bed for occasional use—for guests, for example—bedding can be kept in a near-by cupboard when the bed is folded away. Adults will require a sturdier type of bed than children, and naturally if you plan to cater for couples you will need a spare space-saving bed big enough for two. Most models have legs that automatically unfold. Check that the folding action is safe and easy to manage, and that the legs have an adequate locking device to hold them in position.

The least disguised but nevertheless highly practical space-saving beds are those that stack on top of one another, with interlocking wood frames, or those that are bought in pairs, one bed folding neatly under the other when not in use. The legs of the folding bed are collapsible and castors allow it to be pushed effortlessly underneath its twin. The mattress stays on the folding bed and there is often room for sheets and blankets too, so that the bed can easily be kept ready for use.

Those disappearing beds so favoured by the movie-makers come in two categories, folding either horizontally or vertically against the wall. Horizontal beds can only be single-sized, so they are particularly suited to children's rooms to provide extra playing space. Special straps retain the bedding when folded against the wall, and the bed can fold beneath a curtained shelf that completely hides it from view. Vertical beds are available in widths from 74 to 137 cm/ 2 ft 5 in to 4 ft 6 in and can be concealed by curtains and a pelmet or within a run

Above: *a vertical bed, with plentiful bedtime reading, can be lowered easily from a recess in the wall, revealing a useful bedside light.*

of cupboards. When choosing a vertically folding bed, make sure that the end is properly counter-balanced so that there is no chance of it falling down, and that the base of the bed is attached securely to the floor. Vertical beds can be stowed away complete with bedding, and head boards are available.

Beds disguised as all manner of furniture are not, as one would think, a product of 20th-century sophistication. In the 18th century, the poet Oliver Goldsmith, in "The Deserted Village", was writing: "The chest contrived a double debt to pay, A bed by night, a chest by day."

The nearest we come these days to a chest that becomes a bed by night is the drinks cabinet that conceals a folding bed. The cabinet swivels round, revealing a single bed that can unfold from its back. Even tables can conceal a bed. In one

model a foam mattress folds in half to fit under a large coffee table. In other models, the table top becomes a head board and the tubular-steel bed with foam mattress is unfolded from underneath. Chairs or low stools can also incorporate beds, but storage for bedding must be provided elsewhere.

Perhaps the most sensible of these disguised beds is the sofa-bed, particularly useful in houses or apartments where there is no spare bedroom and guests must be accommodated in the living-room. Look for a design in which the seat unfolds to reveal a sprung base and a mattress: a convertible sofa should provide a sleeping surface separate from the sitting surface. Sheets and blankets can be left on when the bed is folded.

A decision to buy a convertible piece of furniture obviously depends on whether you like the sofa, the drinks cabinet or table, as well as whether the bed that unfolds from it is comfortable and sturdy. If you approve of the style, these beds can be very handy for occasional guests and for one-room flat dwellers. Horizontal and vertical beds are usually installed for permanent use where floor space is short. Beds that fold one under the other are particularly useful in guest-rooms.

Above and top right: *these horizontal folding bunk beds are an ingenious space-saving idea. When lowered for use, each bunk reveals a practical set of bedside shelves. When raised, the bases of the beds are neat and unobtrusive.*

Below and below left: *a horizontal bed, which never takes up valuable floor space, is fun for these young children to unfold but is strictly for older children to sleep in. Access is by the bars firmly fixed to the wall.*

Below: *it would be difficult to guess that this exciting wall decoration conceals a double bed within an interesting shelving system.*

Portable beds

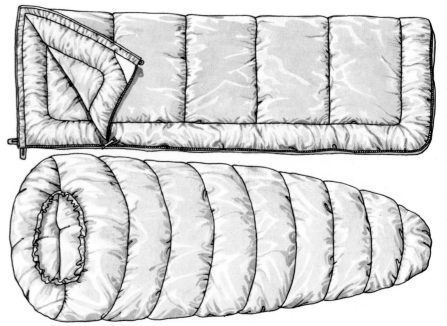

Lightweight portable beds are handy for taking with you when you go to visit friends. Or you can have them stowed in a cupboard for when friends visit you—use them in the garden or on the beach betweentime. Combined with sleeping bags, this kind of bed offers instant accommodation but takes up very little storage space.

Inflatable mattresses

Airbeds are not satisfactory for regular sleeping in the home, but you can use them on the floor from time to time—particularly for children. The waffle-box type will be more comfortable than the more familiar reeded type. You need a lot of puff to fill an airbed—better to invest in a hand or foot pump. Do not use an air-line, and do not fill more than two-thirds full. After inflation, push the cap firmly into the nozzle, and push the valve into the airbed to minimize accidental removal. Obviously you should avoid catching airbeds on anything sharp (small stones, prickly bushes outside the house, sandal buckles, cat's claws, chair legs, etc., inside). However, beds are usually supplied with spare patches, and you can buy airbed repair kits. One airbed model converts into a chair. Some models are specially designed with sides to prevent "roll-off"—the commonest complaint from airbed sleepers.

A safety note: if you are tempted to take your airbed on to the beach, do remember not to use it in the sea or in open water where tides, winds or currents could carry you or your children into deep water and danger. All airbeds should be thoroughly dried before storage, but you should not use heat of any kind.

Roll-up mattresses

Lightweight foam-rubber mattresses are available, which can be rolled up and carried under one arm. Another type simply folds up zig-zag fashion. You can use these on the floor for the odd night, but beware of condensation, which will collect under the mattress after a while. Some camping types are made from profiled foam to allow air to circulate.

Canvas beds

Camping beds will fold up into a narrow roll of canvas. When assembled, a steel frame with legs has webbing suspension strips to support a canvas sleeping surface, for use with or without a camping mattress. The famous patented safari bed has been "adopted as standard equipment by the British Army and by Armies of many other nations . . . and can be assembled in minutes in cramped conditions, on uneven ground, or even in the dark." Should make for sweet dreams! A refined version has flaps at each end to hold bedding in place. Cheaper models are offered without the special suspension strips. Canvas

Of these two types of airbed, the waffle-box is the most comfortable for sleeping on. Keep the reeded type of airbed for the beach.

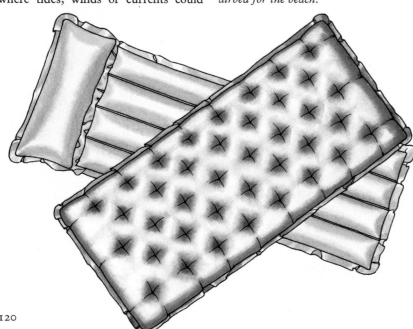

"lugher" beds with folding steel frames can also be used for the odd night's sleep—they are a bit too narrow to provide the average adult with a comfortable night's rest.

Hammocks

Once you become used to the sensation of sleeping suspended from the rafters in a cocoon, you should come to enjoy the experience of a night in a hammock. Sailors and natives of South America have long since adapted to this novel form of bed, but in our society they have not caught on. Hammocks are fine for an occasional night's sleep or a daytime snooze, provided you can find secure fixing points from which to hang them, and provided you feel secure enough. There is on the market at least one very comfortable full-length hanging chair, which gives a much better degree of support, but this is not a portable hammock and requires suspension from a firm fixing in a ceiling joist. It is worth looking in the garden furniture departments of stores for folding beds—there are, for example, hammocks that are slung between a folding frame and do not need wall or ceiling supports.

Sleeping bags

As a convenient form of extra bedding, sleeping bags cannot be beaten. They come in junior sizes up to about 1.4 m/

For versatility, the rectangular convertible sleeping bag wins over the tapered "mummy" shape, but if you want extra warmth, invest in the latter.

56 in long; in small standard sizes up to 1.8 m/72 in long; in large standard sizes up to about 1.9 m/76 in long; in small king sizes up to about 2 m/79 in long; and in large king sizes up to about 2.1 m/82 in long. For comfort, a bag should have an inside length at least 8 cm/3 in longer than the occupant. Check actual measurements carefully; sizes are not standard and words like "king-size" can have different meanings from manufacturer to manufacturer.

Convertible bags are rectangular and they can be unzipped to make a quilt. Two bags of this type can often be zipped together to make a double size. The other type of bag has a tapered "mummy" shape for a snug fit, and although it is better suited for hard camping conditions it is not so useful at home.

The most expensive and warmest bag filling is pure down. This can be mixed with feathers, or feathers will be offered on their own. Polyester fillings are also available for washable bags; a new type called Dacron Hollofil has hollow fibres for greater warm-air retention. Filling thicknesses are indicated by weight—generally speaking, the heavier the weight of the filling, the warmer the bag, but comparisons are only useful when comparing the same size of bag. Obviously, the bigger the bag the more filling there has to be. As an example, polyester fibre fillings for a small standard bag could range from around 737 g to 1.08 kg/26 to 38 oz. The way the bag is quilted will affect its warmth. Simplest "plain" quilting goes straight through from one side to the other, with possible cold spots along the stitching lines. "Walled"-type quilting allows the filling to rest in little channels, so that fillings are evenly distributed at all times. "Double-layer" quilting is a two-layer version of plain quilting, with the aim of eliminating cold spots. It is advisable to use washable cotton liner sheets with sleeping bags.

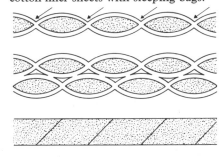

Above: *with friendly-looking sleeping varies from "plain" quilting through "double-layered" to "walled", which is the most effective.*

Below: *for hot summer nights or for a change indoors, a hammock is undeniably pretty and surprisingly comfortable.*

Above: *with friendly looking sleeping bags like these, bedtime is no longer a problem to be reckoned with and can even become a positive pleasure.*

Top right: *this sleeping arrangement may be makeshift, but a comfortable night can be practically guaranteed— and at very little trouble to the host.*

Right: *a foam mattress and a quilt can be used as a bed or as a cosy nook in which to catch up on some reading.*

Pillows

Once you have taken the time and the trouble (and spent the money) necessary to secure a good bed, it is essential to have the right kind of pillows to complete the job of giving your body correct support. A good pillow might last as long as ten years; a cheap pillow could be worn out in two. If a pillow droops when you support it over your outstretched arm, it is worn and should be replaced.

Sleeping with a single pillow, not too thick, is considered medically to be perfectly adequate; it should be regarded as a support for the neck rather than for the head. The pillow should be placed under the neck and the shoulders, not bunched at the top of the bed so that the head is tilted at an uncomfortable angle. If you have broad shoulders and tend to sleep on your side, you might find that you do need two pillows, or at least one very plump one. Some people like to have their head raised because they find it painful to lie flat or have difficulty in breathing. Back-care experts suggest that rather than using masses of pillows to prop yourself up, it is better to incline the whole bed by propping up the legs at the head end. The aim is to keep the whole spine, trunk and head in a comfortably straight line so that muscles can relax for the night too.

Peter Rabbit, Jemima Puddleduck and friends make heirloom nursery cushions.

The modern pillow consists of a strong cover about 48 × 69 cm/18 × 27 in (UK) or 53 × 69 cm/21 × 27 in (USA) filled with natural or synthetic materials. You can find larger and smaller sizes and different shapes: in the USA, queen size means 53 × 79 cm/21 × 31 in; king, 53 × 99 cm/21 × 39 in; continental, 69 cm/27 in square.

Pillow fillings

Down: This comes from the breasts of water-fowl (duck and goose) and consists of light, fluffy plumes with no quills. Goose down is more expensive than duck down. Down makes a soft, light pillow and combines strength with truly buoyant resilience. When in use, the tendrils of the down open and spread out in all directions, grasping air pockets and distributing support. A good down pillow lasts about ten years.

Down and feather: With more down than feathers, this filling must contain not less than 51 per cent by weight of down under UK regulations. Soft and resilient, it gives a good degree of firmness. The greater the down content, the better the pillow's warmth, lightness and long-wearing qualities.

Feather and down: With more feathers than down, this filling must contain not less than 15 per cent by weight of down under UK regulations. Feathers make the pillow firmer.

Curled poultry feathers: These are purified chicken feathers, processed to provide greater resilience.

Polyesters: Sold under the brand names of Terylene and Dacron, these popular man-made fibre fillings are the modern alternative to traditional filling materials. They are soft, with good resilience. Reasonably priced, non-allergenic and the easiest of all pillows to wash, these are ideal for children and invalids.

Latex foam: Made from liquid rubber, latex foam is germ-repellent and non-allergenic. Very springy, it is washable, but with care.

Polyester foam: Chemically made, it is germ-repellent, non-allergenic and washable. Avoid very cheap pillows filled with foam chips; these are lumpy and uncomfortable.

Hop pillows: Dried hops are mixed with feathers or with polyester and enclosed in a ticking. Hop pillows have been used for centuries for their sleep-inducing properties. The secret is a substance called lupulin contained in the hop fruits. Among the first to benefit was George III: "Mr Addington . . . remembered to have heard from his father, an eminent physician, that a pillow filled with hops would sometimes induce sleep when all other remedies had failed; the experiment being tried on the King was attended with complete success."

UK expert Mrs Elizabeth Walker has been researching and experimenting

Above: *stout canvas bolsters and cushions transform a hammock into a thing of comfort. Fresh, bright colours remind one of summer even in the depths of winter.*

Below: *good morning—the sun is up and it is time that everyone else was.*

with blended herbal fillings for many years. She recommends marjoram as the sedative herb, mixed with lavender and thyme as an antidote for headaches and stress. Even a tiny sachet of marjoram can help insomnia, it seems. Cloves and cinnamon can be added to clear the head. Rosemary is recommended for treating nightmares in children, and mint has refreshing qualities. Lemon, verbena and rose petals all add to the sweet smell. Herbs have been used to induce sleep

and restore powers far back into recorded history—certainly records show that Henry VIII had herbs strewn liberally around his bedchamber.

Pillow shapes

If you suffer from neck pain, a "butterfly" pillow is recommended. You can make this yourself from a thinly filled pillow by shaking the filling into each end and then tying the pillow in half. Small figure-of-eight-shaped pillows are also available. A large polyester-filled, boomerang-shaped pillow is good for sitting up in bed. Bolsters, either feather filled or made from solid foam, can be cylindrical or wedge shaped. They are not intended for sleeping, but for "dressing" the bed during the day or as support if the bed is used as a seat.

Pillow cases

It is always a good idea to enclose a new pillow in a washable under-slip as well as an outer case. To avoid wear on your pillow case, make sure it is large enough—about 5 to 10 cm/2 to 4 in wider and about 15 to 20 cm/6 to 8 in longer than the pillow it contains. Pillow shams are not intended for sleeping on; they are often made of quite unsuitable materials. They add a certain something to the bed during the day, but should always be removed at night.

Care of pillows

Down and feather: Air these occasionally outside. Avoid washing unless absolutely necessary, as this disperses oil from the feathers. Pillows badly saturated with spills can be squeezed gently through a warm, soapy solution and rinsed well with three changes of water. Spin dry for two minutes if possible. Hang up by two corners to dry and shake occasionally during drying. The whole process is very time-consuming, and you may opt for the services of a professional cleaner.

Polyester-filled pillows: Wash as above. They should not be dry-cleaned and should never be put in a tumble drier.

Latex pillows: These can usually be sponged clean but, if badly saturated, the whole pillow can be washed, preferably still in its inner case, as latex deteriorates when exposed to light. Wash in warm soapsuds and do not twist or wring. Rinse well. Squeeze out as much moisture as possible into a dry towel. Leave the pillow in an airing cupboard to dry.

Above: *herb pillows are credited with positively magical properties: rest your head on one and forget insomnia.*

Left: *if you should be the owner of a handsome collection of snow-white, hand-embroidered lacy pillows, treat them with care: old fabrics are fragile, so persuade your cats to keep their claws to themselves.*

Duvets

Sleeping under a duvet (alternatively called a continental quilt), a common practice in Scandinavian and mid-European countries, has spread widely in the UK and is growing in popularity in the USA. Traditional duvets were simply large bags filled with goose and duck down; in Swiss and Austrian villages, for example, people would save the down from their geese and ducks to contribute

to the dowry of a young bride. Today's duvets can replace all other forms of bed covering: they trap the body's natural warmth with a layer of very light but bulky filling material sewn between two layers of specially woven cloth.

A duvet weighs between 1.3 and 2 kg/3 and 4½ lb (a typical sheet–blankets–bedspread combination could total about 6.8 kg/15 lb). The body is able to relax more easily under lighter weights, and the warmth-to-weight ratio of a duvet is around four times greater than that of a blanket. Another virtue is that duvets give off almost no dust (they are available with synthetic fillings for the allergy prone). Bed-making becomes easy—ideal for the elderly, the disabled and for children—because you only need to plump out the duvet and smooth its cover.

Duvet covers come in a variety of patterns and colours. It is not usual to cover a duvet (which should be larger than the bed) with a bedspread—the effect would be bulky and impractical—so you may need to conceal the base or boxspring of the bed with a valance.

Rolled up, a duvet is easily stored in awkward places. In use it is ideal for anyone who actively dislikes making beds or has difficulty in so doing.

Choose a duvet of adequate quality to keep you warm without any other covering. Buy a reputable make, either from a responsible retailer or a well-established mail-order source. In the UK, make sure that your duvet conforms to British Standard 5335. This requires a label to be provided telling you the warmth category, or "tog" value, of the duvet, making it possible to compare the insulation rating of different duvets.

Natural or synthetic

Fillings fall into two main groups, natural and synthetic, and within each group there are wide variations in quality and price. The highest luxury class of natural filling is eider-duck down, beyond the pocket of most people New white goose down is cheaper but still expensive, although it makes a luxurious duvet. For downy comfort at a comfortable price, choose duck down.

Feather fillings are vastly inferior to down—as one manufacturer says, "birds have down to keep them warm, and feathers to fly with". Down has no quill shaft, but consists of a mass of soft tendrils that keep you warm by absorbing and holding air, which is warmed by your body. Cheaper fillings may be labelled "down and feathers". This means that the duvet contains more down than feathers, but still probably offers a good buy for those who prefer natural fillings but are working to a limited budget. The greater the down content, the better. The label "feathers and down" indicates more feathers than down, and for the same price you may find that you can buy one of the better qualities of synthetic filling with a higher tog rating.

To prevent the feathers and down from escaping, natural fillings must be contained within a cover of finely woven fabric called cambric. The best construction for natural fillings has "walled channels", which means that the long seams down the length of the duvet are not stitched through to the other side. Tests have shown that this inner wall for duvets containing natural fillings improves the performance of the duvet by about 15 to 20 per cent. Professional dry cleaning is recommended for down- and feather-filled duvets.

Man-made fibre fillings are reasonably priced, non-allergenic and can be easily washed, but when buying a duvet with a synthetic filling be sure it is a branded fibre. Most synthetic fillings are polyesters; one of the newer developments is Dacron Hollofil, which has hollow fibres to trap more air. Synthetically filled duvets can vary from a minimum filling weight of 340 g per square metre/11 oz per square yard to about 425 g per square metre/14 oz per square yard. Higher weights provide greater insulation. Beware of cheap, unbranded duvets.

Generally speaking, a duvet should be about 46 cm/18 in wider than the bed. However, if you can afford it, a wider duvet will be even more comfortable. On double beds, some people prefer two single duvets. Length is also important. If you (and your partner) are under 178 cm/5 ft 10 in, a duvet 200 cm/79 in long will suffice. But if you are taller, buy an "extra long" duvet 220 cm/87 in long. If either of you is taller than 198 cm/6 ft 6 in, find a manufacturer who offers an "extra extra long" duvet.

It is essential to use a duvet cover with a duvet. This is simply a large bag that fits over your duvet like a giant pillowslip and can fasten along the edges with a zip, snap fasteners or with ties. Covers are made in similar fabrics to sheets—you may be able to make your own out of redundant sheets—and should be washed as frequently as you would a top sheet, so you will need at least two for each bed.

Cleaning a duvet

Follow carefully any "care" instructions on your duvet or duvet package, and always use your duvet with a washable cover. If you spill something on your duvet, remove the cover as soon as you can and gently sponge the duvet with warm, soapy water, taking care not to wet the filling too much. Try to smooth the filling away from the area of the stain before starting to sponge.

Duvets with synthetic fillings can be washed, and the best container for this operation is the bath. Knead the duvet gently in warm, soapy water, rinse well and squeeze dry. Hang it well supported on two parallel lines. Down and feather-and-down duvets will benefit from an occasional shaking out of doors on a fine day. Have them professionally cleaned when necessary; never use a coin-operated dry-cleaning machine.

Light and hygienic, a duvet needs only a good shake—outdoors on a fine day—and it is ready to go back on the bed.

Sheets, pillow cases and duvet bags 1

The linen department is where you head in a large store in the search for sheets. Sadly, however, linen (which comes from the flax plant) has become a luxury, although it is a life-long investment if you can afford to pay the price. Linen is blissfully comfortable, strong and durable, and is one of the few fibres that is actually stronger when wet, so constant washing will not affect its life-span.

Cotton, too, has become very expensive because of the massive price increases in the cost of the raw material, but luckily many manufacturers still offer all-cotton ranges. Cotton sheets are beautifully absorbent and feel more and more comforting the older they get. Percale is the name to look for on the finest grade of cotton, but some names used to evoke feelings of quality are in fact no true guide: cotton may be misleadingly billed as Egyptian, linen as Irish, embroidered sheets as Swiss. Variations on the cotton theme include crinkly seersuckers (named after a type of seaweed), which provide an easy-care if less comfortable finish, and flannelette, a warm, brushed cotton, comforting for young and old.

The majority of modern sheets are now blends of cotton and man-made fibres, usually in a 50:50 ratio. The most common blend is cotton and polyester—polyester is sold under brand names such as Terylene and Dacron in the UK, Fortrel and Kodel in the USA. Modal is a newer fibre development, with good wet-strength and resistance to shrinkage—the brand name is Vincel. Manufacturers claim that these blended sheets combine the pleasant feel of cotton with the easy-care benefits and shrink-resistant qualities of man-made fibres. Opinions of users differ, but all agree that it is a boon not to have to iron these sheets.

All-nylon sheets are available with smooth or brushed finishes in pastel or deep-dyed shades. UK research has shown that these are popular, but, significantly, they are used for the beds of children and guests rather than by the people who actually buy them. Nylon is very easy to wash, dries quickly and needs no ironing. Slightly less nasty are the Modal/polyester blends. Many people

Above right: *pretty floral duvet bag teamed up with plain pillow cases. A mix of patterns and plain colours is more interesting than a matching ensemble.*

UK Bedding Chart

Bed size	Flat sheets	Fitted sheets and divan trims	Quilt covers	Blankets
Small single 90 by 190 cm (3 ft by 6 ft 3 in)	180 by 260 cm	90 by 190 cm	140 by 200 cm 140 by 220 cm	180 by 240 cm
Standard single 100 by 200 cm (3 ft 3 in by 6 ft 6 in)	180 by 260 cm	100 by 200 cm	140 by 200 cm 140 by 220 cm	180 by 240 cm
Small double 135 by 190 cm (4 ft 6 in by 6 ft 3 in)	230 by 260 cm	135 by 190 cm	200 by 200 cm 200 by 220 cm	230 by 250 cm
Standard double 150 by 200 cm (5 ft by 6 ft 6 in)	230 by 260 cm 275 by 275 cm	150 by 200 cm	200 by 200 cm 200 by 220 cm	260 by 250 cm
King size 180 by 200 cm (6 ft by 6ft 6 in)	275 by 275 cm	180 by 200 cm	230 by 220 cm or two 140 by 220 cm	250 by 300 cm

USA Bedding Chart

Bed size	Sheets	Blankets
Twin 39 by 75 in	72 by 108 in	70 by 90 in
Extra-long twin 39 by 80 or 84 in	72 by 120 in	70 by 100 in
Full, or double 54 by 75 or 80 in	90 by 120 in	80 by 90 in
Queen 60 by 80 in	90 by 120 in	90 by 90 in
King 76 by 80 or 84 in	108 by 120 in	90 by 108 in

cannot stand the clammy feel of synthetic sheets—they are non-absorbent and slippery and attract an unpleasant build-up of static electricity, and are best avoided. "Satin" sheets are advertised promising nights of glamour, but as these are made from nylon (Celon) you are more likely to get hot and bothered than sensuously slithery. Originally, satin was made only from silk, and it is still possible to obtain silken sheets to order from certain high-class stores at very high-class prices.

Sheet sizes
Never rely on store labels that simply say "single" or "double"—always check the exact dimensions. The best way to ensure comfortably fitting sheets is to measure carefully the actual width and length of your mattress plus its depth. To these measurements add about 30 cm/12 in to tuck in at both sides and at top and bottom. Your sum goes like this:

To estimate sheet width:
1 × width of mattress +
2 × depth of mattress +
2 × tuck-in allowance of 30 cm/12 in
(i.e. 60 cm/24 in)

To estimate sheet length:
1 × length of mattress +
2 × depth of mattress +
2 × tuck-in allowance of 30 cm/12 in
(i.e. 60 cm/24 in)

You will find that inches are still given alongside the metric measurements on most packs; in the UK you may also find sheets in the shops in the old Imperial sizes of 70 × 104 in, 90 × 104 in and 108 × 117 in.

Fitted sheet sizes correspond exactly to the mattress size—they are a boon for bed-making, but are awkward to fold and store. Their life-span is significantly shorter than that of the flat sheet as the

wear is concentrated in one place, a disadvantage they share with sheets that are too small.

Once you have sorted out the right sizes of sheets for your beds, it is helpful to mark the corners of your sheets with S for single, D for double.

Pattern and colour
Co-ordinated ranges of bed linen abound, comprising sheets, pillow cases, pillow shams, duvet covers, valances, bed-spreads, curtains, wallpapers and even carpets. Patterns can be mixed with plain pastels or strong deep-dyed colours, or with co-ordinating patterns. You can have florals of all kinds, geometrics, lacy patterns, scenic woodlands, ging-hams, your national flag or designer originals. Many famous fashion designers have turned their creative talents to bed linen, including Mary Quant, Bill Gibbs, Zandra Rhodes, Halston and Yves St Laurent. One US manufacturer has bought the right to turn Picasso into sheets, bedspreads and curtains (most purchasers are framing them). For children, almost every cartoon and story-book character is available for snuggling up to at night, including Snoopy, Mickey Mouse, Mister Men, Paddington Bear and Holly Hobby.

If you yearn for colour but possess a cupboard full of old white cotton (or even linen) sheets, you can dye them at home, very successfully, in the washing machine. Tie-dye techniques create effective patterns, and colour-fast fabric paints can be used to print stencils or potato cuts. You can add ribbon or braid trims, fabric frills or bands, but make sure that trimmings are washable and colour fast, and are washed and pre-shrunk before sewing.

After all your efforts over the dye-

tub, you will appreciate why deep-dyed sheets are more expensive to buy than the paler colours and why they should be washed separately at first.

Disguising the bed base
Many modern bed bases or boxsprings, covered in brocade tickings to match the mattress, are an eyesore. You can buy or make valances to conceal the base and match the sheets or bedcover. A newer development is a fitted bottom sheet with a valance attached.

Try to maintain a co-ordinating theme throughout the linen for one bed, as you will not want to change the bed right down to the valance every wash day.

Above and below: *modern methods of deep-dying mean colour-fast bed linens in new, vibrant shades.*

Left: *plain white duvet bag cheered up with a hand-stencilled border.*

Sheets, pillowcases and duvet bags 2

When it comes to wash day, always follow the manufacturers' instructions carefully: keep the care labels in a special place. Wash deep-dyed sheets and towels separately for the first few washes. If you send sheets to a laundry but keep pillow cases to wash at home, you could end up with variations in colour due to differences in the washing powders.

White cottons and linens: By machine: very hot (95°C/203°F), maximum wash. By hand: hand-hot (48°C/118°F). Spin or wring. Iron with hot iron when damp. If sheets have any kind of special easy-care finish, refer to makers' instructions.

Coloured cottons: By machine: hot (60°C/140°F), maximum wash. By hand: hand-hot (48°C/118°F). Spin or wring. For special finishes, refer to makers' instructions. Iron with hot iron while still quite damp.

Coloured nylons, polyester/cotton blends, modal/cotton blends, modal/polyester blends: By machine: hand-hot (48°C/118°F), medium wash. By hand: hand-hot (48°C/118°F). Cold rinse, *short spin*, or drip-dry. Makers claim non-iron properties, especially with use of a tumble drier. However, many users remain sceptical and prefer to iron cotton/synthetic blends. Use a *cool* iron set for the synthetic part of the blend, not an iron set for cotton or you will collect a sticky deposit on the base of the iron which is very difficult to remove, and you will spoil your sheets if you persist. Ironed sheets are easier to store.

Removing stains

Treat all stains quickly. The longer they are left, the more difficult they will be to remove. If treated quickly, washing powder and water will usually do the trick. Apart from stains that should be soaked in cold water first, it is best to use only warm suds. Always test chemicals and solvents on an inconspicuous corner of the fabric first. When applying a chemical or solvent, always place the area to be treated over absorbent cloth such as an old piece of towelling. To avoid a ring, first treat an area around the stain and then work towards the centre of the stain. After treating with a solvent and before the solvent fluid has dried wash in good rich suds immediately. Be careful when using preparations marked poisonous—keep them out of children's reach; wash cups or basins thoroughly afterwards. Always treat flammable liquids with care: those that give off vapour should only be used in a well-ventilated room, and care should be taken not to breathe in the vapour.

Stain removal is a tricky business, depending upon the length of time between the staining and the treatment, the type and age of the fabric, etc. For stains on particularly treasured items, it is always best to seek professional treatment.

Blood: Blood stains are very difficult to remove unless treated quickly. If the stain is obstinate, send the article to your launderer or dry-cleaner. Soak articles in cold water as soon as possible. Never use hot water as this will set the stain. Enzyme detergents are useful. If the stain is an old one, treat it with cold water containing a few drops of ammonia. Allow the ammonia to soak into the stain for two or three minutes, then sponge with cold water until the smell of ammonia disappears.

Candle grease: Hardened deposits can be sandwiched between two pieces of absorbent paper and ironed, using as many clean pieces of paper as necessary. Follow with dry-cleaning solvent, working from the edge to the middle of the stain. Coloured wax may need final treatment with a little methylated or surgical spirit. Sponge this off well and launder.

Chewing gum: Scrape off as much as possible with a knife blade. Residue may respond to freezing with a block of ice. Otherwise try a dry-cleaning fluid or a proprietary grease solvent.

Coffee: Deal with spills immediately or staining may result. Mop up as much liquid as possible with a clean cloth, but do not rub. Wash immediately in a solution of 25 g/1 oz borax to half a litre/1 pint of warm water. Rinse well.

Eggs: Egg stains can usually be removed with an enzyme detergent. Soak stubborn stains in one part hydrogen peroxide to four parts water, plus a few drops of ammonia. Soak for not more than 30 minutes, although white articles may be soaked overnight. Rinse well.

Fruit juice: Stretch the stained part over a bowl and pour warm water (40°C/104°F) through the stained material. Some fruit stains change considerably with time and, on drying, may be difficult to remove. If this has happened, professional treatment is advised.

Grease and oil: Dab the stain with liquid detergent as soon as possible. If badly stained, soaking in liquid detergent solution may be necessary.

Ink: Soak in cold water to loosen stain, then wash in the usual way. Stubborn stains on white cotton can be rubbed with a piece of lemon dipped in salt; then stretch the stained area over a bowl and pour boiling water through it.

Ball-point ink: Dab with a pad soaked in methylated spirit (careful—it's flammable). Work inwards and renew pad whenever necessary. Stains will sometimes respond to undiluted liquid detergent. Then wash.

Felt-tip ink: Lubricate the stain with glycerine before sponging or laundering. For stubborn stains, try several applications of methylated spirit (flammable), changing the cotton pad frequently.

Lipstick: Some lipstick stains may be

removed with oil of eucalyptus, but if this is not successful send the article for professional laundering.

Mildew: Mildew is usually caused when fabrics remain damp in airless conditions, e.g. the ironing basket. It is very difficult to remove, so try to avoid it forming. Soak white cottons and linens in one part bleach to 100 parts water with 1 tablespoon of vinegar. Soak other white fabrics in one part hydrogen peroxide to four parts water. Rinse well. There is no safe home treatment for coloureds, but regular washing in rich suds should reduce marks.

Mud: Marks on washable fabrics should wash out quite easily with a solution of good, rich suds.

Perfume: Sponge stain with methylated spirit. Launder to remove fresh stains

Above: *an alternative to the temptation to buy several sets of sheets and pillow cases in different designs: buy the same pattern in more than one colour. This gives you variety without risking chaos.*

Right: *in a simply decorated room, bed linen with a bold design becomes the focal point. Complete the picture with a matching quilt.*

Top: *the dramatic effect of patterned bed linen can be emphasized by using material with a complementary design to make a roller blind.*

Far right: *checked or striped, flowered or pastel—bed linen today is as plain or fancy as you wish.*

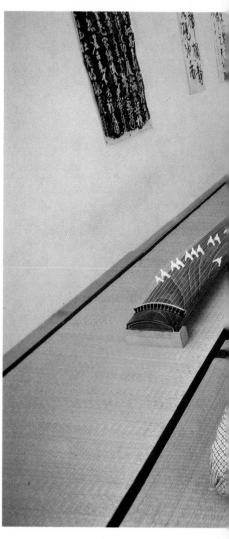

on washable fabrics. Rub dried stains with glycerine or methylated spirit first.

Rust: Moisten the stain with lemon juice. Do not let the juice dry on the fabric. Rinse quickly in water containing a little ammonia. Rinse out ammonia. Never use liquid bleach, as this will not remove the stain and is certain to rot the fabric eventually.

Scorch marks: Moisten light stains, then soak in glycerine. Wash thoroughly. If stain remains, soak in one part hydrogen peroxide to four parts water plus a few drops of household ammonia (test on a corner of the fabric first). If fibres are damaged, there is no remedy.

Tar: (Comes from the beach on children's feet, even in the best of families.) Scrape off surplus, then treat the stain with a grease solvent or with petrol, with an absorbent cloth underneath (be very careful if using petrol and keep well away from naked lights). Wash in hand-hot, rich suds.

Tea: Tea stains on washable fabrics can usually be washed out in good, rich suds. Very difficult stains should be treated with hydrogen peroxide. This can be used on most fabrics, but is not suitable for all colours, so test on a corner first. Use in proportion of one part 20-vol. hydrogen peroxide to four parts cold water. Soak coloureds for not more than 30 minutes, but white articles may be soaked overnight.

Wine: Do not allow stain to dry. Sponge with warm water immediately. The residue should be removed in normal washing. Red wine stains are the worst, and must be dealt with at once.

Blankets

Blankets come in a wide variety of sizes, which differ from country to country and even from maker to maker. (For exact measurements, consult the bedding chart on pages 126 and 127.) When you shop for blankets, remember that they should be as wide as your sheets but need not be as long. If you mean to use the blanket as a throw-over or bedspread—and many blankets are so good-looking that it would be a shame to hide them away under a counterpane—measure the width of the mattress and add to it twice the fall from the top of the mattress to the floor, and your blanket will skirt the floor on each side of the bed.

A good blanket combines warmth with lightness, and for this it is still difficult to beat pure new wool. Wool generates a lot of warmth for very little weight and, if protected from moths and properly cleaned, will last for years. Best-quality wool blankets will be labelled "merino". In the thistledown class are fine cashmere blankets (still available) and luxurious long-pile mohair.

Blankets made from synthetic fibres are also widely available. They are often considerably cheaper than wool, and also more acceptable to asthma and allergy sufferers. Synthetics are easier than wool to wash, dry far more quickly and have no moth-appeal. Acrylics and nylons are much in use, either on their own or blended with other fibres. When buying, it is best to pay as much as you can afford for a quality branded item—blankets should give sterling service for many years.

Cheap rayon and rayon/cotton mixtures often lose all their initial fluffiness after the first wash and can also shrink badly. Cotton cellular blankets are easy to wash and are particularly useful for children's beds in summer.

Blankets are usually made by weaving, either in a conventional "solid" form or in a cellular construction. Cellular blankets can also be knitted in a lacy pattern; available in many colours, these can make very pretty bed covers, particularly when used over deep-dyed blankets that tone or contrast. For maximum warmth you should always use another covering, no matter how thin, on top of a cellular blanket so that you benefit from the warm air trapped in the blanket's waffle surface. There is also a newer type of non-woven blanket in which a web of loose fibres is "needled" into a firm fabric; this makes a blanket that is light, warm and strong.

Britain is famous for its fine, woven blankets of merino or cashmere in pastel and deep-dyed shades, finished with satin bindings. There are also the traditional wool tartans of Scotland and the soft, subtle mixtures from Wales, often heavily fringed. American-Indian blankets, woven in designs that vary from tribe to tribe, are much sought after, and large Asian-Indian embroidered woollen rugs make good, heavy, warm blankets or bed coverings.

The range in designs of printed man-made blankets is enormous: they come abstract in endless colourways, they come figurative—and they come in animal-skin prints that are highly realistic and certainly more ecologically acceptable than the real thing.

Blanket care

Do not allow blankets to get too dirty before cleaning. Follow the maker's instructions carefully (and keep them in a safe place with other care labels). While it is easier to have blankets dry-cleaned because they are so heavy when wet, it is usually possible to wash most types of blankets at home—most machines will take them; simply consult the machine instructions. You can also wash blankets by hand, using the bath if possible. Try to select a fine day. Use warm water and soap flakes, and add water softener in hard-water areas. If you wish you can even tread your blanket with bare feet. Avoid over-rubbing, which can cause felting. Move the blanket gently in the suds with a kneading action. Rinse thoroughly at least three times to prevent a dull, lifeless appearance. You can spin or wring loosely between each rinse and before hanging to dry—preferably supported over two lines 1 m/3 ft apart and out of the sun, though choose a day with a good breeze to speed drying. It should only be necessary to iron bindings, and blankets should be aired thoroughly before storing. You may find the pile benefits from light brushing. Blankets not being used should be stored in a polythene bag; add a moth-repellent for wool blankets and for blends that contain even the smallest amount of wool in the mixture.

Shiny blanket binding can be bought by the metre or yard in large stores and will add a fresh look to old blankets. Using this binding, you can cut up old blankets to make attractive cot sizes.

Fleecy, pure wool underblankets and acrylic pile imitations are available for use under sheets to give extra warmth in cold weather. They are washable, and manufacturers say that you can sleep directly on top of them if you wish.

Electric blankets

It is reckoned that a cold bed is also a damp bed, attracting moisture from the air. A bed can contain around 2 litres/ 4 pints of moisture in an average winter, and the easiest way to warm a bed is with an electric blanket. The sale of electric blankets is controlled by stringent safety regulations. Low-voltage overblankets, which can be left on all night, have thermostatic controls and automatic cut-out safety devices. Used over a top sheet, they only require an additional light covering. Unwired sides and bottom can be tucked in, and they are usually machine-washable. Electricity consumption is low. Electric underblankets must be switched off before you get into bed (with the exception of special low-voltage all-night models). These also incorporate safety cut-outs, and bedside controls give a choice of up to five settings. Underblankets are best taped to the mattress with the eyelets provided, as this avoids rucking.

Safety notes: Never buy second-hand electric blankets: safety regulations have been tightened only within the last ten years. Follow the maker's instructions carefully: they are there to be read. Never use a blanket before it is dry. Never switch on to help it dry out, but allow it to dry unaided. Make sure the blanket you buy conforms to relevant safety regulations. Never plug an electric blanket into a light fitting, and do not use it with an adaptor into which another appliance is plugged. Never use a blanket when creased or folded, and do not fold it to store. Store flat on a spare bed if possible, or roll it. Never use an underblanket as an overblanket, or vice versa. Check frequently for frayed edges, loose connections at the plug and controls, scorch marks, damage to the flexible cord and displaced heating wires. To check wires, hold the blanket up to the light—wires should be evenly spaced and not touch anywhere. Return blanket to the maker if there are any signs of damage, and have the blanket serviced regularly.

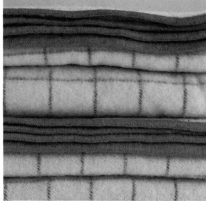

The bottom drawer is not the best place for spare blankets—store them instead in an airy place, but away from direct heat. Synthetic blankets or those that have been mothproofed need no further care. Woolly blankets that have not been proofed need moth-deterrents—rings, mothballs, moth powder or even spray are all efficacious, but remember to give your blankets a good airing before use to get rid of the lingering smell. If you lack suitable storage space—and blankets are bulky things—you might pile them neatly on the spare bed or, as a last resort, spread them under a mattress.

Bedspreads

A bedspread gives a neat finishing touch to a bed when a duvet or a quilt is not used. It can be removed entirely at night or simply be turned back (some designs are specially lined for turning back). Some bedspreads are quilted like comforters to provide additional night-time warmth.

There is an enormous range of styles and fabrics for bedspreads. Basically, they fall into two groups: throw-over or non-fitted styles, and fitted or tailored ones. Fitted or tailored spreads can reach to the floor or, if the bed is trimmed with a valance, they can reach down just far enough to cover the mattress area. Tailored styles can have straight, box-pleated or frilled edges, or they can be finished with scallops. Throw-over styles are often heavily fringed or braided.

Skimpy bedspreads look meagre and mean, so measure your bed carefully and add to the mattress width twice the depth from the top of the mattress to the floor. Fabrics need to be crease-resistant and hard-wearing. Ideally, paler, lightweight bedspreads should be washable, as they depend for their fresh effect on being scrupulously clean.

Candlewick is the traditional fabric for bedspreads. A tufted fabric, usually in simple two-tone designs, but more pleasant by far in a single colour, it can be made of cotton or man-made fibre blends. Hard-wearing, machine-wash-able and crease-resistant, candlewick is popular for throw-over styles.

Cotton is also used for heavy, woven bedspreads in simple, traditional patterns—white or cream are always popular. Cotton throw-over spreads from India are inexpensive and attractive—you can find them in simple striped patterns or in more expensive hand-blocked prints. Colours can fade, so keep them out of bright sunlight and preferably have them dry-cleaned.

Tapestry-effect bedspreads are made in throw-over styles in intricate patterns. They can be made from many fabrics, including cotton and man-made fibres. Delicate, frilled bedspreads can be made from plain or printed nylons or polyesters. Sometimes the flat top of the spread is quilted to add weight and warmth.

Lace spreads are still available and very popular. They can be made from traditional cotton or from polyesters such as Terylene. Use them over a deep-coloured blanket or cotton spread for maximum effect.

Crocheted and knitted spreads can be very effective when created from scraps of wool knitted into squares. Luckily crochet is quite quick, and you can create a lacy heirloom within weeks, rather than the years of work entailed in lace-making or patchwork.

Many firms specialize in quilted bedspreads or comforters which can be informal throw-over styles or tailored. Simple all-over patterns are available, or you can have complicated pictorial designs which can follow the outlines of a printed fabric. Some firms specialize in elaborate quilted appliquéd designs. It is possible to have your monogram embroidered on your spread, or you can add your initials yourself.

Manufacturers who offer co-ordinated ranges of wallpapers and fabrics often have a service for making up bedspreads to complete a bedroom scheme. You will also find bedspreads increasingly as part of co-ordinated bed-linen ranges, which may also include ready-made curtains.

Caring for bedspreads

The wide variety of fabrics and fibres from which bedspreads can be made make it difficult to give generalized washing instructions. Usually, heavier spreads benefit from dry-cleaning. Make sure when you buy your spread that you know what it is made from, and enquire about the best way to look after it. Keep all care instructions in a safe place, preferably in a file, a drawer or a pigeon hole, with your other care labels.

Right: *as fine as a spider's web, this hand-made lace bedspread adds a delicate touch to the imposing bed and stands out clearly against the burnt-orange background.*

Bottom right and far right: *different coverings on the same bed demonstrate how effectively a spread can be used to disguise and transform a bed. A long, sausage-shaped cushion sewn into the off-white bedspread gives the effect of a double-sided sofa. With a change of bedspread the bed becomes a blue, cloud-scattered sky, with the sun at the end emerging between two cloud cushions.*

Above: *bedspreads do not have to be expensive or a great labour of love. This plain white cover is set off by the patchwork head board.*

Right: *a bedspread of knitted patches in effective colours and patterns.*

Quilts and comforters

Quilts are deservedly popular in the USA, where they are also known as comforters. They can be quilted or smooth, plain or patterned, matt or shiny, and usually overhang the bed at least 22 cm/ 9 in on either side. It is not necessary to use a bedspread over a quilt that generously overlaps the bed—indeed, the effect would be bulky and ugly. To conceal the base of the bed, you can buy matching valances, called skirts, petticoats or dust ruffles. You can also buy matching pillow shams with some quilts —pillow cases that turn your pillows into cushions for daytime use.

Sold to standard US bed sizes, quilts are labelled accordingly twin, double, queen or king. They are filled with washable polyesters or, more luxuriously, with down or down and feather mixtures. Pure down is the warmest, lightest filling, but it is not washable and therefore may not be suitable for children and elderly people.

In Britain, quilts (traditionally called eiderdowns, although down from the eider duck has long since priced itself out of the market) have been largely displaced by the fashion for duvets—continental quilts. However, at least one large group of stores sells American-style comforters with polyester filling and reversible covers. Smaller traditional-sized quilts are also still available for those who prefer sleeping with sheets and blankets. These are usually in sizes 8 cm/3 in wider than the bed and are filled with feather and down mixtures or, more commonly, with polyester fillings such as Terylene.

When buying a quilt with a synthetic filling, look for the brand names of the well-known fibre manufacturers, who keep a strict eye on quality. It is also worth remembering that the greater the weight of the filling the thicker and warmer the quilt will be, but take care to compare quilts of the same size. Single quilts, for example, may be offered with polyester fillings in weights such as 510 g/18 oz, 625 g/22 oz or 795 g/28 oz, whereas in double sizes weights are 680 g/ 24 oz, 795 g/28 oz and 1.1 kg/40 oz.

Care of quilts

Be sure to keep any care instructions provided by the manufacturer. Quilts filled with down, or feathers and down, should be professionally dry-cleaned. Do not use coin-operated machines.

Quilts filled with polyesters are usually washable, although this will depend on the covering material, so always check with the manufacturer's instructions. A domestic washing machine is usually too small to allow the free movement necessary if the filling is not to be disturbed. Therefore, use either a large-capacity machine in a launderette or wash the quilt by hand in the bath. Use a gentle, squeezing motion, with a warm water and detergent solution. Rinse thoroughly several times, then squeeze or spin dry for not more than one minute. Drip-dry. A tumble drier may be used if it is large enough to allow the quilt to tumble freely. Do not use an iron or hot press as this could damage the filling.

If a quilt has been dry-cleaned, it is important to air it thoroughly for at least twenty-four hours to disperse dangerous solvent fumes before replacing it on the bed.

Below: *drying in the wind, a prettily designed quilt that would encourage any child to go to bed on time.*

Right: *even the most unwilling person with a needle and thread would not find it difficult to make this bright and bold appliquéed quilt.*

Far right: *an original and dramatic nautical design for a quilt that can be used later as an attractive wall hanging.*

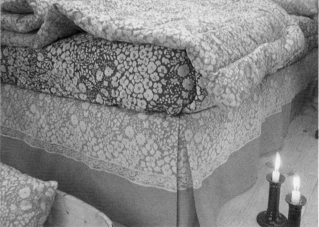

Above: *an enticingly comfortable bed enhanced by a matching sheet and quilt or comforter. The matching lace-edged valance hides the legs and is not difficult to attach to the bed's base.*

Left: *illustrating how Scandinavians use their quilts to best advantage, the base and mattress of this bed are covered with fitted sheets to create a piled-up or layered effect.*

Patchwork

Above: *traditional patchwork quilts are expensive to buy but rewarding to make. They look equally good on a bed or hanging on the wall.*

Below: *two quilts with simple, regular motifs have been teamed together with great effect in this bedroom. Variations of the garden-basket design on the bed cover have been popular for more than a hundred years.*

When the first settlers left Europe for the Americas they took with them traditional English and Welsh three-layer coverlets, their plain tops decorated with intricate patterns—flowers, leaves, shells and geometric shapes—picked out in quilting stitch. They had many uses, as room dividers between families in the cramped shipboard quarters, as bed furniture, food covers or warm shawls.

Because of the shortage of new fabrics in the early years, the quilts were patched as they wore out with random fragments of old clothing and were rechristened Crazy Quilts. New quilts were pieced from tiny, geometric scraps of scarce, imported prints from India. This piecework of patchwork made the best and most economical use of every morsel of fabric, the expensive chintzes highlighted by alternating shapes cut from the cheaper white home-spun. But as the American cotton industry got under way in the 1850s, enough material became available for the planning of extravagant colour schemes and the making of appliquéd quilts, where the design was cut from one fabric and "laid-on" by whip-stitch or embroidery to the block. Sometimes motifs were geometric or stylized everyday objects and plants, sometimes figures and flowers were cut from printed materials to give the impression of fine embroidery. However made, these quilts were usually reserved for "best".

Young girls were started on simple sewing as soon as they could hold a needle and every bride was expected to have at least twelve tops in her hope chest. On the announcement of her engagement a "quilting bee" was called and friends and relatives came together to sew blocks, each embroidered with the maker's name and occasionally biblical quotes, to make an Album or Presentation Quilt. Religious communities like the Amish and Mennonites and immigrants from Germany, Holland and Ireland all brought their own distinctive styles, and patterns were exchanged with relatives back home.

The women of America gave their quilts many and glorious names: some were household—Basket of Scraps, Pincushion, Churn Dash, Log Cabin; some marked political and social events—Whig Rose, Rocky Road to California, Washington Salutes Miss Liberty, Victory; some, like Mary Totten's Rising Sun, included the names of their seamstresses; some were descriptive—Chained Loops, Tumbling Blocks, Nine Patch; some were religious like Job's Tears and Jacob's Ladder and there were myriad star patterns.

Above: *the log-cabin design, made with narrow strips of material, and the star pattern, made with squares and diamonds, look difficult but can soon be mastered.*

How to make patchwork

Most quilts are constructed in three layers: the **top**, which can be a plain ground colour with a design of elaborate quilting stitches or tufting (the origin of the modern candlewick); a laid-on or appliquéd design; or pieced geometric patchwork. Designs are usually sewn together in blocks from a few inches square to several feet square and set together, often with lattice strips in between and edging borders. The **filler** or **batting** in older quilts was cotton, though substances as diverse as old blankets, corn husks and newspapers were used. The modern alternative is a Dacron or polyester batt. The **backing** is plain muslin or cotton sheeting, or printed cotton for reversible quilts. The back is often cut larger, excess fabric being folded to the front to bind raw edges.

The layers can be joined in two ways, either by a running stitch (i.e. backstitch) or by tufting and tying—threading short lengths of strong yarn through the quilt at regular intervals and knotting the loose ends on the right side in tassels.

It is possible to spend months and even years making a single quilt, but this step-by-step guide can easily be adapted for machine-sewing over a weekend, or scaled down for the more ambitious to hand-sew. It includes all the basic techniques required in pieced quilt-making. Experience gained from the immediate results of machine-sewing a simple first quilt can be an inspiration to attempt a more complicated, hand-sewn "heirloom" quilt.

If you want to find out more about quilting, contact your local library, museum, adult education institute, women's group or craft shop for details of reference books, exhibitions, classes and stockists.

Ready-made hand- and machine-made quilts are available in interior design and craft shops. Old quilts can be bought in antique shops, at house sales and in design shops.

Left: *small, wedge-shaped pieces of material are used to make the looped motifs for this quilted pattern, based on the "double wedding ring" design.*

Roman stripes pattern

Size : measure the top of the bed, adding 10 cm/4 in on each side for fullness.

Making the pattern : on five-to-one graph paper, work out the size of blocks you want to work with. On a standard double bed, for example, these are some of the possible variations:

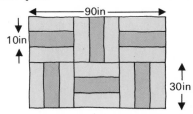

A. 6 blocks 75 × 75 cm/30 × 30 in each divided into three 25 × 75 cm/10 × 30 in strips. Cut only 18 strips to make the whole quilt.

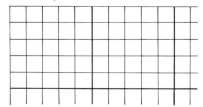

B. 54 blocks 25 × 25 cm/10 × 10 in. Cut 162 9 × 27 cm or 3⅓ × 10 in strips.

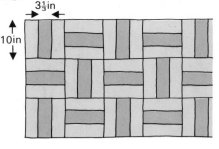

Colour scheme : this pattern is strongest if plain colours and prints are sewn in the same positions throughout. Crayon, or write in colours on graph.

Material required : count numbers of units of the same colour. Draw a rectangle on graph paper to represent a metre or a yard of fabric—taking into

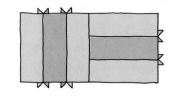

account the fabric's width. Pencil in units that will fit within the graph, allowing 6 mm/¼ in seam allowance around each unit. Now calculate the amount of material for each colour.

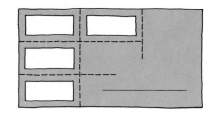

Choosing fabric : fabrics should all be of the same weight. Soft, pre-shrunk, colour-fast cottons, calicos, cotton and polyester mixes, ginghams and muslins are best. Try to avoid 100% synthetic fabrics. Test for colour-fastness by dipping a corner into hot water and ironing on to white tissue.

Cutting : Roman stripes have only one easy pattern piece. The template should be cut from card, thin plastic, or, for large-pattern pieces, use fine sandpaper which holds the fabric still. Draw full size of pattern piece plus 6 mm/¼ in seam allowance on all sides. Cut out. With a hard pencil draw each pattern piece on wrong side of fabric. Cut out pieces. When the template is worn, cut a new one. Cut only one thickness of fabric at a time. Sort pieces into blocks and thread together until needed.

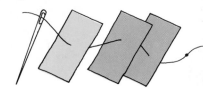

Sew pieces right sides together along seam allowance either by machine or by fine running stitch, eight to ten stitches to 2.5 cm/1 in. Use a good strong cotton or polyester thread, a 7 or 8 sharps needle and a thimble. Press all the seams to the side, preferably using a steam iron for a neater finish.

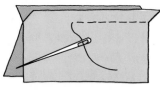

Set : arrange blocks in finished pattern. Sew together in rows. Add borders if any. When top is finished, press gently.

Quilting or tufting is traditionally done in frames, but it may be carried out in individual blocks, although this requires careful basting. Thread should match fabric, i.e. cotton for cotton.

The quilting here follows the outlines of the blocks. Lay out the backing, batting and top, right side up, on the floor. Baste the layers together around the edges 5 cm/2 in on either side of where the line of quilting stitches will run.

Set the machine at ten stitches to 2.5 cm/1 in and sew close to seam lines. Hand-sewn running stitches should be 3–4 per cm/8–9 per in.

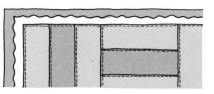

Bias-bind edges or fold excess backing in front, turn in and sew. Do not press.

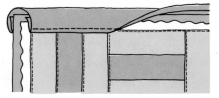

137

Multi-purpose bedrooms

Sleep is one of the main activities to be planned for in a bedroom. So how best can we induce it? This chapter investigates the processes of sleep, the simple rules of health and habits that contribute to its soundness and how our surroundings can influence both our sleep and our dreams. But the bedroom can be used for a great many more purposes than sleep. Love-making usually takes place in the bedroom, and the design of the room and the bed can increase and heighten your pleasure. It is also an ideal room for the pursuit of hobbies that require peace and privacy—reading and writing, sewing and painting. The chapter also deals with convalescing in bed and explores all the comforts with which you can surround yourself, as well as exploring the possibility of turning the bedroom into an electronic amusement centre of push-button-controlled sound, television and lie-in movies, lights, curtains and rotating beds. It looks, too, at those eminently practical bedroom adjuncts, the boudoir and the dressing-room, now making such a welcome comeback, and at the ultimate relaxation, a book at bedtime.

Multi-purpose bedrooms
Sleep

By Dr Ian Oswald
of Edinburgh University Hospital

A day in the fresh air, a good meal, a laze in a warm bath—and thence to relax between warm sheets and drop off to sleep. While a sense of luxury and sensual delight certainly help bring contentment and allow sleep's swift onset, the earlier exercise in the fresh air and a naturally contented disposition are of greater importance. The bedroom, the bed, the bath can give pleasure and convenience, but let them do so as ends in themselves —enjoy them, yes, but don't look to them to ensure sleep. Man evolved over the years to receive sleep's restorative gifts when he *needed* them after toil, and with no regard for the damp, dirty, hard floor of the cave, the hut or the cowshed.

The activities of the day wear out our bodies and our brains. Wearing-out is always simultaneously accompanied by rebuilding within the tissues, but during the day the wearing-out rate exceeds the rebuilding rate, whereas in sleep the reverse is true. This is because energy resources are now directed to inner needs and so rebuilding predominates. Everywhere in the body the manufacture of proteins, those bricks for renewal of the structure, goes on faster during sleep. Sleep is, as Macbeth put it, ". . . sore labour's bath, balm of hurt minds . . . chief nourisher in life's feast."

Why do we fall asleep? Primarily because we have come to that time of the 24 hours when we usually fall asleep, for we have a very powerful inner, or biological, clock. We can reset this inner clock after we have flown halfway round the world, but it cannot be reset at once. For a few weeks we are sleepy and inefficient at times when the local clocks say that we should be awake. It is also worth remembering that many of those people who say they simply cannot fall asleep at night would have no difficulty if, for a few weeks, they had been rising at five to milk the cows.

Then, too, we fall asleep in the face of monotony, or when we are bored, warm or restricted in our movements. This can happen to the passenger in a train, or, more seriously, to the driver on a motorway. It is, however, merely a shallow nap. Long, deep slumbers spring only from within, not from the quirks of our surroundings. The heavy sleep of youth gives way with the years to the broken sleep of later life: it is as inevitable a feature of ageing as wrinkles. Women find both harder to tolerate than do men, and they consume nerve and sleeping pills in larger quantities. More important, some individuals become more resentful of their broken sleep than others, whatever their sex: generally these are people who have a sense of heavy responsibility, or who are born worriers.

Surroundings for sleep

Granted that our sleep depends more upon us than upon our surroundings, we can still fashion our surroundings to give us what peace they can. We are each of us different, so there is no special colour or lighting scheme that helps to induce sleep, save the one that you like and to which you have grown accustomed. Familiar landmarks give us a better night than do strange surroundings: hospitals are notorious places for giving us poor sleep. There is a basic fear of the dark in many infants (and chimpanzees too), and it is not pampering the child nor a shameful weakness of character in an adult to provide, and go on providing, some source of light throughout the night. At the other extreme, if the urge to sleep is strong, we will do so in the strongest sunlight. But, as one may see on the beach, the sleeper covers his head with a newspaper or turns away from the glare, just as many of us like curtains thick enough to exclude morning sunshine. I am probably not alone in my annoyance at bright cracks of light at the edges of the windows.

Irritation is a very individual matter and in the bedroom it is noise that most often provokes fury: many middle-aged people blame noises for the brokenness of sleep that really stems from their own advancing years. I know one woman who blamed her daytime bad temper on her husband's nocturnal snores. Double glazing with widely spaced panes, and

Studying sleep: *the subject is wired up to an electroencephalograph (EEG for short), which records brain waves. The EEG provides a sensitive and reliable index of the presence or absence of sleep, as well as the type of sleep—dreaming sleep, deep sleep or dozy drowsiness.*

Body movement during sleep is normal and natural and should not be restricted by heavy, tightly tucked-in bedding. During dreaming sleep, muscles relax to a point close to paralysis, but the eyeballs move rapidly behind the lids and limbs twitch slightly. During orthodox sleep (in the absence of dreams) the sleeper will change position fairly regularly, probably a reflex action to aid the circulation of the blood. A normal, healthy person can change position as often as 40 to 50 times a night.

  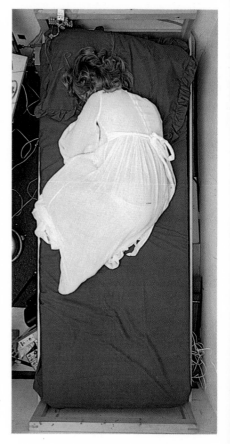

plenty of carpet and soft furnishings to absorb the sharper tones, will reduce noise disturbance and should have a high priority for shift workers. Apart from ear-plugs or separate rooms, I fear there is no simple cure for snorers—best of all to love him so much that even his more discordant notes seem a lullaby.

Personally, I always wake an hour or two before it is time to rise, and if I check the time by fumbling for my watch, or putting on the light, I wake myself up much more. What I now covet is one of those digital clocks that run off the mains and tell you the time by luminous numbers. Then perhaps I could take a quick peep, know I didn't have to get out of bed for a long time, and drop off again.

Beds themselves can mar sleep if the mattress offers inadequate support, and the knobbly old pillow can be another source of trouble. It is surprising how ready people are to purchase new armchairs in which they spend two or three hours a day, yet they are reluctant to part with an ancient mattress on which they spend eight hours of each day. A mattress should be firm, in order to support the body rather than throw a strain on the joints and ligaments when the muscles, that hold us together by day, go limp by night. This is especially important for people with back trouble. Worst of all is a sagging base below the mattress, which causes one to gravitate downwards towards one's partner, then to fight it out in a central furrow.

Food, drink and sex

There are simple rules of health or habits of life that contribute to the soundness of sleep. Both alcohol and sexual intercourse at night will both certainly promote quick sleep onset, but the alcohol often impairs the sex and actually makes sleep worse in the later part of the night—bad dreams, shaky feelings and gastritis. Some people persuade themselves that they need a drink by day or that they sleep better after a drink at night. They don't: alcohol by day means tenseness by the evening, and alcohol at night is one of the biggest causes of insomnia. If you want to drink something at bedtime, have a hot, malted-milk drink. It first relaxes you and then prevents disturbing hunger-pangs later in the night. Remember, though, that one should give oneself time to overcome the unfamiliarity of unaccustomed bedtime foods or a new mattress. Unfamiliar foods, at unusual times of night, disturb sleep. Coffee is another bedtime beverage that the sound-sleeping youngster can take at night, but is definitely not for adults or light sleepers.

People who are losing weight, whether through dieting or worry, sleep worse. Chubbier chaps sleep longer. On other counts, we must, of course, recognize that overweight is about the commonest health problem of developed countries, so not-too-thin and not-too-fat is best. One way to enjoy food more without getting fatter while simultaneously ensuring better sleep is to take more and regular exercise, preferably in the fresh air and, even better, in a wind. Most middle-aged people take far too little exercise, and if they took more they really would enjoy better-quality sleep. Naturally, the cure does not happen overnight: one needs time to gradually become fit first.

And what of dreams? Do they matter? Can we influence them by our bath or our bed? Stories about needing to dream in order to stay sane are merely fanciful, and in the ordinary course of events nothing will stop us dreaming anyway. The point is that although we all dream for hours every night, our sleepy brains cannot hold on to more than fragmentary memories of those dreams. If we are interested, we can train ourselves to be more aware of them while we have them. Once again, it is a matter of personal taste, offering the keen dream-observer more in the way of dinner-party conversation than real insight into deep psychological complexes from which he might understand and change himself. Most dreams remain unremembered partly because they are ordinary accounts of everyday events. So if we enjoy our baths and our beds we can expect to dream a little about them, and to like the dreams, too. Let us all then enjoy the bathrooms and the bedrooms of our dreams.

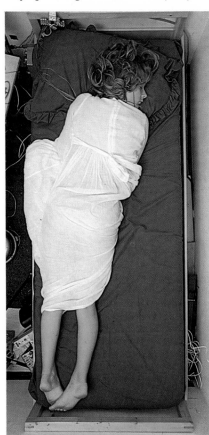
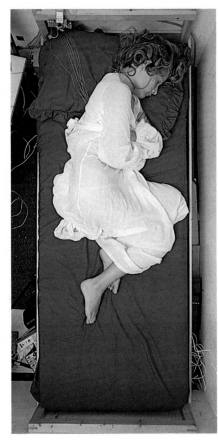
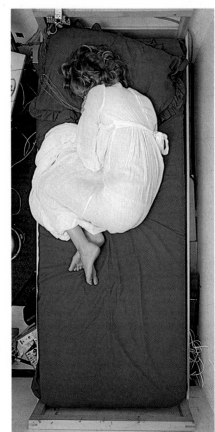

Multi-purpose bedrooms
The designing male

by Roger Baresel

Before: *a seducer at work, engraved by William Hogarth in 1736.*

My first close encounter was, in fact, not in my own bedroom but in my parents' spare bedroom, then occupied by the Austrian *au pair* (cultural exchange, I believe it's called). Admittedly, at the time my thoughts were far from decorative styles, being more concerned with first-night nerves. However, recollecting in tranquillity, I do recall our appreciation of my mother's discreet bedside lighting, which served to hide pubescent embarrassment, the imaginative use we made of her penchant for scatter cushions and the ease with which the duvet was flicked back into place as we heard the parental key in the front door.

Since then, a considerable amount of field research into bedroom decorative styles has led me to the conclusion that how you express yourself in the bedroom is a vital factor, and to the drawing up of the five rules for successful seduction.

Rule 1: do as you would be done by. If you're not relaxed in the bedroom, how can you expect anyone else to be? I am put in mind of the tragic tale of a friend of mine who failed to observe this rule—he didn't master his own bedroom. He invested in a load of goat-skin rugs, otter-skin scatter cushions and sundry other wildlife accessories to lend an air of The Great Outdoors to his lair. Unfortunately, he developed an allergic reaction to the props, making him an extremely unattractive prospect and destroying his sex life for the following two months. So don't be over-ambitious when decorating your sin pit, and don't mortgage yourself to the hilt on a lot of mail-order bedroom equipment. The most important piece of equipment you'll need you were born with.

Rule 2: keep it simple and keep it clean. The first room I ever designed especially for seduction had one overwhelming architectural advantage: it was a bed-sitter. For those of you who haven't experienced life in a one-room flat, the flying start it offers you is that you don't have to devise any beaux stratagems to pop into the bedroom—once you're through the door, you're there, the bed is unavoidable and sometimes the only place to sit.

But of course this is all a bit presumptive, so you do need what is known in the trade as an "ambience". Those were heady student days when *la dolce vita* was a kettle that worked and a clean shirt once a week whether one needed it or not. However, imagination being none the poorer for straitened circumstances, the reasoning ran thus: what is a student's role in life? To study. How does he do that? By means of books. And so books, hundreds of them (few of them mine), became the *leit-motif* of this humble abode. The floor was richly carpeted with piles of leather-bound editions, most of them open or book-marked with a tie. Books were stacked on window sills, and on and in the refrigerator. One corner of the bed was propped up with books where the leg was missing but, by way of counterpoint, only one book lay on the bed—Rupert Brooke's poems, as I recall. The whole decor was reinforced by a spot of Beethoven chugged out on one of the earliest electric-model gramophones. The effect was indicative of a serious but passionate nature, and it worked.

Rule 3: a place for everything and everything in its place. Of course, there are no rules that require you to confine your activities to the bedroom and, in fact, a bit of geographic extemporization can do wonders for a flagging affair. However, bearing in mind the comfort factor, which increases with age, it is vital to get the bedroom on your side. A lascivious friend sprained his wrist drawing heavy velvet curtains in a hurry, so don't let the fitments take over.

Start with the bed. Is it big enough? A small bed is only briefly romantic and can cause severe midnight bruising. And, of course, a bed doesn't have to be a bed. I once shared a closet (laid horizontally) with a girlfriend (also laid horizontally) which, when stuffed with blankets and cushions, proved comfortable and cosy, although I did bang my head on the shoe rack once or twice. But back to bed, which, according to the OED, is a thing to sleep on. Its ideal dimensions are wide enough for sleep but narrow enough to encourage cuddling. Once, in an opulent mood, I acquired a bed the size of a small swimming pool, but my partner and I had to use torches and whistles to locate each other during a power failure. Height is also important—you can do yourself a nasty injury falling out of bed on to a hastily discarded stiletto-heeled shoe.

It is quite easy to spend a lot of time in bed, and for this reason I have devised the Casanova trolley. This handy adjunct is no more than a cheap dining trolley with a quasi-Persian cloth thrown loosely over it, and it does the work of two butlers. The top deck carries the musical equipment (an essential accessory—see Rule 4) and a bottle of wine, a jug of beer or a bucket of champagne, according to your circumstances. The lower deck, cunningly concealed by the drapes, houses the less public accessories, including a bank of switches to dim the lights, draw the curtains, lock the door and so forth. The trolley stands at your shoulder like a silent retainer, ready at the drop of a pillow to indulge your slightest whim. Very handy—every bedroom should have one.

Rule 4: music is the food of love—play on it. The dangers of a bedroom silent but for the rattle of trains at the end of the garden cannot be overemphasized so, after the bed, give your sound system top priority. A transistor radio can look and sound tinny—and so, by association, may you. Your hi-fi supplier will advise you on the most suitable type of equipment, but I can offer you my own favourite record selection.

For purely functional splendour, I recommend Sibelius' *Karelia Suite*—rhythmically compulsive, but the swelling climax is a bit fast so watch out. The adagio from Gluck's *Don Juan* is longer and more climactic, and carries my ★★★★ rating. Romance is best captured (but kept within bounds) with Prokoviev's *Romeo and Juliet*, while Bach's *Double Violin Concerto* is almost impossibly romantic. If you fancy something a little more raunchy, Rod Stewart is your man. More laid back, and slower, is the maestro Eric Clapton. Finally, as an epilogue, I recommend the quiet, reflective passion of Albinoni's *Adagio in G*—a beautiful way to wind down.

One warning before leaving the music department: beware the clock radio. Mine once switched itself on inopportunely in the middle of the night with a concert of Bavarian marches. I put my back out and was laid up for a week.

Rule 5: before decorating, always ask advice. A cunning ploy is the indecisive bedroom. The bedroom should be in a permanent state of being between decor schemes, Louis XV at one end of the room, late Warhol at the other and a stepladder in between. Thus the artistic advice of the other party can be sought— an excellent pretext for crossing the threshold. Another recommendation is that the light should be operated by a silk tie suspended from the fitment—Old Etonian or Squash and Rackets Club are favourites and obtainable in all respectable cities.

A brief word, however, on mirrors— they're as hard to handle as quicksilver. A ceiling mirror can be a positive deterrent (a hundredweight of plate glass suspended over your naked butt by four screws is a Damocletian danger) and side mirrors dispense views of the anatomy that are either alarming or ludicrous.

Ultimately, you're on your own in the bedroom—figuratively speaking—and no amount of fancy fixtures will justify a bad performance. So the best advice is: put in lots of practice.

After: *the seducer has won the lady's heart.*

Multi-purpose bedrooms
The sensual female

by Bonnie Molnar

My greatest orgasms have been outside: on beaches, in the mountains, under trees and over rocks. Afterwards I usually find sand in the wrong places or burs in my hair, not to mention welts, scratches and insect bites. So I have to admit that even if the bedroom is not the most exciting place for making love, it is the most comfortable. Or should be. You owe it to yourself and to your complex female sexuality to make it so, and I think the way to do this is to listen to your senses. Once you are through that bedroom door, they should run the show, no matter what your interior decorator, mother or bedroom book has to say.

Take touch. Everything in your bedroom should be pleasantly touchable. Starting from the bottom, and keeping yours in mind, make sure the floor is covered with something soft that you will not mind rolling around on and that will cushion the patter of your little feet as you run back and forth with towels and grapes and things.

Occasionally you will get up off the floor and into bed. It doesn't matter what it looks like, though I am all in favour of fantasy-building canopies and posters, and your man will probably appreciate something he can support his feet against when he does the missionary bit. But for us, the most important thing is the mattress. It should be big enough so you can roll over each other without falling off, and hard enough so when you really want to brace yourself for some good thumping, your feet do not sink in up to the ankles.

Never have a bedspread that is so uncomfortable, valuable or perishable that you cannot forget it. One of the things that makes bedrooms such a bore is feeling you have to peel the bed every time you use it. The money you save on the bedspread might be put towards satin sheets. I know they are tacky, but all that sensual slither will cut your foreplay time in half.

If you like big, downy pillows, terrific, but have at least one firm one to support whatever bit of anatomy you are offering. Avoid having too many blankets. All that bulk and weight only restricts movement and discourages cuddling. Anyway, your bedroom should be warm enough to allow for nude frolics in all seasons, or you may find your nipples erect with cold rather than anticipation.

Now for your ears. Everyone knows that music helps over the slow bits, camouflages some of your more awkward squeaks, and is good to wake up to. A radio, you may think. But if you are both inspired by Donna Summer in the living-room, and then can only find the football or "Madame Butterfly" on the bedroom radio, you will wish you had installed an extension speaker to the main sound system.

Far from being a squeaker, I think sighing, groaning and even screaming add an uninhibited *je ne sais quoi* to it all. However, if you have ever had a nervous hand suddenly clamp down on your mouth, or been kissed purely to cut your serenade in half, you know what it does to your spontaneity, not to mention your orgasm. And there is always Alfred and Martha next door. So if you are noisy, or would like to be, look into soundproofing.

Naturally, the sense you rely on most is your sense of sight. If you failed to use it properly when you chose your mate, use it to advantage now by being terribly clever with the lighting. For example, make sure your curtains can graduate the amount of light they let in, so if you stay in bed all Sunday, it will not be spent squeezing each other's blackheads. Check all your lamps to ensure they do not shine in your eyes, no matter what position you are in. I always keep candles and matches somewhere handy, but with a dimmer switch you can adjust the light according to your mood without spilling wax all over yourself and the sheets.

If things are going well between you, you will be on your back pretty often, and if they are not, you will probably spend plenty of time lying in bed discussing where the relationship went wrong. Either way, you will be staring at the ceiling more often than you think. If your bodies can take it, admiring yourselves in the mirror is gratifying as well as arousing, but the engineering and expense involved in putting a mirror on the ceiling are frightening. The alternative is plastic mirror sheeting, which can be stretched on a wooden frame.

You will, of course, devote thought to colours. Cold colours like blue and green can fail to get those juices flowing. On the other hand, I once spent five days in a very strange hotel, where the walls were lined with red suede. Apart from feeling as if I were trapped inside a varicose vein, I wore myself out trying to live up to all that throbbing colour. If you think about it, you can discover the colours that turn you on without knocking you out, and also flatter your skin tones.

Nostrils should do more in bed than quiver with anticipation. There is nothing erotic about hexachlorophene or Babbling Brooks Air Freshener, but what they say about musk is true. It leaves a warm, sexy scent on you and the sheets that mingles perfectly with your own particular spices.

So if you have a bedroom that smells good, looks good, sounds good and feels good, and a good man to enjoy it with, "good taste" can surely go and sit in a book on the coffee table.

Hobbies

Both Rossini and Winston Churchill recognized the merits of working in the bedroom. Indeed, they wrote some of their best works sitting up in bed. The bedroom is a personal haven, a retreat from the communal areas of the house and perfect for the pursuit of hobbies, whether they be composing overtures, writing a history of the Second World War or sorting a stamp collection.

Collectors of stamps, coins or shells, postcards or photographs, butterflies or rocks can transform the plainest bedroom into a highly individual sanctum. The only additional furniture you need is a good-sized work-table, and display shelves or cabinets.

Painting, however, requires greater organization. Ideally, the easel should be placed where it need never be moved or dismantled and where a natural northern light falls on to the canvas. A net curtain over the window helps the artist by diffusing the constantly changing daylight. Brushes, palette and paints are less easily mislaid if kept together on a small trolley, which can be conveniently pushed against the wall when not in use.

For dressmaking, thick pile rugs and carpets should be replaced with vinyl or plastic-coated cork tiles; these can be easily swept and will not engulf dropped pins and needles. Reserve a large work-table for cutting out and machining. Lengths of material and trays of cottons, pins, patterns and scissors will take up one or two drawers. An upright chair is necessary for machining, but a comfortable armchair is more suitable for hand sewing. (If your sewing is confined to the family mending, a robust trolley is all you will need; the top can be used as a work-surface for small patching jobs and as a base for the machine, while scissors, thimbles and cottons can be stowed away on the lower deck.)

If music is your forte, either playing an instrument or listening fervently to records, choose a bedroom in a distant part of the house where you are unlikely to disturb less appreciative members of the household. If this is not possible, soundproofing your room can be the answer. It is easier and cheaper, however, to line the room with soft and irregular surfaces such as open bookshelves, curtained wardrobes and walls and deep-pile carpets. These all soak up noise, unlike hard, smooth surfaces, which augment and reflect it.

The bedroom, synonymous with privacy, is where one feels most relaxed doing exercises. The bed itself can be

A loom provides an unusual focal point in this bedroom, which has been divided into sleeping and working areas.

used for some keep-fit routines, but the floor—with a comfortable rug—is better for the more disciplined physical jerks, particularly the tummy tighteners and press-ups. Pendant lamps and jutting pieces of furniture should be banished from the exercise area so that arms and legs can swing and gyrate unimpeded.

Reading and writing in the bedroom require little specialist equipment. Thick carpets and curtains and well-fitting doors will help keep the room warm and quiet. For those people who like to read or write in bed, a swing-over table with an adjustable sloping tray is all that is needed to make these solitary pursuits comfortable and relaxing.

Left: *to give the home dressmaker full advantage of the best light, this sewing machine has been allocated a bench directly beneath the window. Paper-thin roller blinds diffuse bright sunlight, cutting out glare, and an adjustable table lamp spotlights trickier seams.*

Far left: *watching the television, reading and listening to records are easy to incorporate into bedroom life since all three may be done from the bed itself.*

Left: *an elegant partition divides the bed from the music- and reading-room; when it is pushed back, the two areas unite into an open-plan basement bedroom. Wall-to-wall carpeting and deep bookshelves help deaden sound.*

Above: *an artist's studio and bedroom combined: the glass extension, rising well above the main room, throws natural light from all sides on to the canvas. The artist's work, even before it is complete, enlivens the bedroom.*

Relaxing and convalescing

Breakfast in bed is the greatest of all treats, even when the breakfaster in person has to pad to the kitchen to prepare it. The art of laying the tray is not especially esoteric: forethought and a few loving touches guarantee success, whether you cater for yourself, a loved one or a whole family party.

To start with, see that your tray has a raised edge to fence in the load. Then use china with a low profile, sitting squatly on its base—those tall Empire coffee pots that used to be delivered to film heroines by their butlers must have wreaked havoc on the silken covers when they inevitably upset during the retakes. The same applies to the tall, slender vase with its single long-stemmed flower: your love may like a red red rose, but if your love is the least fidgety during breakfast your love will get wet. A short-stemmed rose will smell as sweet, and so will any loving little posy. In the grander country houses, different breakfast sets were assigned to different rooms to harmonize with the decorations: gold-rimmed white china for the yellow room; floral Dresden for the pink room, Danish onion-pattern for the blue. This seems a little grand for life as we know it, but do use your prettiest cups, saucers and plates for the breakfast tray—and your best tray cloth.

Leave all packets in the kitchen: just put the cereal in the bowl and send the milk jug in by its side. The idea is to make everything look as tempting as possible and to allow the breakfaster to postpone the moment of facing the day in earnest. There should also be somewhere to put the tray when it is finished with, since the Sunday papers usually take more time to read than breakfast takes to eat (they also take up a lot of space and it is nice to have somewhere to spread them out without trailing them in the remains of breakfast).

This applies particularly when the tray is for someone under the weather. A swing-over table that can be pushed out of the way after the meal solves the problem for invalid and angel of mercy alike, especially when it is a case not only of breakfast but of lunch, tea and supper in bed as well. But pretty trays, plenty of cushions to lean against, large table napkins to catch the crumbs (and perhaps even the sort of small vacuum cleaner used to clean stairs) should make eating in bed comfortable and pleasant.

Above: *a remarkably cheerful breakfast tray achieved simply by cross-stitch and loving care.*

Top: *recovering from a touch of influenza, our hero finds solace in a hearty breakfast. His absolute comfort is assured—everything is within arm's reach.*

Left: *all set for a perfect start to the day in a bedroom redolent of the very Grand Hotel.*

Right: *room for recovery—the simple serenity could produce an instant cure.*

The amusement arcade

Now that electronics engineers have got their hands firmly on to the bedroom, you can turn what was once just a peaceful refuge from the world into a positive amusement centre. Even the basic pleasure of watching television in bed has been amazingly improved. No longer do you need to squint and crick your neck: thanks to electronics, the picture can be projected on to a large screen, positioned so that you lie back and view in comfort. Alternatively, you can mount the television set on a built-in shelf high on the wall, or suspend it from a track firmly fixed on the ceiling.

But watching TV, or listening to stereo that is controlled from the bedside, or even watching the curtains swish open and shut as if by magic, is only half the electronic bedroom story. The bed itself has been all but taken over, and we now have magical mystery items referred to as "sleeping centres"—which may turn out to be a misnomer, since there is so much built-in entertainment that it would be a pity to miss out on any of the excitement.

In some of these beds you can adjust the sleeping level to any number of positions; others will rotate to face in any direction for a change of view. Some beds, while static themselves, can produce an undulating, massage-like motion to relax you. Others play sweet music into your ear, tell you what time it is in any corner of the world, and wake you up at a prearranged time—having made you a nice cup of tea.

The most amazing of these new inventions—as yet a prototype but dubbed the "Sleep Centre 2002" (what else?)—does all these things and then some. It is, in effect, a circular enclosure containing switches and screens, an icebox and an infra-red grill, surrounding a sleeping platform.

You enter it by means of lighted steps. Naturally, the platform can be adjusted to any height or angle, but there will never be any need to raise yourself in order to gaze out of the window if you want to see who is ringing the front door bell: a closed-circuit TV system linked to an intercom linked to an automatic door-opener enables you to admit approved

Right: *if you can overcome the feeling that Big Brother is watching you, a television built into the wall opposite the bed makes for comfortable viewing.*

guests without stirring. The TV also keeps its seeing eye on other rooms in the house, so you can remain supine, though vigilant, while toying with the buttons on the leisure-panel: these control the radio, cassette recorder, video machine, TV and the stereo system. Moreover, there are special mood-buttons marked "sleep", "wake", "love", "peace". At a touch, by means of music, lighting and

Below: *in the electronic bedroom, you can switch your stereo on and off without moving from under the bed covers.*

bed positions, these buttons create what the bed manufacturers consider to be an atmosphere conducive to these particular states of mind.

We are promised that when this futuristic creation is finally marketed, and you can think of anything else you would like it to contain, its makers will fix it—as long as it can be electronically controlled, of course.

Right: *lie-in movies with video-beam projection TV, which transmits the picture on to a large screen.*

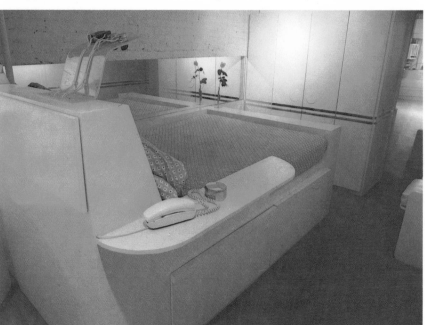

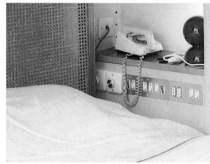

Above: *curtains, lights, radio and television can be operated at the touch of a switch built into a bedside panel.*

Right: *an impossible dream? In fact, this futuristic "Sleep Centre 2002" will be on the market in the 1990s.*

Multi-purpose bedrooms
The dressing-room

The dressing-room has become a much underrated institution. It need not be the great production number of the past, when it was virtually a separate, though connecting, spare bedroom with its obligatory sofa, ample mirrors and wardrobe-lined walls. Few homes today are large enough for such luxuries, and few households run to the valets and ladies' maids who made it all work, since their object in life was to keep their master's and mistress's clothes in impeccable condition.

But it is still a great boon to have a separate area where one bedroom inhabitant can dress without getting into the other one's hair. Such a place need not be a room proper; a walk-in closet, if it is large enough, or even a corner of the bedroom defined as a dressing area, will make life easier.

Organization is the key. Whether you are planning a dressing-room proper, closet space or a corner, this means that all paraphernalia connected with dressing will be concentrated in a single place: not only clothes on hangers, shoes on trees, shirts or blouses on shelves or hangers, but also first-aid equipment for clothes: brushes, pads and spot-cleaners, needles and threads, buttons and—of course—safety pins.

Good lighting and a mirror—preferably full-length—are essential (a hinged mirror, or mirrors set into a corner, will give you a view from all angles). Hair brushes, nail scissors and other toiletries that are needed for last-minute touches should also be kept within easy reach. And to save any last-minute pressing, suits, skirts and trousers benefit greatly if they spend the night not flung over chairs but airing on one of those useful dumb-valets which take the place of the departed "Upstairs, Downstairs" world.

Right: *clothes-storage drawers plus a desk have been neatly tucked under a sloping wall in this sunny dressing-room that doubles as a study.*

Above: *a well-organized dressing area with a curvacious set of drawers for maximum storage space, a spacious dressing-table and well-lit mirror.*

Left: *as well as providing a colourful backdrop, a tie can be picked out at a glance to match the day's shirt in this exclusively male dressing-room.*

Right: *a walk-in closet with open shelves for easy access and a rail for hanging the clothes chosen for the day.*

Multi-purpose bedrooms
The boudoir

The word boudoir is derived from the French *bouder*, to sulk. Lord Byron was often described as having escaped to "his sulking-room" by his disgruntled wife: he spent hours in his study, while the boudoir proper was reserved for Lady Byron, who, indeed, had plenty to sulk about. If we think of boudoirs as an ultra-feminine affair, where ladies in negligées and frilly boudoir-caps wrote letters of assignation to romantic lovers, it is because there was no other room in even the largest house that they could officially call their own.

But sulking is not a feminine prerogative, and neither is the desire for privacy: men, whether or not in a huff, also occasionally like to get away from trouble and strife without necessarily wishing to tinker about in workshop, garage or other masculine-type preserves.

Provided there is a comfortable corner, planned for the purpose, the bedroom is usually the best place in the house to be private in. Whether you arrange your boudoir corner for solitary sulking or for a companionable twosome away from the general hubbub depends on the rest of your domestic arrangements. But don't plan your boudoir corner with too many comfortable chairs or the rest of the household will follow, and instead of escaping to it you'll be running from it to sit in splendid isolation in the multiple living/eating/family room.

Top right: *a Matisse mural will inspire the thinker or soothe those seeking peace and quiet in this well-appointed bedroom-cum-boudoir.*

Right: *an exotic plant and an Empire-period chaise-longue create just the right atmosphere for an hour or two of escapism. A pile of glossy, foreign magazines would complete the away-from-it-all feeling.*

Centre: *comfortable chairs arranged in the corner provide the perfect place for a discreet chat with a friend or one of the family.*

Far right: *overlooking a superb view of New York's skyline, this neatly designed "private corner" is conveniently equipped with a telephone and television.*

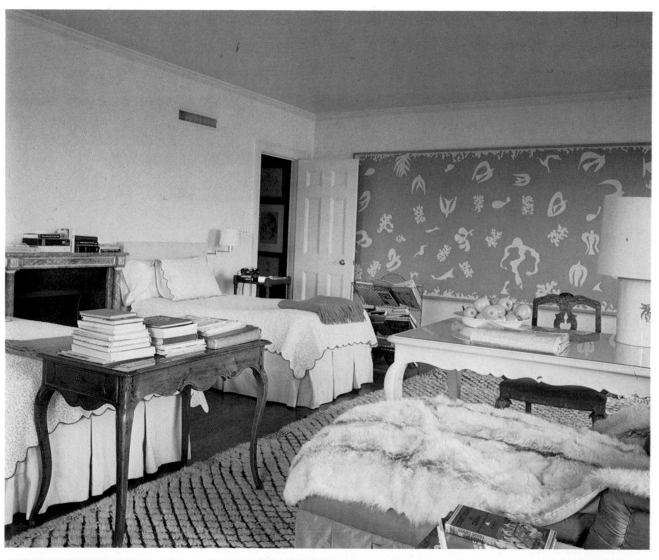

A book at bedtime

One of the best places to establish a personal library is in the bedroom: usually comparatively quiet and undisturbed, it makes a good retreat for the reader as well as the books. Sensible use will also be made of a room that is often sadly neglected and under-used for much of the day.

Bookshelves are most practical when fitted with adjustable shelves to accommodate books of varying heights. Built-in shelves can blend with other fitted storage in the bedroom and, where wall space is limited, you can simply build your shelves upwards and invest in a step-ladder (a small step-ladder with a padded top will double as a bedroom stool). A revolving bookcase is an alternative to conventional stacked shelves and doesn't use valuable wall space. You may also like to place a single shelf by the bed so that your old favourites and any books you are in the middle of reading can be kept close at hand.

Arranging your books is a very personal matter, but it is usually easier to remember authors than titles of novels, and subjects rather than authors in the case of non-fiction. On this principle, the most efficient and easy-to-handle system will have fiction arranged in alphabetical order according to authors'

surnames—say, Kingsley Amis to begin and Yevgeny Zamyatin to end the sequence; and non-fiction in subject sections—biographies, history, languages, poetry, travel and so on. Paperbacks look neater when all shelved together and, depending on how many you have, they may or may not need to be alphabetically arranged. In fact, groupings of paperbacks with an eye to their colour can look very effective and help balance your furnishing scheme.

Precious old leather-bound works—usually fragile—are best placed separately where they will not be unnecessarily disturbed; the best place for these is on the bottom shelf or high on the top shelf. "Coffee-table books" often have more attractive front boards than spines, and you may like to prop them upright on a shelf or lay them flat to display their cover design.

Never dust books individually: if you cannot restrain your duster, confine it to the books' spines. If the top of a book looks dusty when you take it off the shelf, blow the dust particles off

rather than grinding them into the pages (transparent plastic jackets for your more precious books can be bought in stationers and book shops). Remember that direct sunlight is detrimental to leather bindings and paper if the exposure to light is continuous.

Since you are more or less stationary while reading, sometimes for hours on end, keep the room warm and have a really comfortable chair. If you use a desk or writing table, it should be kept uncluttered so that you can pore over your larger books without having to risk moving ink-pots, pens, pencils and jugs of flowers out of the way.

It is always a good idea to have a shelf of reference books, or at least a dictionary, well within reach of the desk or reading chair. Good lighting is essential, particularly when reading in bed. An adjustable lamp poised directly over the book is best. The other requirements for a really pleasurable night-time read, if you are to avoid an aching back and sore elbows, is a good bank of supporting pillows and a book-rest.

Above: *stuffed birds break up the solid line of floor-to-ceiling books.*

Above: *cupboards below the shelves can be used for storing old and treasured leather-bound books out of harm's way.*

Left: *a bed alongside the bookshelves converts into a daytime reading area.*

Right: *the natural alcoves that flank a chimney are ideal for bookshelves.*

Bathroom planning

Before you plan a bathroom you must have a clear understanding of what the structure of your house and your existing plumbing arrangements will allow you to achieve. Naturally, if you are lucky enough to be building a new house, your only limitations—apart from money—are the laws regulating sanitation and plumbing. If alterations to an existing bathroom are to be of a radical nature, or if you are planning a completely new bathroom, it is as well to employ an architect or a friendly builder to advise you on the possibilities and limitations. In recent times most bathrooms have been planned for convenience and economy —the argument being that this is a room where you will only spend a short time, so it would be a waste of money and space to make it anything more than an efficient people-cleaning machine. There are, however, encouraging signs that this attitude is on the decline and the bathroom is becoming one of the most pleasant rooms of the house, where you will want to linger and enjoy yourself. With this in mind, this chapter covers all the basic points of bathroom planning, from how to decide on the most suitable location to the heating and waterproofing requirements, and tackles the difficult problem of combining aesthetics with practicality in the treatment of walls, floors, windows and storage.

Bathroom planning
Creating a bathroom

Until very recently, the bathroom has been the most neglected room in the house, sometimes relegated to a half-landing off the stairs and often draughty, unheated and remote from the bedrooms. Even today, the typical bathroom is generally a small room with the three fittings of bath, basin and WC unit sitting in splendid isolation. This is due partly to the fragmented structure of the sanitaryware industry and partly to the embarrassment—or, at any rate, modesty—which prevails about personal hygiene.

The subject has been exhaustively examined by Professor Alexander Kira of Cornell University, New York State, who has spent the last twenty years studying all aspects of the bathroom. In his book, *The Bathroom**, Professor Kira examines social and psychological attitudes to hygiene and analyses the anatomical needs and physiology of all the bathroom activities. He describes the ergonomic requirements of bathroom fittings, gives design criteria and suggests improvements to currently available fittings.

Considering the bathroom as a whole, he discusses the need for privacy and explores the various other activities for which the bathroom can be used, such as exercising, relaxing, love-making, reading, watching television or simply using it as a quiet retreat. He foresees the time,

in the not too distant future, when the bathroom will catch up with modern kitchen design and will have floor-to-ceiling wall units, each fitting complete with its appropriate storage.

Bathroom location

If there is only one bathroom, it must be easily accessible from all the bedrooms. Preferably, an additional, separate WC unit should be planned to alleviate the inevitable queue in the morning. If there are two bathrooms, plan one for children or guests and a "master" bathroom off the main bedroom. An alternative for the second bathroom is to make a ground-floor "mud-room" with a shower for

returning football heroes or for hosing down the dog, and a large sink for washing boots and garden tools.

Services

After the kitchen, the bathroom is the most highly serviced room in the house, and the resulting conglomeration of pipework with its propensity for attracting dust and creating noise should be concealed. A good light should be provided over the wash-basin mirror as well as general suffused lighting for the rest of the room. Heating should be at a higher level than the average for other rooms for comfort when undressed and to counteract condensation produced by

should be deep enough from front to back so that you can bend over it comfortably for hair and face washing, and wide enough to catch drips from the elbows. Tap controls should be clearly marked, easy to handle and should direct the water well into the bowl. Spray nozzles minimize splashing and wall-mounted mixers make cleaning easier.

WC units

Choose a model with the quietest flushing mechanism and with the longest front-to-back opening, to suit the different shapes and sizes of male and female anatomy. The seat should give good support to the thighs and be easy to clean.

Bidets

Like the wc unit, the bidet should have a good depth from front to back and give support to the thighs. A soap dish and towel rail should be accessible from the sitting position. When space in a bathroom is limited, consider a wc unit with a bidet attachment that provides a hot and cold spray and hot-air drying facilities.

Storage

All bathrooms need cupboards for clean towels, tissues, lavatory paper, sponge bags, sanitary towels, contraceptives and bathroom cleaning materials. A lockable cupboard is needed for medicines, and small drawers for cosmetics. Also needed are shelves for shampoos, talcum powder, bath oils, brushes and combs; racks for sponges, toothbrushes and mugs; rails for towels, bathmats and face cloths; hooks for robes; baskets for dirty linen; bins for non-flushable waste.

Style

If you are a Spartan health fanatic or a hedonistic sensualist, the bathroom should demonstrate these proclivities—bearing in mind, of course, that guests may not share your tastes.

Today, a bathroom can be anything you want it to be. With a little imagination and an understanding of the possibilities that exist, you can make this aspect of your daily life a positive pleasure rather than a functional necessity. After all, whether we like it or not, the bathroom is the one room which every one of us uses every day of our lives, so we might as well enjoy it.

*The Bathroom is published by Viking Press and Bantam Books in the USA, and in the UK by Penguin Books.

the cold surfaces of enamelled fittings and ceramic tiles. Steam from hot water aggravates condensation, and an extractor fan and well-insulated outside walls and roof are essential.

Baths

Baths should not be positioned under windows, which can expose the bather to draughts and lack of privacy. Where baths incorporate shower fittings, they should be enclosed on three sides and be fitted with a shower screen at the shower end. Baths set too low are difficult to clean and make bathing children difficult. The bath should have a good slope to support the back, hand-grips to aid

standing up and a grab rail or pole to help getting in and out. Towel rails should not be substituted for proper grip rails—they are too flimsy.

It is often awkward to clean the far side of the bath and for this a toe recess set into the outer side of the bath is helpful. The controls for the shower mixer and bath water should be set at a good height and should not be positioned under the shower rose. Recessed shelves are needed at a low level alongside the bath and at a high level for the shower.

Showers

The shower tray should be large enough to enable you to move out of the water

stream for soaping and for safety. A seat or foot rest should be provided for washing feet at the dry end of the enclosure, and the tray must have a non-slip finish. The controls should not be positioned under the water source but should be accessible from outside the tray so that they can be turned on before entering. Thermostatic mixers prevent danger of scalding and a grab rail should be fixed to aid stepping in and out of the tray.

Basins

Select the largest basin possible and preferably set it in a counter at a height of 860 to 920 mm/34 to 36 in, which is higher than current practice. The basin

Where's the bathroom?

Few requests to "visit the bathroom" are prompted by a desire to bathe, and the user of the WC unit, in a desire for modesty, often prevents others from shaving, showering and bathing. It is not necessarily the number of bathrooms that contributes to the smooth operation of a household, but rather the distribution of the separate facilities and the degree of privacy accorded them. Some families enjoy lying in the bath-tub together, but feel less at ease about using the WC *en famille*—even nudists have locks on the WC door. It may be that a communal room with a bath plus a separate WC or two—depending on the number of people in the house—would make better sense than two bathrooms that expensively and unnecessarily duplicate every item.

Where should the bathroom be?
If your house is already plumbed, then the whereabouts of water supply and waste pipes will be one of the most important factors when deciding on the location of the bathroom. The standard arrangement in two-storey houses is for the bathroom pipework to be stacked above the kitchen. In an apartment or single-storey house, the bathroom water supply is often back to back with the kitchen plumbing wall. These shared arrangements reduce the run of pipes, sewage outlets and air-exhaust ducts, and are cheaper to install and easier to maintain than a complicated network of piping snaking all through the house.

The bed/bath relationship
Bathrooms are most in demand in the mornings while all members of the household are preparing to face the world and at night when they are ready to crawl back to their beds. The bathroom should obviously be near the bedrooms and, in an ideal world, each bedroom would have a bathroom of its own. If there is room and money enough for only one, then it should be centrally

Above: *the luxury of total privacy enjoyed by the owners of this house has been capitalized by turning an entire bathroom wall into a huge window. A lovely view at bathtime.*

Left: *before converting an attic into a bathroom, as this has been, check with a surveyor that the floor can be reinforced to support the fittings.*

Far left: *not only has the space provided by a landing been cleverly utilized, but this positioning of the bathroom gives it a practical, central location.*

located so that every member of the household, and every visitor, can use the bathroom without embarrassment.

Fresh air and sunlight

A bathroom, with its inevitable smells and steamy atmosphere, obviously needs a generous supply of fresh air but, thanks to the efficiency of mechanical ventilation, fresh air is no longer dependent on the presence of open windows. A view of the outside is undeniably pleasant—more so if your house overlooks fine landscapes or seascapes—but it must be said that the bathroom is one of the few spaces in the home that does not really need daylight or sunlight. As long as you have installed an efficient extraction and ventilation system, a bathroom window can be as small as a car quarter-window, as large as a whole wall (provided you are not overlooked) or even completely non-existent in the case of internal bathrooms.

Embarrassing noises

While it may not matter to you and your family how public your WC is nor how audible its use, it may be a source of unkind embarrassment to guests. If the bathroom or WC shares a thin partition wall with the living area, then a wall of shelving or cupboards will help to baffle sounds. If you have the space, a separate WC, sited near the front door and out of earshot of the living and eating areas, will not only eliminate conversation-stopping moments but will put an end to the trail of guests through the more private parts of your home. Incorporate a shower cubicle and you have a small half-bathroom or "mud-room" for sluicing down dirt-encrusted children before they grab the opportunity of sharing their mess with walls and carpets in the rest of the house.

Rules and regulations

Common sense and building regulations between them dictate certain rules about the location of the bathroom. In Europe and America, regulations require that bathrooms and WCs open into a ventilated lobby and not into any cooking or eating rooms. Consideration for others demands that the WC door does not open directly into a living-room nor into the line of vision of casual callers standing on the front door step.

There is generally nothing to stop you installing a bathroom in the attic space, except perhaps the possible flimsiness of the floor joists. In a basement bathroom you will need a sewage pump incorporated in the plumbing if waste pipes run above the level of the basement floor.

Finally, even in the best-managed households baths and WCs will sometimes overflow—which will always be messy but might also be dangerous if the bathroom is poised above the entry point for electric mains cables—so ensure that you have an adequate overflow system or floor drain.

Above: *this juxtaposition of living and bathing areas is a novel idea and might have been ideal for Handel.*

Below: *to provide refreshing summer-time dips, a duct has been retained as part of this kitchen.*

Above: *a bathroom is more accessible to the family as a communally shared room when the WC unit is located elsewhere.*

Bathroom planning
Basic plumbing

As Prince of Wales, the future King Edward VII of England once said that if he were not a prince, he would be a plumber. There was good reason for his alternative choice of career. His papa, Prince Albert, had died of typhoid, and the heir to the throne himself had just recovered from a near-fatal dose of the same disease caused by bad drains at the house of his hostess, the Countess of Londesborough.

The Prince's illness gave impetus to a sanitary crusade, during which the master-plumber Stevens Hellyer exhorted his fellow craftsmen in London with these stirring words: "Lying there in those strong arms of yours, slumbering in the hardened muscles, resting in the well-trained fingers and educated hands, lies the health of this leviathan city."

Nowadays, the plumbers' hygienic art is no less essential to our well-being, but it is wise to check if those fingers are indeed well trained, and the hands properly educated. If you require the services of a plumber, check that the one you choose is registered with an appropriate association, federation or union. Membership is no guarantee of good work, but a simple telephone call could protect you from being fleeced by a firm of "twenty-four-hour cowboys" who could charge you the price of a new set of taps just to change a washer.

Like any craftsman, a plumber is only as good as his brief, so it helps if you can understand exactly what you are asking him to do. A water system is basically simple, involving few elements—just supply pipes and waste pipes. Complications set in when the bath-tubs, washbasins, bidets and WC units are dotted all over the house, which is why the "wet well" concept attempts to keep all the household's water supply and waste requirements in the same general area, to save long runs of expensive piping.

The water supply

Cold water is supplied to each house by the Water Board. A stopcock, or water cut-off, is located in the main supply pipe before it branches out to the consumer. In the UK, water enters a house through a rising main—a pipe that conducts water directly to the cold-water tank in the roof space. Cold water is then fed via a pipe system around the house, and also to the boiler or water heater. Another

network of pipes distributes hot water to taps and cisterns throughout the house. The cold-water tap in the kitchen is normally the only direct branch off the rising main, and is the tap that is designated drinking water.

In the USA, cold water is supplied under pressure from the municipal water tower. Water runs via the mains pipe, through the water meter and stopcock directly to wash-basins, sinks, bath-tubs and WC cisterns, as well as to laundry machines, air-cooling systems and the boiler or water heater. Supplies of hot and cold water meet for the first time in the mixer taps.

Waste removal

Waste pipes must slope gently to enable the waste from WC bowls, bath-tubs, wash-basins, bidets and their overflows to run down the drain. Flushes of water aided by gravity transport waste from WCs to the main sewage pipes. Air is sup-

plied through a vented soil pipe to equalize the pressure within the pipes and to help sewage to run freely to its underground destination.

All waste pipes bend sharply just after having led out of the appliance. This bend acts as a water trap, which prevents the smell of the drains from rising via the appliance into the house. Used bath, wash-basin and bidet water—known as grey water—meets in the pipe like the tributaries of a river before flowing into the main vented soil waste. A pipe carrying waste from the WC bowl, however, must be connected directly to the main soil pipe with no bends or digressions along the way. Obviously this requirement somewhat limits the positioning of a WC unit.

Pipes

Water pipes are generally made of copper or plastic. The latter are cheap, easy to handle and are used mostly for waste

Above: *today, pipes and cocks are normally concealed or disguised as far as is possible, but in this bathroom the plumbing has been deliberately left exposed, indeed accentuated, and stars as an unusual sculptural feature.*

Top right: *relaxing in the tub of an old-fashioned bathroom can be fascinating: your principal view as you lie back admiring the art of the plumber is likely to be, as here, a complicated array of sturdy pipes and taps advancing from every direction.*

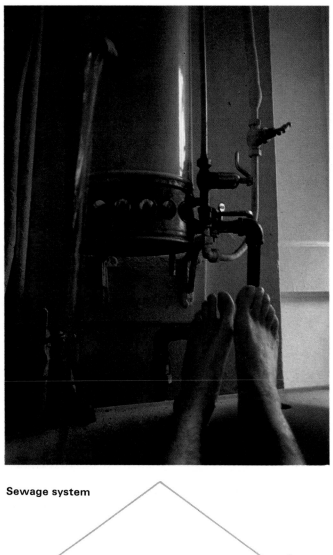

English water system

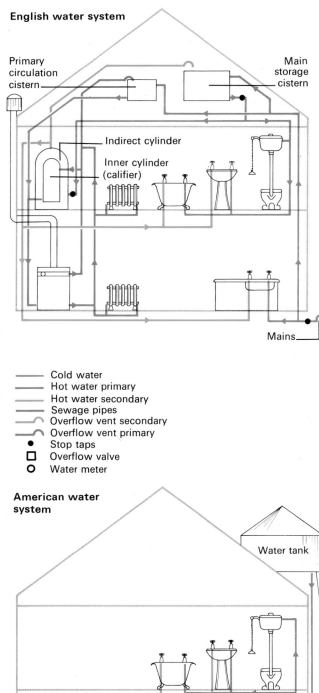

Primary circulation cistern

Main storage cistern

Indirect cylinder

Inner cylinder (califier)

Mains

— Cold water
— Hot water primary
— Hot water secondary
— Sewage pipes
⌒ Overflow vent secondary
⌒ Overflow vent primary
● Stop taps
☐ Overflow valve
○ Water meter

Sewage system

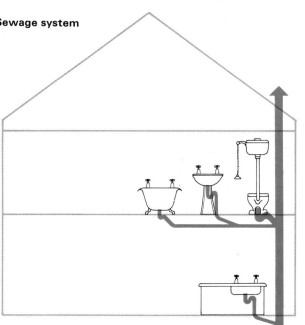

American water system

Water tank

pipes—they are not really suitable for transporting hot water. Copper pipes are neater and less noisy than pipes that are made of plastic.

If you are building from scratch, pipes will most likely be chased into the brickwork and rendered invisible. If you are re-plumbing an old house, you will certainly find it cheaper to run new pipework on the surfaces of the walls, rather than gouging out channels and plastering over. Surface piping can be cleverly boxed in or it can be left boldly exposed to display its own kind of charm.

Cold-water pipes and taps should be lagged to keep out the frost; all hot-water pipes should be insulated to keep in the warmth.

Water pressure

Showers obviously require a certain degree of water pressure in order to work efficiently. This is rarely a problem in the USA, where water enters the house under sufficient pressure to meet most household requirements.

However, in the UK, pressure is built up by gravity as the water runs down through a network of pipes that originate from the tank in the roof space. To obtain sufficient water pressure for a shower, the base of the cold-water tank should be at least 2.8 m/9 ft above the head of the shower.

You and your plumber

Before any work begins, make sure you have a written estimate. A reputable plumber should be able to estimate both for his time and the materials necessary for the job. Check which materials and which fixtures your plumber is planning to use—if you are charged for copper pipes, then make sure that they are copper. Specify the bathroom fixtures you want very clearly down to the last tap, plug-hole and shower head. If you allow the slightest ambiguity, you may find your bathroom furnished with a motley selection of unmatching taps and fixtures from the bargain bin at the local builders' yard.

Do consult the local Water Authority before you start to tamper with the water supply. There are hoards of rules and regulations to fight your way through—but they are there for your own benefit, to prevent you from flooding your home or from spreading typhoid fever around the neighbourhood.

Bathroom planning
Allocating space

A successful bathroom is one that has been carefully planned with the users in mind. People are idiosyncratic in their bathing habits, and the size and the shape of fittings will vary with every set of circumstances. A good starting point would be the standard dimensions for fixtures and the space needed for activity around them.

You will need to tailor space to your needs and choose fittings that suit you. Go to various showrooms to decide which shapes of bath and basin you prefer. If you choose a lower-than-average WC unit (the human body was designed to use a squatting position) you should install a urinal, too—although this is not a common fixture in the home as yet. You can, of course, compromise with a conventional WC unit and a step to raise your feet. Consider, too, each member of the family who will be using the bathroom: wheelchair users, for example, need wash-basins to be lower and doors wider, and children and old people need special consideration.

What fixtures do you need?

In order to determine which fixtures are necessary, it may help to divide bathroom activity into its three primary categories:

Bathing and showering, for which you will need one or more of the following: bath; bath with integral shower; shower compartment; shower room; bidet.

Teeth cleaning, hand washing and shaving: wash-basin.

Urination and defecation, which require: WC unit; urinal.

The minimum number of fitments is obviously three, one from each category, and more will follow depending on the demands of the household and the distribution of other bathroom facilities around the house. If there is only one family bathroom, it will undoubtedly be used by more than one person at once and some doubling up will be required: a bath and a separate shower, for example, and two wash-basins, while the WC unit and the bidet will need to be screened off for privacy.

Planning for other activities

Alongside these primary functions, there are other activities which all demand thought. If you are blessed with a large bathroom, then it becomes the sensible place to install laundry facilities (with a

near-by linen cupboard). A large bathroom is ideal as an exercise room, solarium or first-aid station, and, of course, a bathroom needs its own storage space for towels, soaps and cleansers, a bin for rubbish, a container for discarded clothes and an airing cupboard for linen.

Exploiting space

Lack of space is most often overcome by doubling up on the activity around each appliance. This works well if only one fixture is used at a time: one could, for example, plan to fit the shower within the same floor space as the wash-basin.

Floor space is, of course, a critical factor, and so is height. Full head height is not necessary over the WC unit, as one either sits on it or stands slightly bowed in front of it; nor is it necessary over the full length of the bath, in which one invariably lies down.

Plumbing and planning

The location of the plumbing plays a major part in the distribution of bathroom fittings, because economy dictates that the run of supply and waste pipes should be kept to a minimum. The plumber's job is simplified if all pipework is located in the same wall. A further simplification is to use the same set of taps for both bath and basin, with a long spout that swivels into position when needed. The WC unit requires the most attention for, unlike baths and basins, which empty into drain pipes, a WC unit requires a soil-pipe waste to take sewage direct to the main drainage system. In most cases, therefore, the WC unit is the pivot of the plan.

How to draw the plan

If you are planning a bathroom from scratch, you should commit your thoughts to paper. Drawing up a plan is never a waste of time, and it is certainly easier to shuffle bits of paper around than cast-iron baths and lengths of copper pipe.

First, make rough, freehand sketches of the four walls and the floor, showing the positions of all fixed features such as alcoves, radiators, doors and windows. Measure the room accurately, using a steel rule—cloth tapes are liable to stretch. Now note the measurements of your bathroom fixtures, actual or planned. Buy some graph paper in a sensible ratio, say 1:20, sharpen a couple of HB

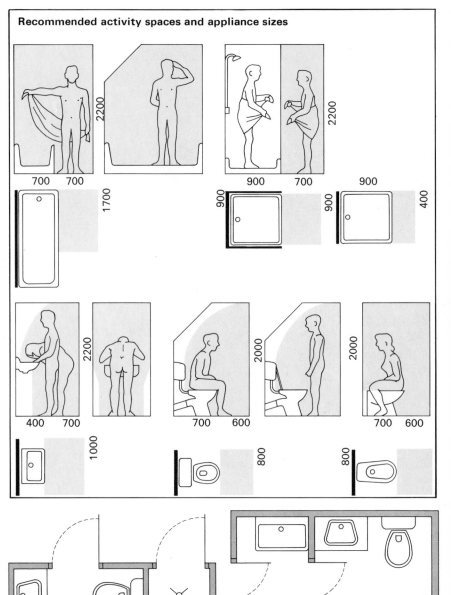

Recommended activity spaces and appliance sizes

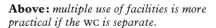

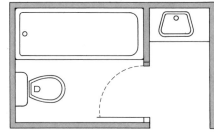

Above: *multiple use of facilities is more practical if the* WC *is separate.*

Above: *this compact plan relies on a doubling up of activity space, but it still manages to provide a utility room with built-in laundry equipment.*

Left: *a wash-basin screened off from the bath and* WC *unit means that shaving, teeth-cleaning and hand-washing activities can carry on regardless of others.*

Below: *full-height headroom is not necessary over the bath-tub, so if your bathroom has a sloping ceiling it is the tub that goes under the eaves.*

Above: *an ingeniously landscaped bathroom makes use of the angles created by the ledges to provide a sense of privacy in a very small space.*

Below: *a novel solution—plumbing fixtures are grouped in the centre of the room : bath and wash-basins this side,* WC *and bidet round the back.*

pencils, have to hand a soft eraser, a pair of scissors and some coloured cartridge paper. Clear your mind, and the table, and you are ready to begin in earnest.

Draw up an accurate scale plan using the measurements and information from your sketches. Do not forget to mark on your plan the swing of doors and windows and the position of essential taps or thermostats. Cut out cartridge-paper shapes to the same scale as the plan, to represent all your appliances—not forgetting that cupboards also have swinging doors. Move the pieces round on the floor plan, with constant reference to the walls (wall-hung radiators and low sills may confound your strategies), until you have reached a satisfactory arrangement with sufficient space for you and your family. Mark on the finished plan the position of all plumbing outlets you may require, and make a note of the wall and floor finishes you have chosen.

Playing with cardboard cut-outs may seem childish, but a properly drawn-up plan does help you (and the builder) to visualize what your bathroom will look like, and it could save you from making expensive mistakes.

Awkwardly shaped rooms

Not all rooms have four walls at true right angles to one another, and if your problems centre round a tiny triangular space with myriad doors opening into it, or a room that is too long or too high, then conventional bathroom arrangements will be laughably useless.

However, the best bathrooms are born out of inventive use of awkward spaces. Almost every room has something in its favour, whether it is a skylight, a lovely old floor, a magnificent view or a charming slope to the ceiling, and just because the room is a bathroom there is no need to smooth out all its character. As in any other room, capitalize on the good features and try to minimize the bad. It is worth spending a little extra to rehang a door, block out an unwanted window, lower a ceiling or raise the floor level to make the room workable, and if there is a choice between saving an interesting feature and saving a few extra steps between bath and basin, it is often more pleasing in the long run to opt for beauty at the expense of super-efficiency. Bathrooms are meant to be relaxing, enjoyable places, and this is what a well-thought-out plan will help you to achieve.

Bathroom planning
Safety first

A bathroom should be comfortable, easy to use and hygienic. Rounded corners and streamlined surfaces make cleaning easier and lessen the risk of grazed shins and nasty build-ups of stagnant water in cracks. Wetness is a natural hazard in the bathroom, and it originates from the following points: the shower—and the shower tray and the sides of the curtain or shower panel when it is in use; the bath and wash-basin splash areas; condensation and humidity in the air; leaking gaskets and blocked plumbing or overflows.

Water will inevitably collect where different materials meet, such as the tiled and painted surfaces of walls, and where different planes meet—the bath surround and adjacent walls, for example, and where screws penetrate the surface to fix soap dishes or mirrors. And water will eventually ruin inappropriate bathroom materials such as uncoated wallpaper, matt emulsions, corrodable metals and jute-backed carpeting.

Protect your bathroom from the effects of waterlogging by laying your plans well in advance:
● Protect wood with three coats of polyurethane varnish.
● Use coving to provide seamless joints between wall and floor.
● Install drip ledges to drain condensation from sloped ceilings or skylights.
● Provide adequate ventilation to combat condensation and humidity—this is most important.
● Ensure that carpeted floors have a waterproof base in case of overflow.
● Use a silicone sealant between glass and window frame.
● Protect the top edge of wall tiles and where tiles are at juncture with bath, basin or shower with silicone caulk.
● Only hang clothes to drip-dry over the bath or, better still, within the shower compartment.
● See that bath panelling or any enclosure round a basin is removable in case there is a leak or any build-up of dampness.

Many a slip

In spite of the relatively small amount of time we spend in the bathroom, 2.7 per cent of all home accidents occur there. A few simple precautions, however, will ensure that you and your family are not among the victims.

Slippery surfaces are a prime con-

sideration. The hard, angular materials used in bathrooms are particularly unforgiving should you fall. If you have a hard but beautiful floor of, for example, marble or ceramic tiles, make sure the bathmat is safely anchored by a non-slip base. Recessed fittings and rounded nosings and corners all help to reduce serious bumps.

After on oily bath, the bath-tub will be like a skating rink. Most manufacturers make baths with an integral non-slip surface; alternatively, a host of non-slip rubber mats are available. Grab rails are not exclusively for the elderly or disabled—anyone may feel dizzy after a long, hot soak. This is due to postural hypotension, caused when the blood rushes to the surface of the skin in an effort to cool it down, leaving the head momentarily in short supply. Although a large bath is one of the most pleasant

things in life, a bath that is too large not only wastes water but you could accidentally slide under the water and drown, especially after a night on the town or taking a sleeping tablet.

For the shower, non-slip trays are essential, and thermostatically controlled mixer valves will certainly reduce the possibility of unpleasant scalds caused by fluctuations in water pressure.

Electrical installations

If you plan to use a hair dryer, heat lamp, telephone, stereo or TV set, or other electrical appliance in the bathroom, you must make sensible and safe provision for electrical outlets. Never touch live electrical appliances with wet hands, since water is one of the best conductors of electricity. In the USA, where voltages are low, you would get a very nasty shock. In the UK, with 240 volts sim-

mering in the wires, you will probably end up dead.

All electrical installations for the bathroom must be fitted by a qualified electrician. This applies especially in the UK, where no sockets are permitted in the bathroom except low-voltage shaver sockets, and all electrical appliances must be wired directly into a fused power supply outside the bathroom. Lights should have pull-cord switches, all heavy machinery (laundry equipment, for example) must be earthed, and lamp holders must have external sockets. Condensation or damp must be prevented from building up around all electrical fittings, however small. In the USA, electrical sockets may be installed in the bathroom provided they are positioned high and are at least five feet from the bath. They must be fitted with waterproof, plastic cover-plates.

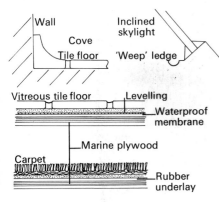

Wall
Cove
Tile floor
Inclined skylight
'Weep' ledge
Vitreous tile floor
Levelling
Waterproof membrane
Marine plywood
Carpet
Rubber underlay

Points to watch: *cove joins between vertical and horizontal surfaces; install drip ledges to catch condensation from sloped ceilings or skylights; lay tiled floors on a concrete screed; give carpeted floors a waterproof underlay.*

Left: *a horizontal grab rail and an inset water-temperature control are both sensible safety features for the shower.*

Below: *soft, absorbent materials covering the units protect the bathroom user from sharp, projecting corners.*

Above: *cork is an ideal bathroom material. Warm to the touch and non-slip, it also protects the floor and walls.*

Above: *classic, ceramic tiles waterproof the bathroom floor and walls and provide the room with an attractive motif.*

Below: *this deep bath is fitted with grab rails and inset ledges to give the bather an easy lift when getting out.*

Heat and humidity

Few environments suffer such radical changes of temperature and humidity as the bathroom. Once or twice a day the atmosphere is subjected to the effects of tubs full of hot water and steaming showers filling the air with droplets of moisture. Unless the room is warm and well ventilated, the moisture will condense and run down the walls, misting up windows and mirrors and adding to the already considerable problems of dampness that beset every bathroom.

There are several forms of instant heat if you have no air conditioning or central heating (or if your existing systems need a boost in winter). A heated towel rail will provide a little background warmth as well as warm towels and, if plumbed into the hot-water system (rather than the central heating), you will enjoy warm, dry towels all summer too. Wall-fixed fan heaters or radiant fires are effective if turned on well before bathtime.

Electric fires should be installed by a qualified electrician, especially in the UK, where regulations governing the use of electricity in the bathroom are stringent. Heaters must be out of reach of anyone standing in the bath and, for safety reasons, switches must be positioned outside the bathroom. Switches within the bathroom must be of the pull-cord type. Infra-red light bulbs can be substituted for ordinary bulbs, but they are not a good long-term solution because their heat output cannot be regulated, they are expensive to replace and need replacing often.

Positioning radiators
It is not so much a question of how many radiators or air-conditioning grilles you have in your bathroom, it is a matter of where you place them. If you have chosen a potentially cold flooring material, such as tiles or marble or terrazzo, then underfloor heating pipes or wires set into the sub-floor will take the chill off the floor

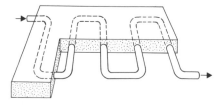

Underfloor heating for the bathroom: heating elements must be sunk into the sub-floor for safety reasons.

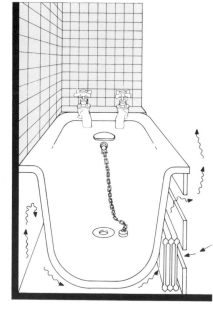

Heating the bath to heat the bathroom: a radiator set between the bath and the bath panel will generate enough heat to warm a small room. The panel must have air vents to allow the warmed air to circulate and do its job effectively.

and heat the whole bathroom effectively. A proprietary heated bath panel, or a radiator set between the bath and the bath panel, will provide sufficient heat for a small bathroom and will also heat the bath-tub so that the bath water stays hotter longer.

Condensation
The only way to cope effectively with condensation is to keep the room warm and allow moisture-laden air to escape through a ventilation outlet or be sucked out by a fan. Fans are often combined with a heating element to give a cold bathroom an extra surge of heat. Internal

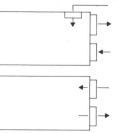

As every schoolboy knows, heat rises and cold air sinks. Position vents accordingly; reverse them if the system is fan assisted.

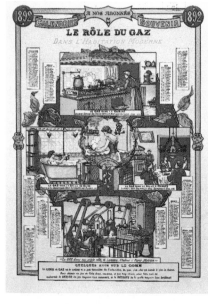

Above: *the bliss of gas heating for such luxuries as hot baths is amusingly depicted in a late-19th-century drawing.*

Right: *an air-conditioning unit fitted unobtrusively into a row of closets.*

bathrooms are a special case, and in order to comply with local building regulations must have a ventilation fan that bursts into activity when the light goes on—and it is certainly a good way to clear the air whether obligatory or not.

Positioning of ventilation outlets and inlets has a great bearing on the efficiency of the whole system. If ventilation relies on natural convection, then inlets should be low and outlets high in the same wall. For forced, fan-assisted ventilation, positions are reversed. With a wall covering such as cork or pine boarding that will temporarily absorb surface moisture, you will have less of a condensation problem than with an impervious surface such as glazed tiles.

Right: *it seems indulgent indeed to have an open fire in the bathroom, but this is, in fact, a gas log-fire which provides the same warmth, glow, even crackle, as the real thing, instantly.*

Bottom right: *if the heated towel rail is connected to the hot-water system, background warmth and the comfort of hot towels can be enjoyed even when the fresh air coming in through an open window is a little chilly.*

Below: *a heating grille slotted into the floor takes away the chill and eliminates the stone-cold feel of the tiled floor, which would be unpleasant for bare-footed early risers.*

Bathroom planning
New life for old fittings

Perverse creatures that we are—turning up our noses at old-fashioned cast-iron baths, lovely wooden WC seats and brass taps. In a headlong dash for hygienic progress, we have substituted plastics, acrylics and stainless steel—and too late we discover that cast-iron baths are deep and comfy, that wooden seats are warm and that generous brass and porcelain taps were things of beauty.

An old-fashioned bathroom full of old-fashioned fittings (provided they are old enough, that is) is not a place to be reviled but lovingly restored, especially if the fixtures function properly. Restoring the fittings does not mean preserving the freezing, steamy, streaming atmosphere that invariably went with them. A beautiful bath, basin or mahogany-encased WC can look stunning in a warm and comfortable setting. There is no rule to dictate that all fittings have to be in the same idiom—if a piece offends, pluck it out and replace it—not with a slavish reproduction or a mean plastic fake, but with a piece that looks good in its own right. Well-designed modern fitments should blend perfectly well and create an interesting contrast of old and new, helped along with subtle lighting and the intelligent use of colour.

Worth preserving?

Chipped or discoloured enamel: Some modern pressed-steel baths have an inner coating of vitreous enamel that has been glazed on to the metal, and such a coating is well-nigh impossible to replace. However, turn-of-the-century cast-iron baths received their coating of enamel once they had emerged from the heat of the ovens, and it is perfectly possible to repaint these. There are extremely satisfactory refinishing processes available for scratched, chipped or stained enamel that entail the careful spraying on of a plastic coating.

Worn-out pipes can be replaced with copper or plastic piping. Special connectors are available to marry up pipes of differing diameters.

Leaking taps: New washers can be fitted to old taps, but major repairs will undoubtedly cost more than their replacement with modern ones, so convince yourself they are pretty enough to warrant the trouble and expense before calling in the plumber.

Inefficient WC bowls and cisterns: There is no point in hanging on to a WC bowl

that does not do its job, and as modern WC units are still made to the same dimensions as the old, it is a simple job to buy a new bowl and refit the old seat or casing. A word of warning about wooden WC seats—research has proved that germs live for a considerably longer period on wooden seats than on plastic ones, so remember to wipe down wooden seats and casings regularly with a damp cloth, using a mild solution of disinfectant. Badly cracked cisterns will have to go, but ball-valves can be replaced. If a new cistern is to be teamed up with a pretty and undamaged old WC unit, then choose a slim-line, low-level cistern that can be hidden behind a false wall.

Above: *this spacious bathroom is furnished like a gracious living-room. The bath is newly enamelled, the taps newly polished and the mahogany panelling around the WC unit lovingly restored. Central heating keeps the temperature comfortably contemporary.*

Left: *the final solution—a pretty little tub, stained beyond repair, gets a new lease of life as a window box on the terrace of a London house.*

Right: *simple setting shows off a lovely old oval wash-basin to great advantage. Taps, tiles and mirror are modern, yet perfectly harmonious.*

Above: *marble bath surrounds and wall panels that are stained and dingy with age will regain their original lustre if professionally repolished. Aged taps can be rescued, too, like the elegant birds at the end of this bath, which have been restored to efficient working order.*

Below: *a deep cast-iron bath will retain the heat of the bath water for much longer than modern enamelled sheet steel. It is comfortable, too—deep enough for total submersion, a feat that is practically impossible in a modern shallow acrylic dish.*

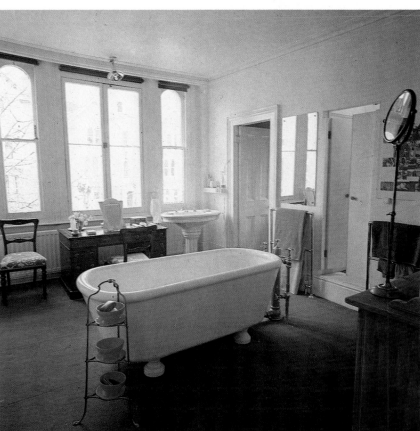

Bathroom planning
Lighting

A bathroom, with its inevitably shiny surfaces, needs gentle, general light to soften the hard edges. There is, however, an important exception to this rule: the light source around the bathroom mirror should be not so much atmospheric as functional, in order to minimize misguided smears of make-up and slips of the razor.

Downlights are effective sources of general light, neither harsh on sleepy eyes nor unflattering to early-morning complexions. They are easily fixed directly on to the ceiling, but are undoubtedly more elegant if recessed and, in low-ceilinged bathrooms, more practical (although it depends on the depth of the joists as to whether they can be installed or not). Downlighters, as the name suggests, concentrate light downwards, shedding a pool of diffused light on the first surface encountered. Thus they are useful not only as general light sources but also for highlighting a work surface such as the wash-basin surround.

A bathroom that is disproportionately tall may be improved by a false ceiling of translucent panels concealing lighting.

Spotlights are best aimed at the ceiling or the walls to bounce an indirect light into the room. Directly beamed at the floor, their glare blinds anyone who walks in their path. Fluorescent strip lights, although efficient and cheap to run, cast a harsh, shadowless light. They should be well baffled in order to screen their slight flickering effect, which is tiring on the eyes.

Efficient mirror lighting for shaving or making up should illuminate the front and the sides of the face. The light should shine on to your face, not into the mirror, and the general light should be carefully positioned so that no glare is reflected by the mirror.

For nocturnal bathroom visits, a night light should make it perfectly possible to fill a glass of water or use the WC. It is also a useful safety precaution in households with young children and elderly people, who may go stumbling sleepily about in the night. There are a variety of these lights available that are safe and cheap to leave on all night in the bathroom, the simplest of all being an illuminated plate that plugs into a wall socket.

Safety is always a vital factor when considering electrical equipment for the bathroom. In the UK, regulations govern the design of bathroom electrical equipment to protect vulnerably wet and naked people from fatal electric shocks. Lamp holders (the metal collar that holds the bulb) must have extended covers to prevent human contact with the live part. Light switches within the bathroom must be of the pull-cord type, although there is nothing to stop you from having a battery of dimmer switches outside the door.

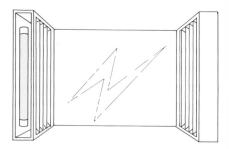

Thin tubes of fluorescent lighting filtered through a louvred baffle throw a good light on the mirror.

Waterproof lights, designed for use outdoors, are perfect for showers.

Below: *naked bulbs are not only dramatic in their theatrical association but also in their effect.*

Above: *a starry line-up of naked bulbs either side of a mirror provides the best light for making-up.*

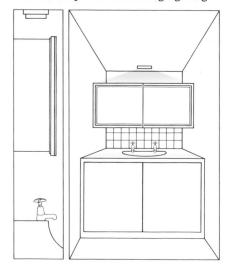

A mistake that is all too easy to make, viewed from the side and the front. A light placed above a mirrored cabinet will throw shadows all over the surface beneath and bedazzle whoever is gazing into the mirror.

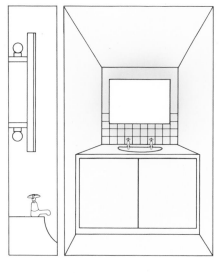

A diffused light is easier on the eye than a harsh, direct light. The profile shows how two strip lights are fitted behind the mirror, bouncing the light off the ceiling and walls. When light shines softly all around the mirror, it presents a shadowless image—much safer for shaving and making-up.

Above: *bulbs either side of the mirror may look rather glaring, but low-wattage ones cast a flattering light.*

Top left: *in this bathroom the light is filtered through a false ceiling of wooden boards, which cast interesting patterns of shadow and light.*

Far left: *thin, transparent tubes, dotted with little lights, are set into the plinth of these units to light you to bed.*

Left: *although more often seen in the kitchen, a fitting set under a wall cupboard throws a good overall light.*

Bathroom planning
Windows

A bathroom window has a doubly important job to do: not only must it let in sufficient light during the day (and air when necessary, of course), it must also create privacy. Until quite recently, frosted and corrugated glass were considered the only answers. Happily, today there are far more attractive ways of resolving the problem.

A sliding screen, such as a Japanese soji, gives seclusion and allows some daylight to filter through, but your lighting will need to be carefully placed so that you don't make a magic-lantern silhouette against the screen at night. Most fabrics can be made up into framed panels, and you will need enough room either side of the window to slide the screen back and forth so that the window can be opened and closed.

Louvres and wooden shutters also filter in light while blocking the view from the outside. These have the advantage of being adjustable, allowing in, at most, maximum light or, at least, no light at all. Pinoleum blinds, too, give a warm Mediterranean glow to a room during the day. Roman and roller blinds are less adept at controlling the light but always look attractive, although roman blinds possibly give rather too furnished a look to a bathroom. Both can be assembled at home and roller blinds can be Hollandized with special fabric paints.

Curtains are perhaps the least versatile window treatment for bathrooms. Although they keep a room warm and block out draughts, they may need to be kept closed during the day—particularly in built-up areas—thus blocking out the light. Their disadvantages, however, are often outweighed by their sheer prettiness. While a flat blind can sometimes make a rather bare bathroom seem even more functional, a pair of crunchy cotton lace curtains would cheer up the whole room. If you have a top-opening window, café curtains—kept permanently closed—may be the answer. Scallop the top hem and hang it from rings or a rod, or simply draw the straight hem through a rod or flexible curtain wire.

Alternatively, the window itself can be treated. Etched or stained glass not only foils the potential peeping Tom but looks splendid and allows in the light—beautifully coloured in the case of stained glass. With this treatment, the window becomes not only self-sufficient, but a work of art as well.

Above: *a porthole window becomes a mirror if the shutters are closed. Mirrors on their reverse sides are used when the shutters are open.*

Top: *this slot window, resembling at first glance a tank of brilliant fish, provides efficient illumination.*

Top left: *a sloping glass roof ensures plenty of light and seclusion.*

Left: *hollow bricks give an oriental screen effect to this bathroom.*

Far left: *rows of shells make an appropriate blind and a pretty sound.*

Opposite: *this vertical louvred blind can be adjusted to allow maximum sunlight or total privacy.*

Bathroom planning
Walls - paper and paint

The more the basic elements in our homes resemble those next door, the more of our time, care and flair goes into creating for them a setting that is unique. Basic bathroom appliances—bath-tub, wc unit, basin—are (thank goodness) our common lot, even though some may have more of them than others and some may own bidets or showers. The shapes and colours of these fitments do indeed vary, but hardly enough to amount to a personal statement: consequently, the bathroom presents a challenge.

Of course, bathroom decorations have to be practical—in other words, as impervious to steam and moisture as it is possible to be. Modern paints and papers are quite robust and there are any number of practically impervious claddings widely, if expensively, available.

The basic choice in paints is between matt, emulsion, vinyl silk and oil-based. Those with an eggshell finish are a wise buy because high-gloss paints aggravate problems of condensation. High-gloss is, nevertheless, fine for the woodwork. Vinyl silk has the advantage of being available in colours which can be mixed to one's own specification.

Some of the most successful bathrooms owe their charm to paper and paint. The first decades of the bathroom's history were taken up with overexcitement about the fact that decent plumbing was becoming generally available. Thus the first bathrooms were temples to hygiene, but now, for fresh and pretty results, bathroom decorators tend to follow the conventions of other rooms in the house.

A scheme that would be unremarkable though pleasant in, say, a modest bedroom—a precise pattern on the wall spiced with clear colour and glossy white—achieves an edge of high sophistication in the bathroom. Or think of the bathroom treated as a conservatory: water and plants are natural allies, even if the greenery is supplied by fern or leaf-printed paper. Flowered papers, lattice-work (actual or in the wall pattern) and bright green floor-coverings can make your bathroom feel like a garden in summer all the year round. The logical extension of this scheme would be to sink a circular bath into a floor covered in grassy-green tumble-twist carpeting and do away with walls altogether, allowing this paradise for Kermit and other frog-princes to form part of a large bedroom, divided by summery screens.

There is, after all, no law that bathrooms must be discreet in colour. Fixtures come mostly in muted tones, but white ones go marvellously with primary colours: in fact, bright colours tend to work best if one is really generous with white to set them off.

It goes without saying that if you use paper you will want to protect the areas most vulnerable to splashing; this can be done with sheets of Perspex, a plastic laminate or a run of tiles. It is wise to bear in mind that steam rises, so papering the ceiling is impractical: the adhesive will be quickly affected by the damp.

Right: *chic, dark brown walls with a rich, tweedy effect that comes from carefully applying several thick coats of shellac or clear but highly glossy polyurethane varnish over a dark and interesting wallpaper.*

Far right: *collector's corner of favourite pin-ups snipped out of their calendar and simply pinned to strips of black paper. Black walls are certainly dramatic, but need to be liberally covered with pictures and mirrors, or the effect will be decidedly funereal.*

Bottom right: *strong, embossed papers, like Anaglypta, are the ideal cover-up for walls that are flaking, cracked or uneven. Paint over the paper with two coats of matt or silk-finish emulsion to enhance the texture.*

Below: *a bathroom with metallic paper must be well ventilated, or the walls will steam up, just like mirrors.*

Above: *read all about the cheapest possible wallpaper. As with all low-quality papers, walls must be properly prepared with lining paper. Two coats of clear polyurethane will prevent the news getting dull with age.*

Bathroom planning
Walls - tiles and textures

Tiles can of course be used decoratively in conjunction with other wall finishes, but a bathroom tiled from floor to wall to ceiling is hard to beat. Glass or ceramic tiles come in endless colours, patterns, shapes and sizes. You can keep things simple, or you can mix designs.

There is one marvellously pretty bathroom that gives a tolerable impression of the Blue Mosque, being entirely clad in blue and white tiles grouped by pattern. These form great tracery motifs behind the bath-tub; then on its panelling there are strict rows of blue tiles, widely spaced with white grouting. On the floor they combine to form diamonds. Alternatively, mosaic tiles enable you to design your own patterns, so that, with judicious lighting, your bathroom can glitter like the rose window at Chartres.

Then there are bathrooms in which tiles have been used to create something as different as a tycoon's office from a typing pool. These are the ones in black terrazzo, wonderful as visual therapy for stultified chairpersons too busy to notice ordinary surroundings.

What can we learn from this dark grandeur? It is that very dark colours make a highly luxurious, if slightly soporific setting. This can be emulated in paint, in cork, in marble papers (much more exciting than marbled plastics, which tend to have an ersatz feel about them) and in stained wood.

Wood is fine for bathroom walls, but timber should be selected with care: softwoods must be pressure-treated against dry rot, which tends to flourish in the warm and steamy bathroom atmosphere, but a hardwood like cedar should survive. So will the glowing polished mahogany that used to encase the great Victorian or Edwardian bath-tub, and also constituted the wall panelling which went with it.

Alas, now that we have recognized its charm, mahogany panelling has become very scarce indeed, and the quest for nostalgia in the bathroom is, on the whole, unrewarding. There are still a few *art nouveau* tiles about, but there is no way of re-creating a turn-of-the-century bathroom in the context of the old and the modest: comfortable bathrooms existed only on the grand scale. And much though we love all that is unpretentious and under-designed, who would exchange comfort for a dip in a tin bath by the scullery fire?

Left: *old, hand-painted tiles are collectors' items now and complete pattern sets are rare, but a colour-matched jumble looks delightful.*

Centre: *brick or brick-work walls can be cement rendered and the surface left sandy, which makes a sympathetic bathroom wall finish. The same effect could be achieved by the use of an exterior cement paint.*

Far left: *old stone walls are often too beautiful to cover up with plaster and paint—but heating needs to be efficient, otherwise the bathroom could become cold and clammy.*

Left: *tongue and groove boarding will smarten up the roughest of walls. With two coats of polyurethane varnish, wood becomes resistant to the effects of wet and steam.*

Centre: *only for the restrained bather—vigorous splashing would soon rot the carpeted bath surround and the elegantly felt-clad walls.*

Far left: *cork is an ideal wall and floor covering for bathrooms—being warm to the touch, it cuts down condensation and provides insulation against heat loss.*

Bathroom planning
Mirrors

To clad an entire wall of a poky bathroom in sheet-mirror can transform the place into something like a ballroom, especially if more mirroring on the opposite wall infinitely reflects the reflection. But the daily sight of self, climbing in and out of the bath a million times over, may be more than some of us can bear.

For the sake of *amour propre*, one should position large stretches of mirror with sensitivity. A bathroom is where cares are meant to be soaked away, and where of all places we are surely entitled to pander to our vanity.

Smoked and tinted mirror is of course more flattering than plain, but to play really safe, use mirror tiles. The smaller they are the better, for the more fractured an image they present the more soothing it is for the ego of those with less-than-perfect bodies.

An alternative to sheet mirror or tinted glass is a gently distorting reflective surface such as that provided by polyester mirror panels. They are so lightweight that they can be fixed to walls not strong enough to take heavy glass.

Then there are the self-adhesive metallic vinyls, which come in various embossings, not all of them attractive, but also in a plain, shimmery silver. It is worth remembering that, because they are applied directly to a wall, its every bump will show and, on a wall in bad condition, distortions may be alarming.

Acrylic mirror has the advantage of being warm to the touch so that condensation problems are kept to a minimum, but it damages easily—the slightest bit of grit in a duster will cause irreparable scratching.

Modest, but potentially the most effective of all reflective coverings, is aluminium kitchen foil. This is fixed with a thin builders' glue that is spread on to the wall, not the aluminium, so that the foil is applied straight from the roll. On a flat surface, its reflective qualities almost equal mirror glass, and if you slightly and deliberately crumple the foil before putting it up, it will look like beaten silver.

No matter what reflective material you use, follow the manufacturer's instructions to the letter when applying it. If the back of a mirror is permanently damp its silver disintegrates. With conventional mirror glass, you should, wherever possible, leave a gap between it and the wall, so that air can circulate. Slices

of thin cork are a convenient means of mounting mirror clear of a potentially wet wall.

Mirror can be effective in small doses. A frieze of mirror tiles around the bath or immediately behind it, or an open-ended mirrored cube for storing bath paraphernalia, or an occasional glint of mirrored glass worked into the scheme all add an extra dimension.

It has also to be said that, even in a bathroom, self-deception ought to have its limits: one properly lit, plain mirror is essential for shaving, making-up and merciless self-scrutiny.

Left: *four mirror-glass panels, arranged around a wash-basin unit, provide an infinitely repeated reflection.*

Below: *smoked glass, encompassing a bathroom, is second to none for creating a highly sophisticated look.*

Above: *in contrast to the surrounding pictures, this antique, bevelled-glass mirror is of a solidly classic design. A glass splash-back, mounted against a black wall, besides safeguarding prints also has a certain reflective quality.*

Left: *angled mirrors, fixed in front of the elegant double basin, effectively show off dazzling white and silver fittings. Light bulbs, incorporated in the mirror, ensure the very clearest image and the looking-glass on a swivel stand is suitable for facial close-ups.*

Right: *a vast acreage of mirror, extravagantly distributed around the room, creates the narcissist's bathroom. Quite apart from being liable to steam up, this could have a rather colourless, bleak effect without the vivid splashes of colour provided by the stools, bath mat and golden bath oils.*

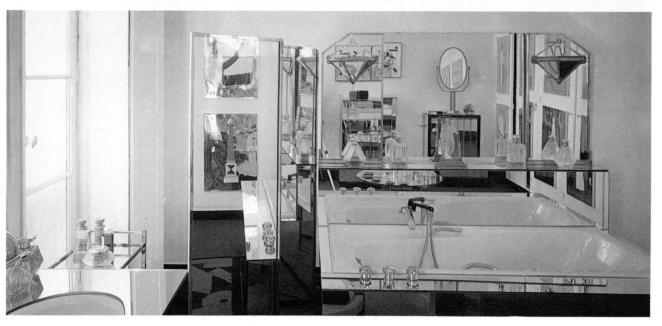

Hard floors

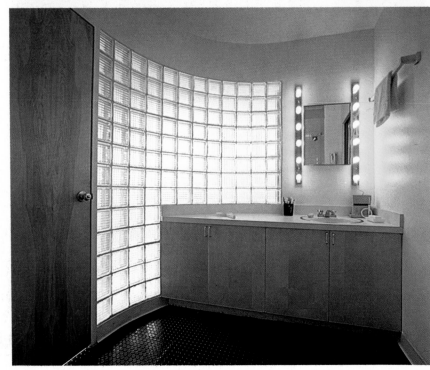

Floor coverings for large rooms generally involve considerations of cost, resulting in solutions somewhat less lavish than our ideal, but in the bathroom there is often scope to indulge our more extravagant inclinations.

At the practical level, the most obvious asset bathroom flooring must have is resistance to waterlogging. This gives easily mopped, smooth floors an advantage over soft carpeting and wood-based floor coverings such as hardboard and chipboard. Smooth flooring is also easy to disinfect—a point to be taken into consideration if the bathroom is combined with the wc.

Slip-resistance is another factor in bathroom flooring. Because many hard surfaces can be slippery when wet, it is essential to provide bathmats beside the bath, shower and, if necessary, the washbasin areas. Hard surfaces, too, may need underfloor heating so that their natural chill will not disenchant the barefoot bathroom users.

When deciding on colour and pattern, think carefully before choosing large, dominant themes that might overpower a small space. Medium and pale shades will make small floor areas look larger, and spilt talcum powder will be less noticeable than on darker shades.

Top left: *a muddy giant has evidently left his imprint on this dramatic black and white vinyl floor.*

Left: *rubber floors are warm and hardwearing and this one, with its nobbly surface, provides an interesting effect.*

Below: *demonstrating the splendour and versatility of marble, this marble-tiled floor matches the walls and fittings.*

Stone floors

Although very costly, stone floors when properly installed will last several lifetimes. They can be very heavy, however, and all stone flooring requires specialist installation on a solid concrete sub-floor. All stone feels naturally hard and cold, but can be combined with underfloor heating.

Marble is the classic floor luxury. Available in large slabs or in thinner tiles, it is available in a beautiful range of varied colours from white and cream through pinks and greens to sumptuous black. It tends to be slippery when splashed with soapy water.

Quartzite is a matt-finished crystalline rock with a small amount of sparkle from its quartz content. Colours include grey, green and gold, and it is available in slabs or tiles. It has a naturally textured, slip-resistant finish.

Slate is hard and impervious, and riven slate, like quartzite, has a naturally textured, slip-resistant finish. Colours include grey, blue-grey and green-grey, and it is available in slabs from 198 × 90 cm/6 ft 6 in × 3 ft, in thicknesses from 9 to 50 mm/$\frac{3}{8}$ to 2 in.

Sandstones, limestones and granites used as flooring slabs make durable, good-looking bathroom floors.

Terrazzo

Like stone floors, terrazzo requires specialist installation on a solid concrete sub-floor. Although costly, its general durability is excellent and it can be combined with underfloor heating. Available in a good range of colours and patterns that can be combined for unusual effects, it can incorporate various aggregates—stone chippings, for example, including marble or pebbles.

Because terrazzo can be slippery when wet, choose a type that contains a non-slip aggregate. A concrete-based material, terrazzo can either be supplied as tiles or cast on site.

Ceramics

Clay floor tiles are available in various shapes, including squares, rectangles and interlocking ogees. They can be plain or patterned, glazed or unglazed. Professional installation is recommended, although some ranges are sold with spacer lugs for do-it-yourself laying. Tiles can be laid on suspended timber floors if these are strong enough to take the weight, but the best base for ceramic is solid concrete.

Ceramic tiles come in a good range of colours and patterns. They are among the easiest floor coverings to incorporate into a complete bathroom scheme because they can be fitted around fixtures such as baths and basins for a co-ordinated effect. When properly fixed, they offer excellent resistance to water, particularly if taken partly up the wall.

Highly glazed smooth tiles are very slippery when wet, so always provide mats for danger areas. Non-glazed tiles offer a better degree of slip-resistance, and non-slip tiles are available, including types with pitted and studded effects. General durability is good, but tiles can shatter if something heavy is dropped on them, so always keep a few spares.

Mosaic

Made from tiny clay tiles, glass or even little chips of marble, mosaic is a covering of small shapes—usually squares—that combine to give a continuous effect. It usually requires specialist installation and can be taken over curved surfaces, including covings at skirtings.

Available in a good range of colours, mosaic can form unusual and complicated patterns and has good durability and resistance to water. Although it can be slippery when wet, the small shapes provide a degree of texture that helps to give feet a grip.

Vinyls

Available in sheet or tile form and in resilient cushioned-type sheets, vinyl is a less expensive form of hard floor covering than those listed before. Tiles are easier to fit around awkward projections, but sheet vinyl can give a one-piece, jointless covering that better withstands water. Both are suitable for do-it-yourself installation and require a smooth, clean, dry sub-floor (on old boards, a hardboard underlay is usually essential). Flexible sheet vinyls can be curved over wooden moulding at floor edges to form a coved finish.

Vinyls are available in a large range of colours, and some imitate ceramic tile designs. It is difficult to find completely plain colours: sheet vinyls are almost totally patterned, and even "plain" ranges of tiles are usually flocked or mottled. Durability is fair to good, depending on quality and installation, and

vinyl is reasonably resistant to water if it is properly fixed at joins and around edges. Slippery when wet, vinyls in bathrooms should not be polished.

Cork

Be sure to buy floor tiles—tiles sold for walls are too thin for floors. Unsealed tiles can be used quite effectively, or they can be finished with several coats of polyurethane. You can also buy tiles already coated with polyurethane or factory-sealed with a wax finish. Wax-finished tiles are the least slippery, but once tiles are sealed avoid extra polishing. The most hard-wearing cork tiles have a clear vinyl wear layer, but these can be slippery when wet.

Thicker types of tiles are not necessarily more hard-wearing, but offer a greater degree of resilience. A smooth, dry, level sub-floor is essential for laying cork; a timber floor will need a hardboard underlay. It is possible to lay cork tiles yourself, but careful cutting and butting together, plus an even application of adhesive, are essential.

Cork is durable and feels warm and pleasant. Its natural brown tones blend well with most furnishing colours, and particularly with well-sealed natural wood panelling and fitments.

Right: *a unique effect has been created for this floor by use of ingenious duck-boarding laid on a flat surface.*

Bottom right: *one of the most hygienic and splash-proof of bathroom floors, ceramic tiles are functional yet smart.*

Below: *this pebbled flooring gives a natural and open-air feel to the room, but requires good low-level heating.*

Soft floors

One of the surest ways to add luxury to a bathroom is to carpet the floor. The feel of soft, warm carpet pile under bare feet is sheer delight and, since bathrooms are not usually very large rooms, the cost of providing carpeting is not excessive. There are, however, snags. Inevitably, bathroom floors get wet, and a damp, soggy carpet quickly loses its foot-appeal. This makes wool or wool-blend carpets inadvisable because they are slow to dry. Instead, use quick-drying synthetics such as nylons, polyesters and polypropylenes.

Bathroom carpeting should never be secured around the edge; it may need to be turned back from time to time to allow the underside to dry. Many carpets with synthetic piles have foam back-

Above: *with carpeting on the floor and walls, and long curtains, this bathroom is invitingly warm and snug.*

Right: *ensconced in a bed of thick pile carpeting, this luxurious sunken bath is very appealing—but it is strictly for genteel bathers.*

ings that can retain unpleasant amounts of moisture in a bathroom unless exposed frequently to the air to dry. Tufted carpets with a foam backing can be loose-laid satisfactorily in small areas, but woven carpets are unsuitable in a bathroom because they usually need stretching and edge-fixing.

The most sensible course is to choose carpeting from one of the ranges now made especially for bathrooms. These have, for example, long, silky piles of nylon or polyester and nylon, with special rubber "waffle" backs to make them quick-drying. They come in a wide range of colours and can be loose-laid so that they can be taken up easily if the bathroom gets waterlogged. They can even be washed if they get grimy.

Loose-lay carpet tiles are also suit-

able for bathrooms. A bonded-pile surface will not seem as luxurious as a long, shaggy pile, but carpet tiles feel pleasant and warm underfoot and are easy to cut to fit around awkward pedestals. They can also be taken up and pegged on a line to dry.

Long-pile cotton carpeting, in the form of rugs in pastel and attractive deep-dyed shades, can be used as a close-

Above: *low-key beige carpeting blends perfectly with a creamy yellow decor.*

Top left: *what appears to be a plank and tile floor is, in fact, a warm rug.*

Right: *the bathroom is not usually the place for boldly patterned carpets, but this dynamic choice works very well.*

Below: *strips of inexpensive coir matting from India are a perfect accompaniment to cork wall tiles.*

fitting carpet. Leave the edges unsecured so that you can take the carpeting up to dry if it gets soaked. Cotton, being so absorbent, makes a particularly pleasant bathroom flooring.

Whatever carpeting you choose, if you know you are catering for a family of regular floor-flooders, it is wise to provide bathmats for use around the bath, shower and wash-basin areas.

Bathroom planning
Changes of level

Sunken bath-tubs are practically synonymous with the Sybaritic excesses of fallen civilizations. Unfairly so, because the major joy of immersing oneself in a sunken bath is the very simple pleasure of being able to reach out for towels, radios and newspapers without heaving oneself half out of the tub.

A bath-tub sunk into a platform gives the bather the same sensations without the structural headaches of carving holes in the floor. Simple steps leading to a raised area around the tub add design interest, practical safety considerations and even additional storage facilities.

Sinking the bath into the floor is quite a different problem—a bath-tub filled with water and a person or two can weigh up to half a ton. Acrylic is, of course, a much lighter material for baths than iron, and is an obvious choice for outsize baths on upper floors. In theory, a floor that can support an ordinary tub can be adapted to support a sunken one, but difficulties will arise if the weight is not correctly distributed through the floor on to the load-bearing wall. Remember that the view from your sunken bath will probably take in the underside of your wash-basin and WC unit, so tidy up their plumbing or box it in.

Home-made bath-tubs
It is quite feasible to make your own sunken bath without resort to expensive manufacturer's one-offs; and simple bathing pools lined with ceramic tiling or marine-grade plywood are certainly more pleasant to look at than bath-tubs of factory-formed plastic.

Right: *to give the illusion of a sunken bath where it would be impractical to hew into the floor, surround the bath with a stepped, tiled platform and add an extra dimension to the bathroom.*

Left: *clever use of space in a small bathroom. The angular ledges and steps create a wealth of visual interest. Smart ceramic tiles are an effective way to deal with overflows and splashings.*

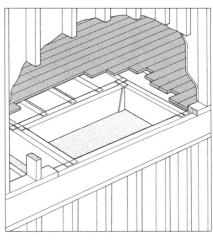

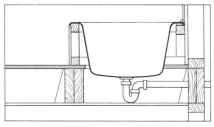

Above: *when sinking a bath, its weight needs to be carefully distributed. Floor joists need checking for strength, and supports should be built up around the lip of the bath to take the main burden.*

Above: *these steps, particularly useful for the elderly and the disabled, afford easy access to both bath and basin. They also provide handy extra seating.*

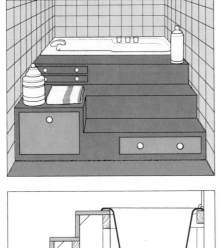

Above: *wide steps add interest and depth to the bathroom. They can also incorporate useful cupboards and shelves.*

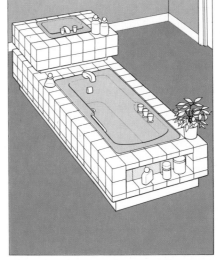

Above: *a broad ledge encasing the bath and wash-basin is useful for concealing ugly pipes and creates compact storage space. The bath surround makes a good place to perch on while drying.*

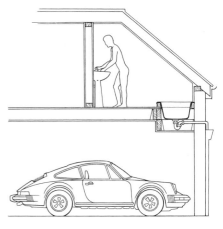

Above: *where headroom in the bathroom is severely restricted, a sunken bath may be the only feasible solution.*

189

Bathroom planning
Storage

Storage for the bathroom is frequently neglected. Often the only facility provided is an inadequate little cabinet, inconveniently placed, or a short, narrow shelf, placed so low over the wash-basin that anyone stooping to wash hair bangs their head. The result in all too many cases is that every available surface—tops of cisterns, ends of baths, edges of wash-basins—is pressed into service, crammed with a litter of face cloths and sponges, soaps and toothbrushes, pastes and powders and lotions and potions all mixed indiscriminately with cleaning cloths and liquids for the bath, wash-basin and WC.

The simple answer is to provide lots more storage. Your bathroom will look neater, work better and be safer. Where space is restricted, plenty of open shelving can cope satisfactorily with a great many items. Leave some shelves widely spaced to cope with tall bottles—you could use one of the adjustable shelving systems sold for living-rooms. Narrow shelves from 100 to 150 mm/4 to 6 in wide take up little room and are very useful.

If wall space is short, make the most of the space you have with a "ladder" of open shelves at right angles to the wall; this can divide two units, such as the wash-basin and WC. Suitable shelving materials include solid timber, painted or well sealed, and melamine-faced chipboard. The latter is particularly useful as it is sold already veneered in standard shelving widths; all you have to do is cut your shelves to the correct length. Glass is traditionally used for bathroom shelves, but it needs to be spotlessly clean to look good and, of course, it can shatter all too easily. Avoid storing glass bottles, jars and mugs over a china wash-basin—if they fall they could chip or crack the basin.

Make sure you have adequate storage space adjacent to the bath and wash-basin. The wide rims on modern baths tend to be used as shelf space, but there is a danger of knocking things off, so provide an accessible shelf for soap, sponge, nail brush, razor, manicure implements, shampoo, hair conditioner and, depending on your age and habits, bath toys, ashtray, drinks, even a good book or magazine. Professor Alexander Kira, pioneer of bathroom design, suggests that this shelf should have a minimum usable depth of 100 mm/4 in, a clear

height of 300 mm/12 in and a minimum length of 400 mm/16 in. He suggests that the wall alongside the bath is the best place for this shelf and that for comfort and safety it should be not more than 460 mm/18 in from the bottom of the tub, "at the shoulder height of the shorter segment of the population".

Similarly, Professor Kira has worked out that one person needs an absolute minimum of 930 sq cm/1 sq ft of storage space alongside the wash-basin. This is where wash-basins fitted into a broad counter-top come into their own.

A bathroom airing cupboard, fitted with wide shelves, provides excellent storage facilities. Hot-water pipes running through the cupboard should be exploited to keep reserves of towels, sheets and clothes well aired and invitingly warm. In larger bathrooms you may have space for further shallow cupboards, which will be handy for storing spare supplies such as lavatory paper and soap. Deeper cupboards or large pigeon holes can be used for storing towels, and sometimes it is possible to make a lift-up

This neat and simple Palaset storage system allows you to mix and match the modules to solve storage problems.

box section at the end of the bath. Covered with towelling, this makes a good place to dry a small child or for an adult to sit. Open shelves and pigeon holes can be screened with a roller blind if you do not want to fit cupboard doors.

There are on the market ranges of fitted bathroom furniture that provide more sophisticated provision for storage, but these tend to be expensive. An alternative is to look instead at ranges for other parts of the house. Wall cupboards sold for kitchens, for example, are often ideal for the bathroom. Whitewood ranges are not expensive and can be given attractive treatments with sealer, coloured stains or paint. There are also small cane and pine racks of shelves sold for living-rooms and kitchens which look very pretty in a bathroom, and hold more than the conventional single bathroom shelf. A row of cup-hooks fixed on the underside of a cupboard or shelf is

useful for face cloths and tooth mugs. A family with two or three small children needs to have at least half a dozen mugs in orbit around the bathroom.

Let your imagination roam free, and storage ideas will abound. Two- or three-tier hanging baskets will take general clutter. Brightly coloured vegetable racks can hold spare lavatory paper and soaps. A long towel rail can be fitted with hook-on bicycle baskets to take sponges and face cloths, while the rest of the rail is left for towels. Or deep shelves can be fitted with plastic washing-up bowls to hold towels. A floor-to-ceiling spring-loaded pole can be fitted with hooks for such things as robes, hot-water bottles and shower caps. Often the junk shop can provide small storage units which, stripped to the natural wood and sealed or brightly painted with gloss paint, can add a touch of personality to an otherwise rather bland room.

One very chic purveyor of bathroom accessories advertises a "make-up centre on wheels" fully fitted with all manner of plastic trays. You could equally well transform an old dinner trolley with bright paint and use plastic food containers with snap-on lids. Line the trolley shelves with plastic laminate for an extra-durable, cleanable finish. Exploit the storage possibilities of your bathroom door with hanging canvas pockets in which to store general odds and ends.

It is often possible to neaten the design of an old bathroom and add extra storage at the same time. Pipes can be disguised with a framework of narrow shelves. When boxing-in pipes, use the enclosed space for storage; even a depth of 100 mm/4 in can be put to use.

Medicines are traditionally stored in the bathroom, but arguably this is not the best place for them since children often use the bathroom unsupervised. Remember that even if you do not have young children yourself, your friends and relations may bring theirs when they visit. Why not keep emergency first-aid materials in the kitchen, and any tablets and medicines in the main bedroom? Drugs, if they are kept in the bathroom, should be stored well out of the reach of children. Lockable cabinets are inconvenient because the key either gets left in the lock, which defeats the purpose, or it gets mislaid, so it is better to choose a cabinet with a child-proof catch.

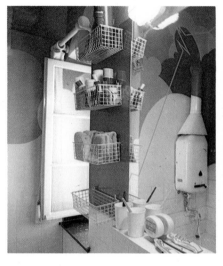

Above: *plastic-coated wire baskets hung on the wall accept all kinds of clutter, from face cloths to spare soaps.*

Left: *a high-level shelf saves valuable wall space. Clear plastic pockets mean accessories can be found at a glance.*

Right: *accessories are tucked away in a cabinet and a canvas wall pocket, so that no clutter interferes with the dramatic spaces in this dark, elegant room.*

Left: *in this well-lit bathroom, a clever high-level shelf for towels and a laminate work-top complement each other, solving storage problems.*

Above: *attractive and convenient, these ample shelves beside the bath are easily accessible and safe, even for a child reaching for towels and accessories.*

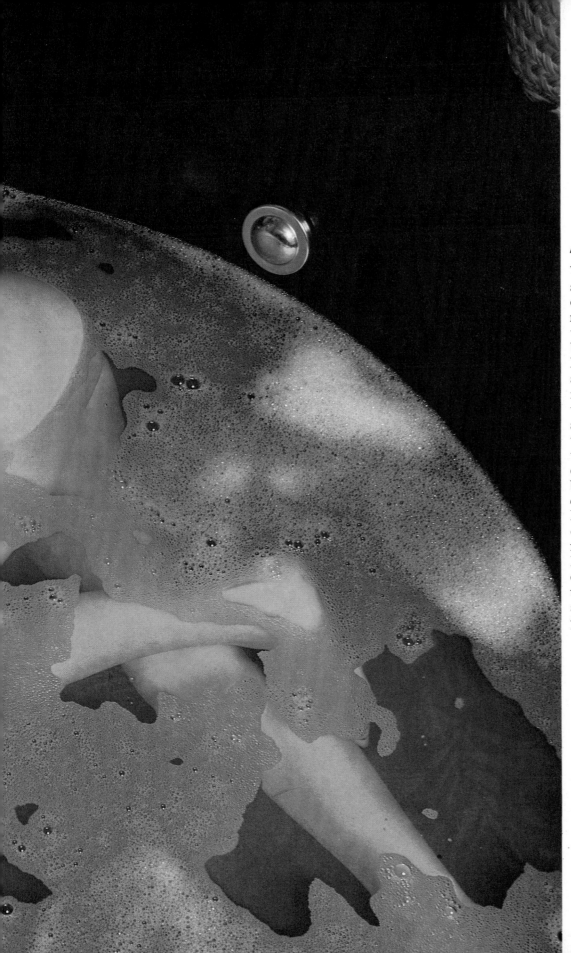

All about baths

When we look at the great pleasure the Greeks and Romans took in bathing, and the exuberance of bathroom designers and plumbers between the middle of the last century and the beginning of the 1930s, it is hard to understand why modern bathroom fittings are so small and mean. Practically the only stylish baths, basins, taps and showers available today are reproductions or renewals of old-fashioned fittings—and grand they are, too, as you will see, with flowing lines and generous proportions, created, I imagine, by talented sculptors and potters who really admired the curvacious stature of their Rubenesque clientèle. Perhaps it is because we have all become so weight-conscious that so many contemporary fittings have an emaciated look. Possibly, this very disregard of ample human contours may be the reason why run-of-the-mill fittings are so uncomfortable and impractical. But, luckily, there are some that are better than others, and this chapter will help you to choose the right bath, bidet, shower, WC, wash-basin and accessories to suit you and your family and make your bathroom a place of pleasure.

All about baths
History of the tub

No great technical problem is involved in making a man-sized dish in fireclay or metal, but either waterpipes or servants are needed to fill and empty it. Nearly 4,000 years ago, in the palace of Knossos in Crete, both were available. The Queen's bath, preserved to this day, is much like a modern tub: both shapes are dictated by the human module.

The Romans, preferring organized public bathing, do not seem to have favoured the solo tub, but after the

Minoan terracotta bath, about 1700 BC.

decline of Rome, most Europeans, if they bathed at all, used simple wooden tubs made by the coopers. Since the hot water, or hot stones to heat it, had to be brought from the kitchen fire, it was customary for the whole family to bathe together while the water remained hot. The bath was often a preliminary to love-making; a board across the tub might carry refreshment, and musicians could attend. Sometimes there was a discreet covering canopy or linen padding inside the tub.

Medieval bather: stained glass from an English manor house, about 1475.

In the 14th century, royalty, at least, boasted separate bathrooms: in London's Westminster Palace there was hot and cold running water, bronze taps, a wooden canopy to the bath, floor tiles and bath-mats. Common folk bathed only in the public hot-houses, known as stews, most of which were also brothels. When these were closed by Henry VIII because they helped to spread disease, public bathing died out in England, as it did in France for the same reason.

From then until late in the 18th century, bathing was primarily a treatment for invalids. A tub with hot water was seldom available except in large country houses having separate bath-houses built over streams or springs. Pepys's diary, covering nine years in the latter half of the 17th century, never mentions his having a bath, and Mrs Pepys apparently had only one, for which she went to a bath-house. Chatsworth, the seat in Derbyshire of the Dukes of Devonshire, was recorded in 1700 as having only one bathroom, but this was graced with marble walls, and a deep bath fitted with "2 locks to let in one hott, ye other cold water to attemper it as persons please". Dr Cheyne, an English hygienist writing in 1724, proposed a revolutionary idea when he advised people to take cold baths at home, three times a week.

The aristocracy of pre-revolutionary France were cleaner than is generally supposed. There were at least 100 bathrooms in the Palace of Versailles. Jacques François Blondel, architect to Louis XV, advised using two baths—one for washing and one for rinsing. Some enormous baths were made in marble, but copper, tin or varnished sheet-iron were more usual. Some baths had heaters attached, fuelled with charcoal or spirit, and some were fitted into elaborate wooden casings. Casanova's bath in Paris was portable, and stood at his bedside, with room for two. For the convenience of the bourgeoisie, the water-sellers of Paris carried bath-tubs in their carts and would deliver them, for a fee, complete with hot water.

At Queen Victoria's accession in 1837, there was no bathroom in Buckingham Palace, but eventually hot water was piped to the portable bath in her bedroom. The manufacturing boom which followed the Great Exhibition of 1851 brought with it a great output of metal baths for the middle classes, in a surprising variety of shapes: Lounge, Slipper, Sponge, Hip, Boot, Fountain, Sitz and Travelling baths.

Below: *Napoleon's bathroom, installed c. 1807, at Rambouillet, France.*

Lord Curzon's bath at Montacute, disguised by Jacobean panelling; 1915.

In 1851, a bath was installed in the White House, Washington, DC, though it is said that there was some opposition to the idea. George Vanderbilt's New York bathroom of 1855, had a marble dado, but the plumbing was all proudly revealed. This sophistication was exceptional: a survey of the 1880s shows that of dwellers in American cities, only one in six had a bath, and in 1895 not a single New York tenement had one.

When bathrooms first appeared in opulent British houses, they were converted bedrooms, unnecessarily large, with wooden furniture, heavy curtains, and even carpets. The architect Edwin Lutyens, who began to practise around 1895, built his first great country houses without bathrooms. When the purpose-built bathroom did appear, it was as a considerable status symbol.

At this time, there were sheet-metal baths, with elaborate mahogany casing carved like an altarpiece, including a top whose polish was all too vulnerable to hot water. The general alternative, a "porcelain" bath, did not remain long in favour. It was stoneware with a vitreous glaze—one great piece of crockery, heavy, expensive, and cold to the touch until it had noticeably cooled the water. The cast-iron bath arrived in about 1880, made with a flat rim, which was covered by wooden casing; the cast roll-rim came later. The enamels with which iron baths were decorated were a source of trouble. They were little more than ordinary house paint, and until the introduction of porcelain enamel around 1910, required constant renewing because the colours faded very quickly.

Porcelain enamel was not porcelain nor was it enamel. It was a hard, vitreous coating, akin to glass, fired on to the metal at high temperature. In most middle-class homes the bath was not cased in, but left open to view. Its exterior was often delightfully decorated with brightly coloured enamel paints stencilled on by hand.

Even servants were now allowed to bathe once a week, and in large houses several small bathrooms were preferred to one large one. The compact bath cell derives from American hotel practice. By 1920, the cast-iron single-shell bath, with the rim squared at the four corners so it could be built into rectangular spaces, was in full mass-production.

Lèse-majesté : French cartoon of Queen Victoria in a roll-rim bath, 1899.

Wood panelling gave way to more practicable materials for casing. The pressed steel bath, about a quarter of the weight of cast-iron, began to take over from about 1950, but had a competitor in the perspex bath. Coloured baths came into fashion: one manufacturer listed 72 colours, pink being so popular that it was offered in 22 shades.

The limit of compactness was reached in the prefabricated bathroom unit, but conversely, as economies recovered after World War II, shower baths proliferated in the USA and the spacious luxury bathroom reappeared. With circular and double baths, some with a shallow end for young children, the ideal of gourmet bathing appears to have been revived.

Right: *hand-decorated cast-iron baths made in Britain, c. 1900.*

Standard shapes and sizes

Understandably, perhaps, prospective bath-buyers are reluctant to climb in and out of baths, testing for size and comfort, but a dry run in the showroom is often the best way to find a bath that suits you. Standard ranges encompass a wide choice of sizes and a confusing variety of built-in contours, ledges and grab rails.

Comfort and safety: The bath-tub is considered by many cultures, notably the Arabs and the Slavs, to be less hygienic than the shower. This is because the bather lies soaking in his own dirty water, but it is this very lying at ease, suspended in warm water, that most people find so relaxing. To be truly comfortable the bath should be gently contoured at one end to support the body —many baths have too steep a slope and are too small. Most people will need a bath at least 168 cm/66 in long and preferably 183 cm/72 in. A seat built into the bath design makes washing movements (particularly of the feet) much easier.

Research has shown that people getting into the shallower US baths tend to maintain an upright position and step into the tub. A vertical grab rail will add considerably to the safety of this operation, providing it is securely fixed. Bathers negotiating the sides of the higher baths more common in the UK tend to bend over, so horizontal grab rails incorporated into the design of the bath or firmly fixed to the wall are a safety point.

The base of the bath should be as flat as possible with a minimum amount of curvature between the bath sides and bottom. A non-slip area is useful if the bath is to be used for showering, or by children or the elderly. Rubber non-slip mats with suction pads will make baths less slippery, but also less pleasant to linger in.

Bath panels: It is common practice to fit a bath against a wall, and frequently into a corner. There is no reason why baths should not be free standing, although this arrangement requires considerably more space. Matching removable side and end panels are available

This extra-long bath allows plenty of room for an adult to relax in or for two children to play in. The solid surround makes a good ledge next to the wall and, on the outside, a comfortable place to perch on while drying off.

Acrylic bath-tubs can be made in dark and interesting colours—at a price.

An unusual colour, such as this peacock blue, enlivens the standard bath.

This broad ledge gives an extra dimension to bathing for both adults and children.

Barry Bucknell's bath is designed to use a third of the hot water of a normal bath.

from the bath manufacturers as extras (they need to be removable to allow access to taps and waste).

Tap positions: Taps are normally positioned at the end of the bath, along with the waste. The waste can be a simple plug and chain, or a more sophisticated chainless "pop-up" type controlled by a knob or lever at the end, or even at the side, of the bath. Many baths offer a choice of tap arrangements: some have no holes and the taps are wall-mounted, others have outlets sited in the corner or separated into two parts—the water controls at the side, convenient to the reclining bather, and the spout at the foot.

Colour: Manufacturers of bathroom fittings in the UK have an agreed range of colours so that different items such as baths, WCs, tiles and so on from different manufacturers will always match, but it is unlikely that different materials such as ceramic and plastic will match exactly. White is the cheapest "colour", then the familiar pastel pinks and blues. More adventurous colours—Pampas and Avocado, for example, sometimes referred to as Group II—are more expensive, and special "fashion" colours cost even more.

In the USA, each of the five major

Vogue Elysian bath in porcelain enamelled cast iron, featuring a safety grab rail, and centrally fixed taps so that the bather can enjoy the luxury of adjusting the water temperature without having to double up to the other end.

sanitary manufacturers has an individual colour range; there are no industry coordinated colours. In general, each of these manufacturers provides around five standard colours and four to six premium or high-fashion shades. At present the colours include blue, green, tan, gold and bone. In addition to the major manufacturers, there are about twelve smaller china producers who make their products in several of the major manufacturers' standard colours.

Bath sizes: In the UK, the British Standard for baths is 1,700 mm long by 700 mm wide/67 × 27½ in. Many other sizes are available, including, for example, metric lengths of 1,500, 1,600 and 1,800 mm, and Imperial lengths of 60, 66 and 72 in. Common widths are between 700 and 800 mm/27½ in and 31 in, with heights commonly ranging from 450 to 550 mm/18 to 22 in. In the USA, bath-tubs are commonly 60 in long, 30 to 32 in wide and 14 to 16 in high.

British	USA
GROUP 1	**STANDARD**
White	Bone
Turquoise	Avocado
Sky blue	Fawn
Pink	Regency
Primrose	Gold
GROUP 2	**SECONDARY**
Avocado	Brown
Pampas	Colonial blue
Honeysuckle	Marble
"FASHION" SHADES	
	Deep Red
	Blue
	Green
	Brown

All about baths
Special shapes and sizes

Baths have changed remarkably little since the Minoans savoured the delights of a long, hot soak; certainly the shape is the same, and the process of making baths has altered little since their revival as necessities rather than luxuries at the end of the last century. Cast-iron baths are still produced in the traditional manner, with a little help from electric-powered tools. The biggest development in recent years has been the introduction of the plastic bath, which is far more versatile in shape. Exactly which type of bath suits your requirements will depend on whether you are looking primarily for longevity, unusual shape or colour, a custom-made bath or one of the traditional designs.

Cast iron, the traditional material for baths, has become expensive but is very rigid, stable and durable. The iron is, in fact, an alloy of pure iron, silicon and carbon with small amounts of other elements, cast in moulds of whatever shape is required. A thick coating of porcelain enamel made from powdered coloured glass is fused at very high temperatures to the inside surfaces of the bath. The result is a bath with a thick, smooth, glazed coating which has very good resistance to staining and general wear, but which can be chipped under heavy impact.

Pressed steel is less expensive than cast iron, and is lighter and easier to handle during installation. Strong, rigid baths are pressed out of sheet steel, which can vary in thickness according to the size and the quality of the bath. The steel is finished with a coating of ground glass, pigments and other materials fused together under intense heat to become the smooth, glossy surface known as vitreous enamel. This coating is not as thick as porcelain enamel, but its wearing properties are similar. It is possible to obtain bath enamel paints in white and in a limited range of colours for re-surfacing old metal baths. Alternatively, you may be able to find a firm to come and do this professionally for you.

Plastic baths are a major modern development, for their comparative ease of manufacture brings colours and adventurous shapes within the pocket of the average householder. Light to install, plastic baths come in good colours with a glossy surface finish. They can easily incorporate moulded seats and back-rests, and also inset trays for soap and face cloths. Plastic baths are warm to the touch and resistant to chipping from knocks, but they are susceptible to scratching and their glossy finish can become dulled with rough use (although in some cases it is possible to restore the finish). If you are a compulsive smoker, stay away from plastic baths because they are extremely vulnerable to cigarette burns, which can cause an ugly, irremovable scar.

There are two kinds of plastic baths, acrylic and GRP (glass reinforced polyester). Acrylic baths are shaped from heated sheets of acrylic plastic (e.g. Perspex) which are vacuum-formed over a mould. To support the bath, a rigid framework or cradle is supplied and it is most important that the maker's instructions for fixing it to the wall and floor are carefully and thoroughly followed. The colour of an acrylic bath goes right through the thickness of the bath. Although a wide range is available, makers are limited to the colours they can obtain in sheet form from the plastics manufacturers.

GRP (glass re-inforced polyester) baths are made from hand-applied layers of glass fibres built up on a mould and held together with coatings of polyester resin. Colour pigments are added by the manufacturer and virtually any shade is possible, so GRP baths can be custom-made to match any other bathroom fitting. In some cases, however, the colour may be only on the top layers of the bath. GRP is stronger and more rigid than acrylic, and is used for larger and more unusually shaped baths. If the bath is damaged, it is often possible for specialist repairs to be carried out by the manufacturer.

Out-of-the-ordinary baths: Study the catalogues and you will find a whole host of bathing options. To fit into a limited space, there are small baths such as high-sided versions of the old-fashioned sitz or hip bath, and even oriental soaking tubs. There are also baths designed to go across corners; these take up a lot of room but look splendid. Free-standing baths will also take up more space, and the plumbing may well prove expensive. The more unusually shaped baths are generally made from plastic: take your pick from a wide selection ranging from clover-leafed baths to heart shapes and from baths for two to the ultimate extravaganza of a four-poster bath.

Above: *a bathing room in a Japanese mountain resort maintains the oriental sense of order, calm and spaciousness with a circular sunken bath, which fills with water from the hot springs below.*

Top right: *what could be more perfect for a bubble bath than a giant champagne glass? Bubbles will coyly cover the bather at the top, but the clear acrylic bowl will not hide an imperfect behind.*

Above: *a tubby bath designed with space and comfort in mind; the bath's contours ensure a luxurious soak.*

Top left: *ultra-modern, but designed with typical Italian flair, this circular glass-reinforced polyester bath incorporates a shower unit, heated towel rails, shelves for soap and scent, and a sliding shower door.*

Left: *even when the only space for a bath is a corner, no problem is posed, as this neat plastic model proves.*

Bath care

To keep a bath looking as good as new clean it regularly, following the manufacturer's instructions if they are available. This prevents a build-up of marks and stains which will be difficult to remove.

The best time to clean a bath is when it is still warm, so encourage members of the family to do their own cleaning. Keep a cloth and appropriate cleaning products handy so that nobody has any excuse for leaving a high-tide mark of unsightly scum round the bath.

Using bath salts softens the water and helps to prevent scum. Make sure they are thoroughly dissolved before you step into the bath—partially dissolved bath salts, with their gritty texture, are not only uncomfortable to sit on but can scratch the surface of the bath. Harsh scouring powders will also spoil the surface. Instead, use one of the many cream cleaners, which are gentle but effective.

A bath can easily be damaged through thoughtlessness. Do not, for example, use it for washing large, sharp-edged items such as venetian blinds, or for developing photographs in chemical solutions. If you must stand in or on the bath to open a window or to clean or paint the ceiling, remove your shoes first or wear clean-soled plimsolls.

Enamelled baths: Special stain removers are available for use on badly stained enamelled baths, but always proceed with caution: try them on a small, unobtrusive area first, such as under one of the taps. Alternatively, try using a paste made from a mixture of cream of tartar and hydrogen peroxide. Apply the paste with a nylon brush, scrub vigorously, then rinse off.

To remove brown stains caused by iron in the water, use a lemon cut in half and sprinkled with cooking salt or white vinegar. Rub the stain with the lemon, then rinse the area you have been working on. Repeat the process if the stain proves to be particularly stubborn.

Green copper stains can sometimes be shifted with a solution of soapy water and a little ammonia. Scrub the mark, then rinse thoroughly.

If the stains are particularly obstinate and cannot be removed by any of these methods, make up a solution of one part oxalic acid to twenty parts of water. Oxalic acid is highly poisonous, so use it with extreme care and only as a last resort. Be sure to wear rubber gloves, and keep children and animals well out of the way. Apply with a soft, clean cloth, allow the acid to sink in for a minute or two, then rinse off thoroughly.

Plastic baths: For everyday cleaning use only a little detergent on a cloth that has been moistened with warm water. If you live in a hard-water area, you may find it necessary to use a cream cleaner from time to time in order to shift lingering stains.

Small scratches and dull patches can be removed with metal polish: apply when the surface of the bath is dry, then rinse thoroughly. For deeper scratches, rub with fine wire wool before applying metal polish.

Substances such as paint stripper, nail varnish, varnish remover and some dry-cleaning fluids will cause damage if they are allowed to come into contact with a plastic bath. Cigarette burns are ugly and difficult to remove, so make sure your bathroom has an ashtray, within easy reaching distance of the bath, for resident and visiting smokers.

Distinctive baths

In the pre-World War II days when A. A. Milne wrote the poem containing the immortal line "Wasn't it fun in the bath tonight", baths were almost uniformly white and dull and the only fun came from such in-bath activities as playing with rubber ducks. Today, however, bathers of all ages can indulge their fantasies on a more sophisticated level. Baths are made in a wide variety of materials that range from regal marble through stainless steel to wood, with its basic, back-to-nature appeal. They can be raised on a dais, lowered into the floor Roman style, even placed outside under the stars.

Most baths that are out of the ordinary are also expensive, but it is still possible to buy old-fashioned, tapless tin tubs, which must be filled with the aid of a bucket. Laborious though this is, it could appeal to anyone with rose-coloured ideas about "the good old days" or with a desire to return to a fairly primitive life-style.

At the other end of the scale there are exotic baths made of glass-reinforced polyester (GRP). This modern material can be used quite safely for large, free-standing baths in shapes such as circles, ovals and even four-posters, without loss of rigidity. GRP comes in a virtually limitless colour range and can be given finishes that resemble other materials—the smooth gloss of enamel, for example—or sparkling metallic finishes. One UK manufacturer of exclusive fittings offers a choice of 36 metallic "colours", including several golds, purple, emerald and brown. Crushed oyster and mussel shells are used for a special, lustrous mother-of-pearl finish.

Using a specially developed process, decoration can be incorporated into GRP baths, either all over or in borders around the edges and such features as the waste hole. Designs include flower patterns or laurel wreaths, Greek key patterns or fleurs-de-lis. You can even have your own initials, monogram or—surely the ultimate bathroom status symbol—your family crest in gold or silver. On the smooth, glossy finishes the effect is similar to hand-painted French porcelain. But the trouble, alas, with plastic and GRP baths is that no matter what they look like or cost, they always feel disconcertingly cheap and the surface scratches easily.

A wooden bath can be a fairly short-term luxury—most wood dislikes water and will eventually warp, crack or rot. Teak is the best wood to use, but it must be bathed in regularly or it will dry out and split. On the west coast of America, wooden tubs situated outdoors on a patio are becoming increasingly popular. The bath is kept filled with freshly circulating hot water, so you can jump in at any time with your family or your friends and neighbours, depending on your modesty threshold.

Free-standing wooden bath-tubs have been used in Japan for centuries, but are an unusual sight in the West. If you wish to install one indoors, make sure your bathroom floor is waterproof, so that any leakages that occur are retained within the bathroom. It may also be a good idea to put a drain in the bathroom floor.

The Japanese call this type of free-standing tub a *furo*. In the USA, authentic *furos* are available from hardware stores specializing in Japanese products. Japanese ritual dictates that the bather sits on a wooden stool called a *koshikake* and washes thoroughly with water from a small wooden bucket called an *oke*. Clean water from the *oke* is used for thorough rinsing. Next, the bather steps into the *furo* (the more slowly you enter the water, the greater the heat you will be able to tolerate) for a long soak. The whole operation is a ritualistic ceremony designed to relax the body and create order in the mind.

It is also possible to have a built-in wooden bath. The advantage of this is that it can be much larger than most standard baths made in other materials, but considerable care must be taken to ensure that the water cannot leak out. The designer of one such bath made of redwood found it took 20 coats of polyurethane varnish to make it entirely waterproof. The owner of another tub made of cedar coated the inside with clear fibreglass resin with good results. Check your local plumbing regulations before deciding on a wooden bath. In some areas of the USA, wooden baths do not meet with local authority approval, although you can always appeal against the decision.

For fostering delightful delusions of grandeur, nothing can match a marble bath. Marble comes mainly from Italy, but also from Belgium, Spain and Greece. Patterns and colours range from pure white with grey mottling, through russet

and white to a richly dramatic black and gold. You will need to check with a specialist contractor that your bathroom floor can bear the considerable weight of a bath made of slabs of marble which may be 19 mm/$\frac{3}{4}$ in thick. Marble baths can also be built up around a basic framework of breeze or Thermalite blocks.

An architect or specialist contractor could also design for you a bath lined with ceramic tiles or mosaic. As with marble, it is essential to employ people experienced in installing custom-built baths: faulty work could endanger the bather and may result in leaks that could damage not only your decorations in other rooms but also the basic structure of the house.

If you cannot afford the luxury of a custom-made creation, do not despair—it is possible to enclose standard baths in marble, wood, tile or mosaic surroundings, which will lift your bathroom way out of the ordinary.

Left and far right: *free-standing wooden tubs have been in use in Japan and China for centuries, and now that they are available in the West there is no reason why they shouldn't catch on. They are attractive, perfect for smaller bathrooms, and economical to use as they take less water than standard baths.*

Right: *since the time of ancient Greece and Rome, marble has been a symbol of beauty and luxury. Simplicity is the key in the design of marble baths: the beauty of the stone should be unrivalled by outlandish design.*

Below: *the standard modern bath would look totally out of keeping in this bathroom, so this bath has been specially designed to blend into its environment. The natural stone used matches the old stone walls, and the oblong shape of the bath is in perfect harmony with the archway and window.*

Above: *this is the ideal bath for people who love to sit and read in the tub. Steps on the left lead you gently into the water, and the submerged seat on the right has water outlets above and around it to warm you with more hot water while you finish your long novel.*

Steam, sauna and whirlpool

Specialized ways to cleanse and revitalize the body have been popular for centuries. The Greeks, Romans, Turks, Russians and American Indians all indulged in the luxury of steam bathing. In Scandinavia, the sauna was popular more than a thousand years ago. Only comparatively recently, however, has it become possible to enjoy such indulgence in the privacy of our own homes.

Steam baths: Steam opens and thoroughly cleanses the pores and invigorates the circulation. Today, steam-bath units can be incorporated into any bath or shower that can be enclosed to keep the steam in. A typical kit has a compact electric steam generator which can be located anywhere in the house as long as it is not more than 15 m/50 ft away from the bathroom, and the steam bath itself consumes very little water and electricity. A timer can be set for anything up to a 30-minute onslaught; this should be topped with a cold shower if you are preparing to go out, or a warm shower if you are going to sleep after it. A reservoir in the steam outlet allows you to add whatever fragrance you like to your steam bath, including ambrosia.

Saunas, by contrast, rely for their effect on dry heat. This makes the body perspire copiously, cleansing the skin, and works like a massage on tired muscles. In Finland, the sauna is traditionally contained in a moisture-absorbing pine cabin beside a lake or fjord. Also traditionally, the participants beat themselves with birch branches or paddles until their skin is red and tingling, then dive into the cold lake or fjord or, in winter, roll around in the snow to tone up their circulation.

Somewhat less Spartan domestic saunas are now available in kit form for installation both inside and outside the home—although you'll have to provide your own birch branches. You can install one in your basement, attic, garage, playroom, spare bedroom or in your garden. The walls and ceiling panels are made from Finnish pine insulated with rockwool, the door is double glazed and fresh air is provided through adjustable vents. A kit comes complete with the traditional sauna stove of heated rocks (thermostatically controlled) on to which you

ladle water from the sauna pail when the dry heat becomes too intense. In lieu of an icy plunge after the sauna, a cold shower completes the ritual.

Whirlpool baths give the body a soothing massage by means of "hydro-air" jets delivered from nozzles set at various points around the inside of the bath. Water is drawn from the bath, mixed with air, then delivered back again as a fast-moving stream of aerated water. The number of nozzles varies according to the model.

Whirlpool bath units are available in a variety of sizes, colours and shapes, including round, cloverleaf and double models, and resemble conventional baths apart from the adjustable nozzles around the sides and ends. The baths tend to be wider and deeper than standard to allow the complete immersion necessary to get full benefit from the massage. Automatic timers are available to control the length of the massage.

"Environment": Perhaps the ultimate in luxury is Kohler's "Environment", designed to be a new dimension in living. Pressing the warm-ambience button, you enter a teak enclosure through a sliding acrylic door. Once inside you choose your "environment" at the touch of a button on the electronic control panel. This ingenious device can simulate anything from tropical rain to Baja sun and from jungle steam to warm chinook winds. These effects are achieved with four heat lamps, four sun lamps, six 24-carat gold electroplated spray heads, a steam generator and two warm-air circulating systems—all of which are operated from a low-voltage power source. Every cycle is electronically timed and interior digital read-outs indicate time lapses.

The cabin has a porthole through which you can look out at a terrarium, an aquarium or the outside world. To further enhance this, you are offered the options of a stereo AM/FM radio and eight-track tape player, air-filled bed with pillow—and an *art nouveau* painting silk-screened on to the translucent back panel.

Top right: *Kohler's "Environment" harnesses the elements to give varying degrees of heat and steam.*

Right: *the whirlpool bath gives a soothing massage with underwater jets.*

Left: *both young and old find the dry heat of the sauna beneficial, and domestic saunas are easily installed.*

History of the shower

No doubt early Man, about whom it is safe and all too easy to generalize, refreshed himself at times under a jetting spring or a waterfall, but notable examples of natural shower baths are sparse until Charles Dickens contrived one under a 150-foot/50-metre fall from the cliffs at Bonchurch on the Isle of Wight. He was known to boast that the drop was 500 feet/167 metres, but even had this

Young boys play under their natural shower bath, the Fogaafu waterfall on Upolu Island, Western Samoa.

been true, he would have been far outclassed by an American lady who took a shower under Niagara Falls—though not, we may safely assume, under the main cataract.

In ancient Egypt, water being scarce, artificial showers of a kind were provided by pouring water from vases. At Tel-el-Amarna, such a shower bath dating from 1350 BC had splashbacks and a shallow trough to stand in, holding only an inch or two of water. The dirty water—too precious to waste—flowed into a sunken vessel to be stored up for subsequent use in and around the palace.

A lady of ancient Thebes, aided by her attendants, is showered from a vase.

Ancient vase design: women showering in streams issuing from animals' heads.

An Etruscan vase painting shows a shallow bath surrounded by Doric columns, each carrying a spout in the form of an animal head. The pipe connecting the spouts provides a convenient rail for the bathers' clothes.

Medieval London had piped water, but until the late 18th century the supply was rationed, few households had more than one tap, and shower baths would not have been permitted. The earliest London example occurs in 1812, when the Lord Mayor, living in the bathless Mansion House, asked the Common Council to install at least a shower. He had to pay for it himself, "inasmuch as the want thereof has never been complained of". Shower baths featured largely in the water cure establishments, but only as a medical treatment, and it is evident that to most patients the idea was unfamiliar.

One proprietor wrote:

"It is no rare thing to see a subject who at this first shower betrays actual terror, shouts, struggles, runs away, experiences frightening suffocation and palpitation; and it is not rare to hear him say, after a few moments, 'so that's all it is'."

Some doctors held that for "white-collar" workers, cold showers were dangerous: by stimulating the blood supply to the head they tended to induce apoplexy; whereas "a navvy, or other muscular machine, with a torpid brain" might take them with advantage.

The British Public Baths and Wash Houses Acts introduced from 1846 warm showers for "the labouring classes" at twopence a turn, including the use of a towel. In 1850, the *Illustrated London News* proposed that "Cleansing Stations of corrugated iron should be situated in the street, to the end that passers-by might repeatedly be encouraged to use them"; these were to be showers. Such curious structures did eventually appear, 40 years on, not in London but in Berlin.

The domestic shower bath of the 1850s stood in a recess or corner of the bedroom. It was a fixture used in conjunction with the ordinary metal tub or hip bath: an overhead tank holding about five gallons was supported on metal legs, one of which was a feed pipe and another a drain pipe. Water was carried upstairs and put into the bath, then raised into the tank by a fixed hand-pump. After use, the water was again pumped into the overhead tank. Finally it ran down via the drain pipe and a tap into a bucket. Among the shower-hats worn, the most common one (often illustrated in *Punch*, the humorous magazine) was a tall, pointed affair reminiscent of the Spanish Inquisition. One ingenious inventor devised a hat with a broad, concave, perforated brim which itself formed the shower—one had only to pour water into it from a jug.

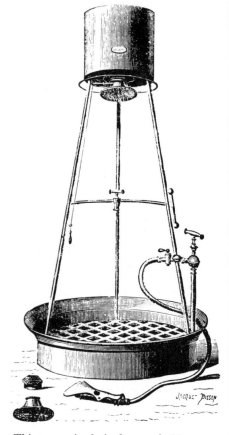

Griffith's patent chair shower, 1859.

This pressurized air shower of 1889 combined overhead shower and hand spray fed from a pump.

The glass shower cabinet, or tub screen, arrived in England from the USA around 1930, and in its more elaborate forms—gold plated, perhaps—became a dominant feature of some prestige bathrooms. Let it be hoped that such cabinets were never so waterproof as might be supposed from the famous Peter Arno cartoon, in which the closed door and the open tap have both jammed; the bather, fully submerged, signals frantically to his wife outside, but what will happen if she does manage to open the door?

But Ogden Nash, the American poet, deserves the last word on showers:
"Some people are do-it-some-other-
    timers and other people are
    do-it-nowers,
"And that is why manufacturers keep
    on manufacturing both bathtubs
    and showers."

Incorporated into this late Victorian bath, a shower enclosure provides spray both from above and from the sides.

A cold shower is of course a character test: Mrs Disraeli, the 19th-century British Prime Minister's wife, remarked that "Dizzy" had infinite moral but no physical courage: she always had to pull the operating chain for him.

In upper-class bathrooms of the 1880s, which were usually converted bedrooms, the imposing hooded bath had a carved mahogany shower cabinet with hinged doors. The shower ran hot or cold, a strong jet or a fine spray. By 1900, cheaper popular models made of sheet zinc had a semicylindrical shower recess, double-shelled and perforated inside to give an overall spray. When compact bathrooms, built as such, began to appear in modest homes, the shower became a simple, overhead rose, set over the bath or over its own shallow trough. A circular overhead ring carried a waterproof curtain of oiled silk. One ingenious variation was to have this ring as a waterpipe, perforated on the inner side.

Singing the praises of a newly invented shower stand, this charming painting by M. Reutlinger appeared as an advertisement in the French magazine Le Panorama Paris *in the late 1890s. In the home, this fitting would be curtained.*

Art deco shower extravaganza, designed by Delamarre for the executive suite in the Chanin Building, New York, 1920s.

Showers 1

Taking a shower is one of the quickest and cheapest ways of getting clean. Children usually love showering, and the elderly often find that stepping in and out of a shower is easier and safer than clambering in and out of a bath. Showering is also economical in terms of both time and money (five or six showers can be taken with the hot water needed for one bath), and is considered to be more hygienic than soaking in the tub because soap and grime are constantly rinsed away by clean running water.

There are many places where a shower can be installed other than the bathroom: under the stairs, for example, or in a bedroom, off a kitchen or on a landing. A shower that is not situated in the main bathroom eases the demand on an already busy room. Modern shower kits and cabinets are relatively simple to set up, but ask the advice of a plumber at an early stage: the type of shower you choose depends largely on the availability of existing plumbing at the proposed site for the fitting.

Basic requirements

To operate satisfactorily, many types of shower require hot and cold water supplies to be of equal pressure. Usually this is not a problem, as the hot-water tank in most domestic systems is supplied by the cold-water tank and will therefore be at the same pressure. The height between the bottom of the cold-water tank and the shower head must be at least 1 m/ 39 in, but preferably double. This height is referred to as the "head of water"; the greater the head of water, the greater the pressure of the spray. When the head of water is too low, a booster pump can sometimes be installed, or it might be possible to raise the height of the cold-water tank.

Ideally, a shower's cold-water supply should flow directly from the cold-water tank, and the connection for hot water should be made as close as possible to the hot-water tank. This is so that the pressure of water reaching the shower will not be lowered too much, if at all, by other taps being turned on and off around the house.

If your existing plumbing proves unsuitable for a conventional shower installation, there are models that take water directly from the mains via an instantaneous water heater fixed adjacent to the shower head. This type of unit will require plumbing into the mains water supply and careful wiring by someone who knows what he is doing. You will not need a tank, but remember that as you increase the temperature the water pressure may decrease.

Choosing a location

If the shower is to be mounted over the bath, you will need curtains or a screen to prevent the water from flooding the rest of the room. Shower curtains are available in a variety of waterproof fabrics, and tubular frames for curtains are sold in kit form. Screens are available in plain or textured plastics and in toughened glass. Soft plastic screens can be folded back, concertina-fashion. The bath may be completely surrounded with shower panels, or it can simply have a folding screen at one end.

Shower trays for separate shower cubicles are usually made from enamelled cast-iron or pressed steel, moulded plastic, fibre-glass or glazed fire-clay, in various sizes and a wide choice of colours.

The tray needs to be completely stable, with watertight seals between tray and wall. The cubicle can be surrounded by a curtain or a more permanent panelled structure, with a folding or sliding panel as a door.

If the shower is fitted into a recess or a small room, the wall should be waterproofed with tiles or perhaps mosaic. Prefabricated shower compartments, complete with trays, are available in moulded plastics or in steel. These units, often in kit form, can be installed in a bedroom or on a landing. One ingenious model has a shower head that can be attached by means of a magnet to any part of the cabinet. Cabinets with tops will contain steam and prevent damage to furnishings from condensation.

For a feeling of well-being, shower in the open air. To get even closer to nature, share the cubicle with a tree.

Showing how simple it is to install a shower: a pole-hung curtain, a tray and just one fixture are all you need.

Above: *elegant, glass-surrounded shower incorporated into the bath. The dazzling chrome fittings are left well exposed to give an unusual scaffolding effect.*

Top right: *life is made easier with a sunken shower tray to contain splashes and a generous shelf within the shower enclosure to hold all you need.*

Right: *a shower can be fitted anywhere in the house—even the conservatory.*

Far right: *this simplest of showers suits the stark design of the bathroom.*

Left: *stereo shower jets beam down into this surreal cubicle. Stacked boulders create a water-baby's fantasy rock pool.*

There are shower fittings to suit all purposes and all pockets. The simplest fitting to install is one that is combined with and controlled by the taps on your bath. A special knob or lever diverts the water from the bath to the shower head, and existing taps can easily be replaced with this type of fitting. Choose a model with a lever that returns automatically to the "bath" position after use or you will get soaked the next time you run a bath. With a more sophisticated version you can adjust the temperature of the water independent of the flow, so that you can turn off the shower to soap yourself and then turn it back on without disturbing the temperature.

Some showers are controlled by thermostatic valves that will maintain the water at a selected temperature, regardless of normal household fluctuations in supply. Some are fitted with an automatic cut-out to stop the flow if the supply fails or drops below a certain pressure. This type of shower usually has two controls: one governs the temperature and the other governs the flow. These controls can be separate knobs, concentric wheels or a single lever that can be moved from side to side to control the temperature and up and down to increase or decrease the flow.

Some shower fittings have a single on/off control, incorporating cold, tepid and hot settings as a safety feature (when there are two separate controls for temperature and flow, it is possible, even for a child, to turn the temperature control to maximum and then to turn on the flow, leading to severe scalding).

Shower heads
A fixed shower head can be installed above the user or at shoulder level. Many people prefer shoulder height because the hair doesn't get wet, but if you want a thorough drenching without stooping, the shower head must be above you.

Some shower heads are adjustable to vary the angle of the spray. A hand-held spray on a flexible tube can be positioned on wall brackets at various heights to cater for the whole family; although it doesn't look as streamlined as a fixed shower head, and it is possible to damage or twist the flexible tube, which disturbs the flow of the water, the detachable fitting is versatile and convenient. It can also allow you to rinse your hair at an adjacent wash-basin.

More than a shower
For shower addicts who want to move a step further than conventional showering, two specialized types of shower are available.

The electronic impulse shower, despite looking uncannily like the first showers invented at the turn of the century, is a relatively new idea in body care. The makers claim that high-powered jets of alternating hot and cold water have a therapeutic effect on both body and mind. Bursts of warm to hot water alternate with cold, with the cold phases gradually becoming more prolonged. This forces the pores of the skin to open and close, stimulating the circulation and releasing dirt, which is rinsed away. The water jets are said to act like a massage on tired muscles and to tone up the circulation and the skin.

If your bathroom is already crowded, a free-standing cabinet is available fully equipped with an electronic impulse shower. It contains four vertical tubes regularly pierced to release a strong spray of water, plus two adjustable high-level spray arms. Virtually the whole body is enveloped in water jets. There is also an overhead shower and a hand shower, so that you can use the unit for an ordinary shower whenever you wish. The pressure of the water may be boosted, where necessary, by a powerful pump, since a balanced hot and cold water supply is required at a constant pressure of 6.5 kg per sq cm/29 lb per sq in (such a pressure is seldom available domestically in the UK).

The temperature of the hot water is adjustable and is then thermostatically controlled. A transistorized pulse generator fixes the bursts of hot water at two seconds, but the bursts of cold can be adjusted to last between one-fifth of a second and ten seconds.

A virtually identical electronic impulse shower unit, without the cabinet, can be mounted on the wall over a bath or in a suitable enclosure. Running costs for this type of shower are about 50 per cent higher than those of a conventional shower, but it is still cheaper than drawing off a tankful of expensively heated water for a bath.

The shower massage is a shower head that delivers water in a series of rapid pulses that range from 800 to 9,000 per minute, for a slow or fast massage. The unit is available in two basic types: those to be wall mounted and those to be held in the hand. It is claimed that water issuing in bursts, rather than in a continuous stream, has an invigorating effect on the user, that it tones the skin and helps to revive tired muscles.

Above: *a sophisticated reproduction ensemble by Czech and Speke.*

Above: *looking like oversized microphones, this colourful pair are the latest design in hand-held shower heads.*

Left: *shower heads with a difference to deliver an invigorating water massage, toning the skin and muscles.*

Above: *an electronic impulse shower in action. Alternating flashes of hot and cold water have a therapeutic effect.*

Above: *a very simple unit, with the streaming translucent shower curtain providing a waterfall effect. The taps are outside the shower area, but within reach.*

Top right: *cleverly designed shower enclosure with mirrors, wall-hung shower head and tiled, sloping floor.*

Right: *a lesson in utilizing the most improbable spaces is learnt by this shower room with its wall-hung or hand-held fitting and vertical wash-basin.*

Left: *a neat shower fitting with a particularly long hose so that even though it is centrally positioned, hair can be easily washed while lying in the bath.*

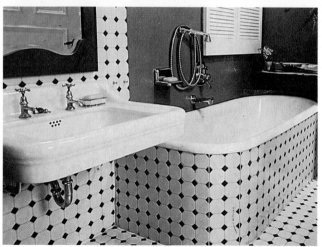

Showers al fresco

A shower taken out-of-doors in warm weather is an immensely pleasurable experience. It is the best way to clean up after messy jobs like heavy gardening, and stops you from bringing dirt into the house. It is a good way, too, to cool off in very hot weather—the next best thing to having a swim. Children, especially, enjoy showering in the garden.

An outside shower can be far less complicated than a normal bathroom shower. There is no need to worry about providing a watertight compartment, and privacy can be provided by a simple screen—but remember that if your garden is overlooked by neighbouring houses, people will be able to see you from above as well as from the side, so you may want to provide a top screen as well as side ones.

Your outside shower can be run from your mains water supply or you can use one of the portable types featured in camping catalogues. With some models, a simple hand pump is used to start a siphonic action: this is controlled by the person taking the shower and gives a gentle spray. A more sophisticated version is powered by a portable 12-volt battery. A "telephone-type" handset and 300 cm/10 ft of hose can be run from any water container, to give 15 minutes' continuous supply from 9 litres/2 gals of water. A collapsible shower booth and drain tray are available as extras.

Left: *an outdoor shower is appreciated equally by muddy little children who require sluicing down before going inside and by their parents.*

Right: *a sturdy container to stand in, a stool for soap and shampoo, buckets of water, hooks on the fence for towels, and privacy are the only props needed for the perfect home-made shower.*

Above and bottom right: *the showers often found at the beach for rinsing away salt water are simply stem pipes with* shower heads attached—ideal for installing outside a beach hut or for pool-side showering at home.

Below: *when attached to the car battery, this camping shower kit is ideal for summer-time showering in the garden and even for washing the car.*

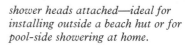

History of the wash-basin

In ancient and medieval households, diners dipped into a common dish, and handed choice morsels to favoured companions. Hand-washing, before and after meals, was not merely desirable, it became a formal and almost obligatory ritual. A medieval poet wrote:

Thai set trestes, and bordes on layd;
Thai spred clathes, and salt on set,
And made redy unto the mete;
Thai set forth water and towelle.

Chaucer was referring to a ritual exactly the same as that described by Homer in the *Odyssey*. A servant called the ewerer brought a jug of scented water and poured

Proving that cleanliness is next to godliness: fixed, circular laver in a 12th-century monastery.

secular bedchamber there would have been a small basin, either fixed in a recess or portable, served via a tap from a metal reservoir, which could be taken to the kitchen and heated over the fire.

By the early 18th century, the bedroom toilet table had become a dainty, portable tripod with a tiny china wash-bowl let into the polished wooden top. By about 1770, it was more substantial, with a larger bowl, and kept permanently in a corner of the room. Endowed with such accessories as a mirror and soap dishes, it served as a shaving stand. Chippendale, Hepplewhite and Sheraton produced countless variations on the basic wash-stand: typical of them was Sheraton's dressing chest of 1803, in effect a combination of both a dressing-table and wash-stand with myriad little drawers for beauty preparations.

About 1830, a more practical form emerged: it resembled a table, had a marble top and splashback, a shelf and one or two large bowls (no longer sunk), each with its matching jug. A lower shelf carried a china slop-bucket with a lid like a shallow funnel. Hot water was brought in a brass or copper can, wrapped in a towel. This arrangement still survives in places where running water and drainage have not reached the bedroom.

Once they did, of course, the wash-bowl became permanently sunk into the marble top, and the piece was given a wooden casing to hide the pipes. The wash-basin had become, in effect, a piece of wooden furniture and remained so right through the 19th century, reaching what many people may consider to be a high point of sombre, obtrusive ugliness during the 1890s.

Around 1880, a cheaper version of the wash-stand was produced in cast-iron. This was not necessarily a simple, utility product: some such stands were fantastically ornate, embodying a mirror frame, shelf, towel rails and coat hooks, all japanned or painted to look like marble, bronze or gold. A fine example by Froy, complete with taps, cost seven pounds—quite a tidy sum.

The cast-iron Pedestal Tip-up Lavatory of 1890 had a hemispherical basin inside which another, slightly smaller, was pivoted. After use, the inner basin was emptied by tipping it; the only advantage of this rather insanitary device

Unusually attractive Victorian wash-stand by architect William Burges (1827–81) for use in his own house.

was that it did not need a waste plug.

By about 1900, improvements in slip casting (using liquid clay in a plaster mould instead of building up solid clay on a mould by hand) enabled the potteries to turn out the one-piece basin

Painting of Pontius Pilate ceremoniously washing his hands; 15th century.

it over the hands, while deftly holding a shallow bowl beneath. The jug fitted into a recess in the centre of the bowl and some bowls had long spouts, which served not only to empty them but as handles. In 1365, the Duke of Anjou had 60 such sets, of gold or silver. Similar, if simpler, utensils were used for private washing: to use them one had to strip to the waist and kneel on the floor.

Private and even royal houses of the Middle Ages had nothing comparable to the elaborate fixed lavers of the monasteries, with their running water, multiple basins, separate taps, recesses for towels and efficient drainage. In an important

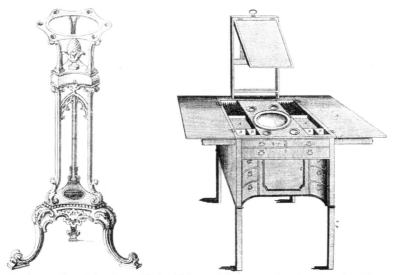

Basin stand and shaving table by Chippendale, 1754; dressing chest by Sheraton, 1803.

complete with upstand (i.e., a low splash-back), overflow and soap recesses. Soon after, the first basins on pedestals appeared, of which some shapely examples were made in the *art nouveau* style.

The first compact, utilitarian bath-rooms appeared by 1900 in mass-built middle-class housing. A plumbed-in wash-basin in a bedroom was, incidentally, still a rare luxury. By 1914, the bathroom basin had been generally transformed. The decorative frills were gone; its plumbing was exposed and it was probably bracketed from the wall, as was the glass shelf above. The latter was known in the trade as a "plumber's delight" because of its habit of falling and breaking the basin. In the bathroom of the late 1920s, brass taps disappeared, gleaming white and shiny chromium plate coming into favour.

During the period when "modern" architects of the *Bauhaus* persuasion were beginning to favour strictly rec-tangular and rather heavy solid forms, even in minor domestic fittings, the wash-basin refused to conform. This was because clayware, fired in a kiln, not only shrinks but changes shape unpredictably: a straight edge may emerge curved, and a sharp angle rounded. The potter pre-fers, and will very often insist upon, curvilinear forms as far as possible. If recent designers of wash-basins have anything to boast about, it is that with feeling for their material, they have pro-duced wash-basins of classical elegance based on subtle ellipses.

Above: *prettiest of late Victorian wash-basins; new techniques enabled the potter to incorporate such details as soap dishes into the overall design.*

Right: *gold-plated taps and art deco surrounds signal Jazz Age opulence in this Manhattan bathroom suite.*

Above: *personal wash-basin of John Brown, Queen Victoria's Highland manservant, on the sumptuously decorated royal train.*

Shapes and sizes of wash-basins

Wash-basins are called upon to perform a multitude of functions, and many people enjoy the convenience of having several about the house. An extra basin in your bedroom is extremely useful: you can wash your hands, your hair, your clothes or your teeth while another member of the family lies soaking in the bath. Consider, too, the convenience for guests of having a basin in the guest-room, while a wash-basin in the WC or cloakroom is useful for family and visitors. In fact, manufacturers of sanitary ware design basins in so many shapes and sizes that all members of the family, and all types of room, are now catered for.

Types of basin: Pedestal basins, as the name suggests, have a central supporting "stem", which is supposed to conceal the plumbing paraphernalia. Before choosing a pedestal basin, however, check with your plumber exactly where the pipes run, or you may find that the pedestal fails to fulfil part of its function.

Wall-fixed basins have the advantage that you can place them at any height. They also look neater than pedestal basins and make floor cleaning easier. They can be hung from specially designed metal hangers which are screwed into the wall, or can be supported by brackets which sometimes incorporate towel rails—useful in a room where space is at a premium. To prevent crashes, it is essential that a wall-mounted basin is firmly fixed. If it is not possible to attach the basin to a load-bearing wall, choose a model that has special brackets, "legs" or a metal stand to give the basin extra support.

Pipes leading to and from wall-fixed models can often be concealed by ducted plumbing. This simply means that the pipes run behind a panel fixed a little way away from the wall, giving a streamlined appearance. Sometimes the basins are semi-recessed into the duct, which is made to finish flush with the basin rim. The space between the basin and the wall is then covered to form a narrow counter-top. With other models the duct can be continued a short way above the basin. When covered, it forms a convenient little shelf.

You can also buy oval, rectangular or circular wash-basins that are designed to be set into a counter-top. If you are doing the job yourself, the type that is easiest to install has a rim that fits neatly over the edge of the surrounding surface.

The rim seals the gap and hides any small deficiencies in the fit. Other models fit under the counter-top and need more skilful installation. Alternatively, you can buy or make a vanity unit. This consists of cupboards covered by a counter-top that is already fitted with a basin.

Sizes: In the UK, standard sizes for wash-basins are 635 × 455 mm/25 × 18 in and 560 × 405 mm/22 × 16 in. Larger and smaller sizes are readily available.

In the USA, about 80 per cent of new wash-basins are fitted into counter-tops. The largest basins generally available are the rectangular 20 × 18 in, the oval

Above: *this narrow basin, designed specifically for hand-washing, is very useful in* WCs *where there is not enough room for a normal basin.*

Right: *pedestal basins, like this one, are very neat and compact and have a pleasing shape. The concealed pipes are encased in the pedestal itself.*

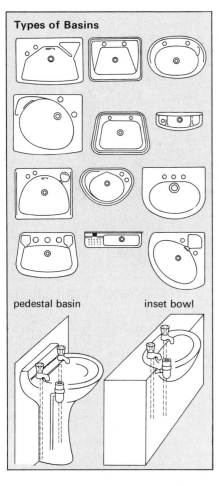

pedestal basin   inset bowl

Right: *a pair of inset basins made of plastic are moulded with their surrounds in one piece for a sculptured effect.*

Bottom right: *basins set into a counter-top can be very versatile in shape, as these two models illustrate.*

19 × 17 in, and the 19 in diameter round models.

Medical and design research has shown that families need the largest basins they can accommodate in terms of both money and space, and that the ideal family wash-basin is 560 to 635 mm/ 22 to 25 in across the front and 300 to 355 mm/12 to 14 in across the back, with an overall depth of 455 to 560 mm/18 to 22 in. While it is unlikely that you will always have room for the ideal basin, the manufacturers fortunately cater for even the most awkwardly shaped rooms. Small basins are available with a depth of only 255 mm/10 in, and other models can be

recessed into the wall or fitted across a corner to take up even less space.

Heights: Pedestal basins usually stand 815 mm/32 in high from the floor to the rim. This is too low for the average adult, who is likely to get backache after prolonged operations such as washing clothes. A wall-mounted basin can be fixed at the more suitable height of around 860 mm/34 in. A basin used only by adults could be even higher—around 920 mm/36 in—while a basin in a child's room could be fixed at a height of about 710 mm/28 in. If there is only one family basin, a small movable step can be provided for children.

215

What wash-basins are made of

Shape and size apart, it is important to consider the material from which a basin is made. The choice is between various ceramics, marble, stone, metals—including zinc, copper and brass—plastic, even hardwoods like teak, each with its own advantages and disadvantages.

Ceramics

Vitreous china is the material most commonly used for wash-basins, whether pedestal, wall hung or inset. A mixture of special clays is cast in plaster moulds to achieve the desired shapes, which can range from elegantly fluted shell shapes to starkly simple bowls, with recesses for soap, sponge and so on. The moulded clay pieces are coated with a glaze, coloured as required, and then the whole piece is fired to a very high temperature in a kiln. The heat makes the clay very strong and durable, and turns the glaze into a tough, smooth coating which is hygienic and easy to clean, and has good resistance to acids and abrasion. Basins made from vitreous china, however, will chip or even crack if you drop heavy objects on to them. Repairs are virtually impossible; in the event of damage, total replacement is usually necessary. For this reason, avoid storing heavy objects such as bottles above a china basin, and take particular care when carrying out work above a basin which involves heavy equipment such as tools or cans of paint.

Glazed fireclay is a stronger, heavier ceramic material which is sometimes used to form a basin and **counter-top** all in one piece, with no dirt-collecting or water-leaking joins—very neat and streamlined.

Metals

Basins made from metals will not crack if subjected to heavy impact, but the finish can be chipped.

Cast iron with an enamelled finish is used for some wall-hung and vanity basins in the US. This material is ex-

Top left: *a plain white vitreous china basin is set off splendidly by an attractive mosaic casing and an impressive marble surround, complete with gold-plated taps.*

Left: *glazed fireclay basin by Armitage Shanks. Fireclay is a good material to use for a basin and surround all in one piece, and here the counter-top provides plenty of room for soap and bottles.*

tremely durable and has a long-lasting, easy-clean finish.

Pressed steel with an enamelled finish is available for inset basins. Again, the finish is long-lasting and easy to clean, but avoid abrasive scouring powders.

Stainless steel, though usually associated with the kitchen, is a practical, easy-clean material for bathroom basins. It is resistant to heat, rust, burns, abrasion, paint stripper and chipping.

Plastics

Acrylic sheet is used for both inset basins or basins and **counter-tops** formed from one sheet of material. While this type of basin is resistant to chipping, the surface is prone to scratching and damage from cigarette burns. Never use harsh scouring powders, but clean with liquid detergent or special cream bath cleaner. Substances harmful to acrylic include paint strippers, nail varnish and nail-varnish remover.

Glass-reinforced polyester (GRP) is used for inset basins. While the range of acrylic colours is limited, GRP can be made in virtually any colour, including shiny finishes that resemble enamel, or pearlized or metallic finishes. Decorative designs can also be incorporated into GRP basins. GRP is vulnerable to damage from burning cigarettes, but manufacturers sometimes offer a specialist repair service, so if the worst happens it is worth making enquiries.

Above: *dark, vitreous china basins look elegant against their stark background. Deep colours are expensive to produce.*

Below: *a bright wall unit that includes a basin and mirror, made from one continuous piece of GRP.*

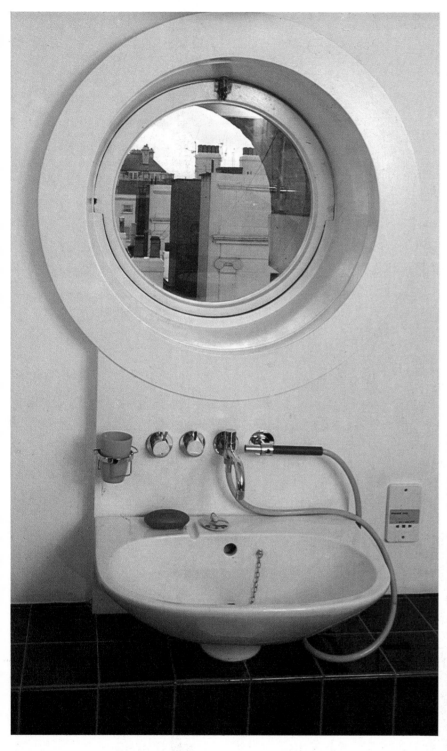

Above: *this hygienic and easy-to-clean stainless-steel basin was designed to be vandal-proof as well as for more genteel use in hospitals and hotels.*

Right: *this fine old pedestal basin, made of fireclay, stands alone and uncluttered by surrounding objects so that its attractive shape and unusual ceramic taps may be displayed to their best effect.*

Above: *this basin, with its shower attachment for hair washing, is set on a platform with a step-up, so one can gaze at the view while brushing teeth.*

Left: *a vitreous china basin with a surround of wood. Avoid heavy objects near china basins because the china is prone to cracking.*

Distinctive wash-basins

In a world of standard shapes and sizes, it is only natural for manufacturers to offer up a complete set of matching bathroom fittings as the ideal. But if conformity is not your style, there is plenty of scope to exercise a little individuality in the choice of your wash-basin.

You may be lucky enough to inherit ornate Victorian or Edwardian china bathroom fittings along with your house; cherish them, if they are in good condition, and see if they can be incorporated into modernization plans. Old-style fittings are back in fashion, and some manufacturers are now making copies of

Left: *as elegant as any Roman drinking fountain, this antique basin combines the soft gloss of old marble with the Italian instinct for perfect proportions.*

Far left: *this exquisitely simple, gold-plated basin in an old Irish castle should be a shining example to all designers of modern bathroom fittings.*

Below: *the luxury of a mosaic-lined basin can be achieved by anyone with the patience to do the job properly.*

elaborate turn-of-the-century designs. Ceramic pedestal basins and inset bowls are available in plain colours, or intricately decorated with flowery patterns. Some of these reproductions are made from glass-reinforced polyester (GRP), with a special finish that looks like hand-painted enamelled china.

Out-of-the-ordinary basins are available in a choice of metals, including hand-beaten brass. (One supplier claims the shape of their basins has been inspired by ancient sacrificial bowls.) A further sophistication is a brass basin plated in a choice of chrome, nickel or copper, and even gold or platinum for those who want to watch their money go down the drain.

Marble is the classic luxury bathroom material: you can, for a fairly reasonable price, purchase a slab cut to hold an inset wash-basin (the slab will need to be about 30 mm/$1\frac{1}{4}$ in thick). It is possible, but very expensive, to order wash-basin and top constructed from one piece of solid marble. Marbled resin imitations such as Corian are, of course, much cheaper, and are already very popular in the USA. Real marble stands up well to normal bathroom usage, but is susceptible to staining, so take care when using hair dyes and tints.

Do full justice to a beautiful basin—do not mar the effect with a set of inappropriate taps. Well-designed taps are, unfortunately, all too rare, but it is well worth the effort involved in tracking them down.

Right: *American designer Sherle Wagner's patterned inset bowl re-creates the charm of a Victorian basin.*

Above: *one-piece, marble-effect vanity unit in durable, man-made Corian.*

Above: *flowered taps suit the mood created by the delicate, plant-like shape of Sherle Wagner's vitreous china basin.*

Right: *this voluptuous wash-stand leaves plenty of space for toiletries.*

History of the bidet

In French, the primary meaning of *bidet* is pony or nag—not inappropriate for an article on which to sit astride. Until quite recent times, few Britons or Americans ever saw a bidet unless they stayed at French hotels, and then were either puzzled because they did not understand it, or embarrassed because they did.

That the bidet serves to clean the private parts has given it an aura of indelicacy, and its contraceptive role one of downright immorality. When late in the 19th century an American doctor preached the virtues of the douche (known incidentally to the ancient Romans) he was imprisoned, but in later years was given partial credit for the reduction of the birthrate in the 1880s—evidence that the real emancipation of women began in the bedroom and the bathroom.

Not until about 1900 is the bidet unblushingly named and illustrated in the non-technical press. At about that date the Ritz Carlton Hotel in New York, having installed these wicked devices, was forced by moral crusaders to take them out again. As recently as 1950, the Hotel Molière in Paris, either to avoid shocking English-speaking visitors, or because these mistook the bidets for WC pans, had a notice above each: "Foot Bath". Manufacturers are still somewhat coy about publicizing their especial value to the many who suffer from haemorrhoids—one reason why the bidet may be considered a fitter companion to the WC unit than to the bath.

Harvard, in his monumental history of furniture (Paris, 1890), found his earliest reference to the bidet dated 1710, when the Marquis d'Argenson was granted audience by one Mme de Prie, and found her seated unconcernedly on this *"meuble utile et discret"*. Madame de Pompadour, mistress of Louis XV, had at least two, elaborate works of art, meant to be displayed and admired. The painter Boucher used one of them as a prop for a full-length portrait of her. The *bidet à seringue* appeared in 1750: worked by a hand-pump fed by a reservoir, it provided an upward spray.

"Femme à sa toilette" by the prolific painter of Parisian life and manners, Louis-Leopold Boilly, c. 1790, an era when it was not unusual to receive guests in the boudoir, hence the lady's unconcerned expression.

In England, the well-travelled among the upper classes imported these French devices and English cabinet-makers began discreetly to make them. They were either concealed in the dressing-closet, or disguised in "harlequin" furniture, so named because Harlequin's act in the theatre was magic transformation. These ingenious pieces open and unfold: a seemingly simple night table by the bed could reveal a wash-stand, toilet accessories, a chamber-pot or a night-stool, and a bidet.

Running water and drainage pipes were not generally to reach bedrooms until well into the 19th century, so that even if the bidet had an outlet, the waste water ran into a concealed bucket. A visitor to the great house at Holkham in East Anglia remarked how the splendour of the open galleries around the stately entrance hall was marred by the morning procession of servants carrying sundry sanitary receptacles to and fro.

Sometimes, Sitz baths—essentially tapered metal bowls just big enough to sit in—were made with double bottoms, the inner one having perforations through which water rose when poured through a funnel at the side. Worked by a pump, this combination of bath and ascending douche was sometimes called a bidet. In such arrangements, the douche had variable nozzles, like a garden hose, and when connected to the water mains, it could act very powerfully. In 1885 it was advertised as "Invaluable in cases of Prolapsus, Seminal Weakness, Piles, Generative Ailments, etc." A Victorian admiral named Beaumont, who was a devotee of the Sitz bath, on which he squatted daily under a waterproof cloak, proclaimed that he was "hatching health". But such treatment belongs more to the "water cure" and the "health hydro" than to the confines of the domestic bathroom.

The "bidification" of the British and American hotel is progressing; that of the domestic bathroom more slowly, aided none the less by the growing popularity of the prefabricated bathroom unit, of which the bidet normally forms a part. Simpler and safer means of contraception have not ousted the bidet, and the elementary importance of its primary function, which many of our grandparents did not even understand, is at last gaining wide appreciation. The little horse is still in the running.

Above: *the ceramic bidet, supplied with a stand, was first advertised in Paris in 1739. One misinformed dealer offered it as "a porcelain violin case on legs"*

Above: *wood-cut of a mid-18th century bidet in use when it still belonged in the bedroom "to take care of the accidental occasions of the night".*

Right: *looking like a cross between a milkmaid's pail and a cowboy's saddle, this Walter Lecuyer bidet was one of the more basic bathroom appliances to appear on the French market in 1889.*

BIDETS

16-6533. Bidet de toilette, cuvette métallique émaillée, pieds pliants en fer peint aluminium, Long. 50 %. *Modèle pratique.* Pds 3ᵏᵍ,200. ...... **1500.** »

Above: *mahogany-encased bidet, hinged discreetly beneath a dressing-table, from Jennings' catalogue, 1880s.*

16-6541. Bidet de toilette dit **"bidet-banquette",** banquette hêtre verni naturel, cuvette faïence blanche, dossier inclinable recouvert liège. Se présente une fois fermé sous l'aspect d'une banquette avec dessus canné. Haut. totale 70 %, siège 49 × 32 %, pds 9 kg. Dimensions ouvert 120 × 32 % .... **11700.** »

Above: *1790s variations on the bidet, advertised in a French catalogue.*

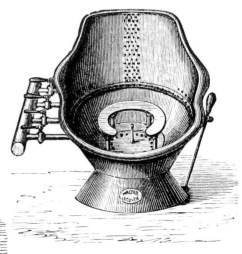

A "hip" or "sitz" bath, equipped with a combination of douches, 1889.

Bidet types and shapes

On the Continent the usefulness of the bidet is fully understood and it is as important a piece of bathroom equipment as the WC unit and the bath—no well-equipped home is without one. For us, however, the virtues of the bidet are still largely unexploited, which is a rather surprising fact considering that we pride ourselves on being among the most hygiene-conscious nations in the world. If you have the space and can discard your reservations you will find that a bidet earns its keep in all sorts of ways. Primarily it is, of course, an invaluable aid to personal hygiene. After using the WC, washing yourself with warm water is far more effective than dry-wiping with paper, so ideally the bidet should be placed alongside the WC unit. Most models are designed so that you sit astride them, but there is at least one range of bathroom fittings that features a bidet enclosed in a box-shaped structure on which the user sits as if it were a chair.

There is an old joke about people thinking that bidets are foot-baths, but the laugh could be on those who sneer, for the bidet is, in fact, excellent for this purpose. It also makes a handy place to dump wet clothes that have been washed in the bath or basin, and it can be useful for rinsing small articles. Philatelists have been known to use the bidet for soaking stamps off envelopes, and it naturally makes a superb place for children to float their ducks and wash grubby hands and knees.

Bidets are usually made from vitreous china in a range of colours to match other bathroom fittings, echoing the design of the WC unit, since the two fittings are intended to stand together if possible.

Below left: *this bidet has been designed to allow for an outward-facing sitting position. It is part of a range of modular, fitted bathroom units.*

Below centre: *the conventional bidet is designed to be sat upon, legs astride, facing the taps. A firmly fixed grab rail helps the user to get up and down.*

Always make sure the bidet is positioned so that you have plenty of room at the sides for your legs and at the back for protruding knees; with some models, this may mean leaving a gap of about 10 cm/4 in between the wall and the back of the bidet.

The simplest type of bidet is fitted with taps for what is known as an *over-rim* supply: you simply fill the bidet with water as you would a wash-basin. This is generally the cheapest and simplest type to install, and is not usually the subject of any special water regulations. Having a rimless bowl, it is also easy to clean. A second type of bidet has a *heated-rim* (sometimes called a flushing-rim) supply with a mixing valve to control the temperature of the water, which enters the fitting from under the rim. A third type can be supplied with an *ascending spray*. Sometimes the heated rim and ascending spray are combined in one model. Special water regulations frequently govern the installation of these more sophisticated types of bidet: there is considered to be a possible risk of water becoming con-taminated from back siphonage created by spray fittings. Check with your local water authority or local plumbing code before you buy your bidet.

Bidets can be fitted with chain wastes or with the more sophisticated pop-up wastes, controlled by a knob or lever. It is also possible to buy a "portable bidet", which is simply a bowl that you fill with water and place over the WC seat. An ingenious American appliance goes a step further: the fitting is plumbed on to your existing WC unit to provide a controlled flow of warm water, followed by a stream of warm air.

Below: *a WC unit fitted with bidet attachments that emit a cleansing douche, followed by a jet of warm air. Mr Bidet, the US manufacturer, claims "it is the most marvellous innovation in personal hygiene ever dreamed possible".*

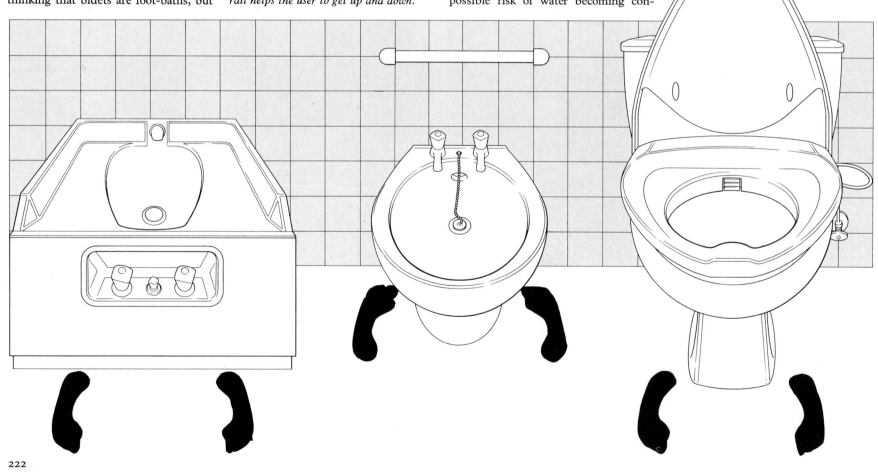

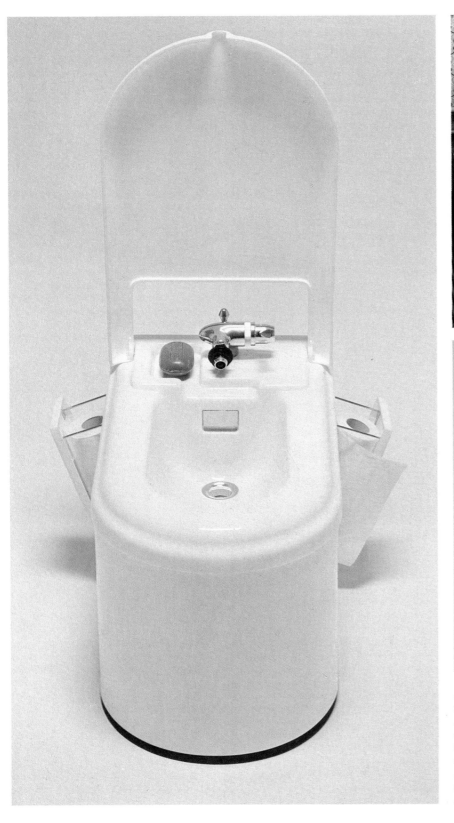

Left: *a fine old porcelain bidet. Hot and cold water issues from under the rim, directly beneath the taps. The wide, rounded ledge gives a comfortable seat to even the broadest fundament.*

Below: *this modern bidet is deliberately styled in the shape of a* WC *unit, next to which the bidet is always meant to stand. This arrangement is intended to encourage personal hygiene.*

Above and left: *a compact bidet unit in a contemporary style, manufactured in Italy by Teuko Guzzini, features lavatory-paper holders and an "over-rim" water supply. The lid folds down and the paper holders slide in to streamline the unit so that it blends discreetly with any bathroom layout, ancient or modern.*

223

All about baths
History of the water-closet

The English language has never had a single, unambiguous, generally agreed word for the throne-like apparatus into which one urinates and defecates.

A *closet* must surely be a small room, or in American usage a tall cupboard, but not the sanitary fitting which it houses. A *lavatory* must be a place or, in America, a utensil in which one washes. *Privy* is properly an adjective (as in *privy closet*) meaning private. *Latrine* is not used in the domestic context. Slang words, such as *bog, loo, can, jakes, john, petty*, are understood only by minorities. Toilet is an absurd genteelism: in the *Oxford English Dictionary* its principal, modern meaning is "the action or process of dressing". Of its many subsidiary, historical meanings, all connected with grooming, "a towel or cloth thrown over the shoulders during hairdressing" will be most significant to the vain and "preparation for execution" to those interested in the macabre. Here, the apparatus itself is to be called a WC unit, and the room specifically designed to accommodate it, a WC.

Top: *remains of latrines at a Roman fort and (**above**) how they might have looked in AD 200. The Roman answer to lavatory paper was the "sponge stick", which a soldier is rinsing in the channel that flowed on under the seats.*

A 20th-century don had to complain of his Oxford college that it denied him the ordinary sanitary conveniences of ancient Crete. There, of all the wonders of Knossos, the one that most fascinates the tourists is the first-known WC. In it there are the remains of a water-flushing system, probably fed from a reservoir, and what was evidently a wooden seat. There may even have been an earthenware wash-out bowl. These date from about 2000 BC. Save for two isolated and experimental water flushing systems, England had nothing comparable until the 18th century.

The Romans were almost as skilled as the Cretans in plumbing. Rome in AD 315 had 144 public latrines; their barracks overseas, as for example on Hadrian's Wall across the north of England, had multi-holers flushed with used water from the bath-houses.

In the monasteries, plumbing was one of the arts preserved through the Dark Ages. The brethren repaired together to the reredorter (i.e., behind the dorter or dormitory), where partitioned rows of seats were ranged above a natural or an artificial stream. At Tintern Abbey on the River Wye, the tide was harnessed to the task of flushing. At St Albans the abbot had a rainwater cistern to flush his "necessary house". Cleanliness, as much as godliness, protected the monks from the ravages of the Black Death.

In the medieval castle the waterless garderobe (another euphemism, derived from the wardrobe where a night stool would be kept) comprised a stone or wooden seat above a shaft that opened into the moat or into a pit. Groups of these shafts were built into the walls, like chimney flues. (In the bishop's palace at Southwell in the English midlands, recesses for the seats radiated round a central shaft.) In Bodiam Castle in Sussex there were at least 20 seats from which to choose. The defensive moats may well have become offensive. As for the pits, the one at London's Newgate Jail, when emptied in 1281, occupied 13 men for five nights. Dirty work, but the men were paid three times the normal rate of twopence each per night.

Domestic WCs were most often built beside, or jutting over, watercourses; London's Fleet River became a notorious source of plague, and Sherbourne Lane, which ran by a bourne or stream, came to be known as Shiteburn Lane. Lon-don's first recorded lavatory with a flushing cistern fed from the main was built by Thomas Brightfield in 1449, but the water authority is unlikely to have encouraged such things, and we hear of no imitators. In 1579, Tower Street had only three privy closets for about 60 houses; the pits for such places were subject to strict building regulations and emptied in the dark by "night men".

Seventeenth-century close stool, japanned and inlaid with mother-of-pearl.

As the Dark Ages lightened into the Renaissance, the close stool or stool of ease became the substitute of the garderobe. It was a richly upholstered box with a hinged lid and a padded seat, containing a pot. An inventory of Louis XIV lists 264 such stools at the Palace of Versailles. Such unsavoury devices might have been superseded from 1596, had more notice been taken of Sir John Harington's book *A Metamorphosis of Ajax* (a pun on a jakes), in which he described in full detail a lavatory bowl and valve-operated flushing system, which he installed in his home at Kelston near Bath. Householders all over Europe continued to empty their chamber pots from the windows into the street, with no more care for passers-by than a warning shout. In England it was "Gardy-loo!" (i.e., *Gardez l'eau*, meaning look out for the water).

In humbler homes, with earth floors, the habit of urinating under the bed was so general that officials known as peter-men were empowered to enter and dig the floors. They were in search of salt-petre, an essential ingredient of gunpowder, formed from crystallized urine. Better bred persons would, at least when the bedroom fire was not lit, use the capacious fireplace.

During the 18th century, the water-flushed bowl started to become popular in England, and even more widely so in France, where it was known as a *cabinet d'aisance à l'anglaise*, or briefly as an *anglaise*. In 1718, John Aubrey, the English antiquary, wrote of a tippler, in which a trickle of water accumulated in a hinged shovel until its weight tipped this up, giving a strong automatic flush at intervals. Queen Anne had "a little place of Easement of marble with sluices of water to wash all down" at Windsor Castle. At Woburn in 1748, the Duke of Bedford could boast of four new WCs, "one of which is within the house".

Around 1759, the ball-valve was introduced to the flushing tank, allowing the latter to be kept full even though the mains water ran only at certain hours. In 1782 John Gaillat, a cook, patented the stink trap and the air indoors became

Bramah's valve closet, 1778. This design, in regular use until 1890, was the most successful of the early systems.

sweeter. A long series of so-called closets then appeared, all of them attempts to produce a perfect flushing system. Joseph Bramah, a cabinet-maker, produced the best system in 1778 by improving on Cummings's valve closet. Bramahs were still in production in about 1890, and similar models were being used in the early

1930s, when there was one in the premises of the Royal Institute of British Architects.

In 1844, after 53 overflowing cesspools had been found under Windsor Castle, the Prince Consort ordered the installation of lavatories. In 1892, an equerry to the Prince of Wales objected to the fact that newspaper squares were provided as a substitute for lavatory rolls. These had been available since the 1880s, an invention of Walter J. Alcock, founder of a firm which now exports worldwide.

Thomas Crapper (1837–1910), more famous for having his name taken in vain than as a sanitary-ware manufacturer.

Victorian catalogues often illustrate one type of WC unit for the rich and one for the poor: the hopper closet, a conical pan flushed by a thin spiral trickle of water, all too simple a design, was advertised as "suitable for Prisons, Mills, etc." About 1870, Mr Twyford, who made the pottery part for the Bramah, noticed that the complex metal parts cost up to 25 times what he was paid for the pottery. He set out to make an all-pottery apparatus. In his Washout Closet, a hollow ledge at the back held about an inch of water and received the deposit; the trap was at the front. The flush rarely cleared the ledge, especially if the water had evaporated.

Mann's Syphonic Closet of 1870 introduced a new principle: a powerful first flush, followed by a slower after-flush, while syphonic action reinforced the clearing. Jennings's Pedestal Vase of 1884 vied with Twyford's for the claim to be the first Pedestal Closet, needing no casing. The Washdown Closet, the

current form, can be made in one piece, and has the minimum of exposed surface and a self-cleaning rim. Around the turn of the century, moulded decorations and transfer patterns went out of fashion; they have only lately returned. With improved design, a head of water was less essential, hence the compact low-level suite, dating from 1895. Effective standards for WC bowl and cistern construction came into force in the 1930s and 1940s along with the technical perfection of the valve.

Mr Shanks of the famous English sanitary equipment manufacturing family once tested a new model by seizing a near-by apprentice's cap, throwing it in the pan and flushing it away. A modern system should pass the stiffer test of disposing of a Ping-Pong ball. Even so, the lavatory bowl is still far

Dolphin-pattern lavatory bowl, 1880.

from perfect. It is too high for a natural squatting position, too low as a target for a standing male, not always wholly self-cleansing, usually too noisy—though the ball-valve in the main supply tank may be more to blame than that in the flushing tank.

It is also extravagant on water: during Europe's drought in the summer of 1976, the Duke of Edinburgh exhorted the British public to conserve water by placing bricks in the cistern. Will the development begun in 2000 BC be successfully completed by AD 2000?

Exquisitely decorated Armitage Shanks lavatory bowl and matching cistern, 1900.

These Closets are made with a Water Seal of 2 inches, thus ensuring reliable trappage, and are guaranteed to flush with a 2 Gallon Cistern.

WCs - shapes and sizes

Medical and design research, so admirably embodied in the book *The Bathroom* by Alexander Kira, has shown that squatting is the best position for humans to adopt when defecating. Common in so-called "less civilized" countries, this position, with the thighs flexed against the abdomen, provides the stomach muscles with the support they need for their pushing action.

"Squat" WC units are made by some

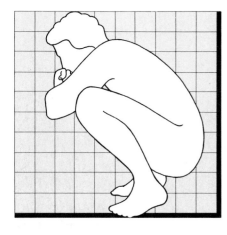

The full squatting position commonly used in less urbane societies is far healthier and more natural than the casual posture adopted in the West.

Western manufacturers of sanitary ware, but almost exclusively for export to countries where the squatting position is normal practice, and not for the home market. Indeed, one manufacturer did make a range for the home market that followed Professor Kira's precepts, but withdrew it because of lack of response from the public.

Unheeding of the Professor's message that objects should be designed to suit the physiology of the body, the common height for WC units in the Western World continues to be around 40 cm/16 in. This is too high to allow a squatting position and leads to what the Professor calls the familiar, casual sitting-on-a-chair posture so often assumed on a standard water closet, particularly by those who read there. In this posture, says the Professor, the individual is essentially passive and unable to do much to aid the body's mechanism.

Even the Professor concedes, however, that Western convention and clothing make it difficult for us to turn to the

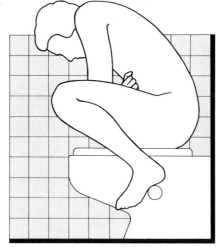

A conventional WC unit that has been modified to accept a semi-squat position, with foot rests for support.

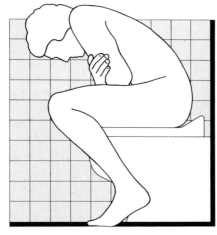

A conventional WC seat modified to slope upwards at the back, giving the extra support that the body needs when in the squatting position.

correct squat WC unit; indeed, it is often necessary to remove clothing in order to use it. The alternative is to continue to use a conventional high model, but to adopt a more healthy posture. We can do this by crossing the arms across the chest, doubling over and drawing back the feet. Those who want to read can put their books or papers on the floor. An alternative is to raise the feet on a small stool or box. Furthermore, carefully designed WC seats are available which are shaped to encourage a more healthy and comfortable position, even when used on a

unit of conventional height. Lower WC units of around 35 cm/14 in are available, and even some 30 cm/12 in, but these tend to be sold for use in kindergartens and schools. It is sometimes possible to lower the bowl height of a wall-hung WC unit to around 30 cm/12 in. Alternatively, you can raise the floor level by a few inches all around the unit to

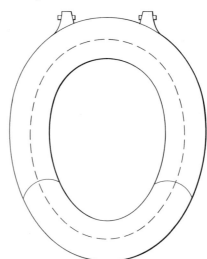

The egg shape of the conventional WC seat has never changed, even though it actually hinders the sitter's balance, support and manoeuvrability.

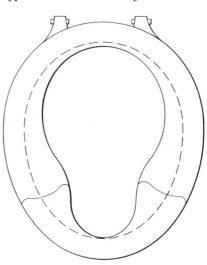

The shape suggested by Professor Kira is elongated to provide comfort for males, and curved to give the thighs the support that is lacking in the conventional WC seat.

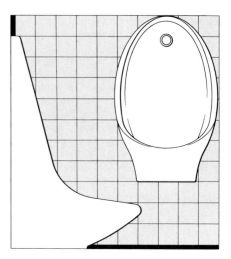

Side and front views of a urinal, normally found only in places such as public WCs and schools. This streamlined design would be useful and not unattractive in a bathroom as company for a low-level WC unit, which is particularly unsuited to male urination.

give the effect of a lower fixture.

Conventional WC units do, of course, have advantages over lower ones. The latter pose a problem for urinating men —or perhaps the problem is more for those who must clean up after them. And the lower the unit, the greater the extent of the splashing. For perfect hygiene, every bathroom should incorporate a urinal, but apparently there is considerable female objection to the idea of introducing special male facilities into shared bathrooms. There is also the problem that older or disabled people, in particular, find low WC units difficult to use.

The disadvantages of low units are not easily surmountable so, added to our inherent dislike of radical change, it is unlikely that we will swiftly adopt Professor Kira's recommendation to start squatting rather than sitting. We would do well, however, to follow the Professor's advice on how we can use conventional WC units to the best advantage.

Right: *stall urinals common in public WCs are practical for males of any height, but are unacceptable in the home.*

Below: *this unit embodies Professor Kira's theories, incorporating the lengthened and curved opening, the reduced height and the lavatory paper close at hand. A pull-down urinal,* **right**, *with an automatic light for night-time use accompanies the WC unit which, although perfect for sitting on, is too low for standing males.*

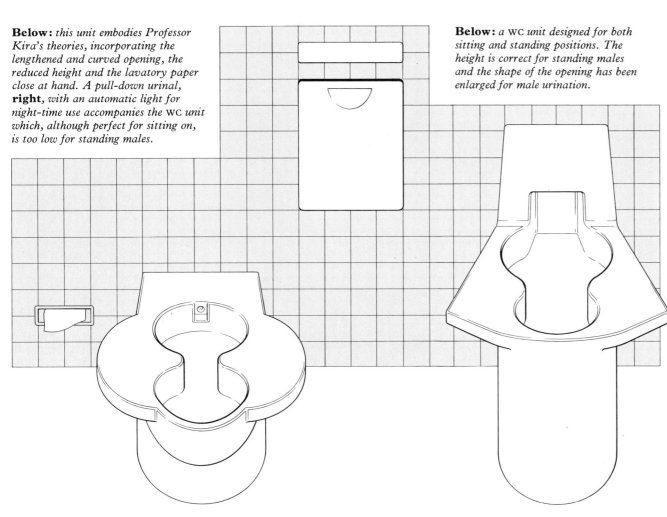

Below: *a WC unit designed for both sitting and standing positions. The height is correct for standing males and the shape of the opening has been enlarged for male urination.*

Above: *a contoured seat and lid that doubles as a comfortable bathroom stool.*

Above: *a compact, unobtrusive and pleasantly shaped low-level WC unit.*

Below: *a unit with a neatly enclosed cistern and a simple flushing system.*

WCs – flushing systems

When WC units were first mass-produced at the turn of the century, they were often superbly ornate yet functional pieces of equipment. Today they have become neat, streamlined and compressed, and some would say that character has been sacrificed for total practicality in the process. There is, however, an ever-widening variety of models and colours to choose from.

Vitreous china, available in white and many colours ranging from pastels to deep, dark shades, is still the material most commonly used for WC bowls. Strong and durable, it has a glazed finish that resists staining and acids. Plastic is used for only a small percentage of bowls and is not recommended; the drawback is that the bowl has to be joined together in sections, creating small crevices that can harbour dirt. Cisterns (flush tanks) can be made from vitreous china or plastic, but remember that plastic is vulnerable to scarring from lighted cigarettes, so remember to provide an ashtray if you have a compulsive smoker in the house.

The high-level cistern commonly found in old houses has now been almost entirely replaced by low-level models measuring about 105 cm/41 in to the cistern top. These can mean that the WC bowl takes up more floor space than with the old type, as the bowl has to be moved forward to accommodate the depth of the cistern (with high-level cisterns, the bowl can be tucked partly under the cistern). The problem can be solved, however, by choosing one of the slim-line cisterns available. If you are converting from high to low, the slim-line is often the most convenient and least expensive choice. Some units are designed to have their cisterns and pipes concealed behind a simple panel known as a duct. This type of unit can be wall-hung on concealed cantilevered brackets.

Special valves are now available to reduce the noise of a cistern refilling with water; new cisterns incorporating these valves are available, and the valves can also be fitted to old cisterns. Automatic flushing valves have been developed to take water directly from the mains supply, but their use is usually prohibited in the UK because the plumbing does not adapt to this system, and in the USA it is confined mainly to non-residential applications.

There is growing concern among manufacturers to develop bathroom appliances that conserve water. In the UK, the normal cistern flushes with 9 litres/2 gals of water, but dual-flushing action cisterns are now available which give a choice of a full flush, or a half-flush of 4.5 litres/1 gal. Some US manufacturers also offer self-ventilating units, which draw in room air when flushed, thus getting rid of any remaining smells, and insulated cisterns to combat condensation, which can occur when a unit is flushed if external conditions are very cold.

The various types of domestic WC units available are as follows:

Washdown: This is the simplest and cheapest type of unit. Water is flushed around the rim of the bowl, and the downward force of the water clears away the waste matter. Although efficient, the action is fairly noisy.

Siphonic: This type of unit has a flushing action designed to create a suction to clear the bowl of waste. Quieter but more expensive than the washdown, it has been considered until very recently far superior. There is a possibility, however, that blockages may occur with some types of siphonic design and also that foul air may pass back into the room. In the USA, a reverse-trap type of unit has a flushing action similar to the siphonic, but only requires a minimum water surface in the bowl of 9 × 8 in, whereas the siphonic requires a minimum surface of 10 × 12 in. A special version of the reverse trap is the US one-piece, in which the flush tank and bowl are made together as one piece. It has the same flushing action as the reverse trap, but draws much of its water directly from the supply pipe to produce a very quiet flush. It also has a very compact, streamlined shape.

Close-coupled: These units have the cistern fitted directly to the back of the bowl, with no connecting length of flush pipe, to give a neat profile. The average close-coupled unit measures about 700 mm/27 in from front to back, the same as a corresponding low-level unit.

Top right: *the sunken bath has been well known for years; this sunken WC unit is an updated Victorian idea.*

Right: *this WC unit has a particularly neat cistern or flush tank, and is flushed by a simple push button.*

a High-level cistern or flush tank.

b Modern low-level cistern.

c Close-coupled cistern.

d Slim-line cistern.

e WC bowl designed to be used in conjunction with a concealed cistern.

f and g Cantilevered WC bowls rest on hidden brackets which fit unobtrusively under the floor finish.

h All-in-one WC unit with an air-intake system to whisk away unpleasant smells.

Above: a vitreous china WC unit with a warm, old-fashioned wooden seat. The black panel behind the WC bowl conceals the cistern and pipes.

Below: modern thinking that low-level WC units are the answer has been translated into the latest design terms.

Above: modern and old amusingly combined—an up-to-date low-level cistern is disguised, with the aid of a mural, as an old high-level type.

Below: this space-age object, designed to be vandal-proof, is a rimless, wall-hung WC unit made of stainless steel.

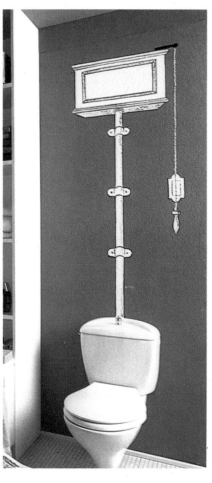

Above: once so familiar, now becoming an increasingly rare sight, old high-level cisterns can be very attractive, especially if given a bright background.

Below: a new approach to WC unit design that requires ducted plumbing and includes storage for lavatory paper.

WCs – sitting pretty

If you decide that, despite all your efforts to enliven it, your WC unit has the rather dull and forlorn look of something that persistently fears the worst, there are various fittings expressly designed to disguise it.

Some designs, sometimes described as *chaises percées*, are simply what our parents or grandparents might have called a commode. Today, however, these elaborate structures, which resemble a chair, are intended to conceal a fully-flushing WC unit, rather than the old chamber pot that required emptying at frequent intervals. Intricate, throne-like chairs with, for example, elaborate cane panels are of course difficult to clean and therefore unhygienic.

An alternative is to "build in" your WC unit by enclosing it in a simple box-like structure with a lift-up lid, perhaps as part of an overall arrangement to provide storage. It could even house the wash-basin as well. You can use solid timber, chipboard or blockboard, or make a framework of wooden battens and panel it with hardboard.

There are various points to bear in mind, however, before you settle for such a structure. Removable panels should be provided wherever access may be needed to pipes or wastes in case of plumbing troubles. And a boxed-in unit may not be so comfortable to use: you will not be able to draw your legs back on either side, for example, in the manner recommended to help stomach muscles in lieu of using the squatting position our bodies were designed to assume. If your built-in structure is to encompass other fittings or provide storage, you should also make sure that you provide unobstructed space above the level of the WC seat on either side to ensure the occupant enough elbow and shoulder room. The finish for any purpose-built housings for WC units should be smooth and easy to clean. Natural wood should be well sealed or painted; wood-based boards such as chipboard can be painted or faced with plastic laminate.

There is at least one range of "fitted" bathroom equipment in which WC and storage units, basin, bidet and bath are all available enclosed in matching box-like units made from chipboard, faced with leather-grained PVC for tops and lids, and plastic laminate for front and sides. The WC bowl, bidet and low-level storage units are all the same height, and units can be aligned to give a stream-lined, fitted effect in the same way that fitted units are available for kitchens.

If you wish simply to minimize the appearance of your WC unit without boxing it in, there are units specially designed to be built in, with the cistern concealed behind a duct or false wall. This type of WC unit can be wall-hung or a special streamlined "back-to-the-wall" design.

Cleaning the WC

It may be stating the obvious to say that keeping your WC scrupulously clean ensures good looks, good hygiene and sweet-smelling air, but it is surprising how many otherwise house-proud people neglect this somewhat unpleasant task for an unhealthily long time—which makes the job far worse in the end.

Clean inside the bowl regularly with a special WC brush, using a disinfectant solution. Cleaning and freshening agents clipped inside the cistern or bowl will clean the bowl with every flush. Periodically, wash out with either a liquid bleach, which should be left to stand in the bowl overnight, or use a special WC cleaner. Never mix the two together, as this can result in very noxious and poisonous fumes.

Bad stains in the bowl of an old WC unit may respond to a paste of cream of tartar and hydrogen peroxide. More drastically, you can apply spirits of salts, but be careful to follow warnings and directions on the bottle as this substance is highly poisonous and corrosive.

Remember to wash down the WC lid and the cistern. More important still, to prevent germs from being transmitted from one member of the household to another, wash the seat and the cistern handle at least once a day with a weak solution of disinfectant. If you keep a small towel for wiping the seat, this should be washed as often as possible. Remember, too, to thoroughly clean the outside of the bowl and the surrounding walls and floor.

If you keep your WC clean and have good ventilation, other forms of air fresheners should not be necessary. To hide smells quickly, however, keep an aerosol air freshener handy. Alternatively, a lighted match allowed to burn its full length will do a good air-cleaning job. If you have a ventilation problem in the WC, keep a large candle burning.

Above: *a mahogany box surrounds an old and prized seat that defies modern theories on low-level squatting.*

Right: *the throne room—in keeping with the grand theme, a modern WC unit is hidden in a "chaise percée".*

Above: *labour of love—a hand-painted wooden seat, personalized with visual jokes and an apt rhyming couplet.*

Right: *ingenious moulded plastic casings inspired by the pneumatic contours of the famous "Michelin Man".*

Above: *close-coupled WC unit and cistern cleverly boxed in with wooden planking to disguise its modern lines.*

Below: *redundant WC bowl, given over to chrysanthemums, lives out its life usefully in a quiet garden corner.*

Plumber's progress

In ancient Rome about 300 gallons of water were used per head per day; a present-day Londoner uses little over 35 gallons. The Romans had pumps, filters, lagged hot-water tanks, mixing taps; their hot tank was refilled from a warm one, the warm one from cold, an economy only lately readopted in the combination tank. Roman pipes of lead (*plumbum*, whence plumber) installed about 2,000 years ago, are still delivering hot water at Bath. An English monk in 1150 enjoyed better standards of hygiene than the average Londoner or New Yorker of 1850. The history of water's course to the tap is not one of steady unimpeded progress.

When the Roman Empire decayed, Europe went unwashed for more or less a thousand years, save in the monasteries. Not until 1237 did the City of London have piped water—it came from Tyburn, near present-day Marble Arch, three miles away. From 1582, water wheels under London Bridge were pumping a more plentiful, if undrinkable, supply.

In 1613, a 38-mile artificial channel, the New River (running from Chadwell, Hertfordshire, to Sadler's Wells), began serving clean water to the highest houses in their lower rooms, and the lower houses in their higher rooms. For a long time householders could fill their tanks from this source only at set hours. Steam pumps (1743), iron pipes (1746) and ball-valves (1748) improved the system.

In 1841, London's noisome Fleet River was recognized as a sewer, and covered in; it still serves. After a series of cholera outbreaks, the great engineer Bazalgette drew up a vast scheme for 83 miles of new sewers, serving over 100 square miles of buildings, which was completed in 1865. From 1846, Doulton's factory had been producing the new glazed stoneware pipes that made sound drains possible.

Right: *built over in 1841, London's Fleet River became the Fleet sewer. Today it runs beneath Farringdon Street and New Bridge Street.*

Constant hot water was provided in the Combined Fireplace, Boiler and Cast-iron Oven of 1806, though it had to be drawn off from a single tap and carried. When cold water first reached the upper floors, hot bathwater was produced *in situ* by a little coal-, coke- or charcoal-fired furnace. For one such heater of 1842, the user was very rightly warned that "when the proper temperature is attained, the fire must of course be extinguished". When piped hot water from the kitchen range became general, there were many fatal explosions, due to the cold tank in the roof space freezing. If the cold tank thawed, the boiler blew up. The cure was to rearrange the system so that hot water could not be drawn unless the hot tank was actually being fed by the cold one; also, a safety valve was added. Coal and domestic labour were so cheap that insulation of the hot tank was unnecessary.

A plumber living in Boston, Mass., about 1850, advertised a mixed system: the kitchen range supplied the bath

Ancient plumbing

Romans understood the principles of running water under pressure, but were unable to put these into practice since they did not have sufficient quantities of metal with which to construct suitably robust pipes. The Pont du Gard aqueduct (right) near Nîmes in France, built during the 1st century AD, illustrates how water had to be carried downhill to its destination.

The jointed terracotta pipes pictured below were found in the Palace of Knossos, Crete. The water was forced to flow faster at the tapered joints, so preventing a build-up of sediment. Thongs were threaded through the eyelets to hold the sections together.

John Doulton, founder of the stoneware firm, became the best pot thrower in London during his apprenticeship to the sanitaryware trade, 1805–12.

(with shower and mixing tap) and the basin, and the cold water tank had to be filled by means of a hand pump, which was probably also used to bring water upstairs.

Gas was in use for lighting from 1812, but even moderately efficient ways of using it to heat water did not appear until

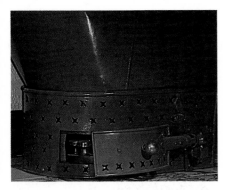

19th-century gas water heater fitted beneath the bath—lethal if not extinguished before bathing.

about 1850. The gas bath had flames playing directly on the underside, and no flue. There was also a portable water heater, a heavy metal pot containing a gas burner whose gas supply was via a rubber tube connected to an outlet on the wall lighting bracket or the gas fire.

In 1868, Benjamin Waddy Maughan produced the first gas geyser—an instant-acting water-tube boiler. Ewart made one which used gas or oil. Early geysers had no safety devices and, unless some complicated instructions were followed, tended to run dry and disintegrate; or go out, fill with gas from the pilot jet, and explode when relit. Ewart's Califont of 1899 could serve any number of remote taps, but it sacrificed the economy of heating the water at the point of use, and it could lead to angry competition between users in different rooms, hoping for a basin of hot water.

Until about 1920, plumbing was generally leaky, for it was customary—in some areas obligatory—to build underneath the bath, and even the WC unit, a save-all tray of sheet lead, sometimes with its own drain plug. An extension of this idea, found in some continental hotels, was to form a completely waterproof floor and skirting with a slight incline towards a drain plug.

Among many plumbing novelties which have failed the test of time is the pillar waste, a rotary bath-plug operated by a handle on a tall vertical tube, serving also as an overflow. It was seldom watertight, hard to clean, and a permanent obstruction to the feet. Even less to be regretted were the tapless baths to be found in a leading London hotel during the 1930s. Water entered the bath through the waste outlet, an event which began with the delivery of a sample of the previous user's residue.

One famous Punch cartoon was entitled "The Plumber's Dream". It showed a fantastic tangle of pipes, bends, bulbous joints, traps and such, festooning a bathroom's walls and ceiling. That sort of thing did tend to happen when houses were old and plumbing new. As a consequence, plumbers were never short of work.

Today, the situation is reversed. Good plumbing is meant to be compact plumbing, as ultimately exemplified in the factory-prefabricated bathroom-kitchen-heating-WC unit. It deserves another cartoon, entitled "The Plumber's Nightmare": apart from connecting its supply and waste, his occupation's gone —at least theoretically.

Left: *designed in 1904 by Ewart, this remarkable geyser, fitted with a shower attachment, was fired by both gas and oil.*

Right: *dredging London's grossly inadequate sewers in the 1850s was a major operation: they had to be cleared before Sir Joseph Bazalgette, Chief Engineer to the Board of Works, could open his new drainage system.*

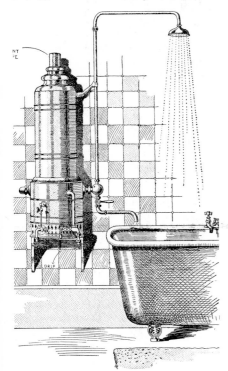

Two extra taps, for health-giving seawater, installed by Nancy Astor in her Kent coast home, 1900. **Right:** *art-deco taps stand like chess queens, 1929.* **Below:** *Shanks's Eureka combination taps for all-in-one bath and shower, 1900.*

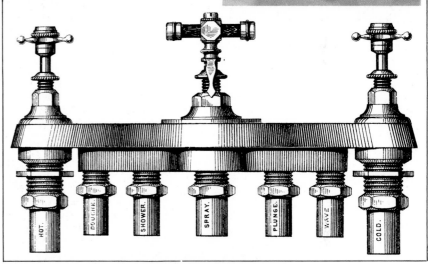

233

Taps: the value of design

Among the most frequently used items in the bathroom are the taps, so when you have the chance to choose new ones make sure they are designed to be comfortable to use and easy to clean. Visit showrooms where taps are mounted on the bathroom fittings so that you can experiment with turning them on and off, remembering that in everyday use your hands will often be wet and slippery with soap.

The majority of quality taps are made from cast brass, which is usually chromium-plated for a shiny silver finish. However, brass-plated taps are also available, and you can find other special finishes such as antique or polished silver, gold, bronze and coloured finishes. Some taps are made completely from plastic, either coloured or chromium-plated. Tap heads can be made from the same material as the spout, or they may feature a contrasting material such as clear or coloured acrylic, onyx in various colours, or other semi-precious stones. Tap shapes range from the streamlined and ultra-modern to the traditional, in-

cluding careful copies of Victorian and Edwardian patterns. There are also fantasy taps that have spouts in the form of swans and dolphins, and even frogs and toads.

Bib taps are designed so that the water comes in from the side, and they are usually fixed to the wall. *Pillar taps* have the water coming up from underneath, and are therefore mounted on a horizontal surface. *Mixer taps* (sometimes called combined taps) for basins and baths can be made in three separate pieces: a cold-water control, a hot-water control and a spout (they may be called spread sets in the USA). Mixer taps can also be made in one piece, sometimes called a "monobloc" fitting in the UK, or a "centerset" in the USA. *Panel tap* sets consisting of two water controls and one spout are available for wall mounting with concealed pipework.

On luxury baths, the water controls can often be positioned on the side of the bath itself, or they can be mounted on the wall at the side of the bath while the spout is placed at the end of the bath.

Special monobloc mixer fittings for bidets incorporate an adjustable spray fitting. Wash-basin mixers are available with swivel spouts that can be turned out of the way—useful during hair washing, for example. In the USA, a spread faucet is available; this delivers water in a splash-free upward arc, convenient for drinking or hair rinsing. With smaller basins, particularly, make sure there is enough space to turn the taps comfortably. Corner taps are convenient for some basins because they are less obstructive during hair washing.

Much work has been done recently on the design of water-saving taps. For example, wash-basins used mainly for hand rinsing can be fitted with a single spray tap with the water coming out at a constant force. Temperature can be controlled by turning a knob. It is claimed that some spray-tap models can save up to 70 per cent of the water needed by conventional taps. They take a long time to fill a basin and therefore may not be convenient for all domestic purposes, but, on the other hand, washing under the

spray is quicker and more economical than filling the basin.

For extra ease of use there are taps that are controlled by levers, rather than by turning a knob, and push-button taps. These types of tap are particularly suitable for use by children, the disabled and the elderly.

Cleaning your taps

Clean taps and surrounds regularly to avoid any excessive build-up of dirt—the area around the taps is particularly prone to a build-up of greasy deposits. Chrome-plated taps should only need a wipe with a cloth wrung out in warm water and detergent, but if they get very dirty you can use a little cream bath cleaner. Special chrome cleaners are available for restoring dulled old chrome finishes. Gold-plated taps should be cleaned with a barely damp cloth using a minimum of rubbing—so that your wealth doesn't disappear too fast. For taps with other special finishes, or made from unusual materials, get the advice of the makers when you buy them.

The internal workings of a tap

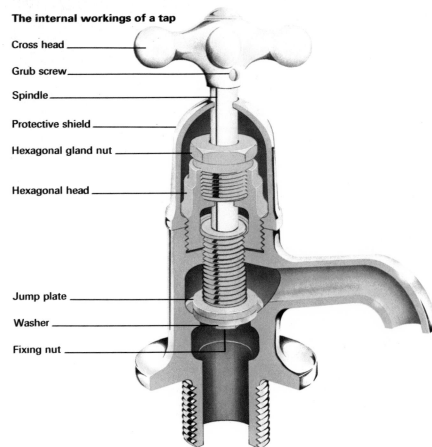

- Cross head
- Grub screw
- Spindle
- Protective shield
- Hexagonal gland nut
- Hexagonal head
- Jump plate
- Washer
- Fixing nut

Above: *brass and gun-metal mixer taps by Czech and Speake.*

Below: *Finnish thermostat mixer taps.*

Above: *chrome and plastic mixer taps.*

Below: *high-quality wall-mounted taps with mixer spout by Czech and Speake.*

Above: *taps for plunge and shower, mounted well up on the wall, leave the bath unencumbered and easy to clean.*

Top right: *brazenly swanning around the bath, these very unusual antique taps add individuality to the bathroom.*

Right: *slender, wall-mounted mixer tap with just the one control to regulate the flow of cold, warm and hot water.*

Below: *these taps and elegant pillar spout have been specifically designed with the user in mind. The high, arched spout facilitates hair washing and teeth cleaning, and the lever taps are ideal for the young, old and soapy-fingered.*

Above: *in the old-fashioned, upright style, these brass taps are very much easier to turn on and off than many of the more recent streamlined designs.*

Left: *if you are the proud owner of a wash-basin as pretty as this one, don't do it the injustice of fitting it with modern fixtures. Instead, complement it with graceful, porcelain-crowned taps.*

Accessories 1

Although your choice of basic fitments, wall and floor coverings set the style of your bathroom, it is the accessories that can make or mar the effect. In a large bathroom there is scope for some imaginative mixing and matching. In a small room, matching accessories look neater and are more restful on the eye.

Fortunately, extensive ranges of bathroom accessories are available in a variety of materials to create the effect that you want. Sealed natural wood, for example, can give a bathroom an informal, even country-house air. It fits in well with cork floors and tongued-and-grooved ceilings, and is particularly suitable in an old house, where the original fittings are still in use.

Chrome accessories, much loved in the 1920s and 30s, are useful to match chrome taps. They gleam satisfyingly if they are kept scrupulously clean, but should be chosen with care as their shapes are not always pleasing to the eye. For those who find chrome too shiny and clinical, satin-finished aluminium is a better choice.

A splash of colour

For a modern bathroom, or one that would benefit from an injection of colour, plastic fittings can be the answer. Many ranges are available, in colours that are bold or gentle, solid or clear, and the styles range from the conventional to the adventurously streamlined.

China and porcelain decorated with flowers, fruit or birds are perhaps the prettiest bathroom accessories. Other ceramic ranges are designed to be fitted into a tiling scheme to provide recessed soap dishes, toilet-roll holders and so on. Some manufacturers of bathroom fittings also make accessories that are colour matched with their baths and basins. And if you feel luxuriously extravagant, you can splash out on (or invest in) accessories with gold-plated finishes. For obvious reasons, never rub these too hard or clean them with scouring powders.

Practical considerations

Before choosing accessories for your bathroom, always make sure that they can be cleaned easily and that they meet your requirements. Are the towel rails, for example, large enough for your family? Each of your needs should be matched carefully against the ability of a particular fitment to meet them, and it is important not to get carried away.

Check, where necessary, how the fittings are to be fixed to the wall, and whether or not the fixings will be visible. If screws are needed, make sure you use ones that will not rust, and match them to the fittings where possible. Round-headed chromium-plated screws look best for fixing chromium fittings. Screws are often included in the pack with the fittings, so undo all the wrappings very carefully.

When choosing where to fix your accessories, act out the sequence of events involved in using the bathroom. Remember that if anyone slips on a wet floor, their immediate reaction is to grab any fitting that projects from the wall, so make sure that all fittings are sensibly positioned and firmly fixed.

Right: *a varied collection of dishes and bowls, soap-racks and mugs which are both practical and decorative.*

Above: *durable chrome fittings include two very useful items : an extendable shaving mirror and a shampoo dispenser.*

Left: *these low-cost moulded plastic fittings would add style to any modern bathroom.*

Right: *if your bathroom is decorated with brightly patterned wallpaper, accessories should be simple and plain.*

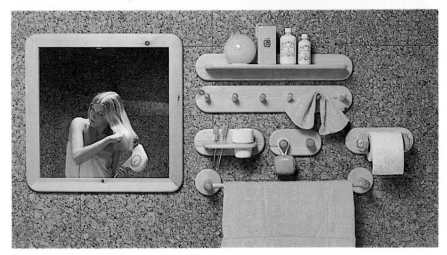

Left: *a range of chunky bathroom accessories in polished pine complements a cork-tiled wall.*

Below: *a washing-line in the bathroom need not be cumbersome or unsightly. This one neatly retracts when not in use.*

Above: *for the all-modern bathroom, Perspex towel rails and shelves look effective when brightly adorned.*

Below: *matching accessories in neutral tones accommodate and display towels, brushes and other paraphernalia.*

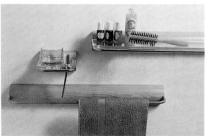

Accessories 2

Once you have acquired the basic bathroom accessories, you can take your time to find the extras. Keep an open mind as you look round the shops—various kitchen accessories, for example, can be put to good use in a bathroom, and junk shop "finds", which give a room character, can often be renovated at little expense. Remember, too, that there is no reason why functional objects should not be decorative as well—indeed, the challenge of decorating a room lies in achieving this dual purpose.

Mirrors: Before you buy, consider the size of mirror you need. A full-length mirror, if it is not free-standing, should be fixed firmly to a wall—not to the back of a door (all mirrors are heavy and need to be firmly fixed with heavy-duty screws, or hung from a strong chain). Small mirrors come in all shapes from the conventional to the bizarre—instead of an ordinary square mirror you could, for example, buy one shaped like a butterfly or a guitar.

Mirrors are often sold with frames that match a basic bathroom range. Alternatively, use an old picture frame, but make sure the framing is watertight or condensation will ruin the mirror. Old mirrors, found in junk shops and on market stalls, sometimes give a slightly distorted reflection—a disadvantage if you need to use the mirror for making-up or shaving, so choose with care.

Mug and glass holders: A wall bracket holding a single glass or mug is totally inadequate in a family bathroom. Instead, arrange a row of beakers in toning or contrasting colours on a narrow shelf near the basin, or fix a row of cup hooks beneath a shelf and hang up a selection of mugs.

Soap holders: These can be free-standing, wall-fixed, built into a recess, or made so they float on the surface of the bath water. The most practical designs incorporate some kind of drainage—soap lasts longer if it is not left lying in a puddle. If you cannot find a modern soap holder that appeals to you (some have awkward projections on which to bump elbows or shins), look for pretty Victorian china soap dishes, sometimes sold with the jugs and basins they were originally made to match. For a bathroom with chrome fittings, you could buy a "matching" salad shaker. Fill it with a selection of soaps, then hang the handles over one of the bath taps.

Waste bin: Unless you provide somewhere for people to put their rubbish, you will find grubby cotton wool and empty toothpaste tubes tucked behind the bath taps or on the window sill. An open bin means that rubbish is constantly on view. A better idea is to have a small pedal bin or, if you have a large family, a swing-top bin.

Seats: If your bathroom is big enough, a cane or wicker armchair is useful for putting clothes and towels on while you are in the bath, or for sitting on after the bath while, wrapped in a bath towel or robe, you indulge in a leisurely pedicure. In a small bathroom, you could box in the space at the end of the bath. Make a foam-filled towelling cushion to put on top. Cork-topped bathroom box stools, as well as providing somewhere to sit, give you extra storage space for spare bathroom paraphernalia.

Clothes hooks: Few bathrooms have enough of these, so you end up trying in vain to hang your dressing gown and night wear on a hook already occupied by two hot-water bottles and a shower cap. If a whole row of hooks (you need several for flannels, toilet bags and so on) is too reminiscent of school, use camouflage: simply paint the hooks the same colour as the surface to which they are attached. If there are children in the house, a row of hooks within their reach will encourage tidyness.

As an alternative to hooks, you could hang your clothes over an old-fashioned, free-standing wooden towel rack, stripped of its thick brown polish and brightly painted, or on a wooden valet stand.

Locks and handles: Try to co-ordinate these into your overall scheme. If there are children in the house, make sure they can reach and manipulate the handles. You should also be able to unlock the door from the outside, as children—and adults—tend to panic if they think they have locked themselves in.

Ring holders: The easiest way to lose a ring is to take it off to wash your hands, then watch it roll off the side of the basin and disappear down the waste or into an inaccessible corner of the room. Old-fashioned china ring holders, made in the shape of a hand or antlers, can often be found in antique shops.

Magazine racks: Piles of magazines on a chair or on the floor look untidy. The answer is a magazine rack, either built into a recess beside the bath or WC unit, or free-standing (bamboo racks are light to move for cleaning).

Above: *a motley selection of containers borrowed from the larder looks perfectly at home on the bathroom shelf.*

Below: *clever detailing on the angled edge of this vanity unit work-top ensures a permanent home for toothbrushes and the usually elusive toothpaste tube.*

Above: *soap dishes to make you smile. A docile pottery cow enjoys a bath, and could double as a butter dish. Both the cow and the mini-bath soap dish are from a range of amusing accessories by Christopher Strangeways.*

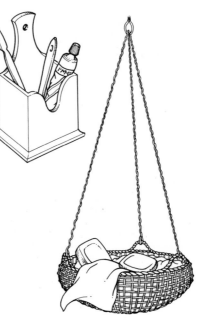

Left: *a wooden salt-box holds the family's toothbrushes and a hanging basket stores soaps, lotions and cosmetics that normally clutter the shelves.*

Left: *bentwood looks good anywhere, and these generously sized towel rings are as practical as they are pretty.*

Far left: *selection of wicker baskets and plywood barrels is perfectly in keeping with the country style of this wood-planked bathroom. Glass storage jars are ideal for supplies of cotton wool or bars of coloured soaps.*

Bottom left: *bathroom corner resplendent with good ideas: sufficient hooks to accommodate everybody's towels; a rack for magazines beside the WC unit; and a wall-hung basket above the cistern for bits and pieces of clutter.*

Below: *colourful wooden cut-out cheerily offers an outstretched arm for towels and a peg for soap-on-a-rope.*

Towels and towel rails

One of the cheapest and easiest ways to put the simplest bathroom into the luxury class is to make sure that there is always an adequate supply of large, clean, dry towels. Conversely, however grand your bathroom fittings, if your towels are damp and soggy your bathroom will never attain a five-star rating for comfort.

For reasons of hygiene, each member of the family should have his or her own towel. In large families, you can adopt a simple form of colour-coding so that each person always uses a towel of the same shade. Alternatively, some stores and many mail-order suppliers will embroider names or initials on towels for you, or you can embroider or appliqué large initials for yourself. And the height of luxury is for each member of the family to have a large, all-enveloping towelling dressing-gown.

Buy the best-quality towels that you can afford. Poor-quality towels will be annoyingly non-absorbent and have weak edges that will easily fray. Compare towels of different qualities in the shops, looking for dense, tightly packed, springy loops. It is wisest to buy from a store with a good name, or buy a well-known brand name.

Cotton, the traditional fibre for towels, is pleasantly absorbent and adequately durable, but it shrinks and takes a long time to dry. Some makers are experimenting with cotton/rayon blends for the looped pile; this reduces shrinkage and makes the towel quicker drying. It is common for the foundation fabric of the towel to be made from a 50/50 polyester/cotton blend while still using all-cotton for the loops; this makes the towels stronger and reduces shrinkage. Cotton/polyester towels dry more quickly, and it is claimed that absorbency is not affected; you must judge for yourself. Linen is still used for small, smooth-woven "huckaback" hand towels. These dry quickly and are easily washed.

A wide range of towel sizes is available, and you may find that some makers have reduced sizes to help offset the rising cost of raw materials. Check on the package the actual size of the towel you are considering, and its fitness for the purpose you have in mind. Do not be misled by meaningless descriptions such as "bath towel". A hand size, for example, might be anything from 51 cm by 76 cm/20 in by 30 in to 51 cm by 101 cm/

20 in by 40 in. Bath sizes can vary from 68 cm by 112 cm/27 in by 44 in to 76 cm by 137 cm/30 in by 54 in. The description bath sheet is also used, and this can be from about 76 cm by 152 cm/30 in by 60 in to 101 cm by 152 cm/40 in by 60 in or even larger. The easy rule is: for after-bath use, buy the very largest size of towel you can afford—it is a simple but lovely luxury.

Naturally, you will want your towels to blend with the rest of your bathroom colour scheme. Patterned towels may be printed, or they may be made by the jacquard weaving process, which creates a pattern from loops of different colours and sometimes varies the height of the loops as well. Plain colours range from palest pastels through to deep dyes, which even include black. Deep colours are more expensive because of the cost of the dyes, but you can quite satisfactorily dye old towels to new, deep shades. It is fashionable for one side of the towel to have a velvet finish, made by shearing or cropping off the tops of the loops. The visual effect is very appealing, but these towels can be annoying to use because the absorbency on the velvet side is considerably reduced.

It is a good idea to wash new towels before you use them. Absorbency is improved, and washing tightens the foundation weave so that the loops are held more firmly in place. Should a towel loop become snagged, don't pull it: trim it level with sharp scissors. Keep any instructions issued by the maker—these are often printed on the packaging, so read the packaging before you throw it away and cut out and keep any care information.

Most towels can be machine-washed at a maximum temperature of 60°C/140°F. Spin-dry or wring. Use fabric softeners sparingly; these can make towels less absorbent. Do not iron towels, but using a tumble drier will make them softer and fluffier. Deep-dyed towels should be washed on their own for at least six washes; some of their dye will bleed into the washing water. This will not affect the colour of the towels, but could affect the rest of the wash. Only use bleach on white towels. The most vulnerable part of a towel is its edge, so inspect carefully the edges of towels that you buy and see that they have well-finished hems. When towel edges become worn, you can bind them with tape

Right: *an ingenious space-saving towel rack that was cheap and easy to make from wood and chromium tubing. It is set into an alcove next to the airing cupboard, so that towels and face cloths are kept warm and dry. It makes a useful niche to air small articles of clothing such as tights and socks.*

Below: *absorbent home-made bathmat, that is simply interwoven strips of coloured sponge, adds a cheerful touch to a tiled floor and is a sensible safety precaution. A non-slip mat is essential for hard, smooth, potentially lethal bathroom floors.*

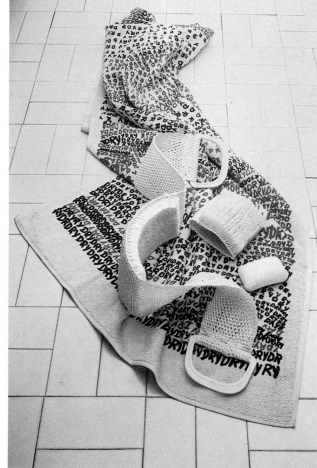

which has been washed and ironed first to pre-shrink it.

Plenty of towel rails for towels to dry on after use will discourage towel sharing. Larger families may find that the rails sold as part of ranges of bathroom accessories are inadequate. They tend to be short (about 76 cm/30 in long), and have to be massed in banks of four or five. It has been estimated that each person needs 60 cm/24 in of towel rail. Consider running your own longer towel rails around the room; make them from painted or sealed wooden dowelling or wooden slats, or from lengths of chromium-plated tubing. Small towel rings, though handy for confined spaces, do not allow a towel to dry properly. Towels should not be hung on hooks because they might tear.

Heated towel rails are a simple luxury. Clip-on rails can be attached to your central-heating radiators in the bathroom, bedroom and even in the passage outside the bathroom. A bank of rails can be mounted above the radiator, or you can connect a heated towel rail to your central heating system or to your hot-water supply (the latter will enable you to have a hot rail even in summer when the heating is turned off). You can also buy electrically heated towel rails; these should be installed by a professional electrician familiar with current wiring safety regulations. It is important that all towel rails are firmly fixed as they tend to be used as grab rails, particularly by children.

Whatever type of floor covering you have in your bathroom, some kind of bath mat is essential. With flooring such as ceramics and vinyl sheet or tiles, the mat prevents wet feet from slipping on the smooth surface. With carpets, the mat guards against the carpet becoming saturated. You may also wish to provide a mat in front of your wash-basin, or your bidet if it is used for washing feet.

It is sensible to have several bathmats so that you can wash them frequently—this is a bathroom item that tends to be rather neglected. A damp, dirty rag of a mat does nothing for your bathroom's appearance, let alone your own morale, health and comfort. Small cotton mats (or cotton/synthetic) which co-ordinate with your towels can be washed easily and are pleasantly absorbent. Old-fashioned cork mats provide a good non-slip finish and feel warm to the touch.

Above: *smart, reversible bathmats made of thick, absorbent towelling are part of the Habitat/Conran range of colour-co-ordinated towels, bathmats and bed linen.*

Top right: *a bath towel with an appropriate message. It teams up with sheets and pillow cases that exhort you to "sleep sleep sleep".*

Right: *on the practical side, bathmats should be big, absorbent and non-slip. From a visual point of view they can add a useful touch of colour to Spartan surroundings of wood and shiny tile.*

Multi-purpose bathrooms

Once you have chosen all the appropriate fittings and decided where to put them, the next step is to enjoy your bathroom to the full. Soaking in a bath, especially after an energetic day, is restorative not only to the body but also to the mind, and if you can do this with a *batterie de bain* at your elbow the pleasure is that much greater. This chapter investigates the properties of soaps and bath oils and the invigorating effect of loofahs. It offers some good advice on how to plan for relaxation both in the bath and out of it —where to put that drink, a book or a radio; and it includes suggestions on turning the bathroom into a mini-gymnasium, a study, a laundry or even a haven for do-it-yourself fanatics.

Multi-purpose bathrooms
Coming clean

We all spend a great chunk of our lives closeted in the bathroom and there are those who argue that the rituals we perform there are fruitless, except to the thriving cosmetics industry, and that the body can keep itself clean very efficiently without our expensive ministrations.

Nobody seems to be against cosmetics on scientific grounds. A lot of today's make-up is as hypoallergenic as technology can make it, and although many people prefer to use ecologically sound, cruelty-free, organic products, and others reject cosmetics totally, some dermatologists argue that make-up can shield the skin against harmful dirt particles. So, according to American dermatologist Dr Bedford Shelmire, you can keep your lipstick and foundation, eye shadow and blusher, but for the health of your skin and your bank balance you should throw out all your cleansers, astringents, masks and hormone creams. Not only does he think that these products are ineffectual but that they can be actively harmful to your skin. The pleasant tingling sensation you experience after applying some lotions is in fact caused by capillaries dilating and over-filling with blood, which can damage blood vessels.

Dr Shelmire also advises against extremes in temperature and rigorous facial exercises which, far from "tightening" muscles, will only cause wrinkles. In place of our exquisitely perfumed, well-packaged and high-priced paraphernalia he would have us use:

Pure Castile soap: Lather the face at least once but not more than twice a day. Use lukewarm water (never hot). Rinse thoroughly, adding one teaspoon of lemon juice to the final fresh-water rinse to help restore the skin's acid mantle.

Liquid paraffin: Use on a pad of cotton wool for pre-cleansing the skin before washing and for moisturizing afterwards. Blot off excess with tissues.

70% alcohol (rose water or witch-hazel): Cleanse oily areas with a solution of one part alcohol to four parts water on cotton pads, repeating until all grime is removed.

A loofah: For epidermabrasion on normal skins only: twice a week, after washing, gently rub the loofah over the face in a circular motion to remove any excess cells.

An egg white: When painted on to the face, allowed to dry and then rinsed off with tepid water, this will act as a cheap, effective face mask.

Although some experts would not be so profligate with what they discard and cosmetic manufacturers undoubtedly will continue to defend the virtues of their own products, all this does seem to be good, practical advice. There is, however, a groundswell of opinion that disputes the whole notion of washing and argues that it is the cause, not the cure, of skin complaints, dandruff and objectionable body odours.

The argument is not simple. It goes like this: the skin has its own ecosystem; it is colonized by benevolent microbes, natural "microbial flora", comprising nutrients and "selective bactericides", including sweat and oleic acid produced by the sebaceous glands, which are there to defend your skin against the invasion of hostile bacteria. Soap and water remove this thin, protective film of oil, leaving the skin open to attack both from inside by overreactive production of oil, and from outside by dirt and harmful microbes, which will adhere more easily and penetrate more deeply. Those who stop washing experience, as one might expect, their hair becoming greasy, body odours becoming stronger and looks of disbelief from friends. However, if you manage to stick it out past this stage the body gradually settles down and re-establishes its natural defences. Hair looks strong and healthy, skin ailments and dryness abate and offensive smells are replaced by a natural, attractive perfume that really is exclusive to its wearer. (In the days when perfumes were needed to disguise vile smells, the bad odours came not so much from unwashed bodies as from the unwashed clothing that retained stale perspiration.) The body's dirt can be removed by gentle abrasion with water and a natural sponge or loofah, and hair can be cleaned by brushing with a natural bristle brush or, more drastically, with "rhassoul", a Moroccan mud rich in mineral salts.

This may seem an extreme view, but it has received some support from skin specialists, who come across many problems caused by over-washing. If it suits your skin and hair and if you look and feel healthier, by all means go ahead. Not washing does no harm to the skin, although make-up should always be removed.

But what if you feel more confident scrubbed from top to toe and your toes curl up with delight at the prospect of breaking the cellophane on a ruinously expensive bottle of French perfume? The prevailing opinion is that you are being conned, that you are the victim of your conditioning from society and the pernicious purveyors of advertising. This may have been true in the past when there was little information about the contents and cost price of products, and when there was little alternative thinking or experimentation going on. But now the information is available and alternatives are many, it seems patronizing to assume that what people do with their bodies is not a conscious choice, especially in a matter as intimate as personal hygiene. Apart from the pragmatic reasons for the things we do, there are the sheer, tactile, sensuous pleasures of self-attention to be savoured. So do what suits you best—after all, you can always lock the bathroom door.

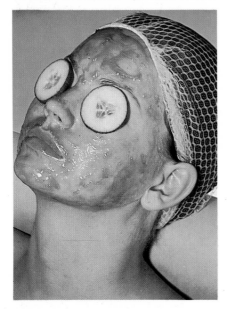

Natural cosmetics are cheap, they smell good and they work. A mixture of yogurt and honey, left on the face for twenty minutes, acts as an effective face mask. Slices of cucumber gently tone the delicate skin around the eyes.

Henna wax is a very effective and natural hair conditioner. For best results, the correct procedure to follow is to comb in the wax after having washed your hair, and then to rub it in thoroughly. To allow the wax to take

effect, wrap your hair in a hot, steamy towel for half an hour before the final rinse. Henna is an oriental shrub with fragrant white flowers—it makes the hair glossy and thick. Pigment extracted from this plant is of a reddish-orange hue.

"Nothing quite like it for cooling the blood"—mud bathing is reputed to be highly restorative and therapeutic. According to Rabyn Blake, who dug this mud pool in his own back yard, it is also a "numinous and sensual experience".

Soaps, shampoos and herbal balms

Vegetable oils and animal fats are the main ingredients of modern toilet soap. These basics go through a number of purification processes and are then "saponified"—that is, turned into soap by means of a chemical reaction involving caustic soda. Years ago, this crude soap was simply allowed to cool and solidify, after which it was cut up into blocks or bars. The end-product contained about 30 per cent water, was very coarse and tended to become brick-hard. Nowadays, further processing reduces the water content, making the soap purer, milder and more effective.

Soap is, in fact, one of the oldest of manufactured products, and there is a particularly grisly legend about the discovery of the soap-making process. A river that flowed past a sacrificial hill was found to be more effective for washing clothes downstream than upstream; this was because the oils from the victims' bodies turned into soap as they passed over alkaline clays on their way down the river—or so the story goes. Soap was certainly being made from animal and vegetable oils in the Nile valley by at least 600 BC. In AD 70, Pliny advised the Romans that the best materials for soap-making were the rendered fat of goats and beech ashes.

In Britain, soap was in use by the 16th century, but only as a luxury. Queen Elizabeth had one bath a month "whether she needed it or not". The big increase in use came only after prime minister Gladstone repealed the soap tax in 1853. Laundry soaps were widely available by the early 1900s, and led to the development of the first toilet soaps in the 1920s.

The function of soap is to cleanse the skin and keep it healthy. To do this without harming the skin's natural processes, most modern toilet soaps are as pure as possible. There are nevertheless considerable differences in formulation and quality. On the one hand, you can find soaps that combine 80 parts of animal fat to 20 parts of vegetable oils. These are relatively low in lather and tend to crack. Although functionally efficient, they are rather harsh. It is possible to increase the creaminess of the soap and the amount of lather it produces by increasing the proportion of vegetable oils and by super-fatting (the process of adding extra oils). This can produce a bar with a very high level of creamy lather, but which wears quickly

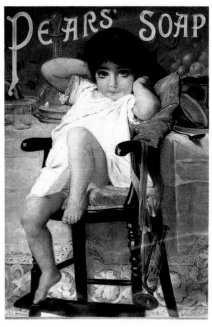

Above: *"Dark and Winsome Child", the 19th-century version of Pears' famous advertisement, extolling the virtues of their product to mothers the world over.*

Right: *a colourful collection of highly decorative and sweet-smelling soaps made by leading manufacturers.*

Far right: *health-giving herbal balms for skin and hair care in the bath. Herbs can be used to cleanse, condition, soften, deodorize, tone and moisturize.*

and will go soft and mushy in water.

Since most of the dirt we acquire is combined with oily substances from the skin, cleansing products need some sort of solvent ability (water on its own is not a good solvent). Solvents that are too powerful will dissolve oil and dirt but may also dissolve too much of the protective layer of sebum on the skin, leaving it excessively dry and flaky. A good modern toilet soap provides just the right amount of solvent action with an efficient lather that will not strip the skin of its natural oils; look for soaps that contain blends of natural ingredients, many of which will be similar to the oils in the skin itself.

Specialist soap-makers cater for the different skin types: avocado and cucumber, for example, are recommended for dry skins, buttermilk for sensitive

skins, sea algae for normal or slightly oily skins. Rosemary is good for oily skins, and glycerine soaps are particularly pure. Experiment with different soaps until you find the one that suits you best.

Shampoos

Most modern liquid shampoos are based on detergent, which is usually combined with some fatty material. Detergent loosens grease and dirt, and then thorough rinsing washes the hair clean. Detergent shampoos leave the hair very shiny but in the long term can dry it out. Creamy soap-based shampoos are kinder to the hair.

Shampoos vary, so experiment until you find one that suits you. Manufacturers add all kinds of things to their shampoos, but beware of gimmicks. There is no truth in the claim that hair can digest protein, for example. Herbs make shampoo smell nice, but there is little proof that the amounts in commercial shampoos have much effect. The same goes for egg—there are only minute quantities in commercial shampoos, and you would do far better to wash your hair in egg yolk and luke-warm water. You can make your own shampoos from the country soap-herb called saponaria, or soapwort. Combine this with camo-

mile for fair hair, and southernwood for brightening and conditioning. Sage and rosemary are recommended for dark hair. Nettles, lime flowers and fennel are also considered to be effective additives.

You may see some shampoos labelled as having a "low pH" value, designed to protect the "acid mantle" of the hair. The pH scale is used by scientists to describe the acidity or alkalinity of any solution. The scale ranges from 0 to 14, and water is neutral at 7. Acid substances have a pH value between 0 and 7; alkaline substances have a pH value between 7 and 14. Hair, skin and nails are all mildly acidic. Untreated hair, for example, has a pH value of around 5.6. Many shampoos are alkaline, and are therefore considered to upset the hair's natural acid balance. Special low-pH shampoos are now freely available from chemists and hairdressers.

It has not been proved that antiseptic shampoos clear dandruff. To control dandruff, try a shampoo with zinc pyrithione, or use one that contains the stronger (and often more expensive) selenium sulphide.

Bath salts and oils

Adding something to the bath water to make it foamy or to make it smell nice considerably enhances the pleasure of bathing. Pine and mineral salts can prove most refreshing.

You can perfume your bath water with small muslin bags of dried herbs; combine them with oatmeal to give the water a milky softness. Recommended mixtures for bath bags include lavender, thyme and lavender, camomile and rosemary. You can add lovage to act as a deodorant. Lavender steeped in boiling water is a recommended footbath.

Bath oils will soften the skin as well as perfume the water. You can buy essential oils from a herbal specialist—the oils are concentrated and very powerful fragrant oils of flowers, herbs, leaves, roots, seeds and barks, and include sandalwood, lavender, rosemary and musk. Add two or three drops to a tablespoon of shampoo to avoid an oily ring around the bath.

It is marvellous bathing in very soft water: it reduces harmful scum, leaves your skin smooth and your hair shiny. You will find, however, that rinsing takes longer than it does with hard water, so be thorough. Many bath salts soften the water, but if you live in a hard-water area you may like to consider having a water-softener plumbed directly into your mains system.

Multi-purpose bathrooms
Face cloths, sponges and loofahs

In order to emerge from the bathroom glowing with that feeling of cleanliness and well-being that makes washing a pleasure rather than a chore, it is essential to have all the necessary cleaning accessories and to keep them in good condition and scrupulously clean.

Face cloths may be bought in squares or in glove form. Finer-textured cloths are easier to wash with and to wash out than the thicker variety, although they wear thin more quickly. In large households, face-cloth identification becomes less haphazard if you allocate a different coloured cloth to each member of the family (this can be done with towels and toothbrushes, too). If you like vibrantly coloured, deep-dyed face cloths, you might find they need an initial laundering before use to remove excess dye.

Face cloths should be boiled at least once a week in water to which a few drops of vinegar have been added. Cloths that have become shiny with soap should be soaked overnight in a solution of water and white vinegar. If you suffer from any skin infection, avoid using a face cloth and simply wash yourself thoroughly with your hands.

Sponges: Synthetic foam-rubber sponges are available in a wide range of sizes, colours and textures, including very fine baby sponges. Although hygienic and easy to keep clean (simply rinse in warm water and a little detergent), synthetic sponges do not last as long or feel as pleasant as natural sponges.

Natural sponges come in a wide choice of sizes, in their natural yellow colour. They can be rather expensive, but their lovely texture and absorbency justify the price. Sponges are gathered from the Mediterranean and other warm seas; they are the soft-tissue skeletons of underwater creatures belonging to the invertebrate phylum *Porifera*. After harvesting, sponges are cleaned in the sea and then bleached and dried in the sun.

Always rinse your natural sponge thoroughly in cold water after using it with soap or with any other alkaline solution, but do not wring it out as this will destroy the tissue. Dry the sponge in a place where air can circulate and never store it in a polythene or plastic bag. Wash the sponge from time to time in clean water, but never boil it because this will harden the tissues. Try not to rub soap directly on to the sponge, as it is quite a job to rinse it out thoroughly.

Loofahs (also known as dish-cloth gourds) are marvellous for getting yourself really clean because their slightly rough texture sloughs off dead skin cells. Loofahs come from the cucumber-shaped fruits of climbing vines of the gourd family, and are green and edible when young. When the skin, pulp and seeds of the fruit are removed, a network of food- and water-carrying tubes is left; this is then dried and flattened. The loofah you buy is completely flat, but when you put it in water it quickly swells to assume its distinctive elongated and rounded shape, which it then retains.

Nail brushes and pumice stones: Every family needs a good, small scrubbing brush for keeping nails clean. The most useful type is the brush that has an extra row of small bristles along the handle. Ideally, you should have one nail brush by every wash-basin and one by the kitchen sink. Train children to use them from an early age.

Pumice stones are pale grey, angular pieces of porous stone formed from the solidified froth of volcanic lava. Kept in the bathroom, or near the sink, a small piece of pumice is very useful for rubbing off ink and hard skin. Moisten well and use with soap, but do not rub so hard that the skin becomes sore.

Toothbrushes: Despite the widespread incidence of dental decay, many people only replace their toothbrushes when they go on holiday or into hospital. You should, in fact, change your toothbrush as soon as it shows any signs of wear, so keep plenty of spares. Your dentist will tell you which type of brush is best for your teeth, and will show you how to use it correctly. You may also be advised to use toothpicks and/or dental floss. Many modern brushes have carefully designed heads with rounded filaments to protect your gums and to aid the brushing action.

*"Rub a dub dub, three men in a tub. . . ."
With all these implements at their
disposal, the butcher, the baker and the
candlestick maker would have had a field
day scrubbing, raking and teasing the
impurities from their pores.*

249

Multi-purpose bathrooms
Relaxing in the bath

The magazine of gourmet bathing, aptly called *Wet* and published in California, tells of the ultimate in relaxing baths: an isolation tank wherein you float in a soundless, light-controlled environment of your own, in water as salty as that of the Dead Sea.

Developed as a therapeutic aid in the treatment of nervous diseases, this isolation tank is now finding its way into domestic surroundings. Its users speak well of it. They report that it induces a state between dreaming and waking, and that on emerging from it they feel infinitely better-looking and more able to face their problems than when they went into their tank.

Now, of course, all but the Spartan school—in and out of the bath as though pursued by Jaws—have always known that a long soak eases tension. The self-indulgent among us prudently provide for extra pleasures: a speaker for music to soothe us; a portable battery-model TV to entertain us; a book rack that fits across the bath for reading, our heads comfortably supported against an air-filled cushion fixed to the bath-tub by suction pads.

Pleasure lovers will also make sure that there is plenty of space for setting down the odd drink or snack. This can take the shape of a wide, purpose-built ledge, part of the casing of the bath itself, or it may be simply a large stool, which can alternatively accommodate bathtime visitors—unless, of course, you provide more comfortable seating.

Once in your bath you won't want too much intrusion from the outside world, but a telephone by the bathside is not to be despised if you enjoy indulging in long, relaxed conversations—and it avoids having to pad, dripping, through the house to answer calls.

Above: *a wide surface surrounds the bath so that all the paraphernalia of relaxing is within arm's reach.*

Above: *designer David Hicks has furnished his bathroom like an elegant living-room, complete with reading stand.*

Below: *strain and tension flow away with the bath water gurgling down the drain in this cool yellow room.*

Above: *the long, luscious soak enjoyed by this languorous girl is enhanced by the armful of mint she is clutching, which infuses the water with its cleansing and soothing properties.*

Above: *this girl is floating in a buoyant saline solution—blissfully relaxed and tranquil—in a dimly lit, totally silent isolation tank.*

Left: *television and telephone are close at hand in this splendid bathroom, which looks more like a living-room. The bath rack has a special mirror to shave by while soaking in the tub.*

After the bath

After the bath is over, how much use does your bathroom get? Does it work for its living—or is it reserved for fleeting visits to the wash-basin, medicine cabinet and WC? Much more can go on in the bathroom than just bathing, and if space is available it can be employed not only in the pursuit of vanity and comfort but to create an escape from the general hubbub of the world outside.

When a deep, lingering bath has thoroughly relaxed you, it is pleasant to continue the therapy by resting awhile on a chaise-longue or on a purpose-built contoured couch—a splendid place from which to contemplate any amount of more energetic pursuits. And if your contemplation proves productive, a writing desk and a telephone will ensure that ideas can be put swiftly into action. From your couch you can also supervise the children's first exploratory water play—with children in the house, the bathroom walls and floor will presumably be both child- and water-proof. If they are not, your life will be full of unnecessary tears and recriminations.

With efficient ventilation and heating to eliminate vapours and keep the temperature comfortable, the bathroom becomes versatile enough to use in a number of unexpected ways. A long counter-top into which a wash-basin is set can make a good work bench for any members of the family who incline towards the do-it-yourself. Of course, only hand tools can be used since for safety's sake there must not be any high-voltage power points in the bathroom, and certainly in the UK no power points would be permitted, but cleaning up afterwards will be marvellously easy for both bathroom and user.

Left: *a contoured couch, purpose-built for the bathroom, is ideal for lounging on after the bath while wrapped in warm, thick towels or in a towelling robe.*

Top right: *superfluous headroom in this* WC *has been exploited as a wine store—not everyone's choice for a cellar, but the space over the cistern can provide much-needed storage in a small house.*

Right: *the Conrans' bathroom is a versatile room to be shared and enjoyed—the perfect location for a restful study, complete with writing table, an open fire and a comfortable couch.*

Above: *the bathroom as a workshop, making clever dual use of wipe-clean walls and studded-rubber flooring.*

Below: *a warm bathroom, comfortable enough to work in, with bookshelves, a telephone and a writing desk.*

Multi-purpose bathrooms
Body beautiful

Even the most flattering of mirrors, artfully designed to make the beholder appear more lissom than an undeceived eye will allow, can only tell little white lies, as Snow White's stepmother discovered. In general, bathroom mirrors and scales reveal the naked truth—and a little trimming is indicated, what better place for it than in the bathroom itself?

Of course, over-indulgence in exercise is never a good thing: don't plan on a *tour de France* on a fixed bicycle, a Paul-Revere gallop on a mechanical horse or a boat race on a rowing machine, without first consulting your heart, your pulse and your doctor. Even gentle gymnastics need to be monitored, and your doctor is the person to tell you how far you can go.

Given the all-clear, a gym in the bathroom needn't be an elaborate affair. Even an occasional swing on a single bar, firmly fixed just below the lintel of the door, marvellously limbers you up—as well as relieving the pressure on minor lumbar aches and pains. But have all fixed equipment professionally installed —you don't want to bring down the walls with your wall-bars, so consult your builder about how much strain your bathroom walls can be expected to withstand.

All electrical equipment must, of course, be professionally installed with due regard to the rules. This also applies to sun-lamps. Sockets may need to be outside the door, and the appliances themselves must be well out of reach of anyone actually in the tub.

Instead of just lying in the bath relaxing, do some gentle exercises to tone up your muscles—though gentle is the operative word, otherwise you'll have tidal waves crashing down on the floor around the bath. Just clench and unclench your muscles—leg and buttock muscles especially—repeatedly until they begin to ache. Washing can also be a form of exercise: a vigorous rub with a loofah not only tones up your skin and stimulates blood circulation, but the actual effort involved does you good too, especially when reaching for awkward places. Copy ballet dancers, with their enviably trim figures, and use the washstand or towel rail as the "barre" for leg and thigh exercises.

Whatever gymnastics you go in for, exercise first and sink into the tub afterwards (or step under a cold shower if you feel really Spartan). Then dry off slowly inside a bathrobe or in a large towel swathed about you like a toga. This is what the Ancient World used to do, and it managed to keep in tolerable shape for a great many centuries.

Useful exercise equipment: To keep in trim, exercise with help from any of the following equipment, all of which is suitable for use in the home: skipping rope; weight-lifting equipment, including dumb-bells, chest expanders, Bullworkers and iron boots; suspended bar; suspended rings; wall bars; exercise wheel (the sort you grab on either side and roll back and forth as if doing press-ups, to tighten the stomach muscles); body shaper (a pulley contraption for exercising the arms and legs); joggers (loose rollers for running on the spot).

More extravagant items: Fixed bicycle; rowing machine; sculling machine (a variation on the rowing machine); electronic impulse exerciser (to tighten flabby muscles); body belt-vibrator; electronic moving mat (for running on the spot instead of around the block).

Right: *poised to cradle the model figure, this immaculately manicured seat sets the scene for body beautification.*

Below: *a 19th-century image of how "la toilette" will be accomplished in the year 2000. The prediction of push-button control may well prove right.*

Above: *assorted weights and exercise apparatus are hung neatly on the wall below a set of keep-fit instructions.*

Right: *father and son relax in their solarium, equipped with infra-red and ultraviolet lighting for a year-round tan.*

Bottom right: *a spidery exercise bicycle keeps company with a chest expander and weights, all for the body beautiful.*

Below: *this bathroom doubles as a gymnasium, complete with floor space for exercising and a set of wall bars.*

Multi-purpose bathrooms
The laundry

There is no law to say that the weekly wash has to be done in the kitchen. Suds and soufflés do not mix, and the bathroom is often the best place for doing the laundry. On the other hand, you will not, of course, find it relaxing to take your bath with the baleful cyclops'-eye of the washing machine inescapably upon you in what amounts to the atmosphere of a launderette, so laundry arrangements in the bathroom need to be carefully planned.

From the practical point of view, the existing plumbing will to a large degree determine the position of the equipment:

the plumber will advise you what adaptations are feasible, and he will also be familiar with the building regulations so far as they affect drainage and angling of new pipes. On safety grounds, your electrician, too, must be consulted. (In the UK it is against the law to have a socket outlet in any room containing a fixed bath or shower.) He will put the lead of your washing machine directly into the wall and position the on/off switch outside the door.

From the visual angle, you may either work the hardware into your existing scheme or hide the machinery away.

Stacked washer/dryers may need only 155 sq cm/24 sq in floor space of their own, so a cubicle with a sliding door to enclose them neatly would not have to be any larger than that, though of course you need to allow a reasonable area of working space in front of it. If there is no spin-dryer and your drying arrangements are above the bath, these can be hidden by a deep baffle. Do not forget to provide space for your accessories: washing powders, bleaches, fabric softeners, sponges all need to be accommodated somewhere near the machine, and a shallow cupboard or a narrow

shelf may be all that is needed. For your dirty clothes you could provide a handsome, stout canvas bag hung from the wall, or a sturdy basket which can double as a bathroom stool. Better still, have two of them and discard your whites into one, your coloureds into the other, and, providing the family learn which is which, you will never have to do any sorting before you attack your wash.

Below: *with careful planning, a washing machine can be fitted neatly into a corner of the bathroom. Washing powders can be stored on a shelf over the bath.*

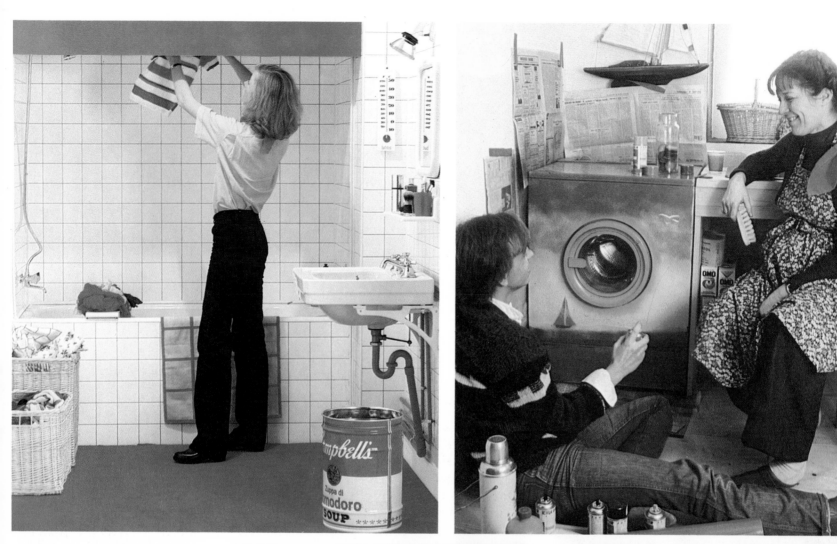

Above: *a cheerful red baffle or pelmet discreetly hides a row of washing that has been hung up to dry in the bathroom.*

Top right: *until the manufacturers become more imaginative, the only way to acquire a washing machine that is as pretty as it is useful is to decorate it yourself with spray paint.*

Right: *designed by Crayonne, this natty, wall-mounted canvas bag is the perfect place to tuck away dirty clothes and linen that are waiting for wash day.*

Far right: *this space-saving and compact bathroom unit consists of a roomy storage area that pulls out from under the sink and, on either side, deep pockets for soiled laundry.*

For children

It is important for children to have a room of their own—a room that is not just a bedroom, but an escape from the adult world where a child's own personality is allowed free rein. When planning a room for a baby, it is important to remember that in next to no time the cherubic and helpless infant will be transformed into a tough little skateboard fanatic. This chapter will help you to avoid the pitfalls of providing romantic decorations and inadequate storage facilities that will soon be outgrown and it discusses the wisdom of allowing children the freedom to reflect their own developing taste, however inappropriate their taste may seem to design-conscious parents. It investigates cots and cradles, both past and present, and on the practical side looks at the vulnerable surfaces— walls that children will scribble on, floors they will spill things on, bathrooms they will flood— and the washable, waterproof and childproof floor and wall coverings that will inevitably make for better relationships all round. With the information brought together in this chapter, you should be well equipped to bridge the decorative generation gap.

History of the cradle

Rock-a-bye-baby, on the tree top,
When the wind blows, the cradle will
rock. . . .

A nonsense rhyme? Not at all: hanging a baby in a tree, to be rocked by the wind, was a primitive habit: a Roman observer in Britain in the second century AD noted that the natives wove cradles into the branches. Nor is it extinct: trees in North American Indian reserves can still be seen festooned with papooses, vertical in their birch-bark cradles, which can also be carried on a mother's shoulders.

American wicker cradle, c. 1620: the child's mother or nurse rested a toe on one end of a rocker, so leaving both her hands free to sew or knit.

Navajo baby strapped into a cradleboard and propped up against a tree stump.

Even so simple a cradle could be dispensed with if the child were swaddled—that is, wrapped from chin to foot in linen bands, like a mummy—forming a neat bundle that could be slung from a tree branch, or laid on the floor by the fireside. Swaddling was a routine matter until the 18th century.

Primitive cradles were hollowed out from halved tree-trunks, and must have rocked easily. Some peoples still make these, with holes along the upper edges for thongs or cords to keep the baby from falling out. When square box cradles began to be made, curved rockers were added. These often projected, so that mother or nurse could sit with hands free to spin, weave or sew while rocking with one foot. She was even freer for other chores if the cradle had a vertical post carrying a cross-piece as a handle.

A basket obviously makes a good baby-container; crib can mean a wickerwork basket, whether or not for human occupation. Motorists still use the "Moses Basket" (in France, a *moïse*)—not the most accurate term, for the biblical original was an "ark" of reeds daubed with clay, purpose-made to float.

Wicker cradles carried to America by the Pilgrim Fathers, known as Mayflower cradles, have been preserved there in such numbers as to suggest that the ship must have been loaded to the

Carved walnut cradle from Tuscany, dating from the late 16th century: it is now in the Horne Museum, Florence.

gunwales, and the Puritans most prolific. Birch has long been recognized as the best wood for cradles, because superstition would have us believe it drives away evil spirits; whereas a child in an elderwood cradle will, at the very least, be pinched black and blue by the fairies.

The word cot for a child's bed is fairly recent; it is Anglo-Indian, from a Hindi

word for any bed, couch or hammock. In modern usage, a cot neither rocks nor swings, but such static rest was a rarity until, in the late 19th century, doctors began to suspect that constant rocking induced brain damage and what they described as artificial anaemia. That it might be possible to rock babies into imbecility was additionally absurd in view of the fact that they were at that time regularly doped with sleeping-draughts based on laudanum or brandy.

This sturdy, square box cradle on oak rockers was made in Pennsylvania in 1780. The body is carved from white pine and the top moulding is of ash.

The swing-cot, hung from above, has several advantages: it is quiet and smooth in action; if it is properly pivoted it will go on rocking for minutes and centrifugal force tends to hold the baby in. An ingenious variation, from the 16th century, offers the best of both worlds: it can be lifted off the hooks from which it swings, and set on the floor to rest on bottom rockers.

Where four-poster beds were in use, the cradle was seldom curtained, because it would be put within the curtains of the parents' or nurse's bed.

The cradle has always been a status symbol, and the most notable examples have served high-born infants. The more important the baby, the larger its cradle—large enough sometimes almost for an adult. A royal baby would have at least two, one for show and the other for everyday use. Two servants, working in turn, were employed solely as rockers— and a mere rocker was not allowed to change the baby's nappy, however urgent its cries. One royal cradle of the 15th century was upholstered with 1,200 ermine skins. Princelings were even coffined in their cradles, and a two-day-old daughter of James I of England was entombed under a cradle of marble within which her effigy lay. The children of

George III (King of England 1760–1820) had wicker cradles costing £13 2s each, probably their second-best, for the future George IV was first publicly exhibited when 12 days old in a nest of white satin, in a gilt cradle, under a canopy of crimson velvet; on either side of the cradle stood a fair mute, employed as occasion required to rock the infant to sleep. Such things were even better in France, where the cradle for Napoleon's son the King of Rome was six months in the building. One made for Queen Victoria in 1850 (her seventh child being due) is described by a connoisseur of the day as "a fine piece which would not have disgraced the latter period of the Renaissance".

The cot has in the past earned itself a bad name, infants being strangled by badly spaced cot-bars, guillotined by dropping side-frames, suffocated by soft pillows and cremated by flammable curtains. There are now government standards for these things, but doctors are still puzzled by cot deaths. There is one easy, partial explanation for them: if an average infant spends half of its time in a cot, will not half of all unexplained infant deaths occur in cots? Most of us die in bed, but that is not to say that beds are dangerous.

Right: *modern cots illustrated in a nursery scene by Sowerby, a 19th-century illustrator.*

Built in 1809, this was one of the first suspended cribs, in which the child could be "soothed rather than jolted to sleep". The frame was of mahogany.

Fantastically ornate crib, *above, a gift for an upstart emperor's only son, inlaid with silver and mother-of-pearl, was given to the infant King of Rome by the city of Paris in 1811. Napoleon was entranced by his son and contrary to convention would boisterously play with him or sit by the crib until the child slept, as depicted, left, by A. Dawant. Each day, the cradle would be carried into the emperor's study and set down by the fire, where the baby could enjoy the spectacle of government. The crib is now in Vienna, birthplace of Marie-Louise of Austria, the King of Rome's mother.*

Cots, cradles and bunks

A new baby will sleep in any kind of container that is warmly padded and deep enough to give protection from draughts—hence that familiar stand-by, a drawer lined with a blanket. Another tradition that goes far back into history is rocking the baby to sleep. The rich employed wet nurses or "rockers" to do the job for them, and it is recorded that the Tudor nurse, Mother Penn, who looked after the children of Henry VIII, had a whole team of "rockers" under her command. Today, a wide range of cribs is available, including many pretty designs in cane and wood. Some of them can be rocked, and one English firm makes a reproduction Tudor cradle—but unfortunately they don't provide the team of "rockers".

To cheer up a crib that is a very simple basic design, you can make a pretty fabric trim—but avoid soft, loose or clinging linings that might suffocate a child. Mattresses for cribs and prams should be firm, and a baby should never be given a pillow. As soon as a baby becomes big enough to move around to any degree, it is time to invest in a full-size cot with high sides.

Safety considerations

The main considerations when choosing a crib, cot or child's bed must be not only comfort and appearance but also, of course, safety. In the USA, federal safety regulations issued by the Consumer Product Safety Commission govern the sale of all cribs, controlling, for example, the spacing between the crib slats. If the bars are too widely spaced, a curious baby, anxious for a peep beyond the confines of a fenced-in world, may get stuck in the railings. In the UK, safety regulations are being introduced by the government, based on the new British Standard BS 1753:1977, Safety Requirements for Children's Cots—a standard that is already being followed by most reputable manufacturers.

Unfortunately, many of the accidents that do occur are caused by second-hand cots that have been stored in lofts and lumber rooms for long periods of time. Old wicker cribs and lovingly-preserved Victorian cradles are often beautifully romantic, but they could turn out to be tragically dangerous, so check thoroughly the safety of any old cot you intend to re-use. Most paints on the domestic market today are lead-free, but you should regard with suspicion cots that have been repainted at any time in the past. The new British Standard prohibits the use of decorative transfers on the insides of cots; do not add any transfers yourself, and watch out for old transfers that may be starting to peel off.

Make sure that the cot is properly assembled and that it is stable and rigid with all the necessary fittings; it has been known for the bottom of a cot to fall out and the child with it. Beware in particular of any kind of projection on the cot, such as the rods on the old style of cot that protruded above the top retaining brackets on the drop side. It is possible for children to catch threads of their garments on projections of this kind, and several cases of strangulation have been recorded.

Ideally, spacing between cot bars should be constant and should not be more than 60 mm/2½ in and not less than 25 mm/1 in. It is important that a child should not be able to climb out of the cot. The internal cot depth should be 495 mm/19½ in, which allows for a mattress depth of 100 mm/4 in. Some mattresses are 120 to 150 mm/5 to 6 in deep, and use of a thicker mattress could present a hazard with a very active child.

Always remove mattresses from polythene wrappers before use and make sure that the mattress fits the cot securely, with no dangerous gaps at ends or sides. This is particularly important if using old-fashioned bow-ended cots.

Folding lightweight cots are available in canvas or chrome-finished metal for travelling babies. Other cots can be adapted to different stages of the child's development. There are bases that can be raised so that a very young, immobile baby can be easily handled, and there are also cots that can be converted into small beds. Some models will even extend into a large bed.

Beds and bunks

Small-size children's beds are available (around 170 cm/5 ft 6 in long) and are sometimes fitted with guard rails. Alternatively, you can buy metal guard rails that clip on to a normal bed. Although young children like the feeling of security provided by a smaller bed, you may not feel that their fairly short-term use is worth the expense.

Where space is tight and two children must be fitted into one small room, bunks are the obvious answer. But choose with care not only the bunk but also the child who will sleep on top. Never put a young child into the top bunk who cannot manage to climb up and down without help, and never put any child up top who is prone to sleep-walking. Make sure that ladders are designed to provide good footholds, with a stable method of attachment to the bunk. Slats are preferable to rungs, which can feel uncomfortable to bare feet. Warn children that climbing up and down the ladder can be dangerous and teach them to use the ladder properly. Fix a light or lights that each child can easily turn on and off when in bed. Bunks with woven wire bases to support the mattress can catch and pull the hair of the occupant of the bottom bunk—some models now have an underside of smooth wooden slats.

Bunks that can be converted into two single beds are useful when children grow older and need less floor space for games—or if you move and can give the children a room each. Make sure the mechanism that locks the two bunks together is strong and child-proof. Some bunks have useful storage drawers that fit underneath—and extra storage is always welcome in a children's room.

Above: *a pampered child is cradled in a giant buttercup and shaded by palm fronds like giant wisps of grass, bringing an air of the garden into the nursery.*

Left: *a simple wicker basket, thickly lined, makes a cot just as snug and attractive as its more costly counterparts, and doubles as a carry-cot.*

Right: *the sides of this bright, graphic cot are removable in sections, gradually unfencing the child as it grows older.*

Top right: *beautifully simple Italian-designed bentwood rocking cradle with a slender stem to support a veil.*

Right: *this versatile cot, equally useful during the day and at night, combines the mobility of a pram with the attractiveness of a wicker crib.*

The nursery

Children's needs change least between the ages of four and 13, so rather than design a room exclusively for a baby, it is best to do so with a child in mind. The room that starts as a warm and quiet nursery for a new-born baby should be capable of evolving into a playroom and bedroom, reflecting the child's changing character as he or she grows. Sensible, flexible storage is highly important. Touches of whimsy are of no significance to a baby whatsoever, and become obsolete in a couple of years. Do not overlook the probability of an expanding brood, so choose the largest room available for your first child.

At the beginning, it is not important for a baby to have a separate room: in fact, most child-care experts are keen on the "bonding" as they call it, of the child and mother, which requires maximum physical proximity. This makes night feeds easier. A very young baby is unlikely to disturb you, but if yours is a constant snuffler, you may prefer a separate room.

Certain special baby equipment is indispensable. A full-size cot is too large to provide a tiny baby with warmth and security. Try instead one of the many attractive cribs on the market, or alternatively have the baby sleep in a carry cot, although a plastic surround can create too much heat. The generally accepted optimum temperature for a baby's room is, incidentally, 64° to 70°F/ 18° to 21°C. Moses baskets are inexpensive, easy to line in a pretty print, and easy to carry. One of these may last till the baby is three to six months old, when a safe, sturdy cot will be needed. Effect the transfer by putting the small crib in the cot a few times, until the child becomes familiar with the scenery.

Apart from a crib and cot, you will need a table or special baby trolley for nappy changing. This should have attachments to prevent the baby rolling off, storage space for clean nappies, pins and cotton wool and be of a height at which you can work without bending over. A baby bath is of equal importance, and can be used later to store toys. Small chairs—the bouncing type or angled plastic baby chairs—are useful, as is a nursing chair for the mother.

Decide in advance where you are going to clean and change your baby so as to avoid walking between bathroom and nursery with a slithery wet bundle in your arms. If you choose the nursery, you will need to install a basin, but bear in mind the havoc a toddler with aquatic interests may later cause.

Left: *nursery units, incorporating a padded changing-surface, can be arranged according to the needs of the child. With its unusually shaped surround it complements the low bed, designed to ease the transition from cot to bed.*

Far left: *there is no need to overprettify a room for a baby : this grand room has been made into a delightful nursery simply by adding a cot, nursery chair and toy basket. A mural of this quality is unlikely to pall over the years.*

Above: *a high-convenience nappy- or diaper-changing area : all surfaces, designed specifically with a baby and its nappies in mind, are easy to clean.*

The inflatable plastic cushion has "wings" to ensure that the youngster cannot roll off. This practical but attractive unit is safe and strong.

Above: *doubling up as an adventure playground, this bedroom is bestrewn with toys ; suspended butterfly kites are entertaining to gaze at from the cot.*

Top: *a lined wicker crib is very suitable for a new-born baby. It is right to place it in the parents' bedroom for convenience and to aid "bonding".*

For children
Toddlers' rooms

A room that only looks good when spotlessly clean may be all right for a tiny, helpless baby, but not for a rumbustious toddler: better to give up before you start and accept that a child's idea of play is an adult's idea of havoc. Provide adequate play space, durable surfaces and plenty of pinboards and blackboards if you want to keep your child happy and yourself in good humour.

Storage, particularly of bulky and oddly shaped toys, needs careful thought. Toys can be kept in big boxes or baskets mounted on wheels, odd bits and pieces can be put in string bags, and larger items, such as prams, can be parked when not in use beneath a work surface.

Fitted wardrobes are more practical than the free-standing variety since they leave more play-space. They are safer, too: a large wardrobe could topple over if a child swings on the door. The best storage systems are those that one can add on to, or with movable shelving that can be swapped for hanging space later on. Choose furniture that is finished with a washable paint or laminate.

Furniture that claims to perform many functions should be regarded with suspicion—it often does what it says, but with drawbacks. For example, there are cots that convert into small beds which may be useful for an only child, but oblige one to go out and spend money on a new cot for a second arrival.

Try not to be seduced by the attractive small-scale furniture on the market. Charming as they are, these pieces have a short life-span unless you expect, or know, a succession of small children to inherit them. If you cannot resist it, limit the purchase to just a table and chair. Cheerfully coloured blocks of foam will provide useful, additional seating when friends come to tea—and are fun for play.

The single most important factor to take into account when designing your toddler's room is safety. Remember that home accidents are the third largest cause of death in children between the ages of one and five. Electric sockets should be the three-pin, shuttered type, electric fires out of reach, and radiators not hot enough to burn bare legs or arms. Windows should be fitted with vertical grilles: horizontal bars are an invitation to clamber. The uprights should be no more than 7.5 cm/3 in apart to ensure that a child cannot poke its head through, then get stuck.

Above: *walls, floor and cot that match down to the knot in the wood, and the wood-burning stove—which must always have a guard when children are around— help to give this room a Scandinavian look. The cot's pretty embroidered curtains provide plenty of scope for children's games.*

Right: *this sensible safety grille is more attractive and less imposing than the more common vertical bars.*

Far right: *reflecting the traditions of the Orient, this playroom is spacious and ordered yet fun for the toddler. The gaily painted boxes provide excellent storage for toys and clothes.*

Above: *an abacus can be kept long after childhood, and here it is given a permanent but unobtrusive niche.*

Left: *a window cut into the wall transforms a partition into a play area, with storage space above, illustrating intelligent use of space.*

Top: *disposable and cheap, painted tubes of plastic or cardboard are fun to play with and useful for storing toys.*

267

For children
Stimulating surroundings

There is surprisingly little information on the effects of physical environment on young children, but common sense dictates that children brought up in attractive surroundings, put together caringly, will grow up with the greatest contentment.

Shapes and colours

Psychologists have evidence that children are affected by the colours that surround them: very bright primary colours, for example, can be over-stimulating; green, conversely, can be calming and blue depressing. But there are also indications that shape and form are more important to children than colour. For example play blocks, often a child's first toy, are of interest not so much for their colour, but for their shape and feel. And the shape of a room, especially if it is an odd one with nooks and crannies and sloping ceilings, is far more likely to be the touchstone for nightmares or for imaginative games than the colour of the walls.

But while bearing these points in mind, also remember the truism that children should not be overcosseted and must learn to adapt.

Colour and design alone do not make a perfect environment. Heating should be balanced, and lighting bright enough not to strain the eyes. A special nightlight or a central light on a dimmer switch should be provided for the child who really fears the dark.

A suitable floor surface needs to have a dual purpose: comfort for the child, practicality for the mother. Carpeting fits the first, but not so well the second, requirement. Cork, vinyl, linoleum or rubber are the best surfaces.

Walls represent the boundaries of a child's world, and are a source of enormous fascination: damp stains and uneven plastering soon become dragons or witches in the child's eye. They will be kicked, picked, drawn on and generally beaten up, and to counteract the assault paint should be durable and washable, i.e. gloss or vinyl emulsion. A wallpaper should not be so expensive that you grieve if it is spoilt—vinyl wall-coverings are more practical and hard wearing than ordinary wallpaper. Steer away from special nursery wallpaper because children are notoriously capricious, quite capable of dropping Paddington Bear in favour of Snoopy.

Above: *for sunny dispositions from an early age, yellow is an encouraging colour. Large cork pinboards present an ever-changing montage of pictures.*

Above right: *sheepish radiator grazes in green pastures. Young children appreciate a little humour in their surroundings.*

Left: *big yellow bus parked at the end of an attic bedroom. The fascia, full of interesting peepholes, conceals bunk beds and lights for bed-time reading. The bus sign doubles as a nightlight.*

Right: *sheets of cardboard with a washable, plastic coating cover both walls and floor. Kids can scribble to their hearts' content with water-based felt pens.*

Far right: *a colourful and inspired lesson in shape recognition.*

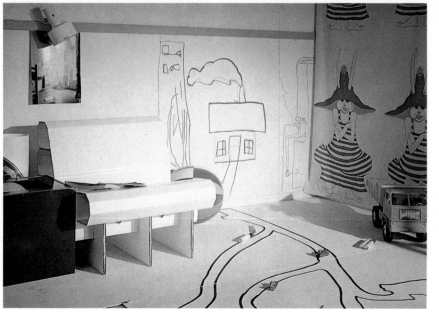

Room for growth

By the age of five, at the start of "real" school, a child's life-style will start to change. There will be a greater degree of independence from the parents and the child will spend more time alone playing or drawing, and later reading, pursuing hobbies, doing homework or simply day-dreaming.

To take in these changes, the bedroom must evolve into a place where the child has privacy, and which will be conducive to homework as well as play.

If you want to encourage your child to do more homework than day-dreaming you should make the chore as attractive as possible by providing a comfortable desk and chair and pleasant surroundings. A desk has the advantage of drawers, with the exception of the old-fashioned, school type with sloping top, which may not always shut properly because it is often packed with too many books. A table or fitted work-surface can be supplemented by an office filing cabinet for storing pens and paper, and can also be used for messier pastimes.

Make sure that the desk and chair are the correct height—it can affect posture for the rest of a child's life. A ready guide for the proper height of a desk is the level of the fingertips when one's arm is held hanging at one's side. So that it may be maintained as the child grows, either the desk or, more conveniently, the chair should be adjustable. For the latter, a revolving office stool is ideal.

As desks or tables and chairs move into your child's bedroom and the need for storage—for anything from dolls' houses to tennis rackets—increases, you may find floor space being whittled away. One needs to be aware of this because, even though a child has ceased to literally live on the floor, this will still be used for various hobbies and larger toys like train sets and model farms. If there is a right moment to carpet a child's room, it is at school age, because there will be less risk of damage to the carpet. Also, the extra warmth and reduction in noise will be appreciated.

Adequate lighting is important. Not only should there be a decent light by which to read, but its switch, and one for the main light, should be within reach of the bed. There is no fear like that of waking in the pitch dark after a bad dream, no agony worse than being unable to go to the lavatory because it is too dark to see the way.

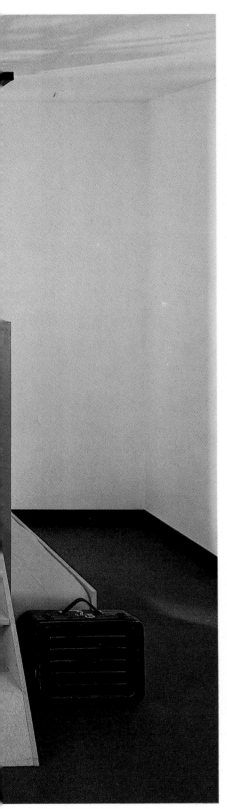

Left and above: *growing up in an interesting environment. The supporting turret at the head of the bed, lined with striped canvas, can become whatever a child's imagination dictates. The steps, on the other hand, conceal a more distinct function. A well-lit desk on the lower level is a positive encouragement to study and has plenty of room for storage.*

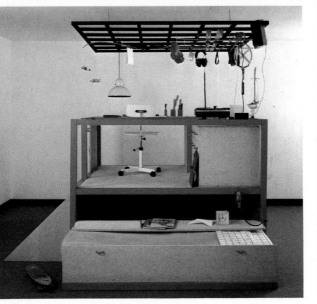

Left and above: *a sturdy, timber-framed structure, just 2 m/6 ft 6 in square and filled in with chipboard panels, makes room for everything a boy could want. The surrounding space is left free for* *football practice and other such boyish pursuits. Like a captain on his bridge, the young owner works from a commanding position. Come bedtime, a divan slides out from under the platform.*

Above: *huge wall-tidy made of remnants cut into jolly shapes and stitched on to a canvas backing. A cheerful way to preserve childish treasures from the tyranny of parental tidiness.*

Room for sharing

Many babies share their parents' room for the first few months of life. This may be convenient when the baby occupies a small crib, but might be tiresome when the time comes for a move into a large cot; not only may the cot prove an encumbrance but the child might waken feeling cheerful, if not rowdy, at the parents' bedtime.

At this stage it is generally better to move your child into a spare room, or an older brother or sister's room. Beware, however, of putting a baby in the same room as a child who might be tempted to "help" by picking up the baby when it cries, thus running the risk of dropping it. Also take into account that small children who share a room tend to keep each other awake.

Bunk beds are the practical solution to shared rooms, but can be dangerous for very young children, who may fall either while climbing up or while fighting on the top storey. Consider keeping bunks as single beds until the children understand the hazards. Choose bunk beds

carefully—some are well designed, others have unsafe ladders or are not securely fastened together. Making bunk beds is hard work unless you have fitted sheets and duvets, or sleeping bags—simple enough for a child to manage.

Each child should have a personal section of storage space, and perhaps a pinboard or separate corner of the wall. Artificial divisions can be created with screens and storage units placed at right angles to the walls, though children rarely stay on their own side of the fence.

It obviously depends on the children's temperaments as to whether they share a room happily. About the age of nine or ten children start becoming aware of their individuality and sex, and need more privacy.

Sharing can be of positive benefit in teaching tolerance and learning to live with others. Conflicts mostly arise when friends are entertained: a child often wants the right to be alone with his or her particular friend and this calls for tactful organization.

Above: *practical and economical bunks are ideal for a holiday house. Note the ingenious and firmly fixed ladder for hopping into the top level.*

Above: *an imaginative way of stacking bunk beds when not in use. The lower bed is pulled out from beneath the upper one, as are the two large storage trays. Centrally positioned lamps are adjustable so that one child can read while the other sleeps undisturbed.*

Left: *a sliding partition doubles as a blackboard and provides some privacy as the children grow up.*

Right and far right: *the colourful blind in front of the bunks hides them from view during the day, provides a cosy atmosphere for sleep and allows the child on the top to sleep even if the one on the bottom is still romping around. The drawback of using roller-blinds is that they can easily be put out of action, especially by small hands grabbing and pulling, so they are not suitable for rumbustious children.*

Splashing about

Children make an awful mess in bathrooms. Their primary aim is to flood the place and they never hesitate to use other people's towels, powder and precious bath oil. A bathroom used by children should therefore be well and truly waterproof, warm, practical and its cupboards, especially the medicine cabinet, secure. A sunken bath surrounded by thick-pile carpet may be luxurious, but ridiculous when it comes to bathing the baby.

Babies in particular have special needs in the bathroom. If you dress the baby there you will need some kind of nappy-

or diaper-changing table and storage for all the paraphernalia that goes with the job. A special baby bath is useful since a full-size bath-tub is frightening for a tiny infant, and uses an unnecessary amount of water. A substitute for a baby bath is a large wash-basin, if care is taken. A heated rail is useful for warming the baby's towels and clothes.

One or two adaptations will have to be made for toddlers, not least a fairly waterproof and non-slippery floor surface. Cork serves the purpose well and also makes a warm, sound-absorbent wall

covering. Vinyl or studded rubber are both good coverings for the floor.

Wash-basins can be set into plastic laminate surfaces with lockable drawers and cupboards beneath, which provide plenty of space for keeping bathroom odds and ends. If you have a large family, two wash-basins are an advantage, preventing all sorts of crises where a horde of children have to be ready for school at the same time. The problem of height can be overcome with a simple step-up or sturdy stool in front of the wash-basin. Existing lavatory seats can be

fitted with special removable child-size seats for safety and comfort.

Basic safety precautions: if the bath does not have a non-slip surface it should be fitted with a special rubber mat. Taps should be carefully positioned, the hot one easily identifiable from the cold. The hot water should not be scalding. Light fittings must be totally enclosed, and switches must be either outside the door or cord-operated. Doors should not lock on the inside. A lever handle is easier for wet, perhaps frightened, hands to manipulate than a round doorknob.

Above: *here, the kids are trying the grown-ups' side for size. The wooden cross-bars are attractive and provide the necessary multilevel towel rails. Slithering in and out of a sunken bath is a joy to children with alligator instincts.*

Left: *hanging on the airing-cupboard door, baskets for children's underwear look attractive and are easy to reach— a simple solution if tidy storage is something of a problem.*

Far left: *washing is easier for children in a split-level bathroom: a raised floor to one side of a unit brings taps and plugs within easy reach, while the razor, high above the lower level, is only accessible to an adult. Bright fittings and a toothpaste dispenser will lure the most reluctant child to wash; non-slip, studded rubber flooring is impervious to overenthusiastic splashings.*

Left: *with its narrow proportions, this converted corridor, cheerfully decorated, makes a very suitable children's bathroom. A corner bath can easily fit two children at a time and it has a wide ledge for rubber ducks and boats.*

Above: *slotted into the bath surround and resting on battens fixed to the wall, an adjustable plank is a simple and effective way to accommodate growing children in the bathroom. It is particularly important to lay non-slip floor tiles beneath this fixture.*

275

One-room living

When you first leave home you will probably rent a room that is far from perfect, but with energy and very little money you can make it a room that you and your friends will really enjoy. Many of the most original furnishing ideas shown here have sprung from an impecunious ingenuity. There are all sorts of ways to divide space into the various functions it will have to house. This chapter explores the possibilities of changing the floor and ceiling levels, and of putting up screens and partitions to help the subdivision process in a room that may be a first home, or a room within the house for a teenager, an independent grand-parent, even a lodger or an *au pair*. This chapter discusses colour, pattern and lighting as some of the cheapest and easiest ways to transform a dreary room; it looks at furniture that folds away or serves a dual purpose, and at versatile storage, planned, like the room, to lead a double life.

Planning for a double life

Before you start designing for one-room living in earnest, you must decide precisely what the function of the room will be. Do you want to sleep in your living-room or live in your bedroom, or attempt a room which is both? Will extensive cooking and washing facilities be required and, if so, does this entail additional plumbing and ventilation? No one wants to sleep in a miasma of fried fish and chips, or do a huge pile of washing in a tiny, enamelled hand basin.

To create the simplest, most functional house-within-a-room, it is best to adopt the attitude "here is the bed and here I live" and avoid too much disguised and flexible furniture, fold-away kitchens and bath-tubs that serve as bases for tables. If, however, the bed happens to be a splendid four poster, or you have a lovely brass bedstead, it will make a splendid main feature.

Similarly, the best method of dividing the room is the simplest: a screen or a blind hung from the ceiling, or storage units brought out at right angles to the wall. A high-ceilinged room could be divided horizontally into a sleeping gallery for an agile person.

The hardest shape to adapt to one-room living is, unfortunately, the most common—a square or nearly square box with one window and one door. Use the window as a starting-off point for deciding how to arrange the room. Would you prefer to sleep or eat by it?

The positioning of large pieces of furniture, such as bed and wardrobe, must be carefully thought out. Placed by the door, forming a lobby round or over which you look into the room, they often look less conspicuous than if they face you as you enter. The dull back of a wardrobe can then be disguised with mirror or foil, or softboard for pin-ups and posters. The most effective way of apparently doubling the area of the room is by the use of mirror, particularly opposite the light source.

Having painstakingly and cleverly arranged your room for maximum comfort and efficiency, you may well find yourself still hard up for space. Turn then to boats and caravans for ideas; nowhere else is storage and space used by necessity with so much imagination.

Right: *the "greenhouse" treatment works best in a big room. No need to disguise a bed that provides such useful seating.*

Above: *a second floor suggested by a platform with storage beneath in this well-organized room.*

Top left: *an ideal room for an agile student. The platform bed leaves plenty of space for a work and dining area.*

Top right: *a penniless couple use their possessions to stunning effect in a simple, practical room.*

One-room living
For grannies and teenagers

It is debatable who can be more stubbornly independent: a widowed grandparent living with a son or daughter, or a rebellious teenager "trapped" by family life. For both, and for the *au pair* who is treated as a member of the family, a private retreat that reflects their taste and character is of great importance.

Unless your elderly relative is very fit, choose a centrally located room where the rest of the family can conveniently keep an eye on the occupant and hear a call for help. The ideal environment for elderly people is one in which they feel they still lead an independent, useful life, though in reality they are being cared for. The room should be much more than just a bedroom. It should be filled with memories: photographs, china, pictures and prized pieces of furniture. Above all it should be cosy and restful, and as such it may become a pleasant retreat for younger members of the family.

There should be shelving for treasures, a comfortable chair or two (not too soft or low), radio and television. The radio and a good reading light should be within easy reach of the bed. The bed itself should be of medium height and easy to make. A small circular table saves space and has no sharp corners for an elderly person to bang against. If space is really short, a canvas pannier slung over the arm of a chair will take care of books or current knitting projects.

A heater with visual warmth provides a comforting glow as well as being safe. As elderly people are much affected by draughts, trouble should be taken to exclude these at doors and windows. Lighting should be soft, local, and include an adjustable reading or sewing light. Grandparents dislike wrestling with cushions and fitted bedcovers every time they want a rest, so the bed should remain exactly that and not masquerade as a sofa.

If space permits, consider a few useful additions: an electric kettle, for use in bed; a sliding table with an adjustable tilting top; an upright piano; a dog or cat basket plus occupant; and plants, which besides being attractive could provide a welcome interest.

At night, sheer curtains let down from a cotton "roof" transform a novel bed, desk and storage unit into a delightful house-within-a-house.

Unlike the older, frailer members of the family, any self-respecting teenager given the independence of a private room is likely to misuse the privilege by deafening the rest of the family with music. Take some elementary soundproofing precautions: thick carpets, heavy curtain material and timber are all sound-absorbent; so are irregular features such as doorless cupboards. Priority should be given to a site for the record player and racks for records, and ample storage should be provided for the endless collection of clothes, games, sports equipment and amusements. Scrubbed orange-boxes are cheap and adaptable.

Young people enjoy sitting on large cushions and bean-bags rather than bulky chairs, and in this way one can compensate for space taken up with storage. To complement the seating, you could provide a low coffee table.

While the floor may take a beating from spilt coffee and wine and will need to be easily cleaned, the walls will be in for a rough time for other reasons. Do not hang anything too heavy on plasterboard and always use proper picture hooks. Use masonry nails to minimize damage to brick walls, and try wallpaper paste for posters—never Sellotape. For postcards and photographs, provide a large piece of softboard and some bright pins.

Above: *a slatted-wood blind can be pulled down to hide the bed during the day without blocking out the light.*

Above: *giving a room character is more a matter of imagination than money. Here, inexpensive furniture such as the bamboo tables, Chinese matting and a cheerful old stove make a child's room a welcoming retreat.*

Left: *a cleverly placed bed means extra wall space for shelves and storage units and gives a square room the illusion of being a far more interesting shape. During the day the bed becomes a sofa scattered with cushions and with the pillows disguised in cushion covers.*

281

Self-contained

Adding cooking, dining and washing facilities to a one-room flat can transform the room into a delightful and orderly mini-house. Equally it can create a lamentable jumble of washing-up and toothbrushes; of bulky tables and chairs competing with a bulging dresser which threaten to squeeze human beings out through the door. To this chaos will frequently be added the stale smell of yesterday's fry-up.

A self-contained arrangement, preferably in the former style, would suit a self-sufficient grandparent or grown-up child, an *au pair* or living-in servant, a rent-paying lodger or your first one-room flat. Whoever it's for, plan the conversion carefully. Decide where the sleeping, eating, cooking and washing areas will be in relation to the best position for the sink and ventilation, which should be as near the cooking area as possible.

Extractor fans, wall-mounted or ducted into the ceiling, are the best answer for ventilation, though they need careful siting and tend to be noisy. Existing windows could be louvred.

Cooking facilities
It is amazing how much food can be produced with the barest essentials. An electric kettle, one gas or electric ring and a pressure cooker is enough to produce a substantial meal. There are excellent small-scale ovens and fridges on the market: an electric cooker with two rings, an oven big enough for a roast and space between for grilling and warming plates stands 419 mm/16½ in ×

457 mm/18 in; fridges, wall hung or free standing, with ample room for one person's food, stand about 558 mm/22 in × 482 mm/19 in and include an ice-making compartment.

For those who feel they can live without a Sunday roast, there are plenty of ingenious alternatives to ovens and cookers. The electric skillet will fry, steam, stew or bake, and there are also electric casseroles, grills and grill-barbecues for steaks and chops. Used imaginatively, these can produce adventurous meals—and for guests as well. Perhaps the tidiest idea is a unit that incorporates a small sink, refrigerator and hob and can be shut away from view when not in use.

Washing and bathing
It is unlikely that the room will be large enough for full bathing facilities; the law in the UK requires that a WC unit be separated from the cooking area by a lobby or at least two doors. If there is room, remember that a bath need not be full size but can vary from sit-up tubs to those that fit into a corner. Showers take up less space and are economical, but harder to disguise.

Even if the bath is shared with the rest of the house there must be a sink in the room. If much washing-up is done the sink should be a stainless steel one, as enamel basins chip easily. You could provide a separate plastic or pottery bowl that will sit in the sink for hand and teeth cleaning. A tenant may not share the same water system as the rest of the house, and the best choice for him or her

would be a multi-point gas heater hidden in a well-ventilated cupboard.

If you or your tenant has a horror of lonely hours spent in drab launderettes, you could even invest in a mini washing machine. One that measures only 380 mm/15 in × 482 mm/19 in will take about 1 kg/2 lb of washing. For drying there are many types of clothes driers, telescopic racks and airers that can be folded away when not in use.

You, your tenant and the law: in Britain, a tenant living in the same house as the landlord and receiving board is not en-

titled to have his rent fixed by a tribunal, and is not fully protected under the Rent Act. It is, however, a criminal offence for a landlord to evict a tenant in residential accommodation without a court order for possession.

It is difficult to summarize the American tenancy laws because rules differ from state to state, but in general they are based on English law. All states permit a landlord to evict a tenant by giving legal notice, followed by legal action, although details of notice to quit vary considerably.

Above: *the major elements of a house are drawn neatly together, leaving plenty of living space. Cooking and storage areas can be hidden away by blinds, and additional free-standing storage acts as a room divider.*

Far left and left: *a room that works equally well as an office and as a one-room flat. The two-sided desk allows office equipment and personal things to be stored separately. The mirrored wall fits both roles and makes the room appear far larger than it is.*

Right: *a room divider-cum-closet supports the sleeping platform, and the dressing-table becomes a desk or table top in this elegant, dual-purpose room.*

One-room living
Camouflaging the bed

In any one-room flat the bed is generally the bulkiest item of furniture, and for convenience it often needs to be disguised. The way in which the bed is best presented depends largely on the dimensions of the room. In a big, open room, a screen or curtain will simply and efficiently hide the bed from view. However, where a screen would swamp the room, camouflage the bed with a cover, or make it into a decorative focal point with the use of cushions and hangings. In limited space, a bed that will convert into comfortable seating or even a work-top for day-time use is often the only practical answer.

Left: *when the room is being used during the day, this bed, cunningly disguised as a cupboard, can be quickly and effortlessly hidden from view.*

Above and top left: *in a secret hideout, suitable for wheeling and dealing, there is no room for both table and bed so one neatly converts into the other.*

Above: *multi-coloured cushions, stacked high on the bed, disguise the bedhead* *and provide the room with a decorative and luxurious focal point.*

Right: *in this dual-purpose room, candy-striped bolsters double as pillows and arm-rests. The continental quilt is well camouflaged in its matching print.*

Convertible sofa-beds

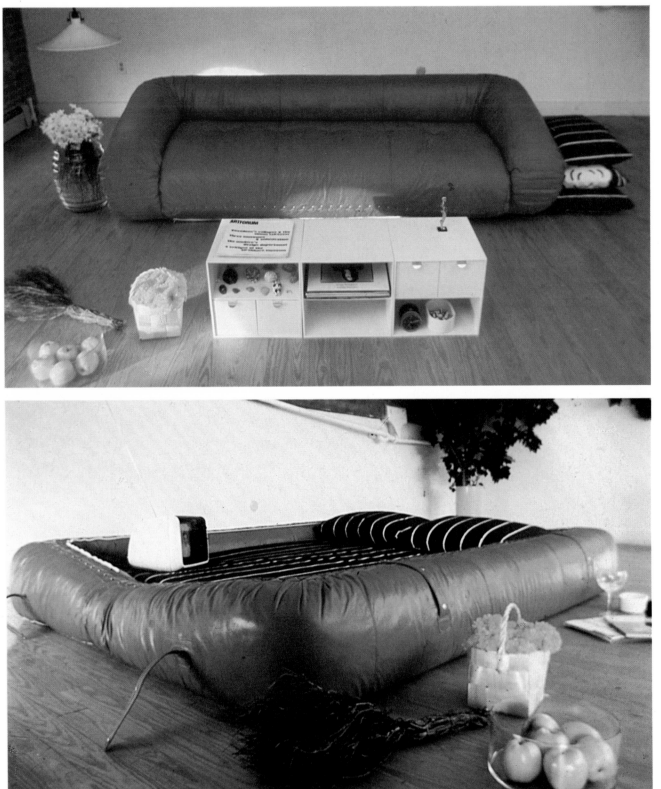

Due to the very nature of one-room living, it is often necessary to combine the greediest space-eaters, the bed and the sofa, in one piece of furniture: the convertible bed.

When choosing a bed-sofa, ensure that it is not too tedious to convert. Beware, too, of one that is neither a comfortable bed nor an adequate sofa. Many convertibles that make good beds are too deep in the seat to sit on comfortably during the day. Others are visually marred by untidy upholstery ridges and furrows. Buy the best you can afford.

The most comfortable convertibles are those that present one surface for sleeping on and another for sitting on. One bed-sofa that fulfils this requirement has a mattress that doubles over to make a very comfortable day-time sofa; another is a sofa incorporating a conventional mattress which, at the tug of a lever, simply folds out from underneath the sofa's cushions.

Left: *this classy Italian bed-sofa is large and comfortable and can be converted from its role as a daytime sofa to a night-time bed easily and quickly.*

Right: *a unit seating system that converts into either a double bed or a single bed with a chair beside it. The bed is made up with a duvet in preference to sheets and blankets, which take up more storage space.*

Above: *in a one-room flat, where space is at a premium, a bed-sofa can be the most practical solution, provided it is positioned so that it can be converted without too much rearrangement of the rest of the furniture in the room.*

Right: *a new design in the traditional style—a craftsman-built wooden settle that unexpectedly converts into a comfortable full-size double bed.*

Versatile storage

Storage is always a problem in a small space, but nowhere more so than in a self-contained room. Cooking and washing equipment, clothes and bedding all have to be stored separately, and you may well need more storage space than purpose-built units can provide. A little imaginative thought can reveal some well-disguised and practical solutions.

When casting around for ideas it helps to look at the interior designs of boats and caravans, where everything is on a small scale and one finds drawers under beds, shelves above windows and doors, and narrow shelves on the inside of cupboard doors. Remember that the underside of a shelf is a useful storage spot—specially made sliding baskets

can be attached to it, or the lids of screw-top storage jars can be fixed to it, so that after use the jars are simply screwed back into place. Walls can be utilized with knife-racks, hooks and canvas or plastic wall pockets. Wire flower baskets suspended from the ceiling in the kitchen area make attractive containers for fruit and vegetables.

The extent of kitchen storage will depend on how much cooking you intend to do, but at the very least room must be found for tea, coffee, mugs and a kettle. Shelves wide enough for plates, with hooks for cups and with one or two trailing plants, look attractive and store a surprising amount.

When choosing storage units, fitted

Top left: *a free-standing storage unit filled with books makes an attractive wall decoration and solves a problem for a hoarder of old magazines. Unusual basketwork drawers provide storage for clothes in this one-room flat.*

Left: *a large purpose-made tray, hung from the rafters by strong webbing straps, makes good use of the ceiling as a means of storing possessions that are not in constant use.*

Right: *an ingenious pulley system, quite in keeping with this amusing though functional room, allows a basket of goodies to appear at the merest touch.*

or loose, look for versatility in their appearance—for furniture that looks equally at home in the bedroom and the sitting-room. A frilly dressing table, for example, has no place in the self-contained room. Long cupboard doors can be divided horizontally into two to look less obviously like a wardrobe; wall-to-wall storage, though space-saving, can be visually dull if not broken here and there, perhaps with a recess lined with mirrored glass to give a sense of depth. An attractive alternative to this type of storage or to built-in cupboards is a large *armoire*, complete with hanging space, drawers and shelves. Even chairs and tables can give you extra storage space. A table with drawers is more use-ful than one without, and one with a folding or sliding flap is a great asset. Wooden chests can be cushioned and used as seating.

A primary goal is to achieve a sense of space. Oddly enough, this is some-times created if shelves and cupboards are brought out at right angles to the room, perhaps dividing the sleeping and living areas, leaving walls free for paintings, mirrors or hanging carpets to divide them vertically. A free-standing column with shelves and cupboards on both sides can make a useful and effective division in a room.

Yet for all that versatile storage aids one-room living you will find tidiness of the utmost importance.

Above: *from this entrance, set into storage units, the room appears larger, undiminished by bulky cupboards.*

Below: *a high bed, an open-sided table and attractive miniature shelving all provide storage for sundries.*

One-room living
Zoning

If you are only temporarily ensconced in a one-room flat, it would be impractical to make structural alterations to partition off the various living areas. Visual trickery, however, is cheap and easy.

Floor, walls and ceiling can each be effectively divided up with splashes of colour and changes of texture. Spreading rugs around the sitting and sleeping areas is a simple way to create floor zones—things look particularly attractive on stained, waxed or painted wooden boards—or you could paint the floor a different colour for each zone. For a more permanent effect, carpet the general living area and lay linoleum tiles where cooking and dining takes place. Wallpaper, paint and hangings can divide up a wall, and the ceiling may be painted to make highlights of colour.

One cunning use of space—and a trick that costs nothing—is to arrange the existing furniture in conversational U-shapes: a sofa with attendant armchairs, a table with chairs on three sides, a bed and drawer units—these can all form an effective U-shape. This leaves the walls free of clutter and visually defines the various zones. In partitioning off corners and slices of a room, curtains and screens come into their own.

Skilful lighting can do much to create zones within a one-room flat. Dark, ugly recesses and vast chimney breasts can be made less oppressive by the creative use of spotlighting, floodlighting and the shadows they create. Dimmer switches give even more scope for lighting illusions and can change a room's atmosphere by a turn of the knob.

Below and bottom: *in this room, mobile storage units trundle effortlessly into position to separate one area from* *another. A deep-pile carpet divides the living area from the polished boards of the storage and work zones.*

Left: *a finely woven drape, separating the bed from the living area, breaks up the space and provides privacy.*

Above: *a louvred blind camouflages the bed without completely cutting off one portion of the room. The stiffened fabric slats can be drawn back when the division is not needed.*

Below left: *this one-room city flat has been imaginatively split into three with blocks of free-standing cupboards. A central reserve for relaxation is flanked on the one side by a bedroom corner and on the other by a dining area over-looking the towers of Manhattan. The woolly rug and Mexican wall hanging add to the illusion of three rooms.*

Splitting the floor and ceiling levels in a one-room flat has the same exciting effect on a room as landscaping has on a garden. It is a practical measure because the resulting areas can be more distinctly divided from one another, and the effect is also visually stimulating.

There are many ways to incorporate different heights and depths into one room, depending on the dimensions of the room. In a large, lofty room, an extreme change of level can be achieved with a high sleeping platform equipped with a ladder or stair. In a more modestly sized room, a low wooden dais can easily be built at one end, over the existing floor if necessary, making a well-defined eating or sleeping area. Lowering either whole or part of the ceiling by installing a false ceiling makes a high room cosier, and if the new level is built strongly enough the space in between the two ceilings can be used for storage. Resting a wide shelf on wall-mounted battens is a simple way to lower one section of the ceiling, but easier still is a length of fabric stretched across the area.

Split levels, of whatever sort, are always particularly effective when balancing out a room for one-room living. The simple rules to remember are that the overall weight of a timber-jointed platform on the floor structure should not exceed 25–30 kg per square metre/5–6 lb per square foot, and that local building regulations may limit the floor area over which you can reduce the height of the room. If you plan to do any major structural work to floors or walls, first consult a reliable surveyor.

Left: *a high-level platform removes the sleeping area from the main living quarters and makes maximum use of the space available. The ladder that gives access to the platform also acts as a partition between two living areas.*

Right: *in this open-plan room, a solid partition and a step down to the sunken bed helps the psychological transition from living to sleeping.*

Top right: *a happy compromise between private bedrooms and open-plan living: the furniture has been built-in, partitioning the private domains, so that each child has an equal slice of this large attic as well as a share in the communal recreation area.*

Right: *a stepped dais that raises the bed level also provides seating, shelving and drawers. Access to the bathroom is kept open to create a feeling of space and to allow light from the bathroom window to penetrate the living area, but the WC and bidet are privately partitioned.*

Spare rooms and sick rooms

What a pleasure it is to stay with friends who have put thought and care into planning and equipping their spare room to accommodate guests. The secrets of the successful guest-room and the perfect host are not difficult to decipher, yet they are rarely put successfully into practice. This chapter explains the simple virtues of doing as you would be done by, of planning your guest-room as an hotelier would plan the rooms in a first-rate hotel. It shows how guests can always be made to feel relaxed, how to deftly arrange guest bedrooms and bathrooms so that everything guests might need is close at hand and in the place they might expect them to be. It deals with those all-important welcoming touches, such as freshly picked flowers on the dressing-table and a nightcap by the bedside. It explains how you can create extra sleeping space and washing facilities, how to turn the spare room into an extra family room when it is not accommodating guests, and how best to cater for the special needs of those who are ill, old or disabled.

The guest-room

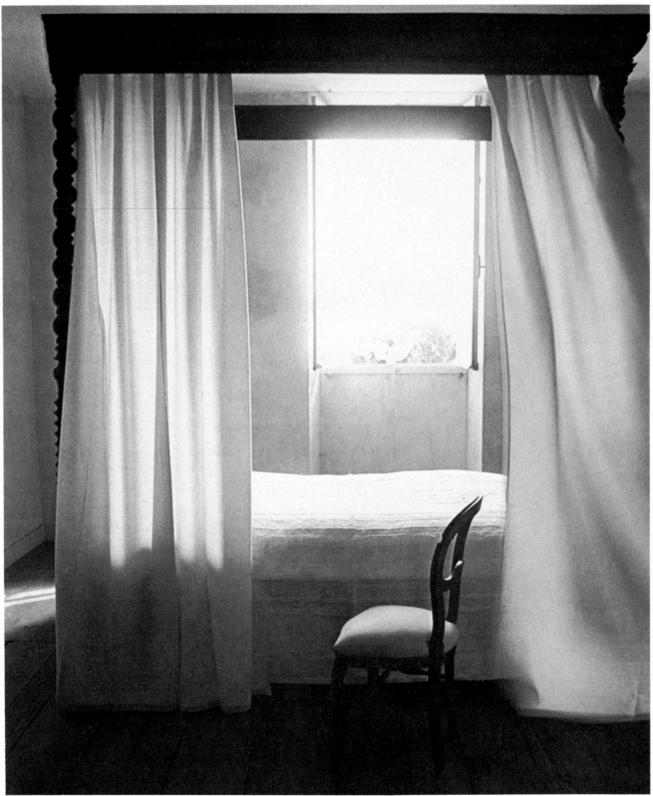

"And mighty proud I am (and ought to be thankful to God Almighty) that I am able to have a spare bed for my friends." Thus wrote Samuel Pepys in his diary for 1666, proving that being able to accommodate overnight guests was as desirable than as now—although whether he puts all his guests in the spare bed together is not clear.

Too often today, however, the guest-room is the forgotten room in the house; uninterestingly decorated, it becomes a dumping ground for odd, unwanted pieces of furniture, its cupboards stuffed with discarded clothes. This might be fine for the host, who rarely goes in there, but not for the guest who spends a gruelling night on a lumpy mattress, with nowhere to hang his clothes.

Ideally, the guest-room should be comfortable and friendly, a natural extension of the rest of the house. It should be neither too masculine nor too feminine, but a room in which an aged aunt or a teenage nephew will feel equally at home. Aim for a relaxed and ordered atmosphere, and avoid intimidating guests by strewing fragile objects around —you won't be pleased if something breaks, and your guests will be mortified.

Lighting should be atmospheric, but

Left: *this curtained bed makes the most of the morning sunshine.*

Below: *bunk beds are ideal for small bedrooms—each guest can read or sleep in comfort without disturbing the other.*

the last light of the night should switch off from the bedside so that guests won't be faced with negotiating a trip over a foreign floor in the dark. The best way to find out whether your guest-room lighting is doing its job properly is to test it yourself: try reading while pretending that another occupant is resting.

Guests are unlikely to require wall-to-wall storage, but there should be a spacious hanging cupboard and a chest of drawers. If the cupboard has a deep shelf where suitcases can be stored, so much the better. A dressing table should have a large, well-lit mirror and plenty of space for hairbrushes and other essentials, and a shallow drawer will score high for stowing small objects, such as the contents of pockets. A comfortable arm-chair to relax in with a reading lamp close at hand will help to turn the guest-room into a home-from-home. And fortunate indeed is the guest who has a bathroom installed *en suite*; if this is not possible, a wash-basin in the guest-room will remove some of the revising of time-tables that usually becomes necessary when an extra person has to share the family bathroom.

Unless your guest-room is frequently occupied, rather than forget it exists, you could use it between guests as a sewing-room, a study, or even ensconce an upright piano and use it as a music-room. A spare room with a neglected air frequently communicates unwelcoming sensations to the sensitive guest.

Above: *instead of leaving your attic to the cobwebs, convert it into a spacious spare room. The sloping roof adds character to the room, giving it a snug, almost chalet-like appearance.*

Left: *twin beds are often the most practical sleeping arrangement for a guest-room. The green and yellow scheme of this simply decorated room is dramatic and refreshing.*

Far left: *a matching bedspread and curtains bring charm to a small guest-room. Fresh flowers next to the bed complete the spring-like theme.*

The perfect host

When it comes to playing the perfect host, few of us are in a position to rival the legendary standards of the Astors and Vanderbilts or, more recently, the Duchesses of Windsor and Argyll. Gone are the days when hosts had to ensure that guests' shoes were cleaned overnight, that their cars were whisked off by the chauffeur to be washed and their clothes were unpacked, pressed and laid out by the valet or the lady's maid. Gone too are the days when exhaustive records were kept of every visitor's favourite foods, of what they last had to eat at your table and who they sat next to.

Nowadays the role of the host is thankfully less daunting; all it requires is plenty of easy hospitality and a little thoughtfulness. The guest-room should obviously contain the essential elements: a comfortable bed or preferably twin beds, good lighting and adequate storage. It is the finishing touches that say "welcome": a posy of fresh flowers on the dressing-table will make the room look fresh and well cared for. A tray with glasses and a bottle of Malvern water, a box of tissues and a wastepaper basket, the bed invitingly turned down, an electric blanket and a bedside radio all make your guests feel that you care about their comfort.

Check that all the lights work, make sure the guest knows where all the switches are, and provide a torch in case the guest needs to locate the wc in the night. Bath towel and hand towel should be neatly laid out and face cloths should be provided along with somewhere for the guest to hang them when they are damp. The thoughtful host will also provide a fresh bar of soap, bath oil or foam, a new toothbrush and toothpaste and some eau-de-Cologne.

Tell the guest what time the family rises in the morning and what time breakfast is served, and offer an alarm clock and the option of a breakfast tray in bed. Have plenty of clothes hangers, free drawers and shelf space—smelling more of lavender sachets than mothballs. All guests will appreciate a supply of writing paper and envelopes, a cheerful selection of books and current magazines, a soothing nightcap to retire with and sincere wishes for pleasant dreams.

As you reap what you sow in the field of hospitality, you can then look forward to being royally entertained yourself.

Left: *a selection of ivory-backed brushes add a subtle touch of luxury.*

Opposite: *plentiful storage, a handy shelf for small items, and a bed that converts into a sofa by day combine to make this a practical guest-room.*

Bottom left: *bunches of flowers, however simply arranged, mean a great deal in terms of welcome.*

Below: *a border of flowers and café curtains make this bathroom homely and comforting in the simplest way.*

Below: *a bedside table covered with a pretty cloth is thoughtfully furnished with a water-jug.*

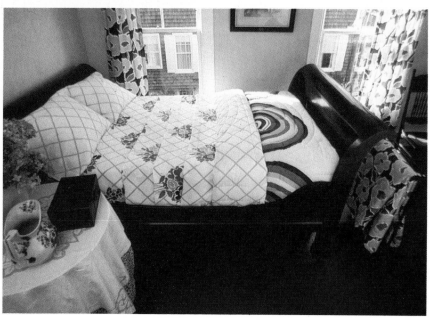

Spare rooms and sick rooms
Extra sleeping space

In a large house with plenty of space to spare for guest-rooms, dinner guests who have missed the last train, visiting relations and the like pose no greater problem than that of finding a clean pair of sheets—and some households, we are told, keep the guest-room ready right down to a made-up bed and biscuits in the tin on the bedside table.

In a small house or flat, however, the solution does not have to lie in creating makeshift camping facilities on the living-room sofa. In fact, unless you have a sofa that converts into a proper bed this is rarely very satisfactory: sheets and blankets that tend to slide about and armrests that get in the way of long legs do not make for a good night's rest, as the morning after's cricked backs and stiff necks too often testify. If you mean to make people comfortable, put them up in a proper bed, even if you have to put up the bed in an unconventional place.

Have a look round your house—is there a tall space, potentially wasted, which could be horizontally sliced by a platform? An inaccessible, unusable space that could take a platform on which to put a mattress? Foam cushioning can be cut to any size, so there is no need to stick with the standard width of 76 cm/ 2 ft 6 in, although anything narrower than 68.5 cm/2 ft 3 in is not recommended. Nor does your bed have to be a traditional 190 cm/6 ft 3 in long—nobody is going to mind spending the odd night on a bed a bit shorter than usual. Provided you use fitted sheets and a duvet (which you can store in a drawer built under the platform when not in use), bed-making can be as easy as sleeping is comfortable.

Overnight beds

There are, of course, any number of ingeniously designed spare beds on the market. There is the sofa that can lose its foam-rubber arms and back to become a highly desirable double bed for the night (it is an answer, too, for people who want comfort for the sitter rather than the sleeper in their one-room abode). There is the folding mattress with a plump bulwark, looking like a life raft when it is opened out, but which straps and doubles up to act as a comfortable living-room couch. There are, as there have always been, sleeping bags, which are the height of comfort for those who are reasonably hardy and request "a

corner of your floor". There are hammocks—for which you need stout hooks in stout walls—and at the other end of the built-in scale there are beds that unfold and unfurl from the most unexpected places. A pivoted bookcase can turn round to display a bed that can be let down like a drawbridge when the need arises, and there is no reason why you should not have a similar arrangement on the inside of a closet door: although if your guests overstay their welcome, the temptation to shut them away, together with their bedding, might be irresistible.

Right: *an object lesson in exploiting potentially wasted space in a high-ceilinged hall. Overnight guests climb up to a platform built across the width of the landing. Roller blinds ensure privacy, duvets ensure easy bedmaking.*

Centre right: *a simple guest-bed replaces the traditional under-the-stairs clutter of muddy boots, vacuum cleaners and picnic baskets. Foam mattresses can be cut to fit a base or platform that is not of a standard size, making a perfectly comfortable occasional bed.*

Below right: *three spare beds stacked in a stair well. Simple, pine platforms are linked by a single ladder—duvets and pillows are stowed away in a box under the bottom bunk.*

Below: *the top of a wide, solidly built-in closet becomes a hidden bed gallery overlooking the dining-room.*

Above: *to bed in the attic—a cosy retreat, but only for the agile. Low-ceilinged niches in the garret are not for granny.*

Top: *a hanging bed floats on high over the living-room, as an integral element of the room's design.*

301

Extra washing facilities

Visitors will appreciate a bathroom of their own—and you will appreciate your guests all the more if they are not closeted in your bathroom splashing themselves with your favourite Cologne. Extra bathing facilities will also add considerable value to your home, so it is worth inspecting every pocket of under-used space with an eye to turning it into a bathroom or WC—however small.

Plumbing installations will be less expensive if you can intersect existing pipe runs. Examine the possibilities of installing showers, WCs or baths in corners of attic bedrooms, in the space under the stairs, slicing off a section of the kitchen or utility room, or even pressing the outhouse or coal-hole into service.

It is possible to cheat on conventional measurements by using mini-sized fitments. Many manufacturers, aware of the need for fitting quarts into half-pint pots, have risen to the challenge and made numerous practical, well-designed and smaller-than-usual items a part of their standard ranges. Many tiny fittings have also been developed and built for specialist usage in boats, caravans or laboratories.

The smallest practical bath is one designed for a caravan: it is only 255 mm/ 10 in deep and 1.2 m/47 in long. There is a small WC designed for kindergartens that is only 300 mm/12 in high, and an upright hand-rinse basin that projects only 140 mm/$5\frac{1}{2}$ in.

Once you have stolen a little extra space by using mini-sized fitments, you can juggle with the rest of the space by slicing off unnecessary headroom over WCs and baths, or non-essential elbow room in the shower. Use awkward angles for built-in storage—however curiously shaped the space, there is bound to be something to fill it.

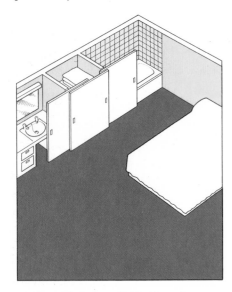

A slice of bedroom, divided into three private cells, becomes an accessible bathroom when the doors are open. When closed, it masquerades as a closet.

Right: *exploiting space in the entrance hall. The closet under the stairs becomes a shower—a curved wall and a flexible concertina door conceal a WC.*

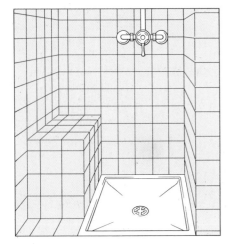

A shower room, however small, will add to the value of your home. Ankles and thighs need less space than elbows.

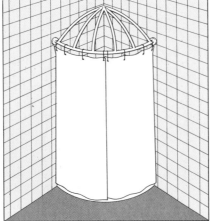

A shower will fit into any corner if plumbing runs near by. Use an angled shower tray and corner curtain fitting.

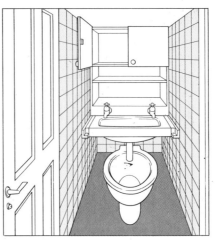

Ingenious double use of a tiny space. A shallow wash-basin slides out on runners and drains directly into the WC unit.

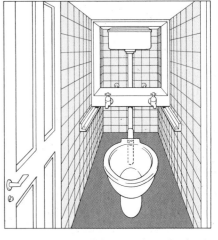

The wash-basin slides back into the depth of space taken up by the cistern. Taps are plumbed into a fixed shelf.

A WC *unit that has found a home in an unlikely but practical spot—a disused but spacious closet.*

Above: *the taps that sprout from a gap in the wood slats are the only clue that the floor in this narrow bathroom conceals a full-length sunken bath. This is an excellent and easily managed arrangement that solves the problem of having to sacrifice the bath for valuable floor space, or vice versa.*

Right: *a window alcove has been employed to provide a space-saving basin, and a pleasant view for the user.*

Far right: *baths can often be made to fit into the most unusual places. This one has been tucked diagonally across an attic corner.*

Left: *this shapely basin has been specially made to curve round the corner, making use of an oddly shaped alcove.*

Bedrooms for the disabled

There are so many types of disability that it would be impossible to lay down one set of rules to cope with the vastly differing needs of, for example, the arthritic, the blind and the paraplegic. At least 5 per cent of the population suffer from some degree of disability. Most are over 50 and experience great difficulty in moving around due to stiffening joints. Some have been disabled from birth and are chair-bound; yet others suffer impaired sight or hearing.

Most of us are "disabled" temporarily at some time—during pregnancy, a long illness or the aftermath of an accident—and everyone finds bending and stretching progressively more difficult with age.

Many of the design points that are intended to help the disabled to live more comfortable and independent lives are therefore worth considering in every household.

Mobility
The wheelchair user faces the most problems because of limited mobility and reach. Floors must be level and easy to traverse—no thick-pile carpets or raised thresholds to doors—and clear of unnecessary furniture (the turning circle of the average-sized wheelchair is 1.4 m/ 4 ft 7 in). Doors must be at least 825 mm/ 34 in wide and hinged on the side nearest the corner of the room, preferably opening outwards from bathrooms and WCs. All locks should be able to be released from the outside.

Heating
Slow movers feel the cold acutely, and hypothermia in bed can be fatal. Rooms should be kept at 17 to 20°C/65 to 70°F. Bedroom fires should not have exposed elements or flames because of the danger of dressing gowns catching fire. Bathroom heaters should never be positioned where they could be touched when standing in the bath or shower (in the UK they must be earthed and connected to power points outside the bathroom).

Lighting
Good lighting is essential for safety and efficiency; bad lighting leads to depression and fatigue. As well as a good general light, individual lights should be provided at activity points. Switches should be at the same level as door handles. Tip switches and pressure switches are useful for those with minimal movement;

pull switches can be fitted with large rings for those who have restricted arm movement. Hinge switches in closets work automatically as the doors are opened. Dimmer switches are useful to lower light levels for television viewing.

Communications
A telephone at the bedside is essential, both for emergencies and for contact with the world outside. Help can be summoned from within the household by bell, whistle, "baby" alarm, intercom, entry phone and videophone. For those with hearing problems, systems can be amplified or fitted with light signals. A telephone attachment (designed originally for busy executives) with pre-programmed cards can make calls for those who cannot dial or hold a receiver. Remote controls for television sets are readily available, and talking books can be hired for those with impaired sight. A "Possum" unit is a highly sophisticated system designed to enable even the most severely disabled person to operate radio, television, telephone, typewriter, curtains, lights and electric fires. The unit is designed so that the controls can be adapted to suit any disability—the electronic wizardry can even be activated by a blow tube. Appropriately, possum is the Latin for "I am able".

Planning the bedroom
The bedroom should be planned with easy access to the bathroom and WC, and not too far removed from family living areas. The bed should be placed in such a way as to afford a sideways view through the window to avoid glare. Wheelchairs need manoeuvring space of at least 1.1 m/3 ft 8 in at one end and on one side of the bed to allow for bed-making. Windows should have low sills, no horizontal bars at eye level and be easy to open. Vertical sliding sashes and high fanlights can be fitted with pull-cords and winding gear. Side-hung casement windows, louvres and horizontal sliding windows are the easiest to operate. For the bed-bound, french windows allow beds to be wheeled out on to sunny terraces.

Beds must be comfortable and at the right height to suit the individual. Old and arthritic people often have difficulty bending at the hips and therefore like a high bed. Chair-bound people need the top of the mattress to be level with the

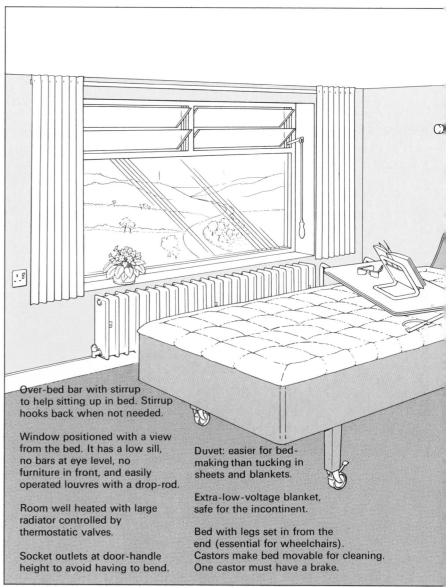

Over-bed bar with stirrup to help sitting up in bed. Stirrup hooks back when not needed.

Window positioned with a view from the bed. It has a low sill, no bars at eye level, no furniture in front, and easily operated louvres with a drop-rod.

Room well heated with large radiator controlled by thermostatic valves.

Socket outlets at door-handle height to avoid having to bend.

Duvet: easier for bed-making than tucking in sheets and blankets.

Extra-low-voltage blanket, safe for the incontinent.

Bed with legs set in from the end (essential for wheelchairs). Castors make bed movable for cleaning. One castor must have a brake.

chair (about 480 mm/19 in). Existing beds can be raised on wooden blocks under the legs, or put on castors, one of which should have an easily operated brake. The legs should be set in from the ends, and a clear 200 mm/8 in space underneath the bed should be left for wheelchairs to approach. Sitting up in bed is easier if a simple rope ladder is firmly attached to the foot of the bed to pull yourself up by. Overhead bars, stirrup grips fixed from a strong ceiling bolt, and electrically operated hoists can help the more severely disabled to move about in bed.

Electrically operated beds can be adjusted to provide a variety of positions from lying flat to sitting up; stand-up beds, which tilt from the vertical to the horizontal, are used for those who cannot bend at all; waterbeds provide continuous body support and prevent bed sores. Day beds or reclining garden chairs are useful for rests during the day. Bad backs will benefit from firm beds or back supports, which will harden up a soft bed and fold away when not required.

Bedding : Foam and rubber mattresses provide good back support and need no

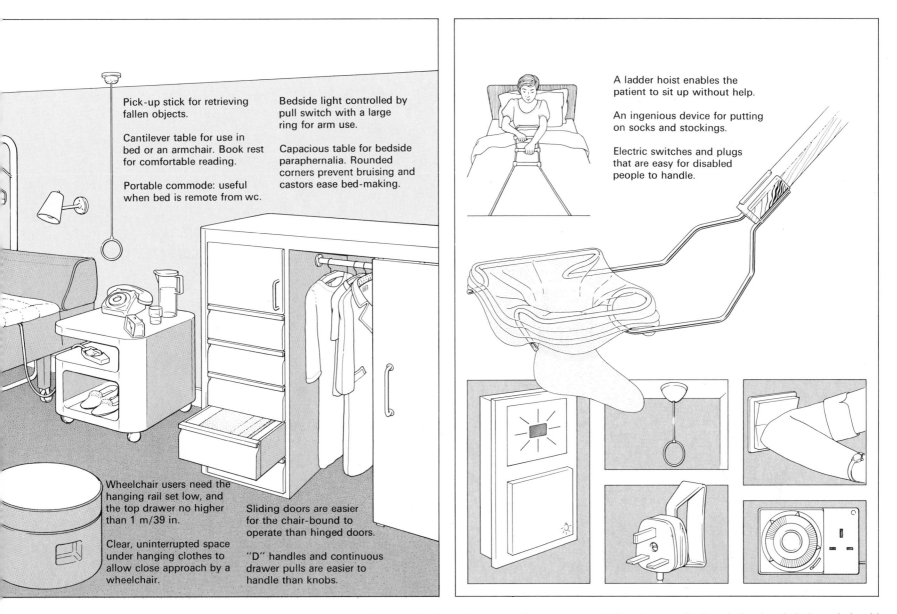

Pick-up stick for retrieving fallen objects.

Cantilever table for use in bed or an armchair. Book rest for comfortable reading.

Portable commode: useful when bed is remote from wc.

Bedside light controlled by pull switch with a large ring for arm use.

Capacious table for bedside paraphernalia. Rounded corners prevent bruising and castors ease bed-making.

Wheelchair users need the hanging rail set low, and the top drawer no higher than 1 m/39 in.

Clear, uninterrupted space under hanging clothes to allow close approach by a wheelchair.

Sliding doors are easier for the chair-bound to operate than hinged doors.

"D" handles and continuous drawer pulls are easier to handle than knobs.

A ladder hoist enables the patient to sit up without help.

An ingenious device for putting on socks and stockings.

Electric switches and plugs that are easy for disabled people to handle.

turning. Bed sores are caused by constant pressure and can be relieved with a wide variety of cushions and rings filled with air or made from latex, polystyrene granules, gel and sheep-skin. Duvets are lightweight and, combined with a fitted under-sheet, ensure that bed-making is kept to a minimum. If traditional bedding is preferred, cellular blankets are warm but light. For the incontinent, there are plastic sheets and mattress covers, and one-way sheets made of porous knitted fabric which can be laid over an absorbent under-sheet. Electric under-blankets can be used for pre-warming beds, but must be turned off before getting into bed, while electric over-blankets with variable heat control can be safely left on all night at the lowest setting. For the incontinent, extra low-voltage blankets are essential for safety. Heating pads give local relief from rheumatic and muscular pain. For safety's sake, all electric blankets and pads should be serviced at least once a year.

Bedside tables must be big enough to accommodate telephone, drinking water, tissues, cosmetics, books, etc. Rounded corners prevent bruising and castors aid bed-making. All furniture should be robust enough to support weight when leaned upon. Cantilevered tables, adjustable in height and tilt, are useful for eating, reading, writing, or painting, both in bed and from armchairs.

Commodes are useful in bedrooms when access to the wc is difficult. There are three basic types: an ordinary armchair with lift-up seat and bucket underneath, which requires frequent emptying; chemical wc unit with a sealed lid which can be serviced as necessary; and a portable wc unit with sealed waste tank and fresh-water cistern which can be flushed 30–60 times.

Cupboards for the chair-bound should have sliding doors or curtains, rather than hinged doors. They should be set out 300 mm/12 in from the corner of the room to allow lateral chair access. Hanging rails for clothing should not be higher than 1.45 m/57 in and drawers no higher than 1 m/39 in. For those who have difficulty bending, no shelves should be provided at low level below hanging clothes. For safety, drawers should run easily and be provided with stops. "D" handles, continuous drawer pulls, and lever handles for doors are easier to handle than small knobs.

Bathrooms for the disabled

Independence immensely improves the morale of a disabled person and it is important that each room in the house should be fitted, if possible, with aids and appliances to make life easier. The bathroom, in particular, is a room where privacy is prized. It should be easily accessible from the disabled person's bedroom, and in a one-bathroom family house a separate WC should be planned if possible (many handicapped people have to spend a long time on the WC). Bathrooms should allow a minimum space of 1.4 m/4 ft 7 in square for wheelchairs to turn in. Floors must be non-slip and, ideally, should have a grating for surface water to drain through. Doors should open outwards or sliding doors should be installed, with locks that can be released from the outside. The bathroom should also have a bell so that help can be summoned in an emergency.

Baths

It may be difficult for a disabled person to get in and out of a bath, but a long soak in a hot bath is generally preferred and considered to be more therapeutic than a shower. The best bath size is 1,700 × 760 mm/67 × 30 in. The bottom of the bath should be flat with an integral non-slip pattern, or made non-slip with a rubber mat or stick-on plastic strips. For the chair-bound, the rim should be 450 mm/18 in from the ground. For the elderly, a higher bath of 550 to 650 mm/ 22 to 26 in may be better, as the rim can be gripped more easily. Low baths are difficult to clean and inconvenient for helpers.

A boxed-in platform level with the head end of the bath makes it easier for a disabled person to transfer from a chair into the bath, and is useful for sitting on while washing legs and feet. Where there is no space for a platform, bath boards and bath seats can be fitted to the bath. Plastic inserts can also be used to convert existing baths into shallow or sit-in baths. Chair lifts and hoists can be fitted to help the chair-bound into the bath.

Sit-in baths offer a compromise between lying down in a bath or standing under a shower. There are also special walk-in seat baths, which have a door at the side of the bath to allow easy access. The door is sealed before the bather runs the water, but unless the room is properly heated the bather can get cold waiting for the bath to fill and empty.

Taps are most accessible if they are positioned at the front corner of the bath. Lever handles and tap turners aid arthritic hands, and mixer taps fitted with a hand-spray are useful for hair-washing and cleaning the bath. Self-closing waste plugs and pop-up wastes help those with limited reach.

Grip rails are essential and should be positioned to suit the individual and the type of bath or platform provided. A vertical pole set firmly in the floor 400 mm/16 in from the tap end of the bath is useful for people of all ages and is particularly helpful with a low bath, but will hinder anyone in a wheelchair. A horizontal rail on the wall side of the bath and a vertical rail at the head end of the bath are minimum requirements. Horizontal bars across the bath do not provide adequate support and impede getting in and out of the bath. A large, recessed shelf set into the wall alongside the bath should be provided for soap, sponges, shampoos and so on.

Showers

For the wheelchair user, the shower tray should be flush with the surrounding floor, with non-slip tiles laid to fall towards a grating. A slatted bench should be provided on the approach side of the shower. This can be hinged to fold upwards when not required. Wheelchair users may prefer to transfer to a shower chair; this is rust-proof and has castors and a perforated seat.

Thermostatic mixer taps prevent scalding and are especially important for anyone with poor sensation. The shower rose should be adjustable in height with a flexible hose fixed to sockets or a rise-and-fall rail, and the shower head should be detachable for hand use. Grip rails fixed at a height to suit the disabled user are essential. Shower curtains are much easier and safer to handle than sliding screens or doors.

WC

The room must be a minimum of 1.4 m wide by 1.7 m deep/4 ft 7 in by 5 ft 7 in to allow for turning, or it may be possible to allow space outside the WC for turning or for transfer to a sani-chair. This is a special chair with an open WC seat; built on castors, it can be wheeled backwards over the WC bowl. The WC door should open outwards and be positioned opposite the WC unit.

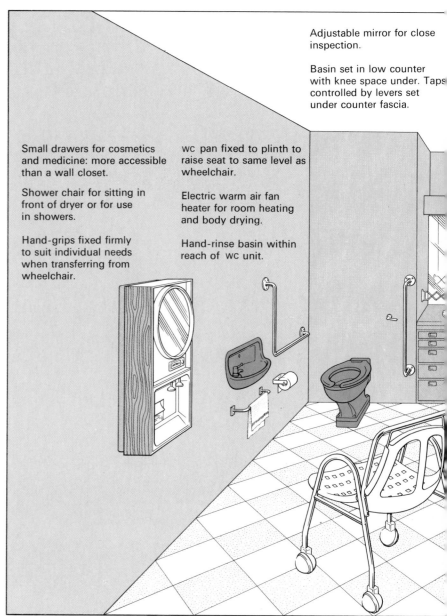

Adjustable mirror for close inspection.

Basin set in low counter with knee space under. Taps controlled by levers set under counter fascia.

Small drawers for cosmetics and medicine: more accessible than a wall closet.

Shower chair for sitting in front of dryer or for use in showers.

Hand-grips fixed firmly to suit individual needs when transferring from wheelchair.

WC pan fixed to plinth to raise seat to same level as wheelchair.

Electric warm air fan heater for room heating and body drying.

Hand-rinse basin within reach of WC unit.

The WC unit must be firmly fixed and the pedestal should not project forward at the base to impede wheelchair access. Ideally, a wash-basin should be positioned so that it can be reached easily by the person sitting on the WC unit.

The average WC seat height of 410 mm/16 in may be too low for many disabled people, although a low seat is better physiologically than a high one. Wheelchair users prefer a seat height of 475 mm/18¾ in. Existing units can be raised with plastic insert seats, which can be moved when not required by other people. Hassocks and foot-stools can be used in conjunction with high seats to improve posture.

Hardwood bench seats are warm and provide more area for support than conventional seats, and open-fronted seats can be useful for men and when using lavatory paper. There are also heated WC seats for people who are hypersensitive to cold, and plastic foam-filled seats for those with skin injuries. Another excellent idea is a combined WC unit and

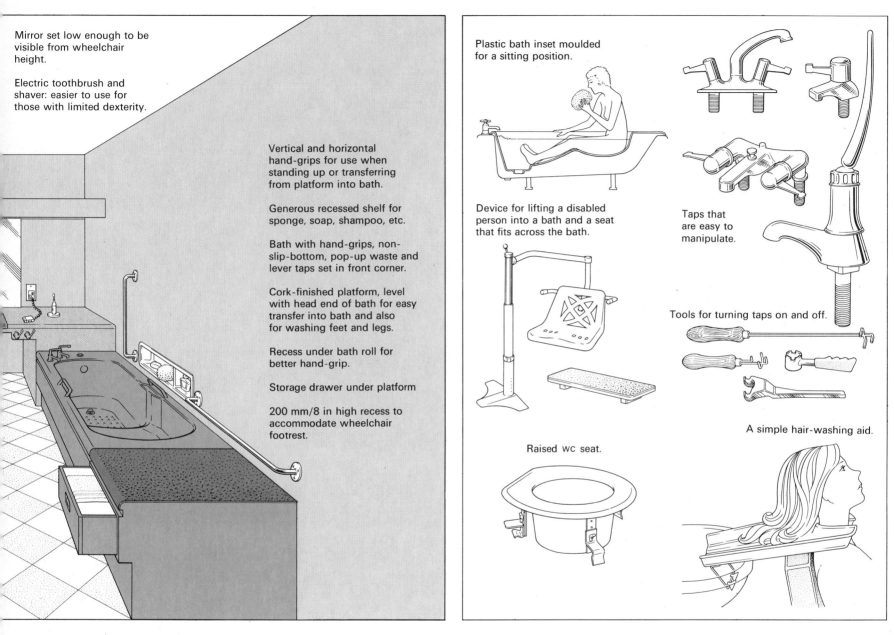

Mirror set low enough to be visible from wheelchair height.

Electric toothbrush and shaver: easier to use for those with limited dexterity.

Vertical and horizontal hand-grips for use when standing up or transferring from platform into bath.

Generous recessed shelf for sponge, soap, shampoo, etc.

Bath with hand-grips, non-slip-bottom, pop-up waste and lever taps set in front corner.

Cork-finished platform, level with head end of bath for easy transfer into bath and also for washing feet and legs.

Recess under bath roll for better hand-grip.

Storage drawer under platform

200 mm/8 in high recess to accommodate wheelchair footrest.

Plastic bath inset moulded for a sitting position.

Device for lifting a disabled person into a bath and a seat that fits across the bath.

Taps that are easy to manipulate.

Tools for turning taps on and off.

A simple hair-washing aid.

Raised WC seat.

bidet, which incorporates a warm-water douche and a warm-air dryer. The controls can be simply operated by an elbow or upper arm.

Grip rails must be provided at a height to suit the user, and in separate WCs horizontal rails should be fixed at both sides, extending as far as the door. Vertical rails at the sides are needed for pulling into a standing position. For wheelchair users, the flushing handle or chain should not be higher than 1.2 m/ 3 ft 11 in.

Bidet
A bidet is helpful for those who have cleaning problems and is useful for treating haemorrhoids. However, a bidet presents the same access problems as the WC unit, particularly for the wheelchair user who would need the rim to be as high as 475 mm/18¾ in. The bidet should have appropriate grip rails firmly fixed.

Wash-basin
Ideally, the basin should be within easy reach of the WC unit. It must be firmly

fixed and, for the wheelchair user, be a non-pedestal type. Basins set in counter-tops provide useful shelf space and can be fixed at any height. Most old people prefer a rim height of 910 mm/36 in; wheelchair users need the basin to be set at 750 mm/29½ in, with the bowl measuring at least 450 mm/18 in from front to back. The front of the bowl should be set as near to the front edge of the counter-top as possible and the basin should have an anti-splash rim. Undersides of basins should be insulated and traps should be

made of plastic to prevent knees being scratched. The knee recess for wheelchair users should be at least 800 mm wide × 300 mm deep/31½ × 12 in.

Basins fitted with lever taps aid arthritic hands. Where these are not allowed by local water-authority regulations, special tap turners can operate taps with crosstops. Remote-controlled, lever-handled taps can help those with limited reach. Mirrors over wash-basins must be set low enough for wheelchair users to be able to see what they are doing.

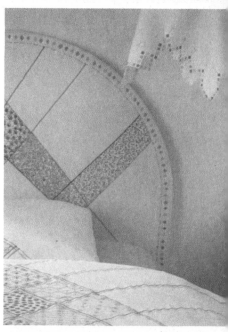

An eye for detail

However efficiently you have planned your rooms, and however beautifully you have furnished them, they will not really become your own until you have added the details that reflect your taste and personality. Although there are many important decisions of detail to make as the rooms are being decorated, it is the personal touches, that you alone can add, that will give the rooms their essential character. This chapter explains the importance of resisting the urge to complete everything immediately. It suggests ways in which the pictures, plants, mirrors and all the other objects that have to be so patiently acquired can be arranged to enliven your bedrooms and bathrooms. It encourages you to think of yourself as an artist creating your own complex three-dimensional landscape, coming back to it again and again, adding a detail, changing a colour, balancing one effect against another and being brave enough to obliterate a whole area of your picture if things do not look right.

An eye for detail
Co-ordination

To establish a sense of co-ordination in a room, a simple but effective trick is to repeat a motif—not necessarily in the same form—on the furniture, walls and windows. The same effect can be gained in a more witty way by creating visual puns—the pairing or juxtaposition of objects that relate by association. Beware, though, of repeating these tricks too often in the same room.

Right: *four butterfly shapes stitch their way up a quilt, growing smaller in the distance until they reappear in a burst of colour on the bedhead.*

Below: *a narrow bedroom becomes a veritable orchard with apples and oranges in bright primary colours glowing on the bedspread and cushions, and ranged along the shelf.*

Far left: *this little girl should have no trouble getting to sleep when she has all these sheep to count—a flock of fluffy wool on the blanket, a large mural and a toy sheep on the shelf.*

Left: *a quilt embroidered to look like a giant blue and white tile co-ordinates cleverly with the unusual tiled bedhead.*

Above: *the bright, bold colours and pattern of this bedspread are reflected in the design of the stained-glass window. The curve of the bedspread's rainbow and of the sun's rays in the corner of the window complement each other perfectly.*

Above: *relax in the bath surrounded by maps of far-away places and the bath becomes a boat, sailing to exotic ports. The maps are protected by two coats of polyurethane to make them waterproof.*

Top: *a tartan rug, a striped bedspread and multi-coloured cushions provide a counterpoint to the pastel stripes on an attic's walls and floor.*

Above: *allowed to remain plain, this old-fashioned radiator would be something of an eyesore. Ingeniously painted to match its background, it becomes an extension of the wall.*

Top: *cherries ripe embroidered on a bedspread are reiterated by a single branch painted on the bedhead. The green of the leaves is repeated in the sheets and pillow cases.*

Murals and illusions

Tempting as it is to let imagination run riot, it would be disturbing to live in a house full of illusions. It is perhaps best to limit illusory effects and murals—particularly *trompe l'oeil*, which can totally deceive the eye even after years—to bedrooms and bathrooms, where possessions are less likely to compete for attention and the walls can be allowed to dominate. Just be sure that you can live with the illusions you have created.

Above: *no one could have bad dreams beneath this fantasy-land bedhead.*

Top: *a magical landscape appears when this blind is drawn over the window.*

Left: *a mural depicting the outline of trees against the sky creates the illusion of a steamy jungle for anyone standing in the shower compartment.*

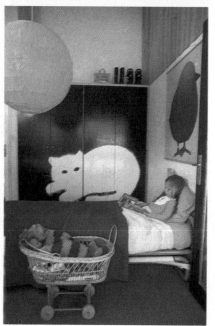

Above: *a bathroom that looks more like the seaside. The bath, raised on a sandy dais dotted with shells, is painted to look like the sea. The stripes on the floor resemble quayside steps to the WC unit, and the cistern is hidden by a jaunty sun umbrella.*

Left: *an oversized furry cat keeps company with an equally large bird, a simple way to create a friendly atmosphere in an otherwise dull room.*

Far left: *more sky imagery, this time with the sky represented by dramatic diagonal blue and white stripes. The clouds are cut-outs, and even the mirror gets the nebulous treatment.*

Top left: *blinds instead of curtains extend the feeling of being literally up in the clouds in this airy bedroom.*

An eye for detail
Walls and windows

You don't need a vast mural to add fun to a room—the simplest details on walls and windows can suggest a sense of humour without demanding total attention. A picture that correlates amusingly with a piece of furniture near by, an individual blind, an ornament placed just where you would least expect it— these are gentler touches designed to bring a smile.

Right: *a large bathroom mirror has a suitably aquatic etching. The lighting is particularly effective in creating an underwater atmosphere.*

Below: *buon giorno—an edging of hand-made lace attached to the bathroom blind makes a gentle morning greeting. Bonjour—in sharp contrast, this dazzling neon light is enough to shock even the groggiest early morning riser into wakefulness.*
Bonsoir—and pleasant dreams for children when this cheerful silk-screened blind is drawn at bedtime.

Left: *a David Hockney painting of spouting taps is tellingly placed in the Conrans' main bathroom.*

Far left: *an obscured glass window is etched with a powerful scene from the First World War. The alcove is painted deep purple, so that the window provides lighting as dramatic as the etching itself.*

Above: *a pair of shapely Alan Jones legs on an expanse of plain tiles.*

Left: *pieces of embroidered quilting are framed and hung near the similarly quilted bed, a novel way to make a room pretty and simple.*

Treasured possessions

The bed becomes the background for a delightful collection of period pieces, carefully arranged with baskets of flowers and bowls of herbs to look agreeably cluttered and relaxed.

Beauty lies, so the saying goes, in the eye of the beholder—particularly, it frequently seems, when the fond eye belongs to a hoarder of "things". But any hoard, collector's pieces or not, can become a personal *tour de force* when stunningly displayed, and the more dramatic the presentation the better even the humblest object will look. Sometimes a collection will benefit from being given a background: a group of old model cars "parked", for example, in front of a framed photograph or print of a stately home. The art is to create an agreeable display that gives inventiveness full rein.

Left: *a highly individual collection of odds and ends has been grouped amusingly together.*

Far left: *an assortment of shells and pebbles is given a new lease of life in a glass jar.*

Below left: *blue and white plates are not often found on a bathroom wall, but here they make a refreshingly different display, enhanced by the matching tiles.*

Below: *the showcase treatment—a jumble of framed photographs and porcelain tea cups and bowls look splendid together in a well-lit cabinet.*

An eye for detail
Bedroom greenery

To be beautiful and decorative, evoke a mood, complement a decorative scheme, define an area or alleviate a dull view: these are the roles of plants in a bedroom—as anywhere in a house. Equally, plants need adequate light, water, air and a suitable temperature wherever they are. However, there are certain senses in which a bedroom is a specialized environment for plants.

It is, for example, one of the least turbulent rooms in a house, and since plants react unfavourably to disturbance, it is worth making a bedroom the venue for your most sensitive specimens.

The bedroom is also a useful convalescent centre for ailing plants. This is because it is likely to be cooler than a living-room, and plants such as ferns and palms, which flag when the central heating is turned up high, may well recover in a cool bedroom.

Third, plants such as cacti, succulents and geraniums, which need plenty of summer sun, must winter in a cool temperature. For this purpose, bedrooms are an ideal solution.

If a bedroom admits little daylight, ordinary bulbs and spotlights used in the conventional way cannot be a substitute: at best, their usefulness to plant life will be as dramatic illumination. It is, however, possible to buy special fluorescent tubes under which certain plants will thrive in otherwise impossible situations.

An old wives' tale has it that plants in the bedroom are harmful to the health because they deplete the oxygen supply overnight. Plants do in fact absorb a tiny quantity of oxygen and emit equally minute quantities of carbon dioxide at night, but this is more than balanced by the oxygen they release during daytime. In any case, the question is academic, because for the human as well as the vegetable occupants of a bedroom, there is no substitute for proper ventilation.

A more entertaining superstition concerns dill and fennel: a bunch hung over the door brings good luck. And a bedroom is clearly the place for *Plectranthus fruticosus*, an evergreen shrub related to the nettle. It is not only decorative, but reputed to cure rheumatism.

Above: *an ultimately dramatic method of displaying a bedroom plant is to make it an integral part of the room's design. In this case it took a custom-built oasis and a desert of carpet to offset the palm.*

Below: *the palm is a very versatile plant, capable of transforming the most conventionally decorated room. Seen through a wide-angle lens, this one's trunk looks much thicker than its 10 cm/4 in.*

Isabella and the pot of basil
A medieval tale of bedroom plant life: this pre-Raphaelite painting by Holman Hunt depicts Boccaccio's gruesome tale of Isabella—who kept her murdered lover's severed head hidden in her bedroom in a pot of thriving sweet basil.

Above: *not only is the window decoratively transformed but back-lighting shows up the attractive translucence of the leaves.*

Left: *a bed—especially a large one—tends to fill a room with repetitively horizontal lines and a plant can effectively alleviate them. Here, a philodendron's upward-snaking shoots and heart-shaped leaves do so admirably. It has been echoed by another incipient philodendron on the opposite side of this sunny room.*

Below left: *there is a tendency for bulbs to be used in ones or twos on the false assumption that this will offset their blooms to greatest advantage. Here the luxurious effect of the narcissi is reliant on the fact that they are planted in a generous clump.*

Cold 7°–13°C/45°–55°F
Several pretty flowering plants prefer cold, for example Myrtle, *Myrtus communis*, Heliotrope, Cherry Pie, *Heliotropium hybridum*, and the Geranium, *Pelargonium* family. Two decorative fruit bearers are Calamodin Orange, *Citrus mitis*, and Kumquat, *Fortunella margarita*. Non-flowering plants suitable for cold bedrooms are Silk Bark Oak, *Grevillea robusta*, and Kangaroo Vine, *Cissus antarctica*.

Cool 13°–18°C/55°–65°F
Richly daubed, the leaves of the Rex Begonia Vine, *Cissus discolor*, Beefsteak Plant, *Iresine herbstii*, and Bloodleaf, *Iresine lindenii*, will add colour to the temperate bedroom. So too will the Cabbage Palm, *Cordyline terminalis*, and the *Dracaena* family, including the Madagascar Dragon Tree, *Dracaena marginata*. The popular Busy Lizzie, *Impatiens wallerana*, and Camellia, *Camellia japonica*, are other, colourful additions.

Warm 18°–24°C/65–75°F
There is no danger of these plants growing too tall for a bedroom. The Dwarf Coconut, *Microcoelum martianum*, is ideal for a particularly small room, growing to 1.8 m/6 ft in about 20 years. The Candle Plant from India, *Plectranthus marginatus*, is low and bushy. The Screw Pine from Polynesia, *Pandanus veitchii*, and Scarlet Plum, *Euphorbia fulgens*, both grow to no more than 120 cm/4 feet.

An eye for detail
Bathroom greenery

Bathrooms and tropical forests have a certain amount in common: they usually lack light and are subject to steamy heat. As a rough and ready rule, plants that thrive in shade and a saturated atmosphere will also thrive in an average bathroom. And by obvious contrast, plants that grow naturally in open and arid desert regions (for example, cacti) will definitely not do so.

There the comparison between bathroom and tropical forest must end: for in reality, the price of domestic heating dictates that bathrooms are anything but constantly warm. Many, if not most, are left to become distinctly cool (say between 13 and 18°C/55 and 65°F) after use. There is only one solution to this problem: measure the mean temperature of your bathroom and choose the plants accordingly.

Otherwise, the well-being of bathroom plants is governed by the same conditions as plants elsewhere in the house. They should not be disturbed unless absolutely necessary; they should never be placed where people might brush against them; while kept well ventilated they should be clear of draughts and, of course, they must be given adequate water and light.

When light is really restricted, for instance in a bathroom that has no windows, or a very small window giving on to a dimly lit area, it is possible to keep plants healthy under strip lighting made for the purpose.

Because ventilation is important to plants, it is good practice to move them for an occasional spell in an open, airy place especially if the bathroom is airless. Indeed, plants in the bathroom, as elsewhere, should be constantly watched for such signs of ill-health as brown leaf edges (often caused by cold draughts) or grey mould on stems (too much humidity in winter). Frequently, the simplest remedy is a change of location.

A bathroom can be a satisfactory, if unconventional, temporary location for plants that flower dramatically over short periods. A hyacinth, for instance, will

give a fine splash of colour as well as a dash of scent. African violets and cyclamen, however, are not recommended as bathroom showpieces since they react unfavourably to being moved. Plants that have grown jaded in a living-room often benefit from a spell in the damper atmosphere of a bathroom.

Space is at a premium in most bathrooms. One way of preventing clutter, and the likelihood of people brushing against your plants, is to place a single telling item in front of a mirror. Well placed, this mirror might double both the foliage and the light.

It is one of the charms of indoor gardening that plants themselves are often seen to best advantage against a dull background. In few rooms is this so often true as the bathroom, which is all too often a clinical place, much in need of softening. Leaves and fronds contrast particularly well with shiny tiles, and a plant with the right shape can disguise an ugly window or hide monstrous examples of the plumber's art.

Top: *charming the bather's eye out of dwelling too long on the blank brick wall is a generous collection of plants, each piece having its own visual interest. Among them are hairy-leaved African Violets and dwarf Neanthe Palm.*

Above: *glass shelves are suitably unobtrusive for this corner. In the background is a Bird's Nest Fern.*

Above left: *one way of giving added impact to a favourite plant.*

Above: *the fitting way to transform a bathroom into a greenhouse. Ferns and succulents enjoy a steamy atmosphere—dry air is their worst enemy.*

Left: *to silhouette hanging plants against a picture window does justice to their overflowing cascades. As a rule, plants grow towards the principal source of light and only ferns and ivies, such as the three Swedish Ivies hanging right, grow symmetrically enough to be used in this way without constant turning.*

Cold 7°–13°C/45°–55°F
Even if you freeze in a badly heated bathroom there are plants that will thrive. Some ivies, including Fat-Headed Lizzie, *Fatshedera lizei*, and Common or English Ivy, *Hedera helix*, favour cold temperatures and a moist but not overwatered soil. These plants, as well as Spider Plant, *Chlorophytum elatum*, like shady rooms, whereas the Fan Palm, *Chamaerops humilis*, likes light.

Cool 13–18°C/55°–65°F
Cool ferns and elegant palms can exotically transform bathrooms. The Dwarf Mountain Palm, *Neanthe bella*, and Kentia Palm, *Howea forsteriana*, will do well. Graceful, hardy ferns such as Asparagus, *Asparagus setaceus*, and Ribbon Fern, *Pteris cretica*, will thrive if watered sparingly in winter. The Umbrella Tree and Umbrella Grass are both suitable for bathrooms.

Warm 18°–24°C/65°–75°F
Plants that thrive on heat grow tall. The Swiss Cheese Plant, *Monstera deliciosa*, can grow to 6 m/20 ft. Parlour Ivy, *Philodendron scandens*, and Valour Philodendron, *Philodendron andreanum*, grow to 1.8 m/6 ft, as do Weeping Fig, *Ficus benjamina*, and the popular Rubber Plant, *Ficus elastica decora*. For the small, hot bathroom try the handsome fern, *Blechnum gibbum*.

An eye for detail
Head boards

The bedhead makes a focal point when you come into the room, so it needs to be pretty; and since it is what you turn your back on as you sit up in bed, it needs to be comfortable to lean against. In the prettiness stakes, you can let your imagination off the leash: even people who insist that their bedroom colours must be "quiet" as an aid to restfulness will hardly be disturbed if something lively, colourful and interesting is going on behind their backs.

As far as comfort is concerned, padding and foam—quilted, buttoned or whatever—is just as soft if covered in bright, cheerful materials. For practicality, choose materials that can be sponged clean, or are of a colour that will not show head marks too quickly. If you choose materials that are delicate, or colours that are pale, have your head board fixed against the wall with light battens that make it easily removable for re-upholstering as the need arises.

Right: *a* DIY *butterfly cut from a sheet of plywood or thin chipboard is stiffened by timber battens and padded with foam. Appliqués on the bedspread repeat the lepidopteran theme.*

Above: *effective illusion—a semicircle of pine planking is inlaid into a wall of diagonal tongued-and-grooved boarding.*

Left: *living in a fairy tale, the bed becomes a drawbridge laid across the grass-green carpet. Story-book murals adorn the walls, and plywood turrets, flanking the bed, turn the head board into a castle. A pretty, painted princess is hurrying away from her tower to make way for real-life equipment, such as telephones and paperbacks.*

Left: *this head board, in keeping with the upholstery and bedcover, is luxuriously quilted and padded. The room is a perfect example of the calming effect of expensive acres of white on white.*

Below left: *a beautifully simple marble-topped island fulfils the varied roles of room divider, head board, bedside table and chest of drawers.*

Below: *under the rainbow, an attic window with a view of the tree tops is an imaginative, if draughty, bedhead.*

An eye for detail
Screens

Screens are evocative, decorative and useful. A well-loved prop in almost every Restoration comedy (erring husbands and flirtatious wives hid behind them when their spouses appeared on the scene unexpectedly), they can give a bedroom an air of light-hearted dalliance. Screens vary widely in style, but exquisitely ornate or plain and simple they can be used in many ways. Useful in large rooms where greater privacy or cosiness is required, screens are also ideal for separating one area of activity from another. A well-positioned screen can change the shape of a room, exclude draughts, hide unsightly clutter or subdue the glare of bright sunlight. And when chosen with care, a screen either modern or antique can be appreciated purely as a beautiful object.

Above: *an effective mixture of styles: an ornate screen heads the bed while a louvred screen provides privacy.*

Top left: *a screen can be used to alter the shape of a room and to divide the sleeping and dressing areas. Provided it is firmly fixed to the floor, shelves can be added for displaying ornaments or, in a child's room, favourite toys.*

Left: *a mirror screen adds new dimensions to a room, particularly to a small room. Its hinged construction makes the screen easy to manipulate, too, so that you can see yourself from almost any angle or from both sides at once.*

Right: *an unusual bedhead made by placing a delicately carved wooden screen in front of a window. Soft light filters through to give the room an intriguingly mysterious atmosphere, with echoes of the Sultan's bedchamber.*

Far right: *when covering a screen with fabric, arrange the material in gentle folds or it will look depressingly reminiscent of a hospital screen. Use a fabric that matches the mood of the room.*

Right: *the Victorians' passion for scrap-books overflowed on to their screens, which they covered with cut-outs.*

Designer's choice

Most people like to design and decorate their bedrooms and bathrooms themselves, only calling in a professional when the complexity of the problem is beyond their experience. Nevertheless, it is the creative work of professional designers, often illustrated in books and magazines, that will by example influence the way you tackle the problems of decorating your own home. The way they set about their work for that small band of affluent people who can afford to employ them, and the paths that lead them to make their decisions, are fascinating and well worth studying. With this in mind I have selected six professional designers, four American and two English, all with very different tastes, who have generously explained and illustrated how they tackled some of the problems of bedroom and bathroom design, both in their own homes and those of their clients. This chapter also takes a look at the ingenious design work that goes into boats, caravans and hotels—all conceived by professionals working to exacting requirements—and suggests ways in which you can learn from their solutions.

Designer's choice
David Barrett

"I work in bed, I eat in bed, I entertain in bed, I even give interviews in bed," explains New York interior decorator David Barrett. "That's why I wanted a bedroom that doesn't look like a bedroom—a unique, multi-purpose room." So when Barrett bought a Federal-period town house in New York City nine years ago and decided to renovate the small upstairs room, he set out to get exactly what he wanted.

"I totally reshaped the room I had picked out as the bedroom," says Barrett, "and I wanted nothing except the presence of the bed to give the room's function away." He also put in the "silvery, not shiny" curved steel walls, the bevelled mirror, oval-sectioned ceiling and custom-made bedside cabinets, mirrored two walls and covered the other two with a deep aubergine velvet, put a red fox fur cover on the bed, placed his African sculptures around the room and found that a large wooden stag he had purchased in London years before made a "perfect head board". The only thing that remained from the room's previous incarnation was the fireplace. "It's a beautiful period piece," he explains, "and with mirror all around it, it just seems to float. Besides, I thought a touch of old would be nice."

Barrett's bedroom is in many ways a night room. "After dinner, when I have guests over, they naturally gravitate in here," he explains. "Then the bed becomes a huge, soft, seven-foot ottoman." The contrast of textures is something that Barrett is acutely aware of. He juxtaposes fur and steel, velvet and wood, mirror and marble. He always has oversize branches in a tall vase on the bedside table. "One of the magical aspects of this room, and one of the main reasons I had the mirrored ceiling put in," he says, "is that when I wake up in the morning the first thing I see are the blossoms—forsythia, dogwood or even autumn leaves, depending on the season, are reflected above me. It's like getting up in the country, being out in the woods."

Barrett's urbane, sophisticated, glamorous room is deceptively practical. "I didn't want any furniture except the bed and the bedside tables in here," he says, "and I planned the curved walls so that all the storage would be hidden behind them and could not be seen at all from the room." The designer also left the window exposed and accessible, and had

shutters made to match the adjacent walls. "When the shutters are closed, the window simply disappears," he says, "and that simply adds to the feeling of confinement that I wanted."

The brightly lit, all-white bathroom is a total contrast to the bedroom. "The basic concept was determined by the physical space," says Barrett. Situated right above the kitchen, the bathroom has the same floor plan—long and narrow. So Barrett divided it into four areas. As one enters there is a washing area, with a bath on one side and a sink on the other. "I'm tall, so I had the sink placed twelve inches higher than is considered normal," he adds. A second area is what he terms "a decorative area" with towels, a carved camel towel rack, and a banquette and storage area upholstered and pillowed in white terry cloth. The third area, which the interior designer deems "the least attractive", is outfitted with a bidet and toilet, and the fourth area contains a stall/steam shower. As in the bedroom, where Barrett has mixed three kinds of lighting—cold cathode under the bed to make it "float", a gooseneck fixture at the head of the bed for reading, and four ceiling-hung chrome fixtures to pinpoint the room's four curved corners—in the bathroom the lighting has been carefully worked out to provide both overall illumination and to emphasize the sink area for shaving and grooming.

"This is the favourite I've ever done for myself. I would hesitate to do this for a client, unless I was quite sure it was what he or she wanted. I work hard dealing with people, their whims, their fantasies and their desires, and I do try to make my jobs unique and to really get to know the person who is going to live in the atmosphere I am going to create." Barrett surveys his bedroom. He enjoys it. It's luxurious and yet somehow simple. "People have called it art deco. It's not," he says. "It's timeless, classic. It will never change. I have everything I want right here. Of course it was expensive, but I was determined to go all the way and have it just as I wanted it to be."

Left: *interior designer David Barrett likes to treat his bedroom as a general living-room. During the day his bed, luxuriously covered with fox fur, becomes a giant sofa from which he can survey his work: curved steel walls, mirrored ceiling and carved wooden stag head-rest.*

Above: *both the camel and pagoda-style bank of shelves accommodate towels in the all-white bathroom.*

Below: *careful illumination highlights the wash-basin area to make shaving and grooming easier.*

Above: *in the bathroom you can step straight from the shower and steam unit to the relaxing after-bath bench.*

Below: *David Barrett totally redesigned his bedroom, leaving only this period fireplace untouched.*

Designer's choice
Alan Buchsbaum

Above: *a feeling of being in a constant state of levitation must result from lying in this dramatic "floating bed", and the predominantly white surroundings aid the illusion. The raised platform which surrounds the bed removes the need for fussy tables and chairs and means that the ceiling can be unusually low without causing inconvenience.*

Left: *the architect, Alan Buchsbaum.*

Architect Alan Buchsbaum, of Design Coalition, is a modest man. Whenever anyone compliments him on the New York loft he renovated recently for a client, he answers, "this is one of the jobs that I'm least proud of. Not because I don't like it, but because it was too easy. It's a simple thing to have done."

Not everyone would agree. The bedroom and bathroom are in many ways spectacular. The architect elected to put the bedroom up on a loft landing and to connect it to a bathroom whose location was already determined by the position of the plumbing. "In any renovation there are problems," says Buchsbaum, "and somehow it always seems to be the plumbing that determines what is going to happen with the design of the space." Once the bathroom space was chosen, the bedroom area was easy. Then the bedroom was co-ordinated with the dining-room situated below it.

"The curious thing about this bedroom," explains Buchsbaum, "is that its ceiling is very low, but I thought it through and was convinced that once you're in a supine position you really don't need a lot of height over your body." So while the overall ceiling height of the loft is 4 m/14 ft, upstairs in the bedroom it's reduced to 2 m/7 ft, and over the bed it becomes 1.7 m/5 ft 6 in—"the lowest ceiling height you can ever get away with," according to the architect. "But," he adds, "because the bedroom floats in the enormous loft, which is more than 88 feet long, it's not claustrophobic." Furthermore, the reduced height above the bed meant the dining area immediately below could have a higher ceiling. "A spatial puzzle," adds Buchsbaum.

The key design element of this bedroom is that there is no furniture in it at all. The mattress is simply inset in a platform, there are no night-tables—magazines and the TV sit on the platform extensions at either side of the bed—and the wardrobe doors hide a dresser.

The bedroom floor, like the floor in the bathroom, is of matt white ceramic

Above: *an exciting bathroom—but to many people (including the building inspector) it could induce vertigo.*

Below: *the architect's plan of the bathroom showing the positions of the bath, basin, shower and* WC *unit.*

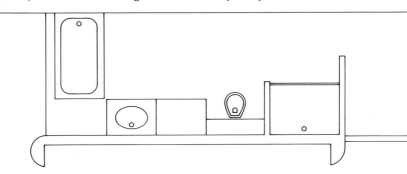

tile, "because", says the architect, "it's the one material that allows for an all-white floor that can be kept clean without too much effort." Some critics have assumed that it's too cold a surface to be comfortable for a bedroom floor. "This is a misconception about tile," says Buchsbaum. "Tile is cold if it is laid on a cold surface, but here it happens to be placed over a platform where the air is warm underneath and around it, so it becomes a pleasant surface to walk on."

In the bathroom, Buchsbaum did manage a few of his design specialities. He topped the sink with a very long piece of marble but left all the plumbing exposed beneath it; one of the things he is especially fond of is the "combination of the elegance of the marble and the reality of the drain pipe."

To some this may be a frightening bathroom. Suspended in space, it has a bath-tub simply let into the floor. The architect wanted to place a railing at the tub's far end, thinking that he might be held responsible if the client slipped on a piece of soap and plunged headlong over the edge. But the client would have none of it, so there is no railing.

Although Buchsbaum says that this is not one of his favourite projects, everybody else thinks it is one of the best jobs he's done. "There's not enough going on here," Buchsbaum says. He does admit that he learnt something about proportion and colour in doing the bedroom. "My client was very influential," he explains. "When it came to choosing a colour, she knew she wanted white, but not pure white. So we mixed a little Alizarin Crimson—a deep, blue-red pigment—in with the white, and although you can't detect that it's not white, it has a bit of a glow and when two walls meet the colour becomes more intense."

The platform carpeting, a pale grey-pink Italian wool, reinforces the subtle colour. "Now that's what I find interesting," says Buchsbaum. "To take a colour like pink, that's *déclassé*, and to make it work, make it lose its usual connotations, and to vary it."

Designer's choice
Tricia Guild 1

Crossing the threshold of Tricia Guild's London home is like stepping into a permanent springtime. Massed bunches of garden flowers fill the air with sweet perfumes, and everywhere you look there are drapes and folds of fresh, pastel-patterned fabrics, piles of lacy cushions and baskets of oddments gathered from woods and fields.

Tricia Guild is the designing talent behind Designers Guild, a small chain of distinctive fabric and furnishing shops that are prettying up the major cities of Europe. There are now eight Designers Guilds, in London, Paris, Bordeaux, Geneva, Munich, Oslo, Madrid and Brussels. Once inside a Guild shop, her message comes over clear and strong. Patterns on patterns abound, confuting any suggestion that such bold mixtures do not work—they do, and beautifully.

"I believe you can mix anything as long as the colours are right," she says, "and that is why we present the style in our shops the way we do. It works even for the amateur decorator, because people are prevented from making errors—everything here 'goes' with everything else. I like to think of it as a relaxed style that is easily emulated, a breakaway from the artificial world of high decoration."

Although she also runs an interior design service, she is keen to encourage clients to do the mixing themselves. "I deliberately present an undiluted image in my shops," says Tricia, "so if people like my style there's no difficulty in putting it together—all the elements are

Continued

Above: *Tricia Guild, advocate of prettiness, softness and a mixture of patterns, at her London shop in the King's Road, Chelsea.*

Far left: *beautiful objects give visual and tactile pleasure to anyone relaxing in the armchair. Walls are covered with softly gathered fabric panels caught top and bottom on wooden rails.*

Left: *beside the bed, an array of little treasures, each chosen not for its usefulness but its pleasing shape.*

Right: *in the heart of the city, a cool retreat—ruched curtains soften the outlook while the cucumber colour scheme and bowls of flowers give a feeling of rural tranquillity.*

Designer's choice
Tricia Guild 2

there and they can water them down to suit their own life-styles or buy the image as a whole."

Tricia started her successful business by selling fabrics with tiny, delicate patterns based on Indian designs. Now her particular style is based on her wide range of fabrics, all with patterns derived from soft, natural forms and trimmed with lace and appliqué rather than the hard-edged geometrics beloved of so many contemporary designers.

On the specifics of bedroom design, Tricia is adamantly open-minded. "I think it is important that one's first impression on waking should be one of relaxed calm. A bedroom should be a retreat from the world, an intensely personal place. Mine certainly is." In her cool, pale green bedroom, Tricia has lined the walls with a delicately mottled fabric gathered on wooden rails top and bottom—a pretty effect and a practical idea, too, as the panels of fabric are easily removable for washing. Her clothes are kept in the adjoining spare-room-cum-dressing-room in a unit made to her own design, the fabric-covered, foam-padded shelves veiled with a softly gathered curtain. She does not like the blankness of closet doors. "If I didn't have a dressing-room near-by, I would have curtained off a section of the bedroom to make a walk-in wardrobe. I don't like a clutter of clothes, but equally I don't want to lock away things I positively enjoy looking at."

In proof of this she lives surrounded
Continued

Above: *a spare room can be a wasted room, but Tricia Guild uses hers as a dressing-room, too. Her clothes are hidden behind curtains, which give a softer look than stark closet doors.*

Far left: *necklaces adorning the mirror in the dressing-room not only look decorative but are conveniently arrayed for quick selection.*

Left: *even in the bathroom every available surface is covered with pretty things, the seashore providing an appropriate theme.*

Right: *a flourish of ferns adds the finishing touch to the pretty pink and white colour scheme in Tricia Guild's comfortable bathroom.*

Designer's choice
Tricia Guild 3

by her beautiful possessions. The dressing-room mirror is hung about with necklaces, and the generous bedside table is crammed with an assortment of pretty pots and boxes, fir cones and vases of flowers. To her, a bedside table is a personal piece of territory on which to display one's favoured bedside things.

Her bathroom is a narrow slot of a room with sunshine streaming in through lace-clad windows. The room is bathed in a golden light that would have been mercilessly destroyed by panes of frosted or reeded glass. It is a pleasant, relaxing room to be in, decorated with the same care and attention to detail that is evident in the rest of the house. The bath is a simple, old-fashioned cast-iron tub. "I hate the idea of plastic—it just doesn't feel right," she says. Her bedroom and bathroom are separated by a short flight of stairs. "It doesn't bother me—I don't mind the walk, and anyway it would have been wrong to impose an unnatural order on this house. Switching the rooms around would have wrecked the beautiful proportions."

When Tricia Guild is working for others, she allows the framework of the house to dictate the style. Light, bright rooms get light, bright treatments, dark rooms are made sombre and smart.

Her own bedroom reflects her personal taste—it is not a blueprint to be adapted for all other bedrooms regardless of the size, shape and orientation of the house and the age and sex of the client. "My bedroom is my dream, really," she muses.

Above: *a bedroom designed by Tricia Guild for a London flat. The effect is soft and luxurious, but more formal and less cluttered than the style she has chosen for her own rooms.*

Right: *a teenager's room in a Paris flat. It was a small room with not much light, so Tricia filled it with warm, apricot colours, a four-poster bed and a corner cabinet crammed with pots and plants.*

Left and far left: *the bedroom Tricia designed for her 12-year-old daughter, Lisa, who loves collecting things and making still-life arrangements of toys and flowers and pictures. The soft, pale blue background is young and bright, and a good foil for Lisa's favourite bits and pieces.*

Designer's choice
John Saladino

"I have tried to break down the Berlin Wall between the bedroom and the bathroom," says New York interior designer John Saladino. "I like to use the same materials and colours in both areas. I think of old-style bathrooms—those white-tiled closets—as being about as relevant as a bomb shelter to what is going on today."

Saladino likes comfortable, sensuous, luxurious spaces, and he knows how to design them. The plan, the colours, the choice of materials, the way he uses space, are all intimately connected to the way he feels his clients should be living. There are no accidents in a Saladino scheme: every surface, every piece of furniture, every accessory is evocative, special and particularly chosen—by him. He thinks before he plans. When asked about his design philosophy on the bedroom, he says, "I prefer to call it a sleeping chamber, because that's just what it is, and the definition serves to remind me

that the bed space must be a serene place of repose."

Colour is a very important part of the Saladino aesthetic. A painter—he studied with artist Josef Albers at Yale University—Saladino was never really schooled in design, and, perhaps as a result, he uses colour lavishly, imaginatively, boldly and subtly. "I am open to the client's feelings about colour," he says. "Some like deep, dark rooms the colour of Burgundy wine, others think of white-washed cottages by the sea. Women have described the bedroom to me as flower-filled and basically a morning environment, whereas men tend to think of it as a night space. So any attempt to lay down rules about what is sensual and what is

Right: *New York designer John Saladino in the apartment he designed for a feminine, vivacious client. The view into the room demonstrates his use of clotted-cream colours.*

Above: *this beautiful and expensive view of Central Park has been emphasized to become a central feature of the bedroom.*

Right: *Saladino has succeeded in capturing the "voluptuous Mediterranean spirit" which he sought for the master bedroom. The round wall behind the bed is part of the "igloo" storage area which provides walk-in housing for clothes.*

not is like trying to pin down the multi-headed Hydra."

The bedroom and bathroom pictured here were designed for " 'a female'—a woman who is constantly on the go, who likes to entertain, who is vivacious and who likes herself." It is done in shades of ivory, peach and traces of pink. "To me this is a sensual room," says Saladino. "The space has a kind of voluptuous Mediterranean spirit—the thick walls remind me of Sicilian or Norman architecture where the structure gives real substance to the environment."

There is a window facing a breathtaking view of Central Park and, according to the designer, "the room floats, because the bed is a sleeping island that

Left: *in the dressing area off the main bathroom, a beautiful antique toilette mirror contrasts well with its modern surroundings, and turns a section of the glass shelf into a make-up centre.*

competes for centre stage with the dramatic window."

"I would never put a bachelor in this room," he continues. "The romantic treatment of the window with its built-in chaise-longue—a twentieth-century resting place for Madame Récamier—is just too obviously romantic, and the antique *armoire*—the client owned that before, but it was never in the bedroom." As for storage, Saladino had a lot of little existing closets torn out and designed an "igloo for clothes": a huge, round architectural form that is an instant means for seeing what is available. "You don't have to rely on your memory and there are no doors to bang, and actually it's a more economical way to build storage, if you have the space, than a series of cabinets with doors." Ambient bedroom lighting is concealed about the storage igloo, and in the rest of the space the light sources are kept below eye level.

One colour is used as an envelope—

walls, ceiling and carpeting are all the shade of "heavy cream". Into the envelope Saladino has placed the bed, covered with a diagonally quilted peach fabric with a low, fabric-covered head board, and a slipper chair upholstered in a peach, cream and pink-striped fabric— "a feminine chair that I would never put in a man's room because it's a direct reminder of the eighteenth-century chairs that women used to sit on while mending their slippers."

Like the bedroom, the bathroom is carpeted in ivory tweed and, since the renovation, the shower opens directly on to the dressing area. The long and narrow bathroom has been made as luxurious and yet as functional as possible. There is a glass shelf for towels which doubles as a make-up console with the addition of a genuine 18th-century toilette mirror. Says Saladino, "I made the client get rid of her reproductions— life is just too short to live with them."

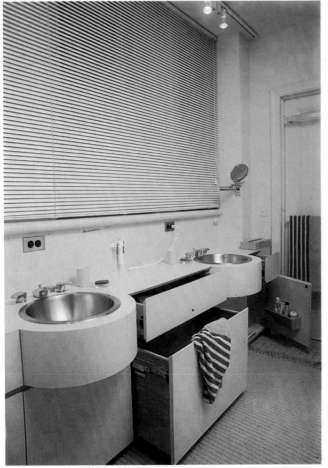

Above: *space beneath the basin is often wasted—here it is utilized to the full.*

Left: *adhering to his idea that the two should be united, Saladino echoes the bedroom's colours in the linking bathroom.*

Far left: *the bathroom occupied by the sons of the house combines practicality with an interesting sculptured effect.*

Designer's choice
Max Clendinning

Above: *designer Max Clendinning pictured in the* pied-à-terre *he designed for an executive working in London.*

"To be a successful designer of people's homes, you have to be interested in people," says Max Clendinning, an architect-trained designer possessed of all the charm of his native Ireland. "My clients end up as my friends," he adds with a smile—which is just as well, considering how much information he gathers about them and their way of life before he puts pencil to paper.

Clendinning cites the example of the couple who were constantly on the move —she with five suitcases, he with one— and the town-house bedroom he designed for them in which he thoughtfully incorporated a flat space for unpacking and a special drawer to hide away the empty cases. Another couple,

who had lived in the same house surrounded by the same furniture for more than twenty years, were again considerately dealt with by Mr Clendinning: "I felt it was very brave of them to bring in a designer at that stage of their lives, and I encouraged them to hang on to anything and everything that meant something to them. Then I designed the house around their things—but that's what I always do. When I've done a place, it stays done until either the clients move or they completely change both their life-style and their possessions."

A Clendinning scheme is tailor-made for each particular client down to the colours of the walls and floors and the design of the shoe rack. Nowhere is this personal approach more necessary than in a bedroom. "I like to meet the client in his or her own surroundings," he says. "Then I can assess how they use a bedroom. Some prefer a living-room with a bed in it, others yearn for a little sleeping

cell off the hall. I take everything into account. If I see they are untidy, then I design a room that is easy to be tidy in. If they are away a great deal, I design a room with no dust traps—a room that is easy to keep clean. I watch how they like to store their clothes, where they discard their shoes, I even count up how many sets of underclothes they have, then I plan accordingly. I once designed a whole house in shades of khaki and black to match the *haute couture* wardrobe of a very elegant lady of fashion."

Clendinning would like to be more adventurous with his bathrooms, and rues the fact that bathrooms come low on people's priority lists. His own preference is for a bathroom big enough to contain a dressing-room: "I feel once you've got up, your time in the bedroom is over—washing and dressing go logically together and I don't really see why you should get dressed in the room you sleep in."

His hallmark, if he has one, is the ziggurat, zigzag shape that breaks up the straight lines of floors and banks of closets, and the shiny walls, painted with layer upon layer of coach-finish paint so that one wall reflects into the other and the corner is lost.

"My definition of a well-designed room", he says, "is a room in which the initial surprise one feels on entering lasts for years."

Below: *staggered closets and drawers have a pleasing line and allow clothes to be filed away in order of length.*

Below: *sunken bath, watery turquoise tiles and thick marble basin give this room a cool, aquarium atmosphere.*

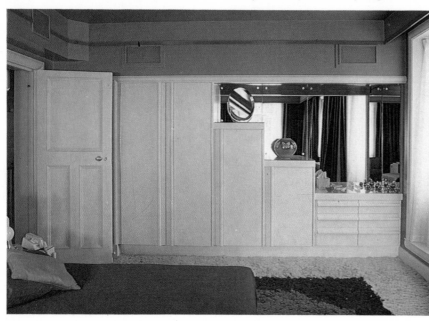

Below: *in a Sussex country house, Clendinning has given this bedroom a magnificently warm glow. The effect has been achieved with painstaking application of layer upon layer of shimmering lacquer paint and an inviting velvet bedspread.*

Above: *with extensive use of marble and shaggy carpeting, the designer has made this a very luxurious bathroom.*

Below: *Clendinning's exciting use of colour and pattern breaks the straight lines of the floor, walls and ceiling.*

Above: *in this bedroom the designer has marked out the storage area with the subtle use of green paint.*

Below: *a "mirror" of shiny paint on the ceiling reflects and accentuates the vivid colour contrast below.*

Robert Bray and Michael Schaible

Robert Bray and Michael Schaible have been partners in the New York firm Bray/Schaible Design Inc. for eight years. They met when they were both at the Parsons School of Design—"Bob was the only person whose ideas I respected," says Schaible—and they worked together in a design firm before deciding to launch out on their own. Today, their deceptively simple, often monochromatic interiors and sophisticated approach to space planning have made them one of the most sought-after design teams in the United States.

The Bray/Schaible approach is direct. Whether they are designing for a large space or a small one, the space itself is the first and often the only consideration. Their treatment of bedrooms and bathrooms is closely linked to the other rooms in a residence. "We like to do the total project," says Bray, "and we're lucky enough to be able to turn down assignments if we're not asked for a total concept." Adds Schaible, "In terms of bedrooms and bathrooms, we try to keep the dressing and bathing areas together, and treat the sleeping area separately. It simply depends on the space that is available."

"In New York City, particularly, one is always cramped for space," explains

Left: *to expand confined spaces Bray and Schaible use mirrors, which in a bedroom they counterbalance with soft shapes and textures and subtle lighting.*

New York designers Schaible and Bray.

Left: *monochromatic interiors and deceptive simplicity are hallmarks of the design team's approach.*

Bray, "so that planning a bathroom requires making the most of an often windowless and small area, making it as light and bright as possible. According to Schaible, these are the spaces that could be claustrophobic, so they like to use lots of mirrors. They try as much as possible to open up the space, and, if natural light is not available, to at least give the impression of a space filled with light and air.

Many of the Bray/Schaible bathrooms are clinically white. Explains Schaible, "We dislike the colours of most standard American bathroom fixtures and find white the only acceptable alternative, and we like to put the toilet and bath-tub on a white tile floor—also grouted with white." Adds Bray, "We prefer to have the walls and floor of the same material, so it makes sense to tile the whole space in white." It also has to do with easy maintenance. "Bathrooms should be easy to clean," says Schaible. "We think of a perfect bathroom as one that can be hosed down."

Lighting is a major consideration to these designers. They believe that it is the quality of light that can determine the function of a room. "In most bathrooms we install two different kinds of lighting," says Bray, "because we think that the experience of taking a bath is a very different one from that of shaving or making up, and that these functions require different lights." So lights are strong over the sink, and on a dimmer switch to control the intensity of the overall light.

In other areas the Bray/Schaible thinking is also very clear. When they can, they try to eliminate clutter by building in storage that is hidden behind mirror and then by organizing and simplifying all the hardware. In the bathroom shown here, they've had a 2.5 m/8 ft towel rack made which simply runs the length of the wall, has no visible fittings and, according to them, "helps to condense the clutter". "This is so much nicer than having four different towel racks all over the place," says Bray, "and you never have to walk into a sea of wet towels."

Bray/Schaible bedrooms are also deceptively plain. The two designers are often asked if bedrooms are masculine or feminine rooms. "We think of them as neuter," they say. "For us, space is neuter—it's what goes into it that can change it drastically. We never do fanci-

Right: *neat closets eliminate clutter.*

Far right: *the designers like walls and floor to be of the same material.*

Bottom right: *one long towel rail really organizes the space.*

Bottom far right: *white is preferred to the standard bathroom colours.*

Below: *elegant architectural taps.*

ful, frilly rooms, but we do use colour once in a while, and when it's a bedroom for two people we want it to be comfortable for both partners: carpeting on the floor and often the walls, lots of soft surfaces—pillows, often a quilted bedcover." Colour depends on the space and the people—some like a light room, some need complete blackout and mirrors. "The immediate thought about mirror is that it's sexual," says Schaible. "It is, of course, but it's also often used to expand the space and it's wonderful if you dress in the bedroom."

How does the Bray/Schaible team work? Effortlessly, to hear them tell it. "We have a serious dialogue with the client," they say, "talk to them about how they feel about sleeping and discuss the limits of the space. We just listen to what they have to say, then go away and start working on it."

343

Hotels, caravans and boats

Above: *in a strange room, your links with the outside world are very important and should be conveniently placed.*

Left: *light, easy-to-move furniture is elegant and effortless to clean around— two important factors in any busy hotel.*

The amenities provided in hotels, motels and, for that matter, boats and caravans deserve a closer look. Where investment is high and space at a premium, it stands to reason that neither of these commodities is wasted.

Designers concentrate on making the very most of space while providing the greatest degree of comfort possible in the circumstances. Their brief also includes the request to keep maintenance costs down: the less time, at least in the case of hotels, that is spent by maids with mops, and the less frequently the decor has to be overhauled, the better all round.

Hotels reckon that furnishing textiles should last for five years and furniture for ten, so care is taken that nothing is too fashionable: styles and colour schemes must not become outdated too early. In the case of newly built hotels, put into use before the structure has finally settled down (as is the case with a good many newly built houses), only emulsion paint is used on the walls, as this is cheapest to replace if cracks should appear—costlier wall coverings go up only when things have stopped moving and dampness has evaporated.

Hotel chains do not attempt to create the once sought-after ambience of a country house: instead, they try to make their guests feel like important executives. Although the telephone may bring service, there are all kinds of time-saving shortcuts: perhaps a little refrigerator in the room, well-stocked with drinks, or a tray set with a kettle, sachets of tea and coffee and long-life milk for the instant cup that cheers. The bathroom invariably has a rail above the bath for drip-drying the executive shirt or the

Far left: *squeezing in bathroom fittings on a boat can pose problems; however, a shower takes up very little floor space and uses a minimum amount of water.*

Above left: *on a boat, the beds and the bathroom are mammoth space fillers and for space economy often have to be eased into the most unlikely looking corners.*

Left: *there is seldom enough storage space on boats: beneath the bed lies a valuable area for closets and drawers.*

Right: *a double bed afloat is a luxury that is feasible only if it can be used for both sleeping and daytime activities.*

executive tights—a device no private bathroom should be without.

Easy maintenance is assured by reducing dust-catching nooks and crannies to a minimum. Surfaces are, as far as possible, continuous and fillets are inserted between pieces of furniture for a flush fit. The bed is high enough for the vacuum cleaner to pass right under, and the bathroom floor is graded towards a drain so it can easily be sluiced down.

Space-saving comes into its own in caravans and boats. It is at trailer shows that the smallest bathroom equipment is seen, and there is no reason why a static household short of space should not reap the benefit of all this ingenuity. Tiny basins, baths and WC units can be married up to domestic plumbing with special connectors.

While no boat-builder really likes to install bunks narrower than 65 cm/2 ft 3 in—and certainly no adult likes sleeping on them—there is an occasional concession in the case of cabin cruisers, where they might be as narrow as 45 cm/ 18 in, which would be sufficient in the home for a slender, overnight child guest, or for a holiday home where a Spartan spirit seems to take over, making discomfort something of a pleasure.

Boats provide plenty of inspired storage ideas, too, as there is no room for free-wheeling objects crashing around the cabin in a force-9 gale. Hammocks are ideal for stowing away lightweight bulky bedding, and the ingenious places that boat-builders find to put lockers and shelves certainly deserves the attention of any home-builder short of space.

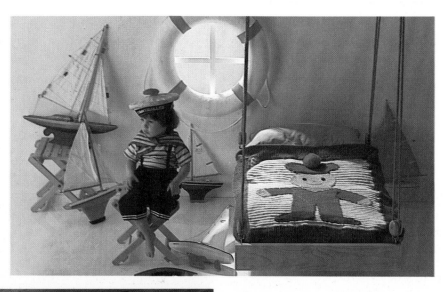

Above: *a hanging bed, a porthole window and a Tam o' Shanter to enchant the would-be sailor.*

Above: *living in a boat necessitates a certain degree of two-tier living: the cabin lies beneath the deck, drawers are slotted under the bed and, here, a WC unit is neatly fitted below a bench.*

345

Designer's choice
Grand hotels

Above: *attention to detail is the true mark of a great hotel, in this case Brenner's Park, Baden-Baden, Germany.*

Left: *the "Bamboo Room" in the Palace Hotel, St Moritz, has an oriental air of luxury.*

Below: *this tiled private bathroom at the Savoy, London, is both smart and grand, but it is also easy for maids to clean.*

Unless you happen to inhabit a well-regulated palace of your own, it is only at the surviving—and, indeed, thriving—really Grand Hotels that you will experience the ultimate in bedding and bathing luxury and catch a glimpse of the way things were for the wealthy before the last world war.

It is at these establishments that out-of-a-job royals tend to make their homes, and that working monarchs stay when they travel. The pages of the hotels' golden guest-books amount to a roll-call of the celebrated from every walk of life. If some of these hotels incorporate the word *Palace* in their names, it is because this is precisely what they were: palatial mansions built for Court favourites, ministers of state and, in the case of the Gritti in Venice, the palazzo that a Renaissance doge called home. And the splendour of the reception areas of the great hotels, with their elegant lobbies, palm courts, huge curved staircases, chandeliers, acres of mirror, Gobelin

tapestries, antiques and paintings is more than matched by the highly civilized furnishings of the suites upstairs.

So, furniture aside, what are the touches of luxury that raise a hired room into the superlative category? There is usually, for one thing, plenty of space: shown to the royal suite of the Angleterre in Copenhagen, even a reigning queen was seen to clap her hands and heard to exclaim, "You mean this is all for me?" There is apt to be a lined and braided canopy above the king-sized bed, which has an immensely comfortable mattress —never any historic lumps, no matter how many royal personages have rested upon it over the years. Good beds are a matter of course in good hotels.

All this, including the splendid bathroom—where the tub may be ancient marble but the plumbing is up to date—emanates a very agreeable air of luxury. This is reinforced by the pleasant design details like subtle, adjustable lighting, efficient door knobs and closet latches,

down to the provision of cut-glass tooth mugs and bowls of fresh flowers.

The management is, after all, in business to cosset you and make you feel like a cherished guest, not an anonymous cypher to be computer processed through the works. This is why the grand hotels take particular pride in good, really personal service. Whether you require a special brand of coffee for your breakfast or tickets for shows that are sold out, everything is miraculously and courteously provided at the touch of a bell.

Some hotel managers plaintively observe that all too few people nowadays really know "how things should be done". Still, while there are yet guests who bring their own monogrammed satin sheets to sleep in, and their own servants (who occupy what are called the couriers' rooms on the higher, less desirable floors) to give a hand in looking after them, we may live in hopes that the very grand tradition of bedding and bathing will last a little longer.

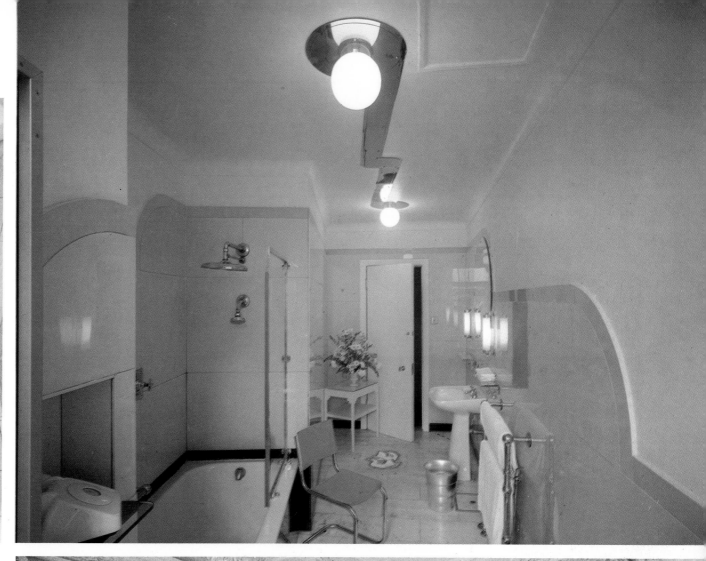

Above: *service indeed! One thing that the Hotel Bristol in Paris could not be accused of is lack of attention to hygiene.*

Top right: *this magnificent bathroom in Claridge's is perfect in every detail down to the flowers and the telephone.*

Right: *aristocratic and even royal though the visitors to the Imperial Suite, Imperial Hotel, Vienna, may be, they can never fail to be impressed by the opulence of the decor, which is in the grand manner of mansions and palaces.*

347

Useful addresses

Terence Conran, who has compiled this book, also runs the Habitat chain of stores in the United Kingdom, France and Belgium, and Conran's in the United States. Many of the items illustrated in these pages can be found in the stores, so we give you a list of their addresses:

Offices (914)-633-8200

UNITED STATES

New York, NY
Conran's at the Market in the Citicorp Center, Third Avenue, Lexington and 54th
(212) 371-2225 Store

UNITED KINGDOM

Birmingham
41-43 New Street Shopping Centre
Bolton
9-13 Knowsley Street
Bournemouth
Parkway House, Avenue Road
Brighton
11 Churchill Square, Western Road
Bristol
Clifton Heights, Triangle West
Bromley
12 Westmoreland Place
Cardiff
14 Wharton Street
Cheltenham
108-110 The Promenade
Coventry
63-64 Hertford Street
Croydon
1111-1114 Whitgift Centre
Edinburgh
32 Shandwick Place
Glasgow
140-160 Bothwell Street
Guildford
4-6 North Street
Kingston upon Thames
14-16 Eden Walk
Leicester
13 Belgrave Gate, Haymarket Centre
Liverpool
17-21 Dawson's Way, St John's Centre
London
206-222 King's Road SW3
London
156-158 Tottenham Court Road W1
London
The Conran Shop, 77-79 Fulham Road SW3

Manchester
14 Dalton Street
Manchester
Southmoor Road, Wythenshawe M23 9DS
Newcastle upon Tyne
Eldon Square Shopping Centre
Northampton
The Grosvenor Centre
Nottingham
144-147 Victoria Centre
Romford
38-42 Market Place
Wallingford
Hithercroft Road
Watford
18 Queen's Road
York
26 High Ousegate

FRANCE

Paris
Centre Commercial de la Tour, Maine-Montparnasse, 11 rue de l'Arrivée, Boîte Cedex 1001
Paris
35 avenue de Wagram
Lille
6 Parvis St Maurice
Lyon
Place des Cordeliers
Montpellier
Centre Commercial, Le Polygone Cedex 0109
Orgeval
La Maison Blanche, RN13
Strasbourg
Centre Commercial, La Maison Rouge, Place Kléber

BELGIUM

Bruxelles 1000
6 Place de la Monnaie

General

Accent on Information Inc., Gillum Road and High Drive, P.O. Box 700, Bloomington, Il. 61701. A non-profit organization serving disabled persons by collecting and disseminating specialized information. Services are available through *Accent on Living,* a quarterly magazine; Accent on Information, a computerized retrieval system; and Accent Special Publications.

Accoustical & Board Products Association, 205 W Tuohy Avenue, Park Ridge, Il. 60068. Manufacturers representing major US producers of accoustical ceiling materials, hardboard and insulation board.

American Innerspring Manufacturers, 1918 N Parkway, Memphis, Tn. 38112. Manufacturers of steel innersprings for bedding and furniture.

American Institute of Architects, 1735 New York Avenue NW, Washington D.C. 20006.

American Plywood Association, Tacoma, Wa. 98401.

Architectural Aluminum Manufacturers Association, 410 N Michigan Avenue, Chicago, Il. 60611. Window and curtain-wall manufacturers.

Association of Home Appliance Manufacturers, 20 N Wacker Drive, Chicago, Il. 60606. Publishes annual directories of certified appliances.

Consumer Protection Center, 2000 H Street NW, Washington D.C. 20006. Gives consumers with complaints appropriate referrals to federal, state and local sources, where problems can be quickly solved.

Consumers Educ. & Protective Association International, 6048 Ogontz Avenue, Philadelphia, Pa. 19141. Educates the consumer to combat fraud and other unscrupulous business activities, and to strengthen the consumer's interests.

Consumers' Research, Bowerstown Road, Washington, N.J. 07882. A non-profit service reporting laboratory tests on a wide range of goods for consumers. Maintains extensive library, including over 20,000 file folders and a large pamphlet collection, and publishes a monthly magazine.

Consumers' Union of United States, 256 Washington Street, Mount Vernon, N.Y. 10550. Tests, rates and reports on competing brands of appliances, food products, household equipment, etc. Publishes monthly Consumer Reports, including Annual Buying Guide Issue in December. Also publishes special reports on particular fields of consumer interests, such as health, family planning.

Cultured Marble Institute, 230 N Michigan Avenue, Chicago, Il. 60601. Gives information to the public about the uses of cultured marble and its advantages.

The Electrification Council, 90 Park Avenue, New York, N.Y. 10016.

Feather & Down Association Inc., 257 W 38th Street, New York, N.Y. 10018. Processors of feather and down and their end products—pillows, comforters, sleeping bags and parkas. Annual convention in New York City.

Furniture Industry Consumer Advisory Panel, P.O. Box 951, High Point, N.C. 27262. Provides a third-party mechanism for resolving complaints involving manufacturing defects in quality of and service for furniture and publishes informational brochure.

Gas Appliance Manufacturers Association, 1901 N Fort Myer Drive, Arlington, Va. 22209. Manufacturers of residential gas appliances and equipment.

National Association of Bedding Manufacturers, 1150 17th Street NW, Washington D.C. 20036. Manufacturers of mattresses, springs and dual-purpose sleeping equipment and supplies. Also holds annual convention in March in Houston, Texas.

National Bath, Bed and Linen Association, 437 Fifth Avenue, New York, N.Y. 10016. Manufacturers of consumer products for the bath, bed and table. Holds an annual trade show in May in New York City.

National Electrical Manufacturers Association, 115 E 44th Street, New York, N.Y. 10017. Publishes material on wiring, installation of equipment, lighting and standards.

National Home Improvement Council, 11 E 44th Street, New York, N.Y. 10017. Includes manufacturers of building products, lenders, utilities, associations, dealers and contractors. They conduct educational and promotional programs to encourage modernizing of homes.

National Housewares Manufacturers Association, 1130 Merchandise Mart, Chicago, Il. 60654. Manufacturers of housewares and small appliances.

National Institute for Consumer Justice, Administrative Conference of the USA, 726 Jackson Place NW, Washington D.C. 20506. Facilitates the remedy of grievances and provides legal recourse for the consumer.

National Supply Distributors Association, 37 Landsdowne Street, Boston, Ma. 02215. Retailers for home improvement items for do-it-yourself stores, such as plumbing, heating, building, hardware and air-conditioning equipment and materials.

National Woodwork Manufacturers Association, 400 W Madison Street, Chicago, Il. 60606. Publishes information on proper care and finishing of windows, sashes, doors and frames, and issues folders on modular standards.

Plumbing & Drainage Institute, 5342 Boulevard Place, Indianapolis, In. 46208. Manufacturers of plumbing tiltings and supplies. Publishes standards and code books.

Plumbing Brass Institute,
221 N LaSalle Street, Chicago,
Il. 60601. Manufacturers of
plumbing brass fittings and
equipment.

Plumbing-Heating-Cooling
Information Bureau,
35 E Wacker Drive, Chicago,
Il. 60601. Maintains clearing
house for consumer inquiries.
Publishes educational materials
on the industry for consumers,
schools, builders, architects and
engineers.

Showrooms

Los Angeles
Home Furnishings Mart,
Los Angeles, Ca.
Permanent exhibit center for
manufacturers in the home
furnishings industry.

New York
Home Furnishings Market,
205 Lexington Avenue,
New York, N.Y. 10016.
Permanent showrooms for
furniture, lamps, fabrics, outdoor
furniture, mirrors and draperies.

Exhibitions

Atlanta Home Furnishings
Market,
Peachtree Center,
Peachtree, Ga.
Twice annually in January and
July; fourteen floors of exhibit
space covering furniture, floor
coverings, decorative
accessories, lamps, mirrors and
picture lines.

Chicago Home Furnishings
Market,
America's National Lamp Show,
Illinois.
Twice annually in January and
June. Manufacturers' new line
introductions of all categories of
home furnishings, lamps,
decorative accessories, summer
and leisure furniture.

Fort Lauderdale Spring Home
Show, Florida.
Annually in March.

Home Furnishings Market Week,
San Francisco, Ca.
Annually in January; largest
combined display of Eastern and
Western manufacturers of
furniture, floor coverings and
decorative accessories.

Houston Home Show, Texas.
Annually in May. Displays of new
home furnishings, appliances,
gardening equipment, etc.

Jacksonville Home and Patio
Show, Florida.
Annually in February. Home
furnishings, housewares and
gardens for all types of homes as
well as a complete antique show.

Miami Home Show, Florida.
Annually in May.

National Housewares Expo,
Chicago, Il.
Annually in January; world's
largest display of housewares
and small electrical appliances.

New Haven Home Show,
New Haven, Conn.
Annually in May; comprehensive
display of new products and
services designed for better living
in our energy-shortage economy.
Emphasis on home decorating
and furnishings.

New England Home Show,
Boston, Mass.
Annually in March; displays of
home furnishings, housewares
and gardens.

Southern Home and Garden
Show, Greenville, S.C.
Annually in March. Display of
building products, home
furnishings, gardens, etc. Also
products promoting the home
building industry.

Transworld Housewares and
Variety Exhibition, Chicago, Il.
Twice annually in January and
July; a complete general
merchandise exhibition.

Winter Home Furnishings
Market, Dallas, Texas.
Annually in January. Display of
home furnishings, floor
coverings, contract furnishings
and accessories.

Bedrooms

Advance Furniture Mfg. Co.,
24180 S Vermont Avenue,
Harbour City, Ca. 90710.

Advent T.V., Advent
Corporation,
195 Albany Street, Cambridge,
Mass. 02139.

American of Martinsville,
Contract Division,
Martinsville, Va. 24112.

Bright Industries,
1900 NW First, P.O. Box 758,
Boca Raton, Fl. 33432.

Drexel Contract Furniture,
Drexel, N.C. 28619.

Fantasy Furniture,
Brownell Hollow Road,
Eagle Bridge, N.Y. 12057.

Linea Plus,
964 Third Avenue,
New York, N.Y. 10022.

Souveran Fabrics Corp.,
509 Madison Avenue,
New York, N.Y. 10022.

Thomasville Furniture Industries,
Thomasville, N.C. 27360.

Beds

American Furniture Co.,
Romweber, 4 S Park Avenue,
Batesville, In. 47006.

Architectural Elegance Inc.,
12200 SW 80 Street,
Miami, Fl. 33183.

Atelier International Ltd.,
595 Madison Avenue,
New York, N.Y. 10022.

Avery Boardman Ltd.,
979 Third Avenue,
New York, N.Y. 10022.

Baker, Knapp & Tubbs,
474 Merchandise Mart,
Chicago, Il. 60654.

Beauti-Glide Co./L.S.I.,
Chestnut & Ninth Streets,
Seymour, In. 47274.

Bedquarters,
964 Third Avenue,
New York, N.Y. 10022.

Borg-Warner Health
Products Inc.,
P.O. Box 28226,
St. Louis, Mo. 63132.

The Brass Collection by
Melvin Wolf,
223 West Hubbard Street,
Chicago, Il. 60610.

Buzan Collection,
2400 Market Street,
Philadelphia, Pa. 19103.

Calif-Asia Co.,
Div. Brown-Jordan,
9860 Gidley Street,
El Monte, Ca. 91734.

Cal-Mode Furniture Mfg. Co.,
9909 W Jefferson Boulevard,
Culver City, Ca. 90230.

Casa Bella Imports Inc.,
1801 Bay Road,
Miami Beach, Fl. 33139.

Chal-Art Crafts Inc.,
11-13 Maryland Avenue,
Paterson, N.J. 07503.

Chairmasters Ltd.,
Annapolis Royal,
Nova Scotia, B0S 1A0, Canada.

Chippendales & Associates,
1783 Merchandise Mart,
Chicago, Il. 60654.

Columbia Bedding Co.,
4520 W Cermark Road,
Chicago, Il. 60623.

Community Metal Products
Corp.,
1213 Circle Avenue,
Forest Park, Il. 60130.

Continental Metal Furniture,
14812 Calvert,
Van Nuys, Ca. 91411.

Core Furniture Intl. Ltd.,
P.O. Box 86,
Sta. Snowdon,
Montreal H3X 3T3,
Que., Canada.

Crest-Foam Corp.,
100 Carol Place,
Moonachie, N.J. 07075.

DIR International Inc.,
48 Brattle Street,
Cambridge, Mass. 02138.

Empire Furniture Factory,
Rattan Works,
4118 Ponce de Leon Boulevard,
Coral Gables, Fl. 33146.

Englander Co. Inc.,
558 Vandalia,
St. Paul, Mn. 55114.

Ficks Reed Co.,
4900 Charlemar Drive,
Cincinnati, Oh. 45227.

Forest Products,
Div. Ludlow Corp.,
Box 40,
Morristown, Tn. 37814.

Forms & Surfaces Inc.,
P.O. Box 5215,
Santa Barbara, Ca. 93108.

Foster Bros. Mfg. Co.,
2025 S Vandeventer,
St. Louis, Mo. 63110.

Furniture Dynamics Inc.,
P.O. Box 426,
Richardson, Tx. 75080.

Galleria Mobili,
Div. D & F Wright Assoc. Inc.,
976 Third Avenue,
New York, N.Y. 10022.

Gem Industries Inc.,
314 Main Street,
Gardner, Mass. 01440.

General Housewares Corp.,
Leisure Furniture Group,
64 Perimeter Center E,
Atlanta, Ga. 30346.

J.L. George & Co. (H.K.) Ltd.,
285 Lake Merced Boulevard,
Daly City, Ca. 94015.

Otto Gerdan Co.,
82 Wall Street,
New York, N.Y. 10005.

Gold Bond Mattress Co.,
801 Windsor Street,
Hartford, Conn. 06101.

Hagen International,
424 Ninth Street,
San Francisco, Ca. 94103.

Hall-Mark Furniture Mfg. Inc.,
2775 E Tenth Avenue,
Hialeah, Fl. 33013.

Harris-Hub Co. Inc.,
15600 S Commercial Avenue,
Harvey, Il. 60426.

Harvard Interiors Mfg. Co.,
4321 Semple Avenue,
St. Louis, Mo. 63120.

Harvard Mfg. Co.,
24300 Solon Road,
Bedford Heights, Oh. 44146.

Hermosa Rattan Co.,
P.O. Box 5688,
El Monte, Ca. 91734.

Heywood-Wakefield Co.,
206 Central Street,
Gardner, Mass. 01440.

Hickory Springs Mfg. Co. Inc.,
P.O. Box 128,
2200 Main Avenue SE,
Hickory, N.C. 28601.

Holland Maid Inc.,
955 Brooks Avenue,
Holland, Mi. 49423.

Horizons Inc.,
P.O. Box 448,
Newton, N.C. 28658.

Hudson Rinsman,
8430 Melrose Avenue,
Los Angeles, Ca. 90069.

Useful addresses

Imperial American Co.,
P.O. Box 878,
Tyler, Tx. 75701.

Inland Bed,
Div. Shore Industries Inc.,
759 S Washetenow,
Chicago, Il. 60612.

International Design Corp.,
3441 W Grand Avenue,
Chicago, Il. 60651.

InterRoyal Corp.,
One Park Avenue,
New York, N.Y. 10016.

Jamison Bedding Inc.,
P.O. Box 989,
Nashville, Tn. 37202.

Jefferson Bed,
448 W 46 Street,
New York, N.Y. 10036.

J.P. Stevens & Co. Inc.,
1460 Broadway,
New York, N.Y. 10036.

Kara Design,
19th St and Allegheny Avenue,
Philadelphia, Pa.

Kaspacians Inc.,
815 S Freemont Avenue,
Alhambra, Ca. 91803.

Kidrest,
143 W 20 Street,
New York, N.Y. 10011.

KT Furniture Div.,
Flair of California,
20100 S Alameda Street,
Compton, Ca. 90220.

Kwik Bed Sofa Corp.,
330 E St. Joseph,
Indianapolis, In. 46202.

Lea Industries Inc.,
P.O. Box 1538,
Richmond, Va. 23212.

James Lee Inc.,
Contempra, 3802,
NE First Avenue,
Miami, Fl. 33137.

Leggett & Platt Inc.,
Metal Bed Rail Div.,
P.O. Box 140,
Linwood, N.C. 27299.

John Leslie Inc.,
P.O. Box 599,
Troy, Mi. 48084.

Elaine Lewis Ltd.,
150 E 58 Street,
New York, N.Y. 10022.

Living Walls Inc.,
120 E 144 Street,
Bronx, N.Y. 10451.

McGuire Showroom,
38 Hotaling Place,
San Francisco, Ca. 94111.

Mirro Craft,
1540 S Hannah,
Forest Park, Il. 60130.

Phyllis Morris Originals,
8772 Beverly Boulevard,
Los Angeles, Ca. 90048.

Motif Furniture Industries Inc.,
2300 S Central Avenue,
Chicago, Il. 60650.

Mount Airy Furniture Co.,
P.O. Box 1247,
Mount Airy, N.C. 27030.

Murphy Door Bed Co. Inc.,
40 E 34 Street,
New York, N.Y. 10016.

Musterring International Ltd.,
3105 Orlando Drive,
Mississauga,
Toronto, Ontario L4V 1C5,
Canada.

National Import Products,
3135 E 12 Street,
Los Angeles, Ca. 90023.

National Slumber Products,
121 W 72 Street,
New York, N.Y. 10022.

Oxford Metal Products Co. Inc.,
2629 Belgrade Street,
Philadelphia, Pa. 19125.

Paragon Designs Inc.,
Evans & Woodhaven Road,
Philadelphia, Pa. 19116.

Parsons Inc.,
507 N LaSalle Street,
Chicago, Il. 60610.

Period Inc.,
P.O. Box 578,
Henderson, Ky. 42420.

Harvey Probber Inc.,
979 Third Avenue,
New York, N.Y. 10022.

Joseph Radak Co. Inc.,
515 Fourth Street, P.O. Box 107,
San Fernando, Ca. 91341.

Lew Raynes Inc.,
40 E 34 Street,
New York, N.Y. 10016.

Restonic Corp.,
1010 Jorie Boulevard,
Oakbrook, Il. 60521.

Romac Metals Inc.,
P.O. Box 836,
Troutman, N.C. 28166.

Romweber Co.,
Batesville,
Il. 47006.

Rubee Furniture Mfg. Corp.,
7-113 Merchandise Mart,
Chicago, Il. 60654.

Rucker Industries,
2670 Rosselle Street,
Jacksonville, Fl. 32203.

R.S. Furniture Inc.,
395 Ste Croux Street,
Montreal, Canada.

R-Way Furniture Co.,
740 S Commerce,
Sheboygan, Wi. 53081.

Scandiline Industries Inc.,
1217 W Artesia Boulevard,
Compton, Ca. 90220.

Schubert Industries,
680-702 Miami Street,
Akron, Oh. 44311.

Sealy Inc.,
Contract Div.,
158 Third Street,
Mineola, N.Y. 11501.

Sevacraft Mfg. Co.,
P.O. Box 5483, 1156 107th,
Arlington, Tx. 76011.

Simmons Co. — Contract Div.,
1870 Merchandise Mart,
Chicago, Il. 60654.

Sleepmaster Products Co. Inc.,
280 Wilson Avenue,
Newark, N.J. 07105.

Smith & Watson,
305 E 63 Street,
New York, N.Y. 10021.

Southern Cross Industries Inc.,
P.O. Box 1597,
Atlanta, Ga. 30301.

Sparta Furniture Div.,
Extensole Corp.,
Sparta, Mi. 49345.

Victor Stanley Inc.,
P.O. Box 93,
Dunkirk, Md. 20754.

Steadly Co. Inc.,
P.O. Box 419,
Carthage, Mo. 64836.

Swan Brass Beds,
1955 E 16 Street,
Los Angeles, Ca. 90021.

Takara/Belmont Inc.,
One Belmont Drive,
Somerset, N.J. 08873.

Telescope Folding Furniture
Co. Inc.,
Granville, N.Y. 12832.

Tenneco Chemicals Foam Div.,
W 100 Century Road,
Paramus, N.J. 07652.

Terry Fabrics Inc.,
74 Coit Street,
Irvington, N.J. 07111.

Therapedic Assoc. Inc.,
225 North Avenue,
Garwood, N.J. 07027.

Thonet Industries Inc.,
491 E Princess Street,
York, Pa. 17405.

Toyad Corp.,
P.O. Box 30,
Latrobe, Pa. 15650.

Tri-lo Products,
2415 W 24 Place,
Chicago, Il.

Tri-Mark Designs,
1006 Arch Street,
Philadelphia, Pa. 19107.

United Foam Corp.,
2626 Vista Industry,
Compton, Ca. 90221.

Warren-Charles Furniture Inc.,
979 Third Avenue,
New York, N.Y. 10022.

West Michigan Furniture Co.,
195 W Eighth Street,
Holland, Mi. 49423.

John Widdicomb Co.,
205 E 58 Street,
New York, N.Y. 10022.

Willow & Reed Inc.,
32-34 111 Street,
East Elmhurst, N.Y. 11369.

Therapeutic Beds

Cadence Furniture Associates
Inc.,
P.O. Box 15795,
Plantation, Fl. 33318.

Chesapeake-Siegel-Land Inc.,
317 E 34 Street,
New York, N.Y. 10016.

DMI Furniture,
P.O. Box 129,
Huntingburg, In. 47542.

Duralite Co. Inc.,
2 Barbour Avenue,
Passaic, N.J. 07055.

Duo-Sofas Inc.,
229 N Frankintown Road,
Baltimore, Md. 21223.

Goodman Mfg. Co.,
2929 "B" Street,
Philadelphia, Pa. 19134.

Frank A. Hall & Sons Ltd.,
969 Third Avenue,
New York, N.Y. 10022.

Lattoflex Inc.,
285 Palisade Avenue,
Cliffside Park,
N.J. 07010.

Scandinavian Design Inc.,
117 E 59 Street,
New York, N.Y. 10022.

Shelby Williams Goodman Inc.,
2929 B Street,
Philadelphia, Pa. 19134.

Sico Inc.,
7525 Cahill Road,
Minneapolis, Mn. 55435.

H. Singer Furniture & Sleep
Products,
Div. Ideal Upholstering Co.,
299 Marlen Avenue,
Montreal H18 4V5,
Que., Canada.

Skandi-form,
1066 31 Street NW,
Washington, D.C. 20007.

Spherical Furniture,
P.O. Box 329,
Boone, N.C. 28607.

Bedding

Abraham-Zumsteg Inc.,
979 Third Avenue,
New York, N.Y. 10022.

Robert Allen Fabrics,
25 Wells Avenue,
Newton Center, Ma. 02159.

Allume,
979 Third Avenue,
New York, N.Y. 10022.

Ambiance,
979 Third Avenue,
New York, N.Y. 10022.

American Drapery & Carpet
Co. Inc.,
33 E 17 Street,
New York, N.Y. 10003.

Amsco Decorative Fabrics,
1136 Bedford Drive,
High Point, N.C. 27261.

Amsterdam Fabricators Corp.,
165 Classon Avenue,
Brooklyn, N.Y. 11205.

Arc-Com Fabrics,
32 E 31 Street,
New York, N.Y. 10016.

Archi-Tex Fabrics Corp.,
38 E 29 Street,
New York, N.Y. 10016.

Art Drapery Studios Inc.,
1347 W Argyle,
Chicago, Il. 60640.

Artmark Fabrics Co. Inc.,
480 Lancaster Place,
Frazer, Pa. 19355.

Associated Draperies,
National Sales Div.,
Field Street,
Box 4701,
St Louis, Mo. 63108.

Associated Drapery &
Equipment Co.,
40 Sea Cliff Avenue,
Glen Cove, N.Y. 11542.

Athol Mfg. Corp.,
P.O. Box 105,
Butner, N.C. 27509.

Barclay Fabrics Co. Inc.,
7120 Airport Highway,
Box 650,
Pennsauken, N.J. 08101.

Bassett McNab Co.,
1032 Arch Street,
Philadelphia, Pa. 19107.

Bates Fabrics Inc.,
1431 Broadway,
New York, N.Y. 10001.

Bayberry Handprints Inc.,
Far Reach Trail,
Putnam Valley, N.Y. 10579.

Bedspreads of California,
Div. of MG Koch & Co.,
2620 S Hill Street,
Los Angeles, Ca. 90007.

Lee Behren Silks Ltd.,
125 Newtown Road,
Plainview, N.Y. 11803.

B. Berger Co.,
1608 E 24 Street,
Cleveland, Oh. 44114.

Berkshire Hathaway Inc.,
Decorative Fabrics Div.,
41 Madison Avenue,
New York, N.Y. 10010.

Joel Berman Assoc.,
116 Greene Street,
New York, N.Y. 10012.

Bloomcraft Inc.,
295 Fifth Avenue,
New York, N.Y. 10016.

Boussac of France Inc.,
979 Third Avenue,
New York, N.Y. 10022.

Boyd Architectural
Wallcoverings,
333 N Baldwin Park Boulevard,
City of Industry, Ca. 91746.

Brandon House Designs Inc.,
8520 National Boulevard,
Culver City, Ca. 90320.

Brickel Associates Inc.,
515 Madison Avenue,
New York, N.Y. 10022.

Bristol Furniture Co.,
2959 NE 12 Terrace,
Ft. Lauderdale, Fl. 33308.

Brunschwig & Fils Inc.,
979 Third Avenue,
New York, N.Y. 10022.

Burlington House,
Div. Burlington Industries,
1345 Avenue of Americas,
New York, N.Y. 10019.

Carousel Designs,
35 NE 40 Street,
Miami, Fl. 33137.

Cartier Mills Inc.,
Div. David & Dash,
2445 N Miami Avenue,
Miami, Fl. 33137.

Henry Cassen Inc.,
979 Third Avenue,
New York, N.Y. 10022.

Cenci Fabrics,
964 Third Avenue,
New York, N.Y. 10022.

Charterhouse Designs Ltd.,
979 Third Avenue,
New York, N.Y 10022.

Chatham Manufacturing Co.,
Dept. AL3A,
111 W 40th Street,
New York, N.Y. 10018.

Clifton Drapery Mfg. Inc.,
11 Circle Avenue,
Clifton, N.J. 07011.

Cohama Decorative Fabrics,
United Merchants & Mfgs.,
214 Madison Avenue,
New York, N.Y. 10016.

Contemporary Hides,
6446 Santa Monica Boulevard,
Hollywood, Ca. 90038.

Contract Decor Inc.,
95 Madison Avenue,
New York, N.Y. 10016.

Contract Fabrics Inc.,
Donald Lampier Assoc.,
2891 Fairfield Avenue,
Bridgeport, Conn. 06605.

Croyden Decorator Fabrics Inc.,
Universal Looms,
7157 Camp Hill Road,
Ft. Washington, Pa. 19034.

Designcraft Textiles Ltd.,
P.O. Box 1344,
Lunenburg,
Nova Scotia, B0J 2C0, Canada.

Design Tex Fabrics Inc.,
275 Seventh Avenue,
New York, N.Y. 10001.

Dolphin Draperies,
4010 NW Second Avenue,
Miami, Fl. 33127.

Drapery Workroom Inc.,
3299 NW Second Avenue,
Miami, Fl. 33127.

Fabric Quilters Unlimited Inc.,
1400 Shames Drive,
Westbury, N.Y. 11590.

Fabricut Inc.,
9303 E 46 Street,
Tulsa, Ok. 74145.

Facade Papers Inc.,
7618 Spafford Road,
Cleveland, Oh. 44105.

Feathre Luv Enterprises Inc.,
P.O. Box 261, Harvard Square,
Cambridge, Mass. 02138.

Fieldcrest,
60 West 40th Street,
New York, N.Y. 10018.

Fortuny Inc.,
509 Madison Avenue,
New York, N.Y. 10022.

Franciscan Fabrics Inc.,
938 Harrison Street,
San Francisco, Ca. 94107.

The Fun Factory,
418 High Street,
Morgantown, W.Va. 6505.

Fun with Furs by Liesel,
190 North State Street,
Chicago, Il. 60601.

Grande Maison de Blanc,
68 E 56 Street,
New York, N.Y. 10022.

James G. Hardy & Co. Inc.,
11 E 26 Street,
New York, N.Y. 10010.

Homecraft Drapery &
Upholstery Corp.,
102 Prince Street,
New York, N.Y. 10012.

Hopkins Co.,
950 King Avenue,
Columbus, Oh. 43212.

Huntingdon Products Co. Inc.,
Div. National Gypsum Co.,
21 Glenn Street,
P.O. Box 247,
Lawrence, Ma. 01843.

Kamola Fabrics,
2117 Pontius Avenue,
Los Angeles, Ca. 90025.

Keller Williams Furniture Mfg.
Co. Inc.,
P.O. Box 14504,
Oklahoma City, Ok. 73114.

Kenney Drapery Assoc. Inc.,
1785 Broad Causeway,
N. Miami, Fl. 33161.

Kirk-Brummel Associates Inc.,
979 Third Avenue,
New York, N.Y. 10022.

Kneedler-Fauchere,
8687 Melrose Avenue,
Los Angeles, Ca. 90069.

Knoll International,
745 Fifth Avenue,
New York, N.Y. 10022.

Kravet Fabrics Inc.,
201 E 56 Street,
New York, N.Y. 10022.

Boris Kroll Fabrics Inc.,
979 Third Avenue,
New York, N.Y. 10022.

Krupnick Bros Inc.,
979 Third Avenue,
New York, N.Y. 10022.

Lady Linda,
295 Fifth Avenue,
New York, N.Y. 10016.

L & B Mfg. Corp.,
2144 Colorado Avenue,
Santa Monica, Ca. 90404.

L & B Products Corp.,
3232 Lurting Avenue,
Bronx, N.Y. 10469.

Hank Loewenstein Inc.,
P.O. Box 22029,
Ft. Lauderdale, Fl. 33335.

Loumac Supply Co.,
900 Passaic Avenue,
Harrison, N.J. 07029.

Luxout Products Div.,
Plastic Products Inc.,
P.O. Box 1118,
Richmond, Va. 23208.

Lyon Metal Products Inc.,
63 Railroad Avenue,
Aurora, Il. 60507.

McCanless Custom Fabrics Inc.,
P.O. Box 1447,
Salisbury, N.C. 28144.

Mann Drapery Mfg. Inc.,
14920 Oxnard Street,
Van Nuys, Ca. 91411.

Master Recessed Systems Inc.,
1800 New Highway,
Farmingdale, N.Y. 11735.

Monroe Kent,
Highway 45,
Aberdeen, Ms. 39730.

Moon Over the Mountain
Patchworks,
900 Park Avenue,
New York, N.Y. 10021.

Morae Designs, Div. Aer-o-lite,
10451 Park Avenue,
Garden Grove, Ca. 92640.

Naco Fabrics,
145 Plant Avenue,
Hauppauge, N.Y. 11787.

Nettle Creek Industries,
Peacock Road,
Richmond, In. 47374.

Norman's of Salisbury,
P.O. Drawer 799,
Salisbury, N.C. 28144.

Norton-Blumenthal Inc.,
979 Third Avenue,
New York, N.Y. 10022.

Overland Fabrics Ltd.,
261 Fifth Avenue,
New York, N.Y. 10016.

Parisian Drapery Co.,
22-08 Morlot Avenue,
Fairlawn, N.J. 07410.

Payne & Co.,
3500 Kettering Boulevard,
Dayton, Oh. 45401.

Perfect Fit Industries Inc.,
303 Fifth Avenue,
New York, N.Y. 10016.

Premier Fabrics Inc.,
30 Lennox Street,
New Haven, Conn. 06504.

T.W. Rattery Inc.,
390 Capital Avenue,
Hartford, Conn. 06103.

Edwin Raphael Co. Inc.,
Infinity Lane,
Holland, Mi. 49423.

Reed Decorative Products Ltd.,
145 King Street W,
Toronto, M5H 1J8,
Ont., Canada.

L.S. Roberts Drapery Co.,
1060 E 15 Street,
Hialeah, Fl. 33010.

Useful Addresses

Royal Drapery Designs,
Div. Royal Design
Products Corp.,
2534 S Kedzie Avenue,
Chicago, Il. 60623.

F. Schumacher & Co.,
939 Third Avenue,
New York, N.Y. 10022.

Scroll Fabrics Inc.,
645 Lambert Drive,
NE Atlanta, Ga. 30324.

Sealy Mattresses,
Merchandise Mart/Space 470,
Chicago, Il. 60654.

Serta Mattress Inc.,
666 N Lake Shore Drive,
Chicago, Il. 60611.

Shapiro & Son Bedspread Co.,
295 Fifth Avenue,
New York, N.Y. 10016.

Skandia Draperies,
Div. Skagfield Corp.,
P.O. Box 753,
Tallahassee, Fl. 32302.

Specifier Contract Fabrics,
Div. United Merchants &
Manufacturers,
295 Fifth Avenue,
New York, N.Y. 10016.

Spectrum/Trend,
Div. Consolidated Food,
261 Fifth Avenue,
New York, N.Y. 10016.

Springs Mills Inc.,
Springmaid Products,
104 W 40 Street,
New York, N.Y. 10018.

Standard Mattress Co.,
801 Windsor Street,
Hartford, Conn. 06050.

Stauffer Chemical Co.,
Westport, Conn. 06880.

Stead Textile,
Chicago Heights, Il. 60411.

Stendig Inc.,
410 E 62 Street,
New York, N.Y. 10021.

Stevens Fabrics Co.,
430 First Avenue N,
Minneapolis, Mn. 55401.

Tilbury Fabrics Inc.,
Grosby Products Div.,
261 Fifth Avenue,
New York, N.Y. 10016.

Tressard Fabrics Inc.,
979 Third Avenue,
New York, N.Y. 10022.

Bathrooms
Baths, Sinks & Toilets

Ajax Hardware Co.,
825 S Ajax Avenue,
City of Industry, Ca. 91749.

American-Standard,
P.O. Box 2003,
New Brunswick, N.J. 08903.

Bathworks & Kitchen Center,
964 Third Avenue,
A & D Building,
New York, N.Y. 10022.

Beylerian Ltd.,
305 E 63 Street,
New York, N.Y. 10021.

California Hot Tubs,
60 Third Avenue,
New York, N.Y. 10003.

Eljer Plumbingware,
Three Gateway Center,
Pittsburg, Pa. 15222.

Formica Corp.,
120 E Fourth Street,
Cincinnati, Oh. 45202.

Kinkead Products,
5860 N Pulaski Road,
Chicago, Il. 60646.

The Powder Room Inc.,
5090 NE Second Avenue,
Miami, Fl. 33137.

Thermasol Ltd.,
Thermasol Plaza,
Leonia, N.J. 07605.

Viking Sauna Co.,
909 Park Avenue,
P.O. Box 6298,
San José, Ca. 95150.

Showers

Alsons Corporation,
525 E Edna Place,
Couina, Ca. 90669.

Dimensional Plastics Corp.,
1065 E 26 Street,
Hialeah, Fl. 33013.

Du Pont 'Corian' Products,
Wilmington, Del. 19898.

James G. Hardy & Co. Inc.,
11 E 26 Street,
New York, N.Y. 10010.

Kempler, George J., Co. Inc.,
160 Fifth Avenue,
New York, N.Y. 10010.

Kent Furniture,
401 NW 71 Street,
Miami, Fl. 33150.

Pryde,
3517 Cardiff Avenue,
Cincinnati, Oh. 45209.

Rain Jet Corp.,
301 S Flower Street,
Burbank, Ca. 91503.

Roman Fountains Inc.,
P.O. Box 10190,
Albuquerque, N.M. 87114.

Showerfold,
5860 N Pulaski Road,
Chicago, Il. 60646.

Tami Products Co.,
3721 Lee Road,
Shaker Heights, Oh. 44120.

Bath Accessories

Allibert Inc.,
315 E 62 Street,
New York, N.Y. 10021.

American Home Accessories,
686 Lexington Avenue,
New York, N.Y. 10022.

Amsterdam Corp.,
950 Third Avenue,
New York, N.Y. 10022.

Artique Inc.,
231 Rt. 17,
Rutherford, N.J. 07070.

Bakit Industries Inc.,
32 E 30 Street,
New York, N.Y. 10016.

Mr. Bidet Products Ltd.,
P.O. Box 1500,
Hollywood, Fl. 33022.

Marie Cook Inc.,
175 S Smith Street,
Lindenhurst,
N.Y. 11757.

Corona Decor Co.,
260 39 Avenue E,
Seattle, Wash. 98112.

Country Craftsmen,
Hillsboro, N.H. 03244.

Decorative Crafts Inc.,
41 Madison Avenue,
New York, N.Y. 10010.

J.C. De Jong & Co. Inc.,
130-15 91 Avenue,
Richmond Hill,
New York, N.Y. 11418.

Detecto Scales,
230 Fifth Avenue,
New York, N.Y. 10001.

Formco Inc.,
7745 School Road,
Cincinnati, Oh. 45242.

General Bathroom Products,
2201 Touhy Avenue,
Elk Grove, Il. 60007.

Grainware Co.,
2600 N Pulaski Road,
Chicago, Il. 60639.

P.E. Guerin Inc.,
23 Jane Street,
New York, N.Y. 10014.

Hall Mack A. Textron Co.,
P.O. Box 328,
Harrodsburg, Ky. 40330.

Harte & Co. Inc.,
16 E 34 Street,
New York, N.Y. 10016.

Hastings Tile,
964 Third Avenue,
New York, N.Y. 10022.

The Walter Hatches,
225 Fifth Avenue,
New York, N.Y. 10010.

William Hunnath Co. Inc.,
153 E 57 Street,
New York, N.Y. 10022.

Karmel Plastics,
49 Richmondville Avenue,
Westport, Conn. 06880.

Kirsh Co.,
309 N Prospect Street,
Sturgis, Mi. 49091.

Koch, George Ltd.,
P.O. Box 358,
Evansville, In. 47744.

Kohler Co.,
Kohler, Wi. 53044.

Kraft Cabinet Hardware Inc.,
300 E 64 Street,
New York, N.Y. 10021.

The F.H. Lawson Co.,
801 Evans Street,
Cincinnati, Oh. 45204.

Lawson Industries Inc.,
7030 NW 37 Street Court,
P.O. Box 47-1066,
Miami, Fl. 33147.

K. Lux Div. K-SH Inc.,
10091 Manchester,
St. Louis, Mo. 63122.

Mottahedeh,
225 Fifth Avenue,
New York, N.Y. 10010.

National Assoc. of Mirror
Manufacturers,
5101 Wisconsin Avenue,
Washington, D.C. 20016.

Nutone,
Madison and Red Bank Roads,
Cincinnati, Oh. 45227.

Paine & Chriscott,
1187 Second Avenue,
New York, N.Y. 10021.

Palmer Fixture Co.,
P.O. Box 905,
Waukesha, Wi. 53186.

The Charles Parker Co.,
101 Park Avenue,
New York, N.Y. 10017.

Paul Associates Inc.,
155 E 55 Street,
New York, N.Y. 10022.

Pfanstiel Hardware Co.,
Hust Road,
Jeffersonville, N.Y. 12748.

Plasco Inc.,
P.O. Box 3585,
Albuquerque, N.M. 87110.

Powers Regulator Co.,
3400 Oakton Street,
Skokie, Il. 60076.

Ritts Co.,
2221 S Sepulveda,
Los Angeles, Ca. 90064.

Rogin Ltd.,
24 E 64 Street,
New York, N.Y. 10021.

Rusco American Bidet,
100 Glendan Avenue,
Los Angeles, Ca. 90024.

Selby Furniture Hardware Co.,
17 E 22 Street,
New York, N.Y. 10010.

Sikes Corporation,
P.O. Box 447,
Lakeland, Fl. 33802.

Taylor, Deane, Imports Inc.,
Suite 9-J-5,
Atlanta Merchandise Mart,
Atlanta, Ga. 30303.

Temple Galleries,
1661 Washington Street,
Holliston, Mass. 01746.

Tennesse Tufting Corp.,
295 Fifth Avenue,
New York, N.Y. 10016.

Tomorrow Designs Ltd.,
979 Third Avenue,
New York, N.Y. 10022.

2001 Products,
240 E 61 Street,
New York, N.Y. 10021.

Vanleigh Contract Group,
323 E 44 Street,
New York, N.Y. 10017.

Vemaline Products Co. Inc.,
455 Main Street,
Wyckoff, N.J. 07481.

Vogue Carpet Corp.,
969 Third Avenue,
New York, N.Y. 10022.

Sherle Wagner Corp.,
125 E 57 Street,
New York, N.Y.

W.J.B. Waite Co. Inc.,
1355 Market Street,
Sp. 572,
San Francisco, Ca. 94103.

Marion Wieder Inc.,
969 Third Avenue,
New York, N.Y. 10022.

Storage

Abstracta Structures Inc.,
101 Park Avenue,
New York, N.Y. 10017.

Alden Supply & Mfg. Co. Inc.,
844 Windsor Street,
Hartford, Ct. 06120.

Bevco Precision Mfg. Co.,
831 Chicago Avenue,
Evanston, Il. 60202.

Best Imports Inc.,
2231 Valdina Street,
Dallas, Tx. 75207.

Biltrite Furniture Mfg. Inc.,
10251 Ray Lawson Boulevard,
Montreal 438,
Que., Canada.

Browne-Morse Co.,
110 E Broadway Avenue,
Muskegon, Mi. 49443.

Brueton Industries,
315 E 62 Street,
New York, N.Y. 10021.

Cameron McIndoo Ltd.,
P.O. Box 488,
Don Mills, M3C 2T2,
Ont., Canada.

Campaniello Imports Ltd.,
665 Fifth Avenue,
New York, N.Y. 10022.

Carter Co.,
186 Alenife Brook Parkway,
Cambridge, Ma. 02138.

Castelli Furniture Inc.,
950 Third Avenue,
New York, N.Y. 10022.

C.I. Designs,
574 Boston Avenue,
Medford, Ma. 02155.

Claridge Products & Equipment,
Harrison, Ark. 72601.

Closet Maid Corporation,
720 SW 17th Street,
Ocala, Fl. 32670.

Cole Business Furniture,
Div. Litton Industries,
640 Whiteford Road,
York, Pa. 17405.

Corsican Furniture,
2437 E 24 Street,
Los Angeles, Ca. 90058.

Crown Industries Inc.,
27 Crane Street,
Newark, N.J. 07104.

Cypress Furniture Industries Inc.,
1195 NW 71 Street,
Miami, Fl. 33150.

Finealum Corp.,
40-42 22 Street,
Long Island City, N.Y. 11101.

Jens Risom Design Inc.,
P.O. Box 300,
Danielson,
N. Grosvenordale, Ct. 06239.

Johnson Furniture Co.,
1101 Godfrey Avenue SW,
Grand Rapids, Mi. 49502.

Kemp Furniture Industries Inc.,
108 W Cola Drive,
Goldsboro, N.C. 27530.

McDonald Products Corp.,
721 Seneca Street,
Buffalo, N.Y. 14210.

Metwood Mfg. Co. Inc.,
N Forney Avenue,
Hanover, Pa. 17331.

Herman Miller Inc.,
Zeeland, Mi. 49464.

Modulo 3 Inc.,
100 Progress Parkway,
Maryland Heights, Md. 63043.

Myrtle Desk Co.,
P.O. Box 2490,
High Point, N.C. 27261.

Pace Collection Inc.,
321 E 62 Street,
New York, N.Y. 10021.

Peter Pepper Products Inc.,
15215 S Broadway,
Gardena, Ca. 90248.

Precision Mfg. Inc.,
P.O. Box 945,
Place Bonaventure,
Montreal, Que., H5A 1E8,
Canada.

Raymor/Richards-Morgenthau
Inc.,
734 Grand Avenue,
Ridgefield, N.J.

Royal System, Inc./Cado
Furniture Inc.,
979 Third Avenue,
New York, N.Y. 10022.

Techniques in Wood Inc.,
Div. TIW Industries Inc.,
P.O. Box 594,
Rochester, N.Y. 14602.

Tecro Collection,
595 Madison Avenue,
New York, N.Y. 10022.

Virco Mfg. Corp.,
P.O. Box 44846,
Hancock Sta.,
Los Angeles, Ca. 90044.

Vogel-Peterson Co.,
Rt. 83 & Madison,
C - 90,
Elmhurst, Il. 60126.

Fortress Inc.,
8801 Beverly Boulevard,
Los Angeles, Ca. 90048.

Frank & Son Inc.,
470 Park Avenue S,
New York, N.Y. 10016.

Jasper Table Co.,
Jasper, In. 47546.

Floors

Borg Textiles of Bunker/Ramo
Corp.,
820 Wisconsin Street,
Delavan, Wi.

Foro Marble Co. Inc.,
566 President Street,
Brooklyn, N.Y. 11215.

Gearhart, Forrest Co. Inc.,
2325 Chestnut Street,
Philadelphia, Pa. 19103.

Glenoit Mills Inc.,
111 W 40 Street,
New York, N.Y. 10018.

Mannington Mills Inc.,
1234 Market Street,
Philadelphia, Pa. 19107.

New York Marble Works,
1399 Park Avenue,
New York, N.Y. 10029.

Patterson, Flynn & Martin Inc.,
950 Third Avenue,
New York, N.Y. 10022.

Phoenix Carpet Co. Inc.,
979 Third Avenue,
New York, N.Y. 10022.

Dan River (Marimekko),
119 W 40 Street,
New York, N.Y. 10018.

Sears, Roebuck & Co., D/733G,
Sears Tower,
Chicago, Il. 60684.

Walls

Agency Tile Inc.,
979 Third Avenue,
New York, N.Y. 10022.

Armstrong Cork Co.,
Liberty & Charlotte Streets,
Lancaster, Pa. 17604.

Custom Laminations,
932 Market Street,
P.O. Box 2066,
Paterson, N.J. 07509.

Fine Art Wallpapers Co.,
979 Third Avenue,
New York, N.Y. 10022.

First Editions Wallcoverings &
Fabrics Inc.,
979 Third Avenue,
New York, N.Y. 10022.

Imperial Wallcoverings,
23645 Mercantile Road,
Cleveland, Oh. 44122.

Paul Kaiser Assoc. Inc.,
4100 N Miami Avenue,
Miami, Fl. 33127.

Marble Institute of America,
c/o John J. Craig Co.,
P.O. Box 9300,
Knoxville, Tn. 37920.

Marlite Commercial Business,
202 Harger Street,
Dover, Oh. 44622.

Northeastern Wallcoverings,
292 Summer Street,
Boston, Mass. 02210.

U.S. Ceramic Tile Co.,
1375 Raft Road, SW,
Canton, Oh. 44711.

Walker & Zanger Inc.,
P.O. Box 241,
Scarsdale, N.Y. 10583.

Wenczel Tile Co.,
Klagg Avenue,
Trenton, N.J. 08638.

Windows, Curtains & Blinds

Acrylium International Inc.,
9950 NW 77 Avenue,
Hialeah Gardens,
Fl. 33016.

Bergamo Fabrics Inc.,
969 Third Avenue,
New York, N.Y. 10022.

Gardisette Inc.,
500 Essex Road,
Neptune, N.J. 07753.

General Drapery Services Inc.,
60 W 18 Street,
New York, N.Y. 10011.

Gurian Fabrics,
276 Fifth Avenue,
New York, N.Y. 10001.

Lewlor Lorentzen Inc.,
720 Monroe Street,
Hoboken, N.J. 07030.

Plastic-View Transparent
Shades,
P.O. Box 25,
Van Nuys, Ca. 91408.

Wamsutta-Trucraft Inc.,
Rt. 286, Saltsburg,
Pa. 15681.

Waverly Fabrics,
Div. F. Schumacher & Co.,
939 Third Avenue,
New York, N.Y. 10022.

Wilcox International Inc.,
564 W Randolph Street,
Chicago, Il. 60606.

Wilson Textile Corp.,
5379 NW Seventh Street,
Miami, Fl. 33126.

Window Modes Inc.,
979 Third Avenue,
New York, N.Y. 10022.

Lighting

Georgia Lighting Supply Co.,
530 14 Street, NW,
Atlanta, Ga. 30318.

Guth Lighting Div.,
Sola Basic Ind.,
2615 Washington Boulevard,
P.O. 7079,
St. Louis, Mo. 63177.

Litecraft/Luminous Ceilings,
P.O. Box 22601,
Tampa, Fl. 33622.

Neo-Ray Lighting Products,
537 Johnson Avenue,
Brooklyn, N.Y. 11237.

Index

Index

Index

Acknowledgements

Photographs:

The publishers acknowledge the kind co-operation of photographers, photographic agencies and manufacturers as listed below.
Abbreviations used are:

t top; c centre; b bottom; l left; r right; Des designer; 100 ID-100 Idées/BR-Brigitte/CH-Clive Helm/CP-Camera Press/F-Femina/FS-Für Sie/GH-Graham Henderson/JT-Jerry Tubby/LW-Elizabeth Whiting Associates/MEPL-Mary Evans Picture Library/MMC-Maison de Marie-Claire/MN-Michael Nicholson/RTHPL-Radio Times Hulton Picture Library/S.Gr-Sun Gravure/SP-Spike Powell/SW-Schöner Wohnen/TF-Tout Faire/TSP-Tim Street-Porter/ZH-Zu Hause

Front cover: c Susan Griggs/Photo: Michael Boys; *and clockwise:* IMS/Photo: Uggla; LW/JT/Des: Christopher Wray; Norman McGrath/Architect Myron Goldfinger; LW/TSP/Des: Tom Wilson; Annie Hatcher/Fantasy Furniture; The Picture Library; *background* Photo: Grandprint
Back cover: Naru

6-7 WET: The Magazine of Gourmet Bathing/Antonin Kratochvil 8-9 Naru 10 t Snark International/Museum of Decorative Arts, Paris 10-11 MEPL 11 t MEPL; b Mauro Pucciarelli 12 tr, br Claus Hansmann; l Bettmann Archive 13 t MEPL; l Snark International; br RTHPL 14 Mansell Collection 15 t RTHPL; bl Archiv Gerstenberg; br Mansell Collection 16-17 RTHPL 17 t, c Ronan Picture Library; b Mansell Collection 18 l MEPL; r RTHPL 19 l Poster Originals; r Ashe Laboratories 20 Paolo Koch 21 l Werner Forman Archive; t Mireille Vautier/Photo: Hélène Decool; c Sally & Richard Greenhill; b Bildarchiv Sammer 22 l courtesy Dr H. Peeters; r detail from Domestic Scene, Los Angeles 1963 by David Hockney/courtesy Kasmin Ltd 23 tl Salmer/Photo: Carlo Bevilacqua; tr Snark International; bl Scala; br Bulloz 24 t Bettmann Archive/Famous Players Lasky; b John Kobal Collection/ from *Diamonds Are Forever,* distributed through United Artists 25 t John Kobal Collection/ from *Harlow,* copyright © 1965 Paramount Picture Corp., Embassy Pictures Corp. and Prometheus Enterprises Inc; bl John Kobal Collection/ from *The Hallelujah Trail,* distributed through United Artists; br John Kobal Collection/ from *The Seven Year Itch,* courtesy Twentieth Century-Fox Productions Ltd 26-7 Naru 28 CP/F 29 tl PAF/Photo: Rusconi; r LW/TSP/Des: Philip Wilson; bl LW/CH/Des: Jane & Jack Tressider 30 t Susan Griggs/Photo: Michael Boys; b S.Gr/100 ID 31 tr CP/SW; b S.Gr/MMC; tl Transworld Feature Syndicate/American Home 32-3 CP/F 33 ct Colorific/Agence Top/Photo: P. Hinous, chez M. Daladier, Architect; tr Transworld Feature Syndicate/American Home; cb The Picture Library; br LW/Photo: Grant Mudford/Des: CVP Designs Ltd 34 l Colorific/Agence Top/Photo: R. Guillemot/Hvitträsk, Finland/ Furniture by Saarinen; tr LW/Lavinia Press/ Des: Hanne & Philip Philipson, Denmark; br LW/CH/Des: Anthony & Janet Harris 35 l LW/TSP/Des: Ken Carlson & Assocs; tr LW/GH/Des: Glynn Smith Assocs; br LW/CH/Des: Richard & Pam Negus 36 LW/TSP/Des: Max Clendinning 37 tr Susan Griggs/Photo: Michael Boys/Des: Douglas Norwood; cl S.Gr/Photo: B. Baert; c LW/SP/Des: Julian Ruthven; cb LW/MN/Des: Billy Gaylord, San Francisco; br Susan Griggs/Photo: Michael Boys/Des: John Stefanidis 38 t LW/TSP/Des: Chiu; cb LW/TSP/Des: Duggie Fields; br John Bulmer 39 tl Transworld Feature Syndicate/American Home; tr CP/SW; b Transworld Feature Syndicate 40 Susan Griggs/Photo: Michael Boys 41 tr Ronald Sheridan; ct Susan Griggs/Photo: Michael Boys; bl LW/TSP/CVP Designs Ltd; br Paolo Koch 42 l Daniel Eifert/Des: Ruben de Saavedra 42-3 Norman McGrath/Robert A.M. Stern, Architects 43 t LW/CH/Des: Terry & Sue Warner; bl CP/SW; br Robert Perron/Des: Robert Shaw 44 t LW/JT/Des: Christopher Wray; b S.Gr/MMC 45 Bill McLaughlin 46 t Susan Griggs/Photo: Michael Boys; l Paolo Koch; b Colorific/Agence Top/Photo: J. Guillot, chez Jean-Michel Beurdeley 47 S.Gr/MMC 48 LW/TSP/Des: Tom Wilson 48-9 S.Gr/MMC 49 t Susan Griggs/Photo: Michael Boys; cb, br S.Gr/MMC 50 t CP/SW; l Transworld Feature Syndicate/Scoop; br LW/TSP/Des: Max Clendinning 51 t Norman McGrath/Des: Gamal El Zoghby; bl LW/TSP/Des: Emanuelle Khahn; br LW/GH/Des: Nicholas Hills 52 Transworld Feature Syndicate/American Home 53 tr CP/ZH; bl Serge Korniloff; br B. Baert/Photo: J. Primois; tl B. Baert/Photo: A.Dovifat 54 b Lawrence Wright; l S.Gr/MMC; r CP/ZH 55 ct LW/TSP/Des: Sally Sirkin; tr The Picture Library; 56 b S.Gr/100 ID CP/F 57 tl Ezra Stoller © ESTO; tr LW/Photo: Mike Shiels/Des: Tony & Gay Firth; b Norman McGrath/Des: William Ehrlich 58-9 Naru 60 b Brecht-Einzig Ltd/Des: Georgie Wolton RIBA; t CP/F 61 Carla de Benedetti 62 tl, tr Christopher H.L. Owen; b Norman McGrath/Architect: Myron Goldfinger 63 Norman McGrath/Architect: Kiviat-Rappaport 64 Christopher H.L. Owen 65 tl S.Gr/MMC; tr Walker Group; b LW 67 t B. Baert; bl Robert Perron/Architect: Will Armster; br CP/SW 69 CP/ZH 70 l Brecht-Einzig Ltd/Architects: Prof. Kammerer & Prof. Belz; r CP/ZH 71 tl CP/ZH; tr Clive Corless; bl Jessica Strang; br CP/F 72 t Norman McGrath/Architect: Edward Barnes/Des: Ben Baldwin; b Habitat 74 t, bl, Friedrich Stüker; br LW/MN/Des: Malcolm Bancroft 75 tl, br Jessica Strang; tr LW/MN/Des: Ken Turner; bl LW/Photo: Neil Lorrimer 76 l S.Gr/100 ID; r Michael Dunne/Des: Barbara Littman, N.J. 77 t Marimekko, Finland; l S.Gr/100 ID; cb CP/BR; br Cannon Mills 78 Michael Dunne 79 tl S.Gr/Fouineuse; tr Norman McGrath/ Architect: Myron Goldfinger; bl LW/MN/Des: John Dickinson; br CP/ZH 80-81 t S.Gr/MMC; b Marimekko, Finland 81 ct Norman McGrath/Architect: Gwathmey Siegel; r Norman McGrath/Robert A.M. Stern, Architects; cb CP/F 82-3 t S.Gr/MMC; b Jessica Strang/Des: Alice Bailey 83 t S.Gr/MMC; b Norman McGrath/Architects: Chimaoff-Peterson 84 Norman McGrath/Robert A.M. Stern, Architects 85 tl Stuart Mager; tr Michael Dunne/Des: Barbara Littman, N.J. bl S.Gr/MMC; br Mondadoripress/Grazia Bricolage 86 l Susan Griggs/Photo; Michael Boys; t Robert Perron/Architect: Louis MacCall; b LW/TSP/Des: Max Clendinning 87 t B. Baert/Photo: A.Dovifat; c Robert Perron/Des: Robert Shaw 88 LW/TSP 89 t Norman McGrath/Architects: Scott Tallon Walker; bl Robert A.M. Stern, Architects/bed: Frank A. Hall/Photo: Ed Stoecklein; r Blind Alley Ltd 90 b CP 90-91 S.Gr/MMC 91 bl S.Gr/MMC; tr, br S.Gr/100 ID 92-3 Norman McGrath/Des: John Saladino 93 t Colorific/Photo: P. Hinous, Connaissance des Arts/chez Malardier/Des: François Catroux; bl IMS/Le Journal de la Maison/Photo: Kolko/Maze; tr S.Gr/100 ID; br Norman McGrath/Architect: Victor Cromie 95 t Carla de Benedetti; bl Mondadoripress/Bricolage; br S.Gr/MMC 96 t Conran Ink; b CP 97 t CP/SW; b LW/TSP/Des: Frank Gehry, Los Angeles 98 Anglo-Persian Carpet Co. 98-99 Michael Dunne/Des: Chuck Winslow 99 t Jessica Strang; r S.Gr/100 ID 101 CP 102-3 Naru 104 cl Mauro Pucciarelli; tr John Bethell; bl Giraudon; br Colorific/Photo: Alan Clifton; cb Historical Pictures Service, Chicago/Betty I. Madden 105 t Angelo Hornak; b National Trust/Photo: John Bethell 109 Robert Harding Associates/illustration by Edmund Dulac for The Princess and The Pea, from *Stories from Hans C. Andersen,* 1911 (courtesy Victoria and Albert Museum, London; reproduced by permission of Brockhampton Press) 112 t LW/GH/Des: Glynn Smith Assocs; b Susan Griggs/Photo: Michael Boys 113 t Marshall & Schule; bl Giovannetti; br Kara Designs from Accessories by Us 114 Robert Perron/Des: Byron Bell 115 Jerry Tubby 118 t Jessica Strang; b CP/ZH 119 bl CP/ZH; tl, tr Christopher H.L. Owen; cr, br Brecht-Einzig Ltd/Architects: Rothermel Cooke 121 tl S.Gr/100 ID; tr Michael Dunne/Des: Jack Ceglic & Joel Dean; bl S.Gr/100 ID; br S.Gr/MMC 122 bl S.Gr/MMC; t Marimekko by Dan River; br CP/SW 123 r S.Gr/ MMC; l Norman McGrath/Des: Katina Meyer 124 Habitat 125 Marimekko by Dan River 126 S.Gr/MMC 127 t Marimekko by Dan River; c Nigel Heed/Des: Flick Ekins; b CP 128 Habitat 128-9 Wamsutta-Trucraft 129 tr Marimekko; br Transworld Feature Syndicate/Scoop 130-131 Mondadoripress/Abitare/Photo: Ballo 131 Habitat 132 t Brecht-Einzig Ltd/Des: Jacqueline de Roemer; bl, c S.Gr/MMC; r LW/Lavinia Press 133 S.Gr/100 ID 134-5 Susan Griggs/Photo: Michael Boys 135 c Susan Griggs/Photo: Michael Boys; tr S.Gr/MMC; b, br Marimekko by Dan River 136 tl Robert Perron/Des: Williams: tr, cr The Joy of Collecting; bl Robert Perron; br CP 137 Marilynn Zipes/quilt by Allison Blythe 138-9 Naru 140-141 Daily Telegraph Colour Library/Photos: Geg Germany 142-3 British Museum, Dept Prints and Drawings/Photos: John R. Freeman 145 CP/ZH 146 Robert Perron/Architect: John Matthews 147 tl CP/F; tr CP; bl Norman McGrath/Des: John Saladino; br Susan Griggs/Photo: Michael Boys 148 t, br S.Gr/100 ID; bl Norman McGrath/Des: Parish-Hadley 149 IMS/Photo: Uggla 150 tl Robert Perron/Des: Robert Shaw; tr Advent Corporation; bl Norman McGrath/Architect: Gwathmey Siegel br LW/TSP; 151 Slumberland/Beaver Public Relations 152 tr LW/Photo: Neil Lorrimer; bl Camera Press/Photo: Peter Warner from Harper's & Queen/Architect: Philip Jebb/Des: Nina Campbell; cr Norman McGrath/Robert A.M. Stern, Architects 153 CP/ZH 154 t B. Baert; bl Norman McGrath/Des: Bray Schaible; br Mario Buatta/Photo: Norman McGrath 155 Norman McGrath/Des: John Saladino 156 Michael Dunne/Des: Jack Ceglic & Joel Dean 157 t Norman McGrath/Architect: Hugh Newell Jacobsen; bl Mario Buatta; br Susan Griggs/Photo: Michael Boys 158-9 Mondadoripress/Abitare 160 Courtesy Charlotte Baden-Powell 162 t B. Baert/Photo: J. Primois; bl S.Gr/MMC; br Marimekko, Finland 163 t Michael Dunne/Des: Jack Ceglic & Joel Dean; bl S.Gr/MMC; br WET: The Magazine of Gourmet Bathing/courtesy Dranoel Nerok 164 Transworld Feature Syndicate/Scoop 165 Patrick Nicholas 167 t, bl Tom Yee; br Daily Telegraph Colour Library 168 Brecht-Einzig Ltd/Architects: Prof. Kammerer & Prof. Belz 169 tl Carla de Benedetti/Architect: Giuliana Corsini; tr Ruben de Saavedra/Photo: Alexandre Georges; bl LW/TSP/Des: Lenny Steinberg, Beverly Hills; br Robert Perron/Ann Dorette 170 l Snark International r B. Baert 171 l B. Baert; tr Colorific/Agence Top/Photo: P. Hinous/Des: Jacques Grange, chez Mme Caracciolo; br Michael Dunne/Des: Bernard Hunt 172 t National Trust/Photo: John Bethell; b Jessica Strang 173 t Vizcaya Museum and Gardens, Miami, Florida; l Christopher H.L. Owen; r LW/TSP/Des: Santa Raymond 174 B. Baert 175 tl Norman McGrath/Des: John Saladino; tr S.Gr/MMC; bl Max Eckert/Des: C. Burke; br LW/JT 176 B. Baert/Photo: J Primois 177 tl Ezra Stoller © ESTO; tr Christopher H.L. Owen; cr LW/TSP/Des: Peter Wilson; bl Susan Griggs/Photo: Michael Boys; br La Maison Individuelle/Photo: Christian Braud 178 l S.Gr/MMC; r Mike Crockett 179 l, br LW/Photos: Mike Shiels/Des: Tony & Gay Frith; tr The Picture Library 180 t Robert Perron/Architect: Nancy Copley; b B. Baert/Photo: J. Primois 180-1 t B. Baert/Photo: M. Nahmias; b Norman McGrath/Des: David Hicks 181 t B. Baert/Photo: Massey; b Norman McGrath/Des: Robert Shaw 182 Colorific/Photo: R. Guillemot, Connaissance des Arts/Des: Jacques Grange, chez Jean-Marie Rivière 183 tl The Picture Library; ct B. Baert; tr LW/TSP/Des: Adrian Gale; b B. Baert/Photo: M. Nahmias 184 t CP/SW; bl P. Monteleoni; br B. Baert/Photo: M. Haas 185 t S.Gr/Fouineuse; bl S.Gr/MMC; br Jessica Strang 186 l B. Baert/Photo: A. Dovifat; tr Colorific/Photo: Guillemot; br LW/CH/Des: Richard & Pam Negus 187 tl Colorific/Agence Top/Photo: P. Hinous/Des: J. Stefanidis; bl S.Gr/MMC; r LW/GH/Des: Nicholas Hills 188 S.Gr/MMC 189 t S.Gr/MMC; b S.Gr/TF 190 Treston 191 tl CP/SW; ct CP; tr LW/TSP/Des: Rupert Lord; bl B. Baert; br S.Gr/MMC 192-3 Naru 194 tl Ronald Sheridan; tr National Trust; bl Sonia Halliday; cb Giraudon 195 l MEPL; r Armitage Shanks/Photo: Angelo Hornak 196 LW/TSP/Des: Khahn 197 tl, ct S.Gr/MMC; tr Angelo Hornak/courtesy Barry Bucknell; b Vogue Bath, courtesy McKelvie, Newton & Nicholson 198 Bildarchiv Sammer 199 l B. Baert; ct Teuco Baths/Photo: Simion, Milan; tr S. Gr/MMC; cb Metlex Inc/Pulse Communications 200 S.Gr/MMC 201 br Max Eckert; bl Norman McGrath/Architect: Robert Brown; tr S.Gr/MMC; tl B. Baert/Photo: J. Primois 202 LW 203 Kohler Co. 204 tl Colorific/Photo: David Moore; ct, bl, br Mansell Collection; tr Ronan Picture Library 205 l Mansell Collection; ct Lucinda Lambton; r Angelo Hornak 206 bl Terence Conran; cb Daily Telegraph Colour Library; br WET: The Magazine of Gourmet Bathing/Photo: Dranoel Nerok 207 tl CP/Photo: Michael Williams; tr Ezra Stoller © ESTO; bl Norman McGrath/Architect: W.S. Ehrlich; br Carla de Benedetti 208 tl Czech & Speake; cl S.Gr/MMC; bl Teledyne/Water Pik; r Nordic Saunas Ltd 209 tl CP/SW; tr Michael Dunne/Des: Horace Gifford, N.Y. bl Camera Press/ZH; br Susan Griggs/Photo: Michael Boys 210 S.Gr/MMC 210-1 Michael Dunne/Des: Tom Moore, N.Y. 211 tr Tony Stone Associates; br Stock, Boston/Photo: Owen Franken 212 tc Lawrence Wright; l from a Dutch Book of Hours/Bodleian Library, Oxford: MS Liturg. 400, f 35v (roll 172f frame 7); tr Angelo Hornak/Victoria & Albert Museum, London 213 tl, bl Lucinda Lambton; r Angelo Hornak 214 t

Acknowledgements

LW/Photo: Mike Shiels/*Des:* Tony & Gay Firth; *b* LW/CH/*Des:* Richard Browner **215** *t* CP/F; *bl, br* S.Gr/MMC **216** *tl* Christopher H.L. Owen; *bl* Armitage Shanks; *tr* Cesame from Marchini & Springorum; *br* LEDA **217** *l* Jessica Strang; *ct* Alan Tye Design Ltd; *tr* Bohlin & Powell, Architects/Photo: Mark Cohen; *br* Norman McGrath/*Des:* John Saladino **218** *tl* Norman McGrath/Architect: Robert Brown; *tr* B. Baert/Photo: M. Nahmias; *b* Transworld Feature Syndicate/Scoop **219** *far l* Sherle Wagner; *br* Pictor; *tr* Elon Tiles; *tr* Du Pont **220** Roger-Viollet **221** *tl, l* Roger-Viollet; *c, ct* Snark International; *cb, br* Mansell Collection; *tr* Science Museum **223** *l, br* Teuco Guzzini; *ct* CP/F; *tr* Bill McLaughlin **224** *cl* Crown Copyright: reproduced with permission of the Controller of HMSO; *bl* after the painting of Housesteads latrine by R. Embleton, copyright Frank Graham; *ct* Angelo Hornak/Crown Copyright, courtesy Victoria & Albert Museum, London **225** *c* Armitage Shanks; *r* Armitage Shanks/Photo: Angelo Hornak; *l* from *Flushed with Pride* by Wallace Reyburn (Macdonald & Jane's 1969)/Photo: Angelo Hornak **227** *bl* Lucinda Lambton; *br* Christopher H.L. Owen; *far r* Wenczel Tile Co. **228** *t* Bill McLaughlin; *b* Cesame from Marchini & Springorum **229** *tl* Bill McLaughlin; *ct* CP/ZH; *tr* Jessica Strang; *bl, cb* Alan Tye Design Ltd; *br* Teuco Guzzini **230** Bill McLaughlin **231** *tl* Lucinda Lambton; *bl* Susan Griggs/Photo: Michael Boys; *c* CP/SW; *tr* S.Gr/MMC; *br* Jessica Strang **232** *t* Mansell Collection; *b* Sonia Halliday/Photo: F.H. C. Birch; *r* Doulton & Co. **233** *tl, ct,* Lucinda Lambton; *bl* MEPL; *tr* Angelo Hornak; *cr* RTHPL; *br* Mansell Collection **234** *tl, br* Czech & Speake; *tr* S.Gr/MMC; *bl* Lönnström Oy **235** *tl* Robert Perron/Architect: Yann Weymouth, Berkeley Apt., N.Y; *tr* Vizcaya Museum and Gardens, Miami, Florida; *cl* Gelardin, Bruner, Cott Inc *cr* Bill McLaughlin; *bl* Michael Dunne/*Des:* Horace Gifford, N.Y; *br* Susan Griggs/Photo: Michael Boys **236** *t* CP/SW; *b* Crayonne **237** *tl, tr, br* S.Gr/MMC; *c* IMS/Photo: Uggla; *bl* Habitat; *cb* Sommer Allibert **238** *tr* Jessica Strang; *tl* Christopher Strangeways/*Des:* Roger Michell & Danka Napiorkowska/Lustre Pottery; *bl* Christopher Strangeways/*Des:* Glynis Clack & Les Rayner/Manor Farm Pottery; *br* B. Baert **239** *tl, tr* S.Gr/MMC; *bl* CP; *br* CP/FS **240** *t* Michael Dunne/*Des:* Horace Gifford, N.Y; *241* *tl* Habitat; *tr* Kaleidoscope/Photo: Clive Boden; *b* S.Gr/100 ID **242-3** Naru **244** *c, r* Syndication International; *l* CP/FS **245** WET: The Magazine of Gourmet Bathing/Photo: Rabyn Blake **246** *tl* MEPL; *tr* Transworld Feature Syndicate/Scoop; **247** S.Gr/100 ID **248** S.Gr/100 ID **249** S.Gr/100 ID **250** *bl* Sunday Times, London/Photo: Sacha; *tr* Norman McGrath/*Des:* David Hicks; *br* Colorific/Agence Top/Photo: P. Hinous/*Des:* J. Stefanidis; *tl* CP/ZH **251** *l* CP/Photo: Peter Warner, Harper's & Queen/Architect: Philip Jebb/*Des:* Nina Campbell; *r* WET: The Magazine of Gourmet Bathing **252** Ezra Stoller © ESTO **253** *tl* LW/Photo: Mike Shiels/*Des:* Tony & Gay Firth; *tr* Tom Yee; *bl* Conran Ink; *br* CP/Photo: Peter Warner, Harper's & Queen **254** *t* Michael Dunne/*Des:* Philippa Naess, N.Y; *b* MEPL **255** *tl* AB Gustavsberg; *tr* CP/ZH; *bl* B. Baert/Photo: M. Nahmias; *br* Tom Yee **256** CP/F **257** *tl, tr* S.Gr/MMC; *bl* Crayonne; *br* CP/SW **258-9** Bruce Wolf **260** *far l* Bettman Archive; *tl* Scala/Museo Horne, Firenze; *b* National Gallery of Art, Washington DC/Index of American Design; *tr* Sinclair Hamilton Collection of American Illustrated Books, Princeton University Library/Photo: American Heritage Library **261** *bl*

Mansell Collection; *tr* MEPL; *c* Roger-Viollet; *cr* Snark International **262** S.Gr/MMC **263** *tl* Susan Griggs/Photo: Michael Boys/*Des:* P. Pradaliné; *bl* S.Gr/MMC; *tr* Mondadoripress/Abitare; *br* S.Gr/100 ID **264** Mike Crockett **265** *tl* S.Gr/MMC; *tr* Jessica Strang/*Des:* Dimity Collins; *br* Transworld Feature Syndicate/American Home; *bl* CP/F **266** *tl* S.Gr/100 ID; *bl* The Picture Library; *r* S.Gr/MMC **267** *l* S.Gr/MMC; *tr, br* Susan Griggs/Photo: Michael Boys **268** Ezra Stoller © ESTO **269** *tl* The Picture Library; *tr* S.Gr/MMC; *bl* CP/F *br* S.Gr/100 ID **270-1** S. Gr/MMC **271** *tl, tr* Elliot Fine/Architect: David L. Hirsch; *bl* S.Gr/MMC; *br* S.Gr/100 ID **272** *t* S.Gr/MMC; *b* CP/SW **273** *t* S.Gr/MMC; *bl, br* CP/F **274** *l* CP/SW; *br* Susan Griggs/Photo: Michael Boys; *tr* S.Gr/MMC **275** *l* Tom Yee; *r* Susan Griggs/Photo: Michael Boys **276-7** Naru **278** Norman McGrath **279** *tl* LW/Photo: Geoffrey Frosch; *tr* The Picture Library; *b* S.Gr/MMC **280** S.Gr/MMC **281** *l* CP/SW: *tr* LW/MN/*Des:* Susan Martin; *cr* IMS/Le Journal de la Maison/Photo: Maze **282** *cr* CP/F; *bl, br* Elliot Fine **283** CP **284** *tl* Bill Mclaughlin; *l* Stanley Tigerman Assocs **284-5** Bill McLaughlin **285** *t* Transworld Feature Syndicate/Scoop; *b* Marimekko by Dan River **286** *t, b* Marimekko by Dan River/*Des:* Raymond Waites **287** *tl, bl* Habitat; *tr, cr* S.Gr/MMC; *br* IMS/Photo: Peo Eriksson **288** *t* Elliot Fine; *b* S.Gr/MMC **289** *l* CP; *t* IMS/Photo: Carl A. Noldin; *br* CP/BR **290** Wolff Olins Ltd **291** *tl* IMS/Photo: Maze; *tr* CP/F; *b* Norman McGrath/Architect: Myron Goldfinger **292** Mondadoripress/Abitare **293** *t* Jessica Strang; *bl* S.Gr/MMC; *br* Norman McGrath/Architects Moore, Grover & Harper **294-5** Naru **296** *l* S.Gr/MMC; *r* Christopher H.L. Owen/Photo: John Zimmerman **297** *t* B. Baert; *bl* Marimekko by Dan River; *br* S.Gr/100 ID **298** S.Gr/100 ID **299** *tl* LW/JT; *bl* Marimekko by Dan River; *tr* IMS; *br* Dan River **300** *t* CP/ZH; *bl* Jessica Strang/*Des:* Alice Bailey; *br* Robert Perron/Architect: Turner Brooks **301** *l* Jessica Strang; *tr* Bill McLaughlin; *br* Norman McGrath/Architect: Tod Williams **303** *tl, ct* S.Gr/MMC; *tr, br* LW; *bl* Christopher H.L. Owen; *cb* CP/ZH **308** *tr, tl, ct, c, br* S.Gr/Jessica Strang; *second from tl* Naru; *third from tl* CP/SW; *bl* Flick Ekins; *cb* Bruce Wolf **308-9** S.Gr/MMC **309** *tl* S.Gr/100 ID; *ct* CP/SW; *c* S.Gr/MMC; *br* Raeanne Giovanni **310** *tl, bl* S.Gr/100 ID; *tr* Mondadoripress/Grazia Bricolage; *br* S.Gr **311** *far l* Robert Perron; *ct, br* S.Gr/MMC; *tr* S.Gr/100 ID; *cb* Jessica Strang **312** *l* Robert Perron/*Des:* Robert Shaw; *tr* Blind Alley; *br* Annie Hatcher/Fantasy Furniture **313** *tl* Norman McGrath/Architect: Tim Prentice; *tr* CP/SW; *bl* S.Gr/TF; *br* S.Gr/MMC **314** *t* LW/TSP/*Des:* Max Clendinning; *bl* S.Gr/100 ID; *cb, br* S.Gr/MMC **315** *tl* LW/TSP/*Des:* Philip Castle; *far r* Jessica Strang; *tr* Conran Ink; *b* S.Gr/MMC **316** CP **317** *tl* LW/TSP; *tr, bl* Jessica Strang/*Des:* Quin Cole; *br* Norman McGrath/*Des:* David Hicks **318** *l* courtesy Samuel & Mary R. Bancroft Collection, Delaware Art Museum/Photo: Courtauld Institute; *t* LW/MN/*Des:* Kate Curry: *b* LW/MN **319** *tl* Roger Phillips; *tr* LW/TSP; *b* LW/MN/*Des:* Dorit Egli **320** Ezra Stoller © ESTO **321** l S.Gr/MMC; *tr, cr* Susan Griggs/Photo: Michael Boys *c* Jessica Strang/*Des:* Candace Bahouth **322** *t* S.Gr/100 ID; *bl* LW/CH/*Des:* Anthony & Janet Harris; *br* Robert Perron **323** *t* B.Baert/Photo: A. Dovifat; *bl* Norman McGrath/*Des:* John Saladino; *br* S.Gr/MMC **324** *t* S.Gr/MMC; *b* CP **324-5** LW/CH **325** *tr* S.Gr/Fouineuse; *bl, br* Dorma **326-7** Naru **328-9** Peter M. Fine **330-1** Raeanne Giovanni **332-7**

Bruce Wolf **338-9** Raeanne Giovanni **340** *bl* LW/MN; *br* Susan Griggs/Photo: Michael Boys; *t* Anthea Sieveking **341** *tl, tr, bl* LW/TSP; *cb, br* LW/MN **342** *tl* Jaime Ardiles-Arce; *bl, br* Charles Nesbit **343** Charles Nesbit **344** *tl, tr* Glynn Smith Assocs; *cr, bl* Jessica Strang; *br* S.Gr/MMC **345** *bl* S.Gr/MMC; *tr* S.Gr/100 ID; *cr* Jack Smith Yachting **346** *tl* Paolo Koch; *tr, br* Ben Martin **347** *tl, b* Ben Martin; *tr* Angelo Hornak

Artists

Maralyn Bruce, Hayward and Martin Limited, Harry Clow, Tony Spalding, Rozelle Bentheim, Pete Saag

The publishers would also like to thank the following:
J W Turnbull of Housesteads Roman Fort
J S Forsyth of Armitage Shanks
Judith Schecter
Barbara Cutler of Frank A. Hall and Sons Ltd
Barbara Douglass of Courtaulds
Beverley Morris of The Joy of Collecting
Elliseva Sayers
Judy Martin
Helen Stell
Charlotte Kennedy
David Ford
Ideal Standard, UK
American Standard, USA
Leisure Showers UK
Vogue Baths
National Bedding Federation UK
National Association of Bedding Manufacturers, USA
Lux Soap

Index by:
Bruce Leigh and Richard Kennedy

Picture Manager:
Sue Pinkus

Additional picture research by:
Elizabeth Ogilvie
Paddy Poynder

Glossary

Some of the English words and phrases used in this book may prove to be confusing or even totally meaningless to the American reader. To avoid any misunderstandings concerning the place for and the use of such items as the duvet and loofah, this list of British/American equivalents will help readers to decipher any unfamiliar word.

bedside table	night table
caravan	trailer
cupboard	closet
duvet	continental quilt or comforter
fridge	refrigerator
hob	cook-top
loofah	Luffa pod used for rubbing the skin in the bath or shower
nappy	diaper
Perspex	clear plastic
power point	electric outlet
reeded glass	patterned glass
tap	faucet
Teasmade	electric teamaker
wash-basin	sink
WC unit	toilet

It should also be noted that the Imperial gallon is equivalent to approximately 1.2 US gallons.